P9-CTB-598

THE THEORY OF
INTERNATIONAL TRADE

WITH ITS APPLICATIONS TO COMMERCIAL POLICY

BY

GOTTFRIED VON HABERLER

ASSOCIATE PROFESSOR IN HARVARD UNIVERSITY;
MEMBER OF THE FINANCIAL SECTION AND ECONOMIC INTELLIGENCE SERVICE
OF THE LEAGUE OF NATIONS

32532

TRANSLATED FROM THE GERMAN

BY

ALFRED STONIER AND FREDERIC BENHAM

HF
1007
.V78
.H11

ST. JOSEPH'S UNIVERSITY   STX
HF1007.V78
Studies in the theory of international t

3 9353 00089 0689

LONDON   EDINBURGH   GLASGOW

WILLIAM HODGE & COMPANY, LIMITED

H F 1007
H 11

German edition, 1933
Spanish translation, 1936
English translation (revised by the Author) :
   First impression, 1936
   Second impression, 1937
   Third impression, 1950

MADE AND PRINTED IN GREAT BRITAIN
BY
WILLIAM HODGE AND COMPANY, LTD.
LONDON, EDINBURGH, AND GLASGOW

PREFACE TO THE ENGLISH EDITION

I am very conscious of the various shortcomings of this book as published in German two years ago. Nevertheless I have agreed to the publication of an English translation without substantial changes from the German original, because I hope that, even in the present form, it will be of some use.

Apart from improvements in detail and statistical researches with a view to verifying and applying to concrete cases the general, theoretical statements, it seems to me that the theory of international trade, as outlined in the following pages, requires further development, in two main directions. The theory of imperfect competition and the theory of short-run oscillation (business cycle theory) must be applied to the problems of international trade. It will soon be possible to do this in a systematic way, since much progress has been made in both fields in recent years.

With regard to the first of these questions, there is the literature which centres around the two outstanding books, *Monopolistic Competition* by Professor E. Chamberlin and *Imperfect Competition* by Mrs. Joan Robinson. In the second field where further development is required, it is not so easy to refer to a body of accepted theory. But it seems to me that a certain measure of agreement as to the nature of the cumulative processes of general economic expansion and contraction is gradually beginning to emerge. By starting or reversing, accelerating or retarding these cumulative processes, changes in the international economic relations of a country may give an unexpected and perplexing turn to events, not predictable on the basis of a more rigidly static analysis. There is certainly a wide field of international economic problems which promises a rich crop if tilled with the aid of imperfect competition and business cycle theory. The theory of commercial policy, in particular, will profit therefrom.[1]

Being occupied by work on a different subject, I have, unfor-

---

[1] *Cf., e.g.*, G. Lovasy, "Schutzölle bei unvollkommener Konkurrenz" in *Zeitschrift für Nationalökonomie*, vol. 5 (1934).

tunately, had no time to revise the book thoroughly along the lines indicated above. I hope, however, to be able to do this on a later occasion.

During the last two years great progress has been made in the technique of Protection. Not only have tariffs been piled on tariffs and quotas on quotas; not only have the old methods been used much more boldly and unhesitatingly than before; but new devices have been invented: clearing and compensation agreements, export and import monopolies, discriminating exchange rates, methods of controlling tourist traffic and expenditure, standstill agreements and so on, with an infinite number of variations in detail. Many interventionist measures, which seemed two years ago either technically impossible or so manifestly undesirable as to be quite out of the question, are to-day adopted without reluctance. I have tried elsewhere[2] to go a little more deeply into the details of the new commercial policy. In the present book I have confined the discussion for the most part to fundamentals. After all, the general principles and the technique of analysis have remained unaltered and are just as applicable to the new as to the old methods. If one has a firm grasp of these principles, it is comparatively easy to apply them to the new techniques of Protection.

Chapters I-VIII have been translated by Mr. Alfred Stonier (with assistance from Mr. Hugh Gaitskell), and Chapters IX-XXI by Mr. Frederic Benham. In translating they both have, I think, improved the original version and eliminated a number of inaccuracies. I am also indebted to Mr. Ragnar Nurkse, who has read the greater part of the manuscript and proposed many improvements. I have taken this opportunity of revising the whole manuscript and making a number of small changes in the text. The section on exchange control has been largely rewritten.

GOTTFRIED V. HABERLER.

GENEVA, *August*, 1935.

---

[2] *Liberale und planwirtschaftliche Handelspolitik*, Berlin, 1934.

PREFACE TO THE GERMAN EDITION

(*Abridged*)

This book aims at a complete and systematic treatment of the main problems arising from international economic transactions. It attempts, especially, to give a thorough theoretical analysis of these problems. . . . I have not followed the traditional practice of beginning with the ' pure ' theory, treating this as the dominating topic and the question of the monetary mechanism as subsidiary. On the contrary, I begin at once, in section B of Part I, with the exposition of the monetary problems: that is, of the mechanism which determines the exchange-value of a currency, equalises the balance of payments, and makes possible the transfer of unilateral payments. This is followed, in section C, by the ' pure theory.' Here I have endeavoured to combine all the valid and relevant doctrines into a systematic whole. For these doctrines are mostly not mutually exclusive, but, on the contrary, supplement one another, either covering different parts of the field, working on different levels of abstraction, or employing different methods of analysis.

I have also endeavoured to avoid the too common practice of placing the theory of international trade and the discussion of trade policy in quite separate compartments without any connection between the two. Instead, I have tried to apply the theoretical analysis to every question arising from trade policy. Indeed, any discussion of trade policy which attempts more than a mere account of the legal and administrative devices in force, or than a statement of the criteria by which the various policies should be evaluated must inevitably consist in the application of economic theory.

In the various places where facts have been cited, they have been introduced not for their own sake but in order to illustrate the argument. The only exception to this is section C of Part II, which attempts a systematic account of the various measures which have served as instruments of trade policy. . .

Some readers will doubtless be surprised that the policy of Free Trade, which is in glaring contrast to the policy actually adopted by nearly every country in the world, should be advocated in this book. The universality of Protection inspires an instinctive distrust of a theory whose conclusions are nowhere accepted in practice. Can a policy which is rejected with such unanimity be correct?

But this is not an argument. It would be absurd to expect economic science to reverse the verdict of its analysis, based upon accepted judgments of value, just because in practice it is consistently ignored. Nobody would dream of asking medical science to change its findings just because everybody followed some custom which it had pronounced injurious to health.

Nevertheless it cannot be denied that the principles stated in this book as 'economically correct'[1] have hardly ever been completely applied. The disagreeable task of having to declare current practice misguided, thereby provoking the accusation of unfruitful doctrinairism, is one which the present volume shares with most scientific writings on international trade. Economists are nearly as unanimous in favour of a liberal trade policy as are Governments in favour of the contrary. It is true that very few writers attempt the hopeless task of proving *a priori* that no case is conceivable in which the 'general welfare' would be promoted by some kind of intervention. Most economists, including the present writer, concede that cases are both conceivable and liable to occur in practice in which tariffs or other restrictions on international trade would be advantageous. At the same time, there is fairly general agreement among them that such cases are on the whole unimportant, so that a policy of complete Free Trade would diverge only slightly from the optimum. The vast majority of economists are convinced that the actual trade policies of nearly all countries are founded upon the crudest errors and have no shadow of justification. Upon this point there is surprising agreement of expert opinion not only among liberals but also among socialists.

---

[1] The meaning of this phrase is discussed in chaps. xiii and xiv.

The fact that nearly all economists unite in condemning Protection explains why some of them devote so much ingenuity to constructing hypothetical cases in which a tariff might be beneficial and why economic works give so much space to such cases. Exceptions are always more interesting, to the scientific mind, than mere illustrations of the general rule. . . . But experience has underlined the truth and wisdom of Edgeworth's judgment: " As I read it, protection might procure economic advantage in certain cases, if there was a Government wise enough to discriminate those cases, and strong enough to confine itself to them; but this condition is very unlikely to be fulfilled."

. . . I am very grateful to Dr. Erich Schiff, of Vienna, for his help with the statistical work.   G. H.

VIENNA, *May*, 1933.

CONTENTS

CONTENTS

PART II

TRADE POLICY

A—INTRODUCTION

B—THE CONSEQUENCES OF DIFFERENT SYSTEMS AND
    MEASURES OF COMMERCIAL POLICY, FREE TRADE AND
    PROTECTION

CONTENTS

CONTENTS

INTRODUCTION.

INTERNATIONAL TRADE.

INTRODUCTION.

§ 1. The Problem of Definition.

The only really systematic theory of international trade we possess is the so-called classical theory, of which practically all the component parts were worked out by such early writers as Hume, Adam Smith and Ricardo.[1] It is characterised, on the one hand, by the doctrine of comparative costs and, on the other hand, by the principle that prices, exchange rates and money flows provide a mechanism which links together the monetary systems of different countries and ensures the automatic adjustment of the balance of payments. In England the classical theory still holds the field and it is accepted by the more theoretically-minded economists in the United States.[2] In continental countries, however, with the partial exception of Italy, it has never found much favour. Criticisms have been frequent, but the critics have not succeeded in substituting for it anything that deserves to be called a new theory of international trade. Certain details of the classical theory have had to be modified, and there has been, of course, much interesting statistical and descriptive work. But the only important theoretical advance has been the application, notably by Pareto, of general equilibrium analysis[3] to the problems of international trade. The classical doctrine—in particular the theory of comparative costs—is exhibited as a special case of the more general theory.

The classical theory starts from the fact that in international trade, as in all other economic activities, it is the individual economic subject who buys and sells, pays and is paid, grants and receives loans, and, in short, carries on the activities which, taken as a whole, constitute international trade. It is not, for example, Germany and England, but individuals or firms located in Germany and England, who carry on trade with one another. The first question, therefore, which has to be answered is whether these economic activities call for a special theory at all. The mere

---

[1] Cf. the exhaustive bibliography in Angell, *Theory of International Prices* (1925).

[2] Notably by those under the influence of Professor Taussig.

[3] Cf. "Teoria matematica dei cambi forestieri," *Giornale degli Economisti* (1894), and "Teoria matematica del commercio internazionale," *Giornale degli Economisti* (1895); also *Cours d'économie politique*, vol. 2, § § 862-78.

fact that a political boundary is involved and that the persons in question are nationals of different countries and, perhaps, speak different languages, is economically irrelevant. It cannot therefore be taken as the criterion of demarcation between one branch of economic theory and another.

The classical school believed nevertheless that there was a fundamental difference between home trade and foreign trade. They pointed out that labour and capital moved freely from one branch of production and from one district to another within a single country. Between different countries, on the other hand, mobility was totally, or at any rate to a great extent, lacking. In the latter case, complete adjustment (i.e. the establishment of the same rate of wages and the same rate of interest everywhere) did not take place. Immobility was accepted quite naïvely by the classical school as the criterion of international trade. They based their argument upon it without attempting to justify its selection on methodological grounds and thus laid themselves open to various objections which have been raised from time to time, particularly in recent years.

An obvious criticism, which certainly has some truth in it, is that the difference in question can only be one of degree. On the one hand, the factors of production are not perfectly mobile within national boundaries; on the other hand, large and, indeed, enormous movements of the factors of production do sometimes take place across these boundaries.[4]

Of course, the classical school did not overlook this fact. Adam Smith stressed the importance of emigration, and J. S. Mill recognised that capital was becoming steadily more mobile and cosmopolitan. Moreover, it is common knowledge that Cairnes introduced the conception of ' non-competing groups ' (i.e. sharply defined groups of labour between which there was no free movement) and pointed out that where such groups existed within a country, the theory of international trade applied to them. Professor Taussig, to whom we owe the latest and most carefully worked-out version of the classical theory, devotes a good deal of space to the imperfect mobility of labour and to the consequent differences of wages rates. It can, perhaps, be maintained that the classical school and their successors have paid too little attention to the significance of these phenomena for the economic development

---

[4] This point is stressed by Prof. J. H. Williams, " The Theory of International Trade Reconsidered," *Economic Journal* (1929), vol. 39, and by Prof. Ohlin " Ist eine Modernisierung der Aussenhandelstheorie erforderlich ? " *Weltwirtschaftliches Archiv* (1927), vol. 26, p. 97; " Die Beziehung zwischen internationalem Handel und internationaler Bewegung von Kapital und Arbeit," *Zeitschrift für National-ökonomie* (1930), vol. 2, and *Interregional and International Trade* (1933).

of the modern world. One may speak with Nicholson of a " lost idea "—lost, that is to say, since the days of Adam Smith.[5] There can, however, be no question of a logical error on their part. If the mobility of labour[6] and capital between different countries were to increase in the further course of economic development, there would be, according to the classical school, no need for a separate theory of international trade. For the phenomena which it tries to explain would have disappeared and with them the distinction between home and foreign trade. But one must be careful to distinguish between the *empirical* question whether the assumptions of the classical school apply to any particular epoch, and the *logical* question whether their conclusions follow from those assumptions.

It has been argued that, even within the bounds of a single country, real capital cannot readily be transferred from one line of production to another,[7] and, further, that the cost of transporting capital goods from one part of a country to another is sometimes much greater than from one country to another. But this argument is irrelevant, since it refers only to specific capital goods already in existence. For capital theory, however, the criterion of perfect mobility is the equality of interest rates. This refers to alternative ways of investing liquid or money capital. If the cost of transporting capital goods from one place to another is high, considerable differences in the price of capital goods will probably exist. But, nevertheless, interest rates may very well tend to equality. The rate of interest need not be higher in San Francisco than in New York, because there is a mountain range and a distance of 2500 miles between them. It must, however, be granted that, if a country is completely shut off from the rest of the world—in the sense that there can be neither movements of labour nor trade in commodities of any kind—no capital can be transferred, even if money as such is able to flow in and out. The necessary and sufficient condition is the existence of some international trade, even if it consists entirely of consumption goods and services (e.g. tourist traffic) and sufficient flexibility to allow an import or export surplus to develop. As will be shown later, capital may then move in the shape of increased imports or decreased exports of consumption goods, thus releasing factors of production for employment in other directions.

The international mobility of capital is restricted not by trans-

---

[5] *Cf. A Project of Empire* (1909), p. 12.
[6] In spite of his internationalism, which was characteristic of the whole classical school, Ricardo spoke of the " natural disinclination which every man has to quit the country of his birth . . . These feelings which I should be sorry to see weakened "—*Principles* (ed. McCulloch), p. 77.
[7] This applies particularly to fixed capital, i.e. to buildings and machinery.

port costs but by obstacles of an entirely different character. These consist in the difficulty of legal redress, political uncertainty, ignorance of the prospects of investment in a foreign country, imperfection of the banking system, instability of foreign currencies, mistrust of the foreigner, &c., &c.

In actual fact, there is to-day very considerable immobility of the factors of production, particularly of labour. Apart from the ' natural ' obstacles, such as the cost of emigration, ignorance of foreign languages, and lack of initiative, nearly all countries impose restrictions on immigration. Moreover, the War and the post-war inflations have seriously restricted the international mobility of capital. This is proved by the persistence of large discrepancies between the rates of interest in different countries. The chief reason is, undoubtedly, that owners of capital have lost faith in the political stability of the debtor countries, where rates are high. Hence they fear expropriation by a depreciation of the exchanges or by exchange restrictions, moratoria, standstill agreements, and other devices of the same kind now in vogue.

Immobility of labour and capital is by no means the only possible criterion for defining international trade. Various alternative criteria, such as the existence of separate currencies and the independent control of monetary policy in different countries have been suggested. Each definition of this kind draws attention to different phenomena, and we shall have to investigate them all in due course; but it is meaningless to inquire which is the ' correct ' criterion of international trade.

§ 2. The Political Conception of Foreign Trade.

The distinction made by governments between home trade and foreign trade is not based on any objective economic criterion, but simply on a judgment of value or a rule of law. Home trade means simply trade within that area, the prosperity of which interests the government in question or is subject to its jurisdiction.

The line of demarcation between domestic and foreign trade generally coincides nowadays with the national frontiers, and foreign trade is identified with trade between different countries. Of course, this need not be the case. For instance, a British statesman may regard trade with Canada as domestic trade. On the other hand, it sometimes happens that people living in a particular district consider trade with other parts of the same country as foreign trade. They may even try, by local tariffs and other means, to protect their own district from ' foreign competition.'

The judgments of value, which determine the political distinction between home trade and foreign trade, are not based on the sort of theoretical criteria which we have been discussing. For a Frenchman or for a German, trade between France and Germany is foreign trade, whether capital and labour are mobile between the two countries or not. It would remain so, even if both countries adopted the same currency, though this is unlikely to happen because of the attitude (i.e. the judgments of value) of statesmen in the two countries. The comparative homogeneity of the economic system of one country and its comparative isolation from other countries are the effect rather than the cause of the attitude of statesmen to the distinction between their own country and the outside world.

It is, at any rate, ambiguous to speak, as some German writers have done, of the ' unity of the national economy.' One can understand by a unified national economy an economy which is carried on by a single organisation, e.g., the collectivist economy of Soviet Russia. Or one can understand by it a totality of separate economies, which are more or less closely connected by trade and exchange. This is, obviously, the sense in which one speaks of the French or German economy. But one can speak in the same sense of the European economy, since the various national economies are inter-related and interdependent. The difference is only one of degree. One can even speak in this sense of the unity of the world economy, though its interdependences are not of a very close character.

Some countries are linked together much more closely than others. It would, therefore, be interesting to classify the various types of connection from this point of view. Thus, at one end of the scale, there are countries which exchange only commodities (e.g., industrial for agricultural products). The interdependence between debtor and creditor countries is appreciably closer. Then there are countries with a common currency or a common banking-system, &c., &c. It may be useful to study the consequences of these various degrees and kinds of relationships, but nothing is gained by attempting to draw a sharp line between those relationships which do and those which do not constitute a single economy.

It must, finally, be emphasised that, in a deeper philosophical sense, even the planned collectivist economy of a country or a family can only be grasped individualistically.[8] Every branch of economics has to do with human actions

---

[8] This is the principle of methodological individualism. *Cf.* Max Weber, *Gesammelte Aufsätze zur Wissenschaftslehre*, pp. 503 *seq.*, and *Wirtschaft und Gesellschaft* (1922), chap. i. *Cf.* also Schumpeter, *Wesen und Hauptinhalt der theoretischen Nationalökonomie* (1908).

and human behaviour.[9] Other phenomena interest the economist only so far as human activity is directed towards them (commodities), or so far as they affect human activity (environment). Economic activities are determined on and carried out by individual persons in a collectivist no less than in an individualist economy. The difference is not that in the latter case economic activities are carried on by individuals, and in the former by the community. It is merely that they are governed by different motives and considerations—in the planned economy by the policy of the central planning authority, in the exchange economy chiefly by the desire for money, power or property.

§ 3. QUESTIONS OF EXPOSITION.

The theory of international trade has to be regarded as a particular application of general economic theory. The theory of marginal utility, which interprets and explains the individual's economic activity as such, must therefore be applicable to those economic activities which, in their totality, constitute international trade. The same holds true also of the propositions of price theory which follow from the laws of supply and demand.[1] We shall, therefore, have to make constant use of these general propositions applying them to the specific assumptions which characterise international trade. How far it is appropriate to assume that the reader is already familiar with these propositions, and how far it is necessary to trace their deduction from the corpus of general economic theory, is of course a difficult problem of exposition.

The arrangement of the present work is as follows. Part I deals with the various phenomena selected by different authors as the criterion of international trade. Section A of Part I is concerned with the problems which arise from the fact that different money circulates in different countries, and that each country has its own central bank and controls its own monetary policy. This phenomenon gives rise to the problem of foreign exchange. Closely connected with it is the problem of the trade-balance and of the mechanism which equalises the balance of total payments and renders possible unilateral payments such as the transfer of reparations.[2]

Section B of Part I deals with the phenomena which result from

---

[9] The question in what way economic activities differ from other human activities cannot be discussed here.

[1] " The general conditions which determine equilibrium are the same for both species of trade [home or domestic trade and international trade]; the principal difference is that in the case of home trade there are one or two more equations." Edgeworth, " The pure theory of international values " in *Papers relating to Political Economy* (1925), vol. 2, p. 5.

[2] We need not discuss the question whether this problem belongs to the theory of international trade in the strict sense or not. The fact that one can also speak of a balance of payments between different parts of a single country with only one currency and complete mobility of the factors of production, shows that the phenomenon in question is by no means confined to the international sphere.

the immobility of labour and capital, i.e. with the theory of comparative cost and all that follows from it. It will have to be shown how the theory of comparative cost is based on the general theory of economic equilibrium. This section is, therefore, concerned with what is usually called the ' pure ' theory of international trade.

The method of discussing, first, the monetary problems and then the phenomena which ' give rise ' to them, is not the most usual.[3] But, as will be shown later, the ' real ' factors (or whatever one likes to call the subject matter of ' pure theory ') are in no way logically or objectively prior to the monetary phenomena. The reversal of the usual order of treatment does not, therefore, lead to different results; it is merely an expository device which appears to offer certain advantages.

In Part II the theory of international trade is applied to the problems of commercial policy. There more use will have to be made of general economic theory than in Part I. For, as already explained, the political conception of foreign trade is determined not by theoretical criteria but by spheres of economic interest. What is foreign trade to the statesman may be home trade from the theoretical point of view. In that case only the propositions of general economic theory and not those of the theory of international trade are applicable to it.

---

[3] It has, however, been adopted widely of recent years. *Cf.* Prof. Ohlin's important work, *Interregional and International Trade,* and among earlier writers Nicholson's *Principles of Political Economy.*

PART I.

A—THE MONETARY THEORY OF INTERNATIONAL TRADE.

CHAPTER I.

INTRODUCTORY.

Our problem is to examine on the one hand the factors which determine the rates of foreign exchange, *i.e.*, the exchange ratio between the currencies of different countries, and on the other hand the mechanism which brings the balance of payments into equilibrium.

It will be best to approach these questions with the help of an example.

Let us imagine a closed economy in static equilibrium. All economic processes have been repeating themselves year by year. Supply and demand, consumption and production, capital depreciation and investment exactly balance one another in every branch of industry and each individual firm is itself in static equilibrium.

Suppose, now, that a political frontier is drawn through the middle of this area, so that it no longer forms a single country, but two countries[1] with separate administrative organs. Clearly this change creates no new economic problem. From the economic point of view, the redistribution and increase of taxation due to the reorganisation and partial duplication of the administrative machine is the same thing as a redistribution of the burden of taxation between taxes and rates. Either one can ignore this change altogether, or one can assume that the new static equilibrium appropriate to it has already been reached.

Suppose, next, that each of the new countries decides to have a separate currency of its own. A law is passed providing that, whereas in one country payments shall continue to be made in ' crowns,' in the other country the crowns which are in circulation shall be changed into ' dollars ' at the fixed rate of five crowns to one dollar; in the dollar country, debts must henceforward be contracted and payments made in dollars. As a result, all prices and all liabilities expressed in money will be divided by five.[2]

---

[1] For the case of more than two countries, *cf.* chap. ii, § 4.

[2] This change in the unit of money which affects equally and simultaneously the monetary expression of all transactions, must not be confused with a depreciation or appreciation of the currency. The latter is produced by an increase or diminution of the amount of money, which leaves the raising or lowering of prices to the forces of supply and demand. The transition to the new price-level is achieved not at a stroke but step by step. Obligations already contracted remain nominally unchanged, while the real purchasing power which they represent diminishes or increases.

13

The new situation, thus created, differs from the preceding one only in the fact that every payment from one place to another across the political boundary now involves an extra act of exchange. A payment from the dollar country to the crown country will require an exchange of dollars into crowns, whereas, beforehand, the amount was simply made payable in terms of the single currency then existing.

It is clear that, under the assumption of static equilibrium, the introduction of a second currency need not in itself produce any economic change. No matter where the boundary is drawn,[3] all economic activities will proceed as before. At the rate of exchange originally fixed the demand for dollars is equal to their supply, and equilibrium will therefore be maintained at this rate. A moment's reflection shows that this must be the case. It has been assumed that each individual's balance of payments is in equilibrium; his receipts exactly equal his expenditure over the appropriate period of time. This implies that the balance of payments between any economic group and the rest of the economy must also be in equilibrium; for the external balance of payments of a group is merely an aggregate of the balances of payments between members of the group and persons outside it.[4]

Of course, this does not imply that the same firms which make payments to the foreigner necessarily receive the payments which balance them. It only implies that, when an individual A in the dollar country pays 100 to the crown country, there must be an individual B in the dollar country whether he is identical with A or not, who is in receipt of 100 from the crown country. This is an obvious corollary of the postulate that every individual balance of payments is in equilibrium.

It is also a matter of indifference whether the debtor or the creditor actually changes dollars into crowns. The importer in the dollar country normally sells the imported commodity for dollars, and the exporter in the crown country pays for his means of production in crowns. The dollars must, therefore, be changed into crowns at some point in this chain of transactions.

In actual fact, the persons who have to make payments abroad, are not normally those who receive from abroad the payments which balance them. Indeed, the two groups are not necessarily

---

[3] It need not be a territorial boundary at all. One might assume that all red-headed men decide to use a special currency for trade with one another.

[4] One speaks, for short, of 'British exports' and 'Germany's balance of trade.' But to analyse these conceptions one must split them up into their component parts, i.e., into the actions of individuals. The " equality between private expenditures and private incomes tends ultimately to produce equality between the commercial exports and imports " (Thornton, *An Enquiry into the Nature and Effects of the Paper Credit of Great Britain* (1802), p. 118).

in direct contact at all. An organisation of some kind is, therefore, required to provide a link between them, so that the supply of foreign currency can meet the demand for it.

The simplest method would be a *bureau de change* prepared to exchange on demand crowns for dollars and dollars for crowns at the current rate of 5 : 1. It would have to start with a certain amount of capital to allow for temporary fluctuations, *e.g.*, seasonal fluctuations due to the harvest. But, under the assumptions made hitherto, all fluctuations would in the long run cancel out.

The modern economic system does, as a matter of fact, contain an arrangement of this kind. A sort of clearing market exists where foreign debts and claims are cancelled against each other. The banks in the various trading countries do business with each other, and there is a foreign exchange market where the various currencies are bought and sold. Moreover, under the gold standard, the central banks act as *bureaux de change*.

The means of payment in international transactions are not for the most part cash, which is only used for small amounts (*e.g.*, by travellers abroad), but bills of exchange, cheques and telegraphic transfers. The distinction between the various means of payment is a legal rather than an economic one; the technical details need not, therefore, concern us.[5] The illustration, favoured by the ordinary textbook, is as follows. The exporter draws a three months' bill on the foreign importer and the latter accepts it, *i.e.*, makes a legally binding promise to pay. The exporter then sells the bill to someone who is buying or has bought goods from abroad. The latter gives it in settlement of his own debt to the foreign firm supplying him, which in its turn receives cash for it from the original acceptor. But it makes no essential difference whether the two payments are made in this way or not. They may just as well be made by means of a book transaction or by the sale and purchase of ready money. It is sufficient to note that there are various different means of payment and that these compete with one another, thus forming in effect a single market where the supply of foreign money confronts the demand for it.

In the stationary economy postulated above, this market is in equilibrium. Our main problem will be to consider what happens when equilibrium is disturbed. But, first of all, it is necessary to classify the items which make up the balance of payments and the different senses in which this latter term is used.

---

[5] An account of them will be found, *e.g.*, in the following works : Goschen, *The Theory of Foreign Exchanges;* article on *Foreign Exchange* in the *Encyclopedia of the Social Sciences* (1931), vol. 6; Flux, *Foreign Exchanges* (1924); Whitaker, *Foreign Exchange* (1933), 2nd ed.

CHAPTER II.

THE BALANCE OF PAYMENTS.

§ 1. Classification of Items.

Before proceeding to the qualitative analysis, let us glance at the more important of the quantitative computations which have been made.

Since 1922 detailed statistics have been published annually by the American Department of Commerce of the balance of payments of the United States.[6] For some years now the Economic Intelligence Service of the League of Nations has published an extensive annual survey of the balance of payments of the more important countries.[7] The most exhaustive investigation of this kind for any single country was that conducted by the German ' Enquete-Ausschuss '[8] which based itself on a system of classification worked out by the International Chamber of Commerce in Paris.

(a) The chief item in the balance of payments is the international trade in commodities. A comparison of the value of imports and exports yields the balance of trade.[9] The German system of classification just mentioned distinguishes on the export side the following items : goods exported in the ordinary way, ships sold to the foreigner, fish sold at foreign ports, home products sold from ships located abroad, international mails carried, electricity supplied to foreign countries, and, finally, goods smuggled out. Some of these items do not appear in the official statistics of foreign trade, which cover only commodities passed through the customs. Such items must be computed separately, but the classification has no theoretical significance.

Of much the same type as payments for commodities are payments for services. These are appropriately called invisible exports and imports. They represent transport services, shipping freights, passenger fares, harbour and canal dues, postal, telephone and

---

[6] *The Balance of International Payments of the United States in 1922*, (T.I.B. No. 144), based on Prof. J. H. Williams, " Balance of International Payments of the United States for the year 1921," in the *Review of Economic Statistics* (1922).

[7] *Memorandum on Balances of Payments*, published in English and French.

[8] *Ausschuss zur Untersuchung der Erzeugungs- und Absatzbedingungen der deutschen Wirtschaft: die deutsche Zahlungsbilanz*, in *Verhandlungen und Bericht des Unterausschusses für allgemeine Wirtschaftsstruktur* (1930). This work has been continued on the same lines and the results have been published at intervals in *Wirtschaft und Statistik*.

[9] The question whether a passive balance of trade should be regarded as an unfavourable symptom is not relevant at this stage.

16

telegraph fees, commercial services (fees and commissions), financial services (brokers' fees, &c.), and services connected with the tourist traffic. There is always the risk that some items may be counted twice over. Thus, if an imported commodity is re-exported at an enhanced price, the difference, even if due to services included in ' invisible exports,' will be reflected in the price statistics of imports and exports. In such a case therefore it should not be counted separately.

The balance of trade and the balance of services can be grouped together under one heading and contrasted with the balance of credit.

(b) The credit balance consists, on the one hand, of the interest balance, or balance of payments on capital, and, on the other hand, of the capital balance, or balance of payments (and repayments) of capital.

The interest balance includes fixed interest on Government, municipal and private loans, variable profits and dividends, rents, &c., and perhaps also the yield of patents, copyrights, cartel dues and so forth.

Under the heading of capital balance one should distinguish between long term and short term investments. Long term capital exports consist in the purchase of shares in foreign undertakings, the repurchase of home securities or repayment of loans contracted abroad, the purchase of foreign holdings in property located at home, &c., &c. Short term capital exports include any increase in the volume of bank balances held abroad, or in the holdings of foreign bills, and any decrease in the volume of commercial indebtedness to foreign countries.

The flow of long term capital is closely connected with the flow of short term capital, and changes in the one tend sometimes to be compensated by opposite changes in the other, so that only fluctuations in both combined affect directly the demand or the supply of foreign currency. Thus, if a German firm floats a loan of 10 million dollars in New York, it need not mean that the supply of dollars and the demand for marks in the foreign exchange market are immediately increased by 10 million and by 25 million respectively. What happens is that a New York bank opens an account in favour of the German firm, on which the latter draws gradually according to its requirements. The long term debt is, therefore, compensated by the creation of a short term asset, and there is no effective demand for currency until and so far as the latter is used up.[1]

---

[1] Of course, it may happen that a short term debt is created first and that it is consolidated later by the issue of long term bonds.

(c) Further items in the balance of payments are Government transactions (salaries of diplomatic representatives, subsidies, reparations, &c.) and gifts of money such as remittances sent home by emigrants.

§ 2. DIFFERENT SENSES OF THE TERM.

Having classified the items which make up the balance of payments, we must now analyse the concept itself. The term ' balance of payments ' is used in a number of different senses, which are apt to be confused with one another. It is very important to distinguish carefully between them, as the failure to do so has led to serious misconceptions.

(a) The term is sometimes used for the amounts of foreign currency bought and sold within a given period of time. In this sense the balance of payments is, of course, always in equilibrium, since the amount bought must necessarily equal the amount sold. The proposition is a mere tautology which follows from this (not very helpful) definition of the concept.

(b) It may refer, secondly, to the payments made, within the period, to and from foreign countries. This is not the same thing as (a) since payment can be made not only by the purchase of foreign money, but also by the transfer of foreign money already held.[2] If the volume of payments made is greater than the volume received, the deficiency will be made up in this way. The balance of payments in sense (b) may, therefore, very well be passive. It cannot, however, remain passive longer than the stock of money lasts. Moreover, it must have been active at some earlier point of time, since otherwise the stock could never have been acquired. Over a long period, therefore, the balance of payments must be in equilibrium in this sense too.[3]

(c) The term is frequently used in the more restricted sense of the balance of payments ' on income account.' This includes the interest balance and the balance of trade and services. If it is passive, then either the capital balance is active, or there is a transfer of gold or foreign currency. An ' unfavourable balance ' is then equivalent to an increase in indebtedness (including the export of shares, and any increase in holdings by foreigners) or to a loss of gold.

(d) There are no accurate figures of the balance of payments in any of the above senses. One must, therefore, be content with

---

[2] Including gold, if the country receiving payment is on the gold standard.
[3] Only a gold-producing country can have a permanently passive balance—if one does not prefer to regard gold in such cases as a commodity rather than money.

statistics of liabilities falling due. If these are all settled, the result is equivalent to the balance of payments in sense (*b*).

(*e*) From the balance of liabilities falling due during a given period, it is only a short step to the computation of the total volume of claims and liabilities outstanding at a given moment. This yields the ' balance of international indebtedness.'

(*f*) For the explanation of the exchange rate it is not sufficient to measure the amount of liabilities outstanding at a given moment or falling due during a given period; nor does it help to record *ex post facto* all the payments actually made during a given period. Economic analysis cannot start with a certain amount of existing liabilities;[4] it has to consider how they are contracted. The willingness to buy and to sell at this or that price (exchange rate) must be studied. In other words the apparatus of demand and supply must be applied to our particular market. The term ' balance of payments ' is then used in the sense of the whole demand-and-supply situation and in this sense it will be used in the following pages.

§ 3. SUPPLY AND DEMAND ANALYSIS.

The exchange rate between the means of payment of two countries is determined, like all other prices, by supply and demand. Since the supply of one currency constitutes the demand for the other and *vice versa*, we may treat either of them as a commodity and the other as money. In the following exposition the foreign currency will be treated like a commodity for which there is monetary demand, and we shall speak of its price in terms of the domestic currency.[5]

In the accompanying diagram, prices (*i.e.*, exchange rates defined as number of units of domestic currency per unit of foreign currency) are measured along the vertical axis, and amounts of foreign money bought and sold along the horizontal axis of a rectangular system of co-ordinates. The demand curve (DD) slopes downwards from left to right. This expresses the fact that people are willing to buy larger amounts of foreign currency at a lower price. This one can explain provisionally by the fact that foreign

---

[4] This point was stressed by Ricardo in his discussion with Malthus. " You appear to me not sufficiently to consider the circumstances [which] induce one country to contract a debt to another. [In] all cases you bring forward you always suppose the [debt] already contracted." *Letters of Ricardo to Malthus*, ed. by J. Bonar (1887), p. 11.

[5] This is in accordance with the method of quotation used on the continent, where exchange rates are expressed as so and so many units of domestic money per 100 units of foreign money. Rates quoted in London mean, on the other hand, so and so many units of foreign money per £1.

commodities become cheaper in consequence of the cheapening of the foreign currency and larger quantities will be imported. The supply curve (SS) slopes upwards from left to right. This expresses the fact that people are willing to sell larger amounts at a higher price, which is to be explained by the stimulation of exports due to the fall of prices of domestic goods in terms of foreign currency.[6] The two curves intersect at P. This means that there is an exchange rate at which the amount of foreign money which can be disposed of is equal to the amount offered for sale. If this price obtains, there is market equilibrium.

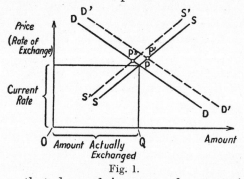

Fig. 1.

Suppose now that demand increases, because of an unfavourable change in the balance of payments in sense (d). In other words there is added to the existing demand the demand of those who now have to discharge additional debts to foreigners. This is represented by a shift of the demand curve from DD to D'D'. It now intersects the supply curve at P'. The exchange rate has risen and the amount of foreign money sold has increased. A rise in the exchange rate may also be due to a reduction in supply, owing, e.g., to a fall in exports. If the supply curve shifts from SS to S'S', the price will rise from P to P" and the amount sold will decrease.

---

[6] The statement that the supply curve slopes upwards from left to right needs qualification. If the amount of money in each of the two countries is held constant, there will be a point at which the supply curve curls backwards and slopes upwards to the left. This means that, if demand increases beyond that point, the amount of foreign money offered for sale will actually diminish (elasticity of supply $<$ 0); for the smaller amount of foreign money offered can buy a larger amount of domestic money. In the limiting case when the price of the foreign currency approaches infinity, i.e., when the price of domestic money in terms of foreign money falls to zero, the supply of foreign money will become very small. (It should be noted that the supply and the demand curve are not symmetrical. The point where the supply curve turns to the left corresponds to that point in the demand curve when the area of the inscribed rectangle begins to diminish.)

These cases are, however, of no practical importance. They are remote from reality chiefly because of the assumption that the quantity of money remains constant. If the quantity of money changes and, therefore, prices change, the demand and supply curves shift. The mechanism of adjustment consists precisely of more or less automatic changes in the circulating medium which produce appropriate shifts of the demand and supply curves.

Here it is necessary to recall the distinction, worked out in § 2, between the balance of payments in sense (a) and the balance of payments in sense (f). Sense (a) refers to OQ (demand actually satisfied, or supply actually sold); sense (f) refers to the whole demand-and-supply situation as represented by the two curves. In sense (a) the two sides of the balance of payment are equal by definition and a statement to the effect that they are equal is a tautological statement. But if we say that the balance of payment is, at a given moment, unfavourable, we mean that at the then prevailing rate (or at a rate which is considered as normal) demand exceeds supply, because the demand or supply curve or both have shifted. The balance of payment in sense (f) is in disequilibrium at a given rate, but equilibrium can be restored by a change in the exchange rate.

In view of the fact that changes are constantly occurring in the innumerable items which make up the balance of payments, it might be supposed that the rate of exchange would continually fluctuate like the price of commodities of which the supply-and-demand curves are liable to shift. But experience shows that under normal conditions the exchanges remain practically stable. There must, therefore, exist a mechanism which regulates supply and demand.[7]

We shall discuss in the next chapter this mechanism under the working of the gold standard. Chapter IV is concerned with the mechanism which operates under a paper currency, and Chapter V provides a synthesis of the two cases.

§ 4. THE CASE OF MORE THAN TWO COUNTRIES.

Throughout the preceding argument it has been assumed that only two countries are involved. But the modern economic system is composed of a number of different countries, each of which trades with each of the others. There is no reason to expect that one country's balance of payments with any other individual country will be in equilibrium. The analysis given above is applicable, therefore, only to a country's balance of payments with all the other countries combined. The mechanism of adjustment operates, however, through the so-called triangular trade, by influencing the balance of payments between countries other than the one directly concerned. In equilibrium the position is as follows. Germany, for instance, pays for its imports from the United States partly by selling machinery to South America, while the South American countries export raw materials to the United States. On the monetary side we can imagine the American exporter receiving in payment from his German customer a bill on Brazil, and selling it

---

[7] In terms of our demand and supply curves the working of the mechanism must be conceived as follows : There is an equalising source of supply (gold reserve of the central bank or exchange equalisation fund); the curve of total supply is therefore horizontal over a certain range. To avoid a depletion of the gold reserve, forces are set up which tend to shift the demand and the supply curve in an appropriate way; prices are changed and the flow of capital is influenced by means of changes in the rate of interest.

to an importer of Brazilian coffee. Actually the whole set of transactions will be financed by the banks, probably *via* the London money market, but that makes no essential difference. The modern banking system acts simply as a partially decentralised clearing-house.

When more than two countries are involved there will be more than one exchange-ratio. Between three countries there will be three ratios (e.g. 1 : 2, 1 : 3, 2 : 3), between four countries six ratios (*e.g.* 1 : 2, 1 : 3, 1 : 4, 2 : 3, 2 : 4, 3 : 3) and between n countries $\frac{n\,(n-1)}{2}$ ratios. Since the various foreign exchange markets are connected by telephone and telegraph, the different ratios must bear a determinate relation to each other. If, for instance, the dollar rate for marks were to rise, while the dollar rate for pounds, and the sterling rate for marks, remained constant, it would pay to change marks into dollars, dollars into pounds, and pounds into marks, until—assuming the dollar rate for pounds to be in equilibrium —the sterling rate for marks had risen proportionately. It is true that if the international money market is broken up by the severance of communications in wartime, temporary discrepancies may arise,[8] but experience shows that they will disappear very soon, even when rates are fluctuating widely.[9] There may, of course, be different rates for cash, telegraphic transfers, bills payable at sight, three months' bills, &c., all in terms of the same currency. But these exceptions are only apparent, since they refer to price discrepancies between what are, in effect, slightly different means of payment.

The situation, however, changes completely when a rigid exchange control supersedes the forces of the market. Then more or less fictitious and independent rates prevail and there is no necessity for a rapid adjustment between them. The problems resulting from this will be discussed later.

---

[8] This applies also to a single exchange ratio, which may be different even in the two countries directly involved.

[9] *Cf.* Graham, *Exchange, Prices and Production in Hyper-Inflation: Germany, 1920-1923* (1930).

CHAPTER III.

THE GOLD STANDARD.

§ 1. DEFINITION.

The term ' gold standard ' may be used in a narrower or in a wider sense. In the narrower sense it signifies a monetary system under which gold coins of standard specification, or gold certificates with 100 per cent. gold backing, form the circulating medium. In the wider sense it covers also the case where notes or silver coins are legal tender, provided they are convertible into gold at a fixed rate. There must, of course, be no prohibition of the melting down of gold coins.[1] Under these conditions the value of money and the value of gold are rigidly linked together and cannot diverge from one another.

If two or more trading countries are on the gold standard, and if there are no obstacles to the import and export of gold, then the different currencies are rigidly linked together. For instance, if an ounce of gold can be coined into a definite number of pounds sterling and into twenty times as many marks, then—still under the provisional assumption that no costs are involved—one can convert at will twenty marks into one pound and *vice versa*. A good analogy, which will be worked out in Chapter V, is that of two vertical cylinders joined by a connecting pipe.

§ 2. THE GOLD POINTS.

So long as the balance of payments is in equilibrium the ordinary means of international payment (bills, cheques, &c.) cancel out and there is no need for the transport and recoinage of gold. But suppose, to take a concrete example, that, owing to a failure of crops or the necessity of paying reparations, Germany's balance of payments with England becomes passive. What happens then?

The effect is that the demand for bills on England becomes greater than their supply. Consequently the value in marks of sterling bills goes up. If the actual cost of recoinage is zero, marks can still be converted into pounds at the rate of 20 : 1. Nevertheless, firms which have payments to make in England are prepared to give a somewhat higher price for sterling bills, since

---

[1] There have been many such prohibitions in the course of economic history, but they were always difficult to enforce.

they can in this way avoid the expense of transporting gold. If, however, the price of bills rises above the so-called ' upper gold point,' it will pay to export gold and to have it recoined abroad rather than to pay the enhanced price.[2] The position of the gold point is determined by the costs of transporting gold; these include, of course, the insurance premium and the loss of interest involved. Corresponding to the upper or export gold point there is a lower or import gold point, which is likewise determined by the cost of transmitting gold. Under modern conditions the actual transmission of gold is undertaken, not by the merchant himself, but either by a banking house which specialises in this line of business or by the central bank itself. The bank is enabled in this way to open an account abroad. It can then draw cheques and sell them at the enhanced rate. After the War it became the practice, instead of actually shipping gold, to earmark it on foreign account. If the Bank of France wished to import gold from America, it would simply have the bullion placed in a special account at New York, ready for shipment should the necessity arise. The Bank of International Settlements has tried to set up an international clearing system to supersede gold movements altogether; but since 1929 there has been to some extent a reaction in favour of the traditional practice.

The complications due to the existence of international borrowing will be considered later. For the present it is assumed that a passive balance of trade cannot be adjusted, even temporarily, in this way.

§ 3. MERCANTILIST IDEAS.

Suppose now that, owing to some factor the effects of which are not purely transitory,[3] the balance of trade becomes passive and the rate of foreign money rises above the gold export point. How long can the outflow of gold continue? Is there any limit to the amount of gold which will be withdrawn from circulation? Must the Government intervene to prevent an inconvenient drain on the currency, or is an appropriate distribution of gold between different countries secured automatically?

It is common knowledge that the mercantilists advocated the restriction of imports and the encouragement of exports, with a view to inducing an active balance and an inflow of gold. " The

---

[2] Goschen's *Theory of Foreign Exchanges* contains a classical statement of the theory. For a detailed catalogue of the determining factors, *cf.* Einzig, *International Gold Movements.*

[3] *E.g.*, a series of poor harvests, the necessity of paying reparations over a long period, or the permanent contraction of a foreign market.

ordinary means to increase our wealth and treasure is by foreign trade, wherein we must ever observe this rule; to sell more to strangers yearly than we consume of theirs in value."[4]

It is only fair to remember that the mercantilist doctrine was a great advance[5] on the ' bullion system ' which was dominant in England till after the beginning of the seventeenth century. This consisted in the rigid control of each separate transaction with foreign countries, with a view, on the one hand, to reducing commodity imports to the bare minimum and, on the other hand, to ensuring that exports should be paid for by an actual inflow of gold. All payments passed through the hands of the ' King's Exchanger,' who had a legal monopoly in the transaction of foreign business.[6]

The mercantilists showed that it was absurd to try and regulate every single transaction, since the only thing that mattered was the balance of total payments. Thomas Mun even went so far as to say that a passive balance of trade with one country should not be interfered with so long as it led indirectly to an active balance with another country. It was on the initiative of the mercantilists, and particularly of Mun himself, that the most burdensome of the restrictions on foreign trade were removed.[7]

The mercantilists are often criticised for taking into account only the balance of trade instead of the total balance of payments; but this criticism is unwarranted. Even in the sixteenth century there was an international credit system and a well-organised international money market. Many of the mercantilist writers referred explicitly to items in the balance of payments other than the trade balance. For example, Thomas Mun mentioned, amongst other things, expenditure on foreign travel, the transmission of gold to Rome, and military expenditure abroad. Certain other items which are familiar today were non-existent or of negligible proportions in the seventeenth century, and it is hardly surprising that the mercantilists ignored them. In any case, omissions of

---

[4] Thomas Mun, *England's Treasure by Forraign Trade* (written about 1628, published posthumously in 1664).

[5] Prof. Schumpeter calls the doctrine of the trade balance "the first step towards an analysis of the economic system." *Cf. Epochen der Dogmen- und Methodengeschichte* (2nd ed. 1924), p. 38.

[6] *Cf.* Tawney's *Introduction* to Thomas Wilson, *A Discourse upon Usury* (1572), reprinted in *Classics of Social and Political Science* (1925). Prof. Tawney observes with some justification, that the devices employed by the Tudors are exactly the same as those resorted to during the War—and also, it may be added, during the depression from 1931 onwards. *Cf.* chap. vii, § 7.

[7] The best discussion of the mercantilist doctrine is to be found in Viner, " English Theories of Foreign Trade before Adam Smith," *Journal of Political Economie* (1930), vol. 38, pp. 249 *seq.* and 404 *seq.*, and " The Balance of Trade " in the *Encyclopædia of the Social Sciences* (1930), vol. 2, p. 399, Professor Viner confines his attention to the English mercantilists. *Cf.* also Heckscher, *Mercantilism* (1935) (2 vols.).

this kind are unimportant compared with other defects of the doctrine.

The mercantilists based their whole attitude to problems of commercial policy on the idea that the accumulation of gold meant an increase in the real wealth of a country. This view was, of course, erroneous. But even if there were any sense in trying to increase the amount of gold in circulation, the method they advocated— namely, Government interference with foreign trade—would not in fact produce this result. Moreover, the fear that there might be an indefinitely large drain of gold unless such action were taken, was totally unfounded. The whole theory rested on very crude notions about the balance of payments. Mercantilism received its death-blow in 1752 when Hume published his *Political Discourses*. This was the first appearance in a systematic form[8] of the ' classical theory,' which was later refined and extended by Adam Smith, Thornton, Ricardo, Senior,[9] John Stuart Mill, Cairnes, Bastable, Taussig, &c.[1] It must now be considered in detail.

§ 4. THE CLASSICAL THEORY AND ITS CRITICS.

Our problem is to explain how equilibrium is restored after the balance of trade has become passive and gold has begun to flow out. The classical solution is as follows. The outflow of gold decreases the volume of money in circulation. Consequently prices fall, exports are stimulated and imports are reduced. In the foreign country where the balance of payments has become active the opposite happens.[2] Gold flows in, the volume of currency in circulation expands, prices rise, imports are stimulated, and exports are reduced. The movement of gold, which is the same thing as the cash payments necessitated by the passive balance of trade, produces a gap between the price levels of the two countries. This in its turn stimulates a flow of goods in the same direction as the original flow of gold, and the flow of goods induces a flow of gold in the opposite direction. The two gold movements, therefore, cancel out and the balance of payments is restored to equilibrium

---

[8] It was demonstrated by Friedrich Raffel that every one of the elements composing it could be found in earlier writers. *Cf.* " Englische Freihändler vor Adam Smith," *Zeitschrift für die gesamten Staatswissenschaften*, supplementary vol. 18. *Cf.* also Viner, *loc. cit.*

[9] His *Three Lectures on the Transmission of the Precious Metals from Country to Country and the Mercantile Theory of Wealth* (1828), reprinted in *London School of Economics Series of Reprints No.* 3, 1931.

[1] A detailed account of the historical development and a practically exhaustive bibliography are to be found in Angell, *The Theory of International Prices* (1926).

[2] Some writers have expressed a fear that the balance of payments may become passive for all countries simultaneously. But this is unlikely to happen until trade connections are established with another planet !

by the movement of commodities. Thus, payment is made provisionally in gold, but finally in goods. To put the same thing in another way: if a country is suddenly called on to make additional payments to foreign countries, its volume of exports and consequently the supply of foreign bills will increase. Simultaneously the demand for these bills diminishes, because imports contract. The bill market returns, therefore, to equilibrium and the exchange falls once more below the gold point.

This mechanism thus preserves equilibrium in the balance of payments. It prevents a complete loss of gold by any one country and ensures an appropriate distribution of gold among the gold standard countries which participate in world trade. The mechanism of the gold standard regulates the movement of gold automatically. It therefore renders state intervention at once superfluous and ineffective. " The exportation of the specie may at all times be safely left to the discretion of individuals. . . . If it be advantageous to export it, no laws can effectively prevent its exportation. Happily, in this case, as in most others in commerce, where there is free competition, the interests of the individual and that of the community are never at variance."[3]

Ricardo never tired of pointing out that, for purposes of international trade, money is simply that commodity which is most readily exchangeable. It, therefore, gravitates like other commodities—only with particular ease—to the place where its value is highest, or, in other words, where the price level is lowest. " If in France an ounce of gold were more valuable than in England, and would therefore in France purchase more of any commodity common to both countries, gold would immediately quit England for such purpose, and we should send gold in preference to anything else, because it would be the cheapest exchangeable commodity in the English market; for if gold be dearer in France than in England, goods must be cheaper; we should not therefore send them from the dear to the cheap market, but, on the contrary, they would come from the cheap to the dear market and would be exchanged for our gold."[4] Ricardo was only putting the same thing differently in the many passages where he attributed the outflow of gold to its ' redundance.' " By relative redundance then I mean, relative cheapness, and the exportation of the commodity I deem, in all ordinary cases, the proof of such cheapness."[5]

Discussion of the particular questions at issue between Ricardo

---

[3] Ricardo, *The High Price of Bullion* (1911), 4th ed., reprinted in *Works*, ed. McCulloch (1846), p. 265.
[4] *Op. cit.*, p. 266.
[5] *Letters to Malthus*, ed. Bonar (1887), p. 13.

and Malthus must be postponed till Chapter VII, where the classical
treatment of the 'transfer problem' is compared with the very
similar discussions of recent years. At the present stage it is more
convenient to deal with certain misconceptions of the scope and
implications of the classical theory as a whole.

On the Continent the classical theory has never found much
favour,[6] criticism being generally directed against the 'quantity
theory of money,' on which it is based. But two varieties of the
quantity theory must be distinguished. The more rigid one asserts
that a given percentage increase or diminution in the quantity of
money will necessarily change prices in the same proportion. But
the classical theory of international trade clearly does not require
so drastic an assumption. It need only postulate that an increase
in the quantity of money tends to raise prices, and that a diminution in the quantity of money tends to lower them, without saying
by how much. The quantity theory in this less rigid sense can
hardly be disputed. There is no advantage in substituting, as
Professor Aftalion wishes to do, for 'quantity of money' the
expression 'total incomes.'[7] Naturally the quantity of money
influences the price level only when it is actually spent, and thus
constitutes an effective demand for goods. Without altering in
any way the meaning of the classical theory one could say 'total
money incomes fall,' ' the supply of money shrinks ' or ' the demand
for goods becomes smaller ' instead of saying ' the quantity of
money diminishes ' or ' there is an outflow of gold.' One could
also speak with Professor Ohlin of a ' shift in (nominal) purchasing
power.'

It has been objected that the gold movements which occur in
practice are too insignificant to overcome such large disturbances
as often arise in the balance of payments. This objection cannot be
dealt with at the present stage, where the assumption is still made
of a purely automatic, ' unmanaged ' gold standard. Under
modern conditions every monetary system is influenced by the
deliberate policy of the central bank and by the mechanism of
international credit.[8] As will be shown later, gold movements
provoke changes in the volume of purchasing power many times
greater than themselves. Under a ' pure ' gold standard, where

---

[6] As typical of the French and German attitude, cf. the various writings of
Prof. Nogaro, and Helfferich, *Money*, p. 599 (vol. 2).

[7] *Cf.* his article, " Die Einkommenstheorie des Geldes " (*Wirtschaftstheorie der
Gegenwart* (1932), vol. 2, p. 376). Prof. Schumpeter has shown conclusively that
there is no antithesis between ' income theory ' and ' quantity theory ' : *cf.* " Das
Sozialprodukt und die Rechenpfennige " (*Archiv für Sozialwissenschaft* (1918),
vol. 44).

[8] For the objection that tariffs, &c., prevent the attainment of equilibrium, *cf.*
chap. vii, § 5.

the circulating medium consisted exclusively of gold, such movements would, therefore, have to be on a much larger scale.

Professor L. Laughlin[9] has objected that between modern
markets which are connected by railroads, telegraph, telephone,
&c., price differences cannot exist long enough to produce sufficiently large movements of goods. This criticism of the classical
doctrine can be disposed of by pointing out that modern means of
communication equalise prices by inducing transactions between the
cheap and the dear market; far from being an objection, this statement calls attention to circumstances which make for a rapid
functioning of the mechanism.

It is perhaps worth while to think out the classical theory
in terms of inter-regional trade.[1] Suppose that, owing to a redistribution of taxation, London or the County of Middlesex has
to make increased payments to Scotland. In that case Scotland's
purchasing power rises at the expense of the South. If the Scotsmen who now have more to spend buy the same commodities
as would have been bought by the Londoners whose incomes have
been reduced, the only effect is a movement of goods from London
to Scotland. More will be consumed in Scotland and less in
London. If, however, the Scotsmen spend their money at home
on commodities other than those which the Londoners have
previously been in the habit of buying, the process of adjustment
is more complicated. The volume of money in Scotland (which
forms the demand for goods there) has increased, whereas in
London it has diminished. Prices, therefore, rise in Scotland
and fall in London, and the discrepancy between the two price-
levels causes goods to flow from London to Scotland. This is
exactly the same process which has been expounded above as
the standard case in international trade. The problem will be
further analysed in chapter VII.

---

[9] *Principles of Money* (1903), p. 369.
[1] *Cf.* p. 11. As Ricardo himself pointed out, " The money of a particular
country is divided amongst its different provinces by the same rules as the money
of the world is divided amongst the different nations of which it is composed "
(*The High Price of Bullion; Works*, p. 282).

CHAPTER IV.

INCONVERTIBLE PAPER CURRENCIES.

§ 1. THE ' BALANCE OF PAYMENTS ' THEORY AND THE ' INFLATION ' THEORY.

The last chapter dealt with currencies rigidly linked together by convertibility into gold. The present chapter is concerned with the opposite extreme, with inconvertible paper currencies, the relative values of which are determined by supply and demand in the open market. The value of one in terms of the other is subject to variations like the price of ordinary commodities. There are no fixed parities or gold points, and a passive balance of payments will cause, not an outflow of gold, but a depreciation of the exchange. There is no fixed point at which depreciation will cease, corresponding to the gold export point in the previous example. On the other hand, depreciation cannot go on indefinitely, except under a progressive inflation. For the relative price changes which are necessary to reduce imports, stimulate exports, and restore equilibrium—and which under the gold standard are induced by the outflow of gold—are here produced by variations in the rate of exchange.[1] The problem is now to find the general principle which determines how far depreciation will go.

During the War, when the gold standard was suspended by one country after another, this question became again one of practical politics; and it was debated keenly, above all in Germany. Two explanations were put forward of the steady depreciation of the mark in terms of foreign currencies. The official view, which was mercantilist in spirit, ascribed it to the passive balance of payments; the critics, on the other hand, attributed the whole responsibility to inflation.

---

[1] Prof. Hollander points out that this factor operates to some extent even under a gold standard—within the limits set by the gold points (" International Trade under Depreciated Paper : a Criticism." *Quarterly Journal of Economics* [1918], vol. 32, p. 678). He concludes that absolute price changes are not required. But as Malthus showed in his review of Ricardo's *High Price of Bullion*, " we know indeed that such a demand (*i.e.*, for goods of the country whose balance of trade has become passive owing to a failure of the harvest) will to a certain degree exist, owing to the fall in the bills upon the debtor country, and the consequent opportunity of purchasing its commodities at a cheaper rate than usual. But if the debt for the corn or the subsidy be considerable, and require prompt payment, the bills on the debtor country will fall below the price of the transport of the precious metals. A part of the debt will be paid in these metals, and a part by the increased exports of commodities " (*Edinburgh Review* [Feb. 1811], vol. 17, pp. 344-5). *Cf.* also Viner, *Canada's Balance of International Indebtedness*, p. 194.

The ' balance of payments ' theory in its naïve form merely asserts that exchange rates are determined by the balance of payments, in the sense of supply and demand. There can be no objection to this ' theory,' but the question is : what determines supply and demand?

The balance of payments theory in its more sophisticated form does try to answer this further question. It asserts that the balance of payments is determined chiefly by factors which are independent of variations in the rate of exchange. In addition to fixed payments, such as reparations and the interest on foreign debts, the demand for many imported raw materials is inelastic because they are not to be had at any price except from abroad.

The fatal weakness of this theory is that it assumes the balance of payments to be a fixed quantity. To use an appropriate metaphor suggested by Mr. Keynes,[2] it applies the theory of solids where that of liquids would be more appropriate. The balance of trade (and also some invisible imports and exports) depends on the relation between price-levels at home and abroad. Even the demand for imported foodstuffs has a certain elasticity. For the same physiological needs can be satisfied either by cheap commodities like bread and potatoes, or by expensive ones like meat and fruit. In a word, the balance of payments is partially dependent on the exchanges; it cannot, therefore, be used to explain them.

This objection was raised by theorists of the ' inflation ' school.[3] They pointed out that the mark would never have depreciated so far if the volume of currency had not been continually increased. It was only the rise of domestic prices that prevented the expansion of exports and the contraction of imports. Otherwise equilibrium would have been restored by the change in relative prices. Exactly the same point had been made more than a hundred years ago by Ricardo, who asserted that ' the exchange accurately measures the depreciation of the currency.'[4] The situation in England during the Napoleonic wars was very similar to that in Germany from 1914 to 1920. The twentieth century has added but little to our understanding of these phenomena, and the correspondence

---

[2] *Cf.* " The German Transfer Problem," *Economic Journal* (1929), p. 6. Mr. Keynes himself compares the balance of trade to a sticky mass.

[3] *Cf.* the various writings of Prof. Cassel; Mises, " Zahlungsbilanz und Devisenkurse " (in *Mitteilungen des Verbandes der österreichischen Banken und Bankiers* [1919]); Machlup, *Die Goldkernwährung,* chap. 15; and Hahn, " Handelbilanz—Zahlungsbilanz—Valuta—Güterpreise " and " Statische und dynamische Wechselkurse " in *Geld und Kredit* (1924).

[4] *Letters,* p. 15. *Cf.* also *High Price of Bullion, passim,* and the celebrated *Bullion Report* which was produced under his influence (reprinted in Cannan, *The Paper Pound of 1797-1821*).

between Malthus and Ricardo still provides the best discussion of the points at issue.

§ 2. The Theory of Purchasing Power Parity.

The view that a fall in the exchange is due to inflation rests on the theory of ' purchasing power parity.' This theory asserts that the relative value of different currencies corresponds to the relation between the real purchasing power of each currency in its own country. The term ' purchasing power parity ' was first introduced by Professor Cassel, who enunciated the theory in its most extreme form. But he did not invent it[5] and his formulation was in any case very much over-simplified. His assertion that the demand for foreign money is determined by its purchasing power abroad is simply not true. Foreign money is normally purchased to settle a debt, and debts are contracted either without reference to prices at all (political debts) or with reference only to particular prices (commercial debts). General purchasing power is rarely considered.

But it is not difficult to guess what Professor Cassel really means. In so far as particular prices tend to equality in different countries, prices in general, or the value of money, will show the same tendency. But experience teaches that absolute equality of all particular prices is never realised. Nevertheless, one can speak of the equalisation of general price-levels, though hardly any of the purchasing-power-parity theorists except Marshall have tried to show in detail in what sense this is possible.

Obviously one cannot mean that the price of every single commodity must be the same in different countries. It is only transportable goods which react directly to price discrepancies at all, and even here discrepancies cannot be reduced in this way to less than the cost of transport. Every commodity has an export point and an import point. The distance between the two ' commodity points '[6] is determined by the cost of transport, including tariffs, insurance, uninsurable risks, interest (since transport takes time), cost of advertisement in the foreign market, &c., &c.[7] If

---

[5] The theory is older even than Ricardo. According to Prof. Angell, the first writer to formulate it clearly was John Wheatley (*Remarks on Currency and Commerce* [1802]). It was also extremely well set out by William Blake (*Observations on the Principles which Regulate the Course of Exchange; and on the Present Depreciated State of the Currency* [1810]). Blake spoke of the relation between Real Exchange (*i.e.*, purchasing power parity) and Nominal Exchange.

[6] As one may call them by analogy with the gold points. It should be noted that the export point is the lower commodity point in terms of domestic price.

[7] Most of these factors are not peculiar to international trade, however the latter concept may be defined.

in a country the price of a given commodity rises above the import point, imports will increase, if it falls below the export point, the commodity will be exported.

Professor Angell has recently urged that, in addition to transport costs, there are other factors which produce permanent price discrepancies. Following Professor Schüller, he mentions lack of information, lack of initiative, selling costs in a new market. None of these factors represents permanent costs of transport (indeed, the first two can hardly be regarded as costs at all), but for that very reason they do not lead to permanent price discrepancies.[8] How long discrepancies due to them will persist is, of course, another question. Some markets react more promptly than others. The stock exchanges and the markets for staple commodities in different countries are connected by telephone and telegraph, and speculation is highly organised. They therefore react to price discrepancies within a few hours. Other markets take days or even weeks to react; but in modern times improved communications and the collection of more and more detailed information about foreign markets have reduced substantially the 'reaction period' of all markets.

Professor Angell draws attention to another fact which in his view is the chief cause of disproportionate price differences. The increase of production which is necessary if exports to the country with the high price-level are to expand, will normally involve rising costs. Under perfect competition this cannot prevent the equalisation of prices. But, according to Professor Angell, there are many cases in practice where it will pay manufacturers to produce the smaller amount at a lower marginal cost, thus making larger profits per unit of the product. Now it is true that market conditions may be of this type, but, even so, they will not give rise to price discrepancies; for exports can be increased without an expansion of total output. Indeed, manufacturers may not even know what proportion of their output will be exported by the traders who buy from them.

The case of dumping (i.e., price discrimination in favour of the foreigner) also provides no exception to the rule, since commodities can be reimported if the price discrepancy is greater than the costs of transport.[9]

Within the limits set by the cost of transport the price of a commodity may vary between different countries. In many

---

[8] As Ricardo pointed out (*Letters to Malthus*, p. 18), lack of information as a disturbing factor could be urged against almost every law of political economy.
[9] For a general discussion of dumping *cf.* chap. xviii below.

cases the two commodity points are a long way apart, and the limits are correspondingly wide. If transport is impossible, or if it is disproportionately expensive,[1] there will be no *direct* connection at all between prices at home and abroad.

Thus it is possible to distinguish, roughly, between goods which are and goods which are not ' internationally traded.' All commodities which are regularly exported or imported, even if only in small quantities, should be classified as international goods; but it is perfectly conceivable that a commodity which is exported from country A to country B may be produced in countries C and D for the home market and neither imported nor exported. Moreover, the list of international goods is continually changing. Whether at any particular moment a given commodity is ' international ' or not depends on whether the cost of transport is smaller or greater than the difference between the marginal costs of production in the countries concerned.

The question what goods are ' international ' depends therefore on the particular circumstances; and the boundary is continually shifting. Goods which have previously been imported will be produced at home if costs in general are reduced (*e.g.*, by deflation), if their particular costs of production are diminished (*e.g.*, by a new invention) or if their costs of transport are increased (*e.g.*, by a tariff). Shifts of this kind may be permanent or transitory or periodic (*e.g.*, seasonal). A great many domestic goods are potentially international goods. The nearer their cost of production is to the export or to the import point the more likely they are to become international goods, as a result of small changes either in the cost of production or in the cost of transport.

The price of international goods in the exporting country coincides with the lower or export commodity point, and in the importing country with the upper or import point.[2] The difference between them is equal to the cost of transport. If it were greater, the flow of goods would increase; if it were less,

---

[1] The first applies to land, houses, labour and commodities with prohibitive tariffs, the second to certain building materials and so forth.

[2] In trade statistics a single class of goods may frequently be found both among the imports and among the exports of the same country. This may occur for several reasons. Thus the imported commodity may differ slightly in quality from the exported commodity, although they are classified for statistical purposes under the same heading. Moreover, goods of the same type may be imported and exported at different moments of time (e.g. seasonal fluctuations), or they may be imported into one part of the country and at the same time be exported from another part of the country. Thus for many years wheat was imported into Western Germany and exported from Eastern Germany. Further, certain goods are imported from one country and then re-exported to another. Finally, there may be occasional exceptions due to imperfection of the market. But the distinction between regular exports and imports does not thereby become meaningless. *Cf.* Taussig, *Some Aspects of the Tariff Question* (1931), 3rd ed.

the flow of goods would diminish. The price of each international good in one country has, therefore, a determinate relation to its price in the other country; and both prices move together. The same argument applies to the price of international goods taken as a whole. Their average price-level is generally higher in one country than in another, since the cost of transport varies between different goods. But if there is no change in transport costs the average price-level rises or falls everywhere in the same proportion; it cannot possibly go up in one country and down in another. If all goods were internationally traded the theory of purchasing power parity would, therefore, require no further proof. But there are also domestic goods; and it is theoretically possible that their price-level may vary even inversely to that of international goods. The theory of purchasing power parity has, therefore, to prove that the two price levels do, in fact, move together.

It seems probable that there is a fairly close connection of this kind.[3] Even if the proportion of international to domestic goods is small,[4] it must not be forgotten that the former include most of the important raw materials, which influence considerably the price of their products. Moreover, the number of international and of potentially international goods is continually being increased by improvements in transport.

We are now in a position to state the theory of purchasing power parity in a precise form and with the necessary qualifications.

(a) It is not true that prices must be the same in all trading countries. Owing to differences in the cost of transport there will be differences in the price of particular articles. It is impossible to say beforehand whether in any particular case they will cancel out, leaving average prices the same, or not.

(b) The theory cannot, therefore, be applied to absolute levels of prices, but only to changes in the price levels.[5] Moreover, there is a direct and rigid connection only between the prices of international goods in different countries, though probably the connection between the price of international and of domestic goods within each country, and, therefore, by way of the former between the general price levels of different countries, is fairly close.

Let P_A be the general price level of country A and P_B the general price level of country B. Let R be the exchange rate

---

[3] Cf. Zapoleon, " International and Domestic Commodities and the Theory of Prices " (Quarterly Journal of Economics [May 1931], vol. 45, pp. 409 et seq.). Mr. Keynes is of the opposite opinion. Cf. A Tract on Monetary Reform, p. 93.

[4] For the United States it is computed at between 5 and 8 %, but the figures are not very reliable. In smaller countries one would naturally expect the proportion to be higher.

[5] Cf. Pigou, Essays in Applied Economics, p. 166.

of currency A in terms of currency B. Then $P_A = P_B \times R \times k$, k representing the difference between the value of money in A and in B respectively. Thus $R = \dfrac{P_A}{P_B \times k}$. The fraction $\dfrac{P_A}{P_B}$ expresses the relation between the two price levels, and k the divergence from purchasing power parity.

Let 1 and 2 represent different points of time. Then $R_1 : R_2 = \dfrac{P_{A_1}}{P_{B_1} \times k_1} : \dfrac{P_{A_2}}{P_{B_1} \times k_2}$ If the degree of divergence from purchasing power parity remains constant throughout (*i.e.*, if in both countries the general price level moves parallel with the price level of international goods), then $k_1 = k_2$ and $R_1 : R_2 = \dfrac{P_{A_1}}{P_{B_1}} : \dfrac{P_{A_2}}{P_{B_2}}$ In this case the change in purchasing power parity, *i.e.*, the relative movement of the two price-levels, is reflected by a proportionate variation of the exchange-rate.

The simplest form of the theory is represented by the equation $\dfrac{R_1}{R_2} = \dfrac{P_{A_1}}{P_{A_2}}$, which holds when the general price-level in country B remains unchanged (so that $\dfrac{P_{B_1}}{P_{B_2}} = 1$), while an inflation takes place in A. In other words, the change in the purchasing power of money in country A is here reflected in a corresponding variation of the exchange rate.

(*c*) It is obvious that the theory of purchasing power parity stands or falls with the hypothesis that k does in practice remain fairly constant. There is no logical necessity for this. The extent to which k changes depends primarily on the comparative importance of international and domestic goods. If the volume of international trade is small, it may even change very considerably. In such cases the theory breaks down completely.

Suppose, for example, that Canadian exports to England consist of wheat—representing agricultural produce in general— and English exports to Canada of electrical machinery, both to the value of 100 million. If, now, England's demand for wheat increases, more will be imported and the price will rise.[6] England has then to choose between two alternatives. She can directly stimulate exports and discourage imports by letting the exchange depreciate. On the other hand, she can hold the exchange constant by reducing the amount of money in circulation. Under a gold standard of the rigid type this is brought about automatically by an outflow of gold, but under a paper currency credit must be restricted in order to secure stability of the

---

[6] Similar results follow a change in supply.

exchange;[7] in either case there has to be deflation in England. The prices of all commodities produced at home, including electrical machinery, go down and wheat becomes comparatively dearer. Thus equilibrium is finally restored, in this case, too, by an increase of exports and a diminution of imports.[8]

In both cases k has changed. The price of international goods is once more, apart from transport costs, identical in both countries. In England the general price-level has fallen, compared with the price of wheat. The price of electrical machinery is affected in the same way as that of other commodities produced at home. The price-level of imports and exports together has therefore risen, relatively to the general price-level in England. In Canada, on the other hand, the prices of international goods have fallen more than the general price-level in Canda, since electrical machinery is now cheaper than before. This is clearly an exception to the theory of purchasing power parity.

An example of the type just analysed was suggested by Professor Viner in a debate with Professor Cassel.[9] In reply, Professor Cassel admitted that the rate of exchange was determined not only by purchasing power parity but also by the conditions of demand for imports. But he maintained that his theory was meant to apply only to the effect of monetary changes operating *ceteris paribus*.

(*d*) In the modern world sudden and violent changes of k are prevented by the reserve of potentially international goods. But over a period of years quite appreciable changes can take place. The question therefore arises whether the theory of purchasing power parity is anything more than an extremely rough approximation to the facts. The answer must be that for one group of phenomena, namely monetary changes, the theory holds true with a high degree of precision. During the post-war inflation, perhaps 99 per cent. of the depreciation of the German mark was due to

---

[7] *Cf.* chap. v below.

[8] Apart from the two cases analysed in the text, there is a third possibility. The increased demand for wheat in England implies a decreased demand for other commodities. Productive resources may therefore be liberated for use in the export industry, and the price of electrical machinery may fall, without disturbance either to the exchange or to the price system as a whole. If purchasing power parity is to be maintained, Canada must expend the whole surplus derived from the sale of wheat on the purchase of electrical machinery.

[9] At Chicago in Jan., 1928 Prof. Viner pointed out, further, that prices can rise in one country and fall in the other if the cost of transport in one direction goes up and in the other direction goes down. The same point has also been made by Prof. Pigou (*op. cit.*) in a more general form. He points out that any impediment to trade in one direction only will upset the purchasing power parity. Prof. Gregory admits that there are exceptions to the purchasing power parity theory, but considers them to be negligible. *Cf.* " Geldtheorie und Handelsbilanz " in *Die Wirtschaftstheorie der Gegenwart* (1932), vol. 2, pp. 370-1.

the rise in prices and only 1 per cent. to changes in relative demand. It is improbable that inflation or deflation will permanently affect k, by changing the relative demand for international and for domestic goods respectively, if the basic conditions of consumers' tastes and technical knowledge remain constant.[1] Moreover, in a violent inflation the disturbing effect of changes in relative demand is clearly quite imperceptible.[2]

(e) The experience of recent years has shown that it is possible, to a quite unexpected extent, to isolate, by means of rigid import restrictions, one country's price-levels from those of the outside world and thus to maintain for a long period an exchange-rate which is quite out of line with purchasing power parity in the ordinary sense. In the more exact terminology of our theory one would have to say that it is possible to produce rapidly large changes in k by the imposition of tariffs and quotas; but, of course, only at the cost of drastically restricting the international division of labour.[2a]

Although the theory of purchasing power parity has therefore only a restricted field of application, the fundamental conception which distinguishes it from the balance of payments theory is both correct and important. While the price-levels of different trading countries may diverge, their price systems are nevertheless inter-related and interdependent, although the relation need not be that of equality. Moreover, as will be shown in the next chapter, supporters of the theory are quite right in contending that the exchanges can always be stabilised at any desired level by appropri-ate, though not necessarily by proportionate, changes in the volume of money.

§ 3. PROBLEMS OF STATISTICAL VERIFICATION.

If the theory of purchasing power parity is to be tested statis-tically, care must be taken to select for comparison those prices which are relevant to it. This presupposes a theoretical analysis.

Attention has generally been concentrated on the index of wholesale prices. But this relates to raw materials, semi-manu-factured commodities and foodstuffs, which are mostly international goods. The high degree of correlation[3] which has been established affords, therefore, not much support to the theory of purchasing power parity.

---

[1] The problem of temporary changes will be discussed in chap. vi.
[2] In the above-mentioned discussion Prof. Cassel made it clear that his theory had been devised primarily to meet this case, and that it presupposed, strictly speaking, fixed demand functions.
[2a] *Cf.* chap. vii, § 7.
[3] In chap. vi it will be shown by statistical examples that even in this field discrepancies persist for fairly long periods when inflation is going on.

Of greater significance is the behaviour of retail prices or the 'cost of living'; for retail commodities are, clearly, domestic goods. Statistical enquiry shows that the absolute price-level of retail goods is usually higher in rich than in poor countries. This is due partly to differences in the cost of retailing, but partly also to the fact that many commodities which appear in statistical tables under the same heading are of higher quality in the more prosperous countries.[4] Moreover, taxes on retail trading and restrictions and regulations of various kinds work in the same direction. All these factors produce absolute price discrepancies and they also prevent the movements of retail prices from corresponding so closely in different countries as those of wholesale prices. It is, therefore, of great theoretical interest that a considerable degree of correlation has been observed.

The problem of comparison between goods of better quality and goods of poor quality exemplifies one of the main difficulties of statistical work. The price levels of different countries include different commodities. Even staple commodities are not completely standardised, and no two markets operate in exactly the same way. A strict comparison is, therefore, impossible. Moreover, the statistical data are very incomplete. Apart from a few raw materials, there are not even the weekly quotations which would be necessary for detailed comparisons, while information about rebates, discounts, &c., cannot usually be obtained at all. On detailed problems of this kind a great deal of work remains to be done. In the meantime one must refrain from drawing hasty conclusions about the relation between the price systems of different countries from the ordinary crude statistics.

The most usual method of determining whether the exchange-rate between two countries is in equilibrium and whether it corresponds to purchasing power parity is as follows. The price-indices of Great Britain and the United States are both put equal to 100 for 1928, when the exchange-rate is assumed to have been in equilibrium. Changes in the two price levels are then calculated relatively to the common base year, and the divergence between them is compared with movements of the exchange. If, *e.g.*, the English price-index fell between 1928 and 1932 from 100 to 90 and the American index from 100 to 60, then the value of the pound in terms of dollars should have decreased by one-third.

This method is, however, inadequate, quite apart from any deficiencies of the statistical data. For one cannot be sure whether

---

[4] This applies not only to the goods themselves but also to the conditions under which they are sold.

there was equilibrium in the base year, or to what extent k has changed. Moreover, even in the simplified case when all goods are internationally traded, and there are no costs of transport, the method is still inaccurate.

Let us consider two periods and two countries. Individual prices change differently from period one to period two, but there are no price differences in either period between the two countries. Then the purchasing power parity would clearly hold in both periods; if each price is the same in both countries, *a fortiori*, the price-level must be the same too, however we define this ambiguous term. From that it does not, however, follow that the price-level in each country will be found to have changed to the same extent between the first and the second period. At least, if we take for each country price index numbers which use values of production or consumption as weights, any difference between the weighting systems of the two countries will produce a divergence in the calculated change of the price-level in the two countries between periods one and two.[5]

This paradox is due to the fact that only fixed-weight index formulæ fulfil the so-called 'circular test.'[6] This puzzle exists also if we drop the assumption that each price is the same in both countries; but it is then veiled by the influence of the price discrepancies. It seems to follow that index-numbers designed for the verification of the purchasing-power-parity theory, should not use figures of national consumption or production as weights.

---

[5] *Cf.* Nurkse, *Internationale Kapitalbewegungen* (1935), p. 151.
[6] *Cf.* Haberler, *Der Sinn der Indexzahlen* (1927), p. 48 *et seq.* Irving Fisher, *The Making of Index Numbers*, 3rd ed. (1927), p. 274 *et seq.*

CHAPTER V.

FURTHER DETAILS OF THE EXCHANGE-MECHANISM.

§ 1. Preliminary Remarks on Monetary Theory in General.

The last two chapters have sketched in outline the workings of a pure gold-standard and of inconvertible paper-currencies respectively. But the monetary systems of the modern world represent generally neither of these two extremes. In the present chapter it will be shown how exchange-rates are kept more or less automatically stable under certain modified types of gold-standard, and how they are deliberately controlled by means of discount-policy.

It has often been pointed out that money finds its purest expression in ' token-money '—such as currency-notes—which as a commodity has practically no value at all. In other words, monetary problems can be expressed in their most general form when we assume a pure paper-currency. Most of the conclusions reached under such an assumption—in particular what has been said about price-adjustments and purchasing-power parity—can therefore be applied without qualification to the special conditions of the gold-standard and of the intermediate types as well.

Before doing so, however, it is convenient to illustrate some of the fundamental conceptions of monetary theory by means of a familiar analogy. In fig. 2 the monetary systems of two countries are represented by vertical cylinders as follows:—

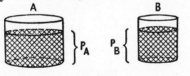

Fig. 2.

In each case the amount of water stands for the quantity of money, the depth of water for the price-level, and the width of the cylinder, as measured by the area of its base, for the volume of transactions, or amount of work which the money has to perform. The functioning of the gold-standard may be represented by a pipe connecting the two cylinders below the water-line and thus ensuring that, should water be removed from one cylinder into the other, a corresponding amount would flow back through the pipe. Thus the level of water in the two cylinders could not in the long run be different. With inconvertible paper-currencies, on

41

the other hand, price-changes would be reflected in relative changes of the two water-levels, representing a shift of the exchange-rate. Changes in purchasing-power parity (± k) would in both cases be represented by the raising or lowering of one cylinder compared with the other.

The volume of transactions is determined, broadly speaking, by (a) the volume of goods and services to be exchanged, (b) the degree of vertical integration or differentiation,[1] (c) the habits of payment, or methods of settling accounts, and the extent of payments by instruments of credit.

Factors (b) and (c) are usually grouped together under the rather vague heading, 'Velocity of Circulation of Money.' But the method of classification is really a matter of convenience. Thus one can contrast, with Professor Mises, the ' stock of money ' with the ' demand for money,' and understand by the latter the volume of trade in the wider sense, i.e., the width of the ' cylinder ' as determined by factors (a) to (c). On the other hand, one may consider it more appropriate to distinguish between determining forces ' on the money-side ' (quantity of money, velocity of circulation, methods of payment which dispense with cash, &c.) and determining forces ' on the commodity-side ' (quantity of goods to be exchanged, &c.)—though the line of distinction is not always clear-cut. One can treat the methods of payment which dispense with cash (settlement at a clearing house and credit as a means of payment) as an increase either in the quantity of money or, with Wicksell,[2] in the velocity of circulation of cash. The method of classification chosen is to a large extent immaterial: the important thing is to analyse the various factors in detail and not merely lump them together under ' demand for money ' or ' velocity of circulation,' as the case may be.

' Bank-money ' deserves special notice. A large proportion of payments—in the Anglo-Saxon countries, where the use of cheques is very widespread, the great majority of payments, on the Continent of Europe a considerable part—is made not in cash but by the transfer of bank-credit from one account to another. Bank-money is also called ' deposit-money ' or ' credit-money.' ' Average volume of short-term liabilities of the banks ' × ' rate of turnover ' = ' total clearing figures ' shows roughly the magnitude of these transactions.[3]

---

[1] Cf. notably Hayek, *Prices and Production*; Holtrop, *Omloopsnelheid van het Geld*, 1928, p. 111; and the German edition of the latter work, " Umlaufsgeschwindigkeit des Geldes " in *Beiträge zur Geldtheorie*, 1933, ed. by Hayek, pp. 144 *et seq.*
[2] Cf. *Lectures on Political Economy*, vol. 2 (1935).
[3] Cf. Neisser, " Umlaufsgeschwindigkeit der Bankdepositen " in *Handwörterbuch des Bankwesens* (1933).

One can regard the expansion of bank-credit as an increase either in the quantity of money or in the velocity of circulation or efficiency of 'real money'; or, again, as a decrease in the demand for money or in the work which real money has to perform. But since bank-money is quantitatively so important and since the banks are able to create and destroy it, the expression 'changes in the quantity of money' seems most appropriate.

Some writers even commence their exposition of monetary theory by postulating a pure credit-system, and introduced cash-payments only at a later stage.[4] But this procedure has the disadvantage of obscuring the fundamental principle that money—of whatever kind—has economic value only because its quantity is limited.

But whichever terminology or method of exposition one adopts, it is necessary to find an expression for the following two relations. On the one hand, there must be a definite relation between cash and bank-money. Needless to say this ratio is not absolutely fixed but varies from time to time. On the other hand, the creation of bank-money under given circumstances has a determinate influence on prices—whether one calls it an increase in the quantity of money or in the velocity of circulation.

We are now in a position to state those elementary propositions of monetary theory which are relevant to the main argument. If the volume of trade and the velocity of circulation (habits of payment, &c.)—or in terms of our analogy the width of the cylinder—remain constant, then the price-level rises with every increase in the quantity of money. If in a progressive economy the quantity of money and the velocity of circulation (habits of payment, &c.) remain constant while the production of goods increases, then the price-level must fall, &c., &c.

It will hardly be disputed that the only easily-regulated factor among the forces determining the price-level is the quantity of money, including credit. The other factors—the quantity of goods to be exchanged and the habits of payment (velocity of circulation)—cannot be influenced so quickly, if at all. A monetary policy therefore which aims at stabilising the price-level or the exchanges must regulate the quantity of money. In this way one can usually counteract other influences on prices, and thus maintain the existing price-level. If, for example, in the course of economic development the quantity of goods to be exchanged increases, prices will tend to fall. Unless this tendency is offset by a change in the habits of payment (*e.g.*, by a growth of methods

---

[4] *Cf.*, *e.g.*, Hahn, *Volkswirtschaftliche Theorie des Bankkredits*, 3rd edn., 1930; Hawtrey, *Currency and Credit*, 3rd edn., 1928; and Keynes, *Treatise on Money*.

of payment other than by cash) it can be prevented only by an increase in the quantity of money. In other words, a larger quantity of money is required to carry through a larger volume of transactions at the same level of prices.

The rate of exchange is determined, as we have shown, by the equation $R = \dfrac{P_A}{P_B k}$. Assuming, to avoid complications, that k remains relatively constant, it follows that $\dfrac{P_A}{P_B}$ must be held constant if it is desired to stabilise the rate of exchange. Any changes in k must be compensated by changes in $\dfrac{P_A}{P_B}$. In either case the desired effect can normally be produced by regulating the quantity of money.

§ 2. PRICE-STABILITY versus EXCHANGE-STABILITY.

Governments generally choose to stabilise either the price-level or the rates of foreign exchange. These two lines of policy are compatible with one another only if foreign countries also follow a policy of stabilising the price-level[5]—that is to say, only by international agreement. But if in foreign countries the price-level is rising or falling, the country in question is faced with the dilemma of either stabilising the exchange rate and letting the domestic price-level move in sympathy with the foreign price-level, or stabilising domestic prices and allowing the exchange rate to move in inverse ratio to the movement of the foreign price-level. In general, stabilisation of the exchange-rate is the line of least resistance, unless price-levels abroad are subject to very wide fluctuations. Movements of the exchange-rate leap to the eye, whereas small changes in the price-level are less clear-cut and attract less attention. When the exchange rate of a country depreciates by 10%, everyone sees what is happening. A 10% rise in the price-level is, on the other hand, not such an unambiguous and striking phenomenon. Both commercial and financial relations with foreign countries are at once sensibly affected by fluctuations of the exchanges. Speculation in the foreign-exchange market[6] develops, unless rates are kept absolutely stable, and international credit-operations of a normal kind are seriously hampered hereby. In financially weak countries—particularly where the memory of inflation is still fresh—every deviation of the exchange from gold-

---

[5] And if k remains constant. If k changes, the exchange and the price-level can both remain constant only if the price-level abroad happens to have shifted exactly parallel with k.

[6] Cf. chap vi.

parity, or even any likelihood of such deviation must lead to a crisis of confidence and to withdrawals of credit. This has been demonstrated once more by events in Germany in 1931 and 1932.

The repeated runs, during the last few years, on the currencies of the Gold Bloc have shown that fluctuating exchanges produce very unpleasant long-period effects. The gains and losses which can be made from the unexpected depreciation of one currency or another have come to be realised more and more widely. People therefore try to invest their money in as liquid a form as possible, in order to be able to convert it at the first sign of danger into some other currency which appears at the moment to offer greater security. The desire for liquidity has led to the hoarding of gold on a large scale and has very considerably strengthened the tendency to deflation, particularly in the gold-standard countries.

For smaller countries in whose economic system foreign trade plays a large part, stabilisation of the exchange is the only possible policy. Particularly if they are dependent on foreign capital, they must sacrifice stability of prices to stability of the exchange, at any rate so long as there are important countries abroad with a fairly stable monetary system to which they can attach themselves. For strong countries another policy is conceivable. Thus Mr. Keynes has for many years advocated for England a policy of stabilising the price-level, with the aim of smoothing out cyclical fluctuations, even at the cost of an unstable exchange-rate with the gold-standard countries. The arguments in favour of stabilising the price-level rather than the exchange cannot be examined here.[7] For this would involve a detailed treatment of trade-cycle theory and trade-cycle policy, and particularly of the problem of price-stabilisation as a means of smoothing out cyclical fluctuations.

Recent years have provided extremely interesting experiences in this field. Since departing, in September 1931, from the gold-standard, England has followed more or less deliberately and with the support of many English economists a policy of stabilising the price-level.[8] This policy enabled the Scandinavian countries and the Dominions to reap the advantages of stable exchange-rates with England—still the centre of world-trade—and with other members of the sterling-group, and to maintain stability of prices relatively to one another.

But as already mentioned the instability of the exchange-rate between the gold- and the sterling-currencies has led to serious

---

[7] Cf. Harrod, *International Economics* (1933). This able discussion is however based on a theory of short-run (cyclical) fluctuations which cannot be accepted as definitely established.

[8] Cf. Benham, *British Monetary Policy* (1932).

disadvantages. The conclusion seems therefore justified that stable exchange-rates, or in other words an international standard of one kind or another, is indispensable in the long run for any extensive exchange of goods and credit on an individualistic basis. A collapse of the international money-system would have to lead sooner or later to a rigid control, in the first instance, of the capital-market. This would necessitate, as will be shown in § 7, chapter VII, also a rigid superintendence of trade in commodities. Whether the international system must take the form of the gold standard is another question. From the purely economic point of view one could equally well picture an international sterling-standard, such as already operates over a considerable part of the world. This is in fact only to a small extent a question of economic theory, and to a much greater extent a question of international politics.

§ 3. Methods of Preserving Exchange-Stability (Gold-Bullion Standard, Gold-Exchange Standard).

(a) The simplest method of preserving a stable exchange is a gold standard in the rigid sense. As already pointed out, its mechanism, which has been described in Chapter III, may be compared to a pipe connecting our two cylinders and ensuring automatically that the level of water shall always be the same in each.

(b) Stability of the exchange can however equally well be maintained under a less rigid type of gold standard. There is no need for the circulating medium to consist entirely of gold.

International payments are normally made not in cash but by cheque or by a bill of exchange. Gold is used only for a small proportion of total payments and that only when equilibrium has been disturbed. Here one can distinguish three main cases. (1) A sudden payment in one direction which does not evoke a simultaneous payment in the opposite direction. This may be compared to an overflow of water out of one cylinder into the other; but a corresponding quantity would flow back through the pipe. (2) A permanent increase in one country's volume of trade, or a decrease in the velocity of circulation. This would be represented by an increase in the diameter of one cylinder; water would flow into it and stay there permanently. (3) An increase in the amount of money. This would mean, in terms of our analogy, that water was poured into one cylinder; a corresponding amount would then drain off into the other cylinder. Experience shows that large movements of gold are required only in the third case. For, in the first case, a transfer of goods is soon stimulated[9] and, in the second case, the expansion, which necessarily takes time, is facilitated by the normal increase in the world's stock of gold.

It should be noted that the policy of preventing any increase in the total amount of money[1] leads in the latter case to unfavourable results. There are reasons for the view, widely held by economists,[2] that if in a closed economy productivity per head increases, it is better to keep the amount of money constant than to stabilise prices. This argument must however be applied with caution to the international sphere. Suppose that productivity per head increases in the United States but remains constant in Europe. Unless the total amount of money increases, there must be a change in the international distribution of gold if the gold-parity is to be maintained. In the United States prices fall, exports increase, imports diminish, gold flows in and prices rise again. In the European countries the amount of money has to fall, although conditions at home do not call for deflation. This would be avoided if the quantity of money in the United States was increased from the start.

To return to the main argument. Since under normal conditions only a small proportion of the gold in circulation is ever likely to flow out, the gold standard can be maintained even if a considerable part of the currency consists of paper-money with only a relatively small gold-backing. To use a picturesque metaphor of Adam Smith's, " a sort of waggon-way (is provided) through the air." This means an appreciable saving to the country concerned, since a substantial amount of gold, which is more expensive than paper, can be dispensed with. If other countries follow suit, prices rise all along the line and the only advantage is that gold can be used more freely for industrial purposes and that factors can be transferred to the production of other commodities.

It is only a further step in the same direction to use the whole stock of gold as a reserve for emergency payments to foreign countries and to make paper-money the sole legal tender.[3] This is called the ' Gold-Bullion Standard.'

(c) If the whole stock of gold is in the hands of the central bank, the latter can use it to buy short-term foreign investments, which, on the one hand, yield interest and, on the other hand,

---

[9] Cf. chap. vii.
[1] Cf. Hayek, *Prices and Production* and *Monetary Theory and the Trade Cycle*.
[2] Cf. the references in Hayek, " Paradox of Saving " in *Economica*, May 1931, p. 161.
[3] Cf. Machlup, *Die Goldkernwährung*, 1925. Ricardo was the first to advocate a gold-standard of this type (*Proposals for an Economical and Secure Currency*, 1816).

are readily convertible into gold. This device, which is called the 'Gold-Exchange Standard,' was practised even before 1914, especially by the Austro-Hungarian Bank, but also to some extent elsewhere.[4] When the Central European currencies were stabilised after the war, most of the countries concerned adopted a dollar-exchange standard,[5] because at that time the United States was the only country really on the gold standard. But Holland, Switzerland and the Scandinavian countries made a similar use of sterling-bills after England returned to the gold standard. When she again abandoned it, in 1931, they suffered heavy losses. Since then the practice has gone out of fashion to some extent, except within the 'sterling area.'

Clearly gold-exchange standards in the proper sense presuppose that at least one country remains on a gold standard of the traditional type. It is conceivable that two countries might adopt a gold-exchange standard relatively to one another. If, for instance, the United States sent gold to Great Britain[6] for investment in sterling-bills, the Bank of England would be enabled in its turn to purchase American bills by the same method, and so on indefinitely. This procedure might be called 'reciprocal inflation.'

If the credit-policy of the central banks was determined in the traditional way by the reserve-proportion, the same gold would form a basis for credit-expansion in more than one country, and a world-inflation would ensue.

The quantity of money is controlled under all varieties of gold-standard by its convertibility into gold or foreign exchange. If prices rise or if because payments to foreign countries temporarily exceed payments from them, there is a demand for gold and foreign exchange at the central bank, a corresponding volume of notes will be paid in and thus withdrawn from circulation. The reserve-regulations, which lay down a definite relation between paper-money and cash-reserves, are intended to prevent the bank from issuing too much paper-money.

In addition to this 'automatic brake' there is also a 'hand brake' operated by the central bank, which both directly and indirectly influences the rates of foreign exchange. This hand brake is the discount-policy.

§ 4. DISCOUNT-POLICY.

In all historical cases of the gold standard, only a part of

---

[4] Cf. Ansiaux, La politique regulatrice des changes, and Keynes, Indian Currency and Exchange (1913), chap. ii.

[5] Cf. Machlup, Die neuen Währungen in Europa (1927).

[6] As already pointed out, the actual shipment of gold can, under modern conditions, be dispensed with.

the note circulation consists of gold and gold certificates and, in consequence, expands and contracts in direct response to changes in the demand for and in the supply of bullion. The remaining part of the note circulation is issued by the central bank not in exchange for bullion but by discounting bills of a standard type.[7] The rate of discount (*i.e.*, the difference between the value at maturity and the price offered by the bank) is called ' bank-rate.' It represents the rate of interest at which the central bank is prepared to lend money against this type of security.

A rise in bank-rate tends, *ceteris paribus*, to strengthen the exchange; a fall in bank-rate tends to weaken it. The mechanism is twofold. Changes in bank-rate affect the exchange, on the one hand, directly by causing an inflow or outflow of short-term investment, and, on the other hand, indirectly by influencing prices. The former effect is immediate but transitory, the latter gradual but permanent.

(*a*) The indirect effect is as follows: It is an accepted principle of monetary theory that a rise in bank-rate leads to a fall in prices and *vice versa*.[8] If the rate is lowered, more bills are offered to the bank for discount and additional money is thus brought into circulation. The goods on which the borrowed money is spent tend to rise in price and gradually other prices rise too. If changes in bank-rate are to be effective, the central bank must, of course, actually be in the habit of discounting bills. Moreover if, *e.g.*, a fall in bank-rate is offset by a tightening up of conditions regarding security, or if the total amount of bills discounted is held constant, then a fall in bank-rate will not cause the amount of money to increase. It has already been shown how changes of price affect the exchange. Here it must be stressed that the relevant commodity-prices only change gradually as the influence of the change in the amount of money spreads through the system.

(*b*) Experience shows, however, that in most cases changes in bank-rate affect the exchange immediately. This happens as follows. Since an appreciable proportion of short-term lending is supplied by the central bank, the latter exercises within limits a control over the money-market. If bank-rate goes up market-rates

---

[7] Generally with not more than three months to run.
[8] *Cf*. A. Marshall, *Official Papers* (1926); Wicksell, *Geldzins und Güterpreise*, 1898 English translation (1936); *Lectures on Political Economy*, vol. 2, English edn., 1935; Mises, *Theory of Money and Credit*, English edn., 1935; Hawtrey, *Good and Bad Trade* (1913); Hawtrey, *Currency and Credit*, 3rd edn., 1928. Keynes, *A Treatise on Money*, 1930, vol. 1, chap. xiii, " Modus Operandi of Bank-Rate." Hayek, *Monetary Theory and the Trade Cycle* (1932). Marco Fanno, " Die reine Theorie des Geldmarktes " in *Beiträge zur Geldtheorie*, ed. by Hayek, 1933.

C

as a rule go up too—though perhaps not to the same extent. The central bank may be regarded as the marginal lender. Moreover, a rise in bank-rate has a strong psychological influence. It is regarded by the other lenders as a danger-signal and they restrict supply accordingly.

A rise in the rate of interest implies, *ceteris paribus*, a fall in the prices of all securities bearing a fixed rate of interest. For instance, if the market-rate of interest rises from 4 to 5%, debentures and other fixed-interest securities clearly become less attractive compared with other lines of investment at the same financial centre. But the consequent fall in their price will induce foreigners to buy. The balance of payments is therefore affected in the same way as by a fall in commodity-prices.

This connection between the rate of discount and the price of stocks bearing a fixed rate of interest allows the central bank to reinforce its discount-policy by 'open-market operations.' By selling or buying, *e.g.*, Government stock in the open market, the bank can produce the same kind of effects as by raising or lowering its rate of discount.

The most powerful, however, of the immediate effects of a rise in the market-rate of interest is to attract the flow of short-term investment away from foreign markets. An inflow increases the supply of foreign money and strengthens the exchange.

This does not, of course, imply that there must be the same rate of interest in all countries or that small changes necessarily lead to movements of capital. The tendency to equality of interest-rates must be understood in the same sense as that of commodity-prices. A rôle corresponding to that of transport-costs, in the wide sense explained about, is here played by the risk-factor. It sometimes requires a considerable difference of interest-rates to induce capital to move. In times of financial disturbances as in large parts of the world since 1931 foreign capital cannot be attracted at any price. All that can be asserted is that a rise of the interest-rate in one country tends, *ceteris paribus*, to attract foreign capital or to prevent it from flowing out.

The form assumed by these short-term capital transactions varies according to the organisation of the money-market. The most significant difference is that some markets react more quickly than others to changes in the rate of discount. This is what will determine whether a given degree of passivity in the balance of payments can be compensated by a small rise in bank-rate or whether most drastic methods of restricting credit must be employed. Under normal conditions a rise in the Bank of England's rate of discount is particularly effective.[1] This is due to the unique position of London as a financial centre. In London there are always large quantities of sterling-bills from all parts of the world being discounted. If the rate of discount goes up, it will pay a foreigner who has debts to settle in sterling to buy a bill payable at sight or a telegraphic transfer on London, rather than to have a three months' bill discounted. The increased rate of interest deters him from borrowing. The supply of foreign means of payment therefore increases immediately and the pound is strengthened.

Further technical details cannot be discussed here. The general principle that a rise in bank-rate attracts foreign capital is established by the fact that normally gold-movements are small in quantity. At the first sign of such movements the rate of discount is altered.

But this of course merely postpones the problem of making the additional payments to foreign countries which are necessitated by the passive balance of payments. Foreigners are induced to lend the difference.[2] For the most part, however, they do so only at short term. If therefore the forces making for a passive balance are more than temporary in their operation, the direct effect of a rise in bank-rate is not sufficient to restore equilibrium. If the depth of water in one of the two cylinders threatens to increase permanently, then the exchange can be prevented from falling only by a decrease in the amount of money. This is ensured by the indirect effect of a rise in bank-rate already discussed.[3]

§ 5. THE INFLUENCE OF BANK-CREDIT.[4]

The mechanism described above is modified by the existence of bank-credit. If the joint-stock banks expand or contract their

---

[1] *Cf.* Hawtrey, *Currency and Credit*, 3rd ed., chap. ix, " A Contraction of Credit," 1928, pp. 136 *et seq.* Whitaker, *Foreign Exchange* (1933). " Report of Committee on Finance and Industry " (Macmillan Committee) § 295, 1931. Somary, *Bankpolitik*, 3rd edn. (1934).

[2] Obviously this part of the mechanism is particularly liable to disturbance, and in times of financial panic it may break down completely. *Cf.* chap. vii, § 6.

[3] The existence of the direct influence is generally looked on as an advantage, because it gives the indirect influence time to operate. Mr. Keynes, however, regards the extreme international mobility of short-term lending as dangerous. He thinks that a rise in bank-rate which is insufficient to lower prices may, nevertheless, be sufficient to attract foreign capital; the central bank may, therefore, be tempted to postpone the adjustments necessary for long-run equilibrium. Mr. Keynes makes certain suggestions for discouraging the international movement of money without weakening the effect of discount policy on prices (*cf. Treatise*, chap. xxxvi, and Mr. Hawtrey's illuminating analysis in *The Art of Central Banking* (1932), pp. 412 *et seq.*). They are reminiscent of the gold-premium policy followed before the War by the Banque de France (*cf.* Mises, *The Theory of Money and Credit* (1935), Part iii, chap. vi, §§ 4, 5).

[4] *Cf.* Taussig, *International Trade*, chap. xvii. Viner, *Canada's Balance of International Indebtedness*, chap. viii. Angell, " Equilibrium in International Trade " in *Quarterly Journal of Economics*, vol. 42, May 1928. Feis, " The

volume of deposits the effective amount of money increases or diminishes without changes in the amount of legal tender. Thus it is possible for ' nominal purchasing power ' to expand in one country and to contract in another without the transfer of gold, if the banks in one country expand credit and the banks in the other country contract it. Gold-movements, therefore, no longer play the same prominent part as in the classical mechanism. But this does not mean that the mechanism as a whole ceases to operate; actually there is no very fundamental difference between the two cases.

The new situation can best be made clear in terms of a world-wide clearing system, such as the founders of the Bank for International Settlements hoped to introduce. This would mean either that the central banks deposit their stocks of gold at the international bank, or even that gold reserves are superseded altogether by credits held there by the central banks. In either case a passive balance of trade in one country would lead merely to a reduction of the reserves of that country's bank and to a corresponding increase in the reserves of other banks; there would be no shipment of gold at all. But the mechanism of price-levels, balance of trade, &c., would nevertheless remain fully operative.

This imaginary case is not very unlike what actually happens. Both the central banks and the joint-stock banks keep money on deposit at foreign banks. The first effect of a passive balance of payment is a shrinkage of these accounts. If the banks affected react by restricting credit—as they normally do—and if the disturbance is only on a small scale, equilibrium can often be restored without either gold-movements or a fall in the exchange.

Professor Viner has analysed a very striking example of this kind in his examination of the Canadian balance of international indebtedness between 1900 and 1913. Canada was borrowing on a large scale from England and from the United States; she therefore had an active balance of payments. This did not however lead to an inflow of gold. The borrowed money was paid into the accounts of Canadian banks at New York, and these ' foreign reserves ' were treated as though they had been cash reserves; extra notes were issued and advances made. Prices therefore rose and imports came to exceed exports. The difference was paid for out of the accounts at New York and there were no gold-movements at all.

Mechanism of Adjustment of International Trade Balances " in *American Economic Review*, vol. 16, December 1926, pp. 593 *et seq.* R. M. Carr, " The Rôle of Price in International Trade Mechanism " in *Quarterly Journal of Economics*, vol. 45, August 1931.

According to Mr. Carr[5] the Canadian example presents certain further peculiarities. He asserts, in contrast to Professor Viner, that in many cases loans were not floated until after prices had already risen. This he takes to be in strict contradiction to orthodox theory. It must be granted that in the case of a rapidly developing country the order of events may quite conceivably be as Mr. Carr maintains. But even so, the expansion of credit is clearly dependent on the foreign loan, and not *vice versa*. If a loan is not forthcoming, then the policy of expansion must be reversed; otherwise the exchange will fall. To determine *in concreto* how the different phases of such a process are related in time one would require weekly or at least monthly statistics; these are unfortunately not often available. But apparent anomalies of the kind suggested cannot in any case throw doubt on the broad functional relationships worked out above.

---

[5] *Cf.* " The Rôle of Price in the International Trade Mechanism " in *Quarterly Journal of Economics*, vol. 45, August 1931, pp. 710 *et seq.*

CHAPTER VI.

EXCHANGES DURING INFLATION.

§ 1. The Significance of Static Analysis.

The preceding chapters have dealt mainly with what may be called the static theory of the exchanges. The equatation $R = \dfrac{P_A}{P_B k}$ has therefore been used with reference to the static equilibrium towards which the price- and exchange-relations between two countries tend to gravitate. The present chapter, on the other hand, deals with dynamic or unstable exchange rates, which represent a temporary divergence from equilibrium, and which carry in themselves the seeds of further change.

It is an error to suppose that static theory ignores the phenomena of change altogether. On the contrary, static theory takes account of them by contrasting the state of affairs before equilibrium is disturbed by changes of data with the state of affairs after the economic system has reached the new equilibrium appropriate to them. Any differences between the two states of equilibrium are then imputed to the change in data as effect to cause. This method of approach is called 'Comparative Statics.'[1]

Suppose, for example, that under an inconvertible paper currency the amount of money is increased by 20 per cent. Equilibrium analysis shows that when the extra money has had time to circulate throughout the system, prices will be higher than before. If one could assume that this change of data involved no further permanent changes except the price adjustments, then in the new equilibrium prices would be higher and the exchange would be lower than in the old equilibrium by exactly 20 per cent. But in actual fact the process of inflation always leaves behind it permanent or at least comparatively long-run changes in the volume of trade and in the structure of industry. The impact effect is a change in the direction of demand. At the points where the extra money first comes into circulation purchasing-power expands; elsewhere it remains for a time unchanged. When the increase spreads to other points, supply, which has begun to adjust itself to the

---

[1] *Cf.* Schams, " Komparative Statik," *Zeitschrift für Nationalökonomie*, vol. 2. (1930).

original change, cannot always be readjusted, since capital will have been sunk in the expectation that the shift in purchasing-power is permanent. Moreover, those who owed money when the inflation began gain permanently at the expense of their creditors. It is therefore most unlikely that all prices will have risen equally or that the average price-level and the foreign exchanges will be higher than before by exactly 20 per cent.

The point of this example is to show not that the rigid quantity-theory is inadequate, but that, even when these complicating factors are taken into account, static analysis is still applicable. The object is still to discover what the conditions of the new equilibrium are, towards which the economic system gravitates when the amount of money has been increased.

§ 2. THE TRANSITION FROM ONE EQUILIBRIUM TO ANOTHER. (PRICE-LEVELS AND EXCHANGE-RATES DURING INFLATION.)

Now it is necessary to supplement the static analysis by examining the intermediate stages between one equilibrium and another. Even in previous chapters this could not be altogether avoided, for the mechanism of adjustment itself involves usually a price-discrepancy incompatible with static conditions. In a country whose balance of payments becomes passive, prices fall, whereas in other countries they rise: this is sometimes necessary to stimulate exports, restrict imports and thus restore equilibrium. The details of this process will be further considered in chapter VII where the 'transfer problem' is discussed.

The present chapter is concerned with certain discrepancies of a rather less transitory kind, which may occur during an inflation. If the successive waves of expansion follow one another so quickly that the economic system has no time to absorb one before the next is upon it, then prices and foreign exchange rates may remain for some time out of equilibrium with each other.

The type of inflation differs according to the point at which the additional money is injected. In a gold-inflation, for example, the producers of gold have the first handling of it;[2] in a credit inflation, the entrepreneurs. The case selected for analysis here is that of a 'budget-inflation,' because in other types of inflation prices do not change sufficiently to show any appreciable dis-

---

[2] For an account of how the additional money spreads from this point, cf. Cairnes, " The Course of Depreciation," reprinted in *Essays on Political Economy* (1873), pp. 53 *et seq.* The historical development of the theory is sketched in Hayek, *Prices and Production*, chap. i. Among recent works, cf., e.g., Mises, *Theory of Money*, pp. 152 *et seq.;* or S. Budge, *Lehre vom Geld*, vol. 1 (1931), pp. 140 *et seq.*

crepancy compared with the exchange. In this case the extra money is first spent by civil servants and Government contractors. The goods they purchase rise in price, the firms producing these goods increase expenditure in their turn, and so the rise of prices spreads gradually to other parts of the system.

Sooner or later the exchange must depreciate. If the successive waves of extra money are spent in the first instance on home products, then average prices rise faster than the exchange depreciates. If, on the other hand, they are used to buy imports, or if costs increase very sharply in the export industries, then the opposite happens.

The German inflation (1914-23) is an interesting case which illustrates the underlying principles. It may be divided for this purpose into four stages :

(a) During the War Germany's foreign trade was kept practically at a standstill by the blockade. Hence the volume of exports and more particularly of imports could not react to price-changes with the normal rapidity. The mark fell therefore in value less rapidly abroad than at home.

(b) In 1919, when the blockade was lifted, the volume of imports increased, the balance of payments became passive and the exchange depreciated more than in proportion to the rise of prices. Had the quantity of money not been progressively increased, equilibrium would soon have been reached by an expansion of exports and a contraction of imports. As it was, some of the extra money was even injected directly into the foreign exchange market to pay Reparations.

The chief reason, however, which kept the depreciation of the exchange ahead of the rise in prices was psychological. Whenever inflation is carried beyond a certain point people begin sooner or later to anticipate that prices will go on rising. Speculation comes to dominate the foreign exchange market and depreciation is accelerated. At a later stage the influence of professional speculation is reinforced by the action of the ordinary public, who begin to hoard foreign currency.

This last factor presents one aspect of a wider process. In the same way as the exchange depreciates faster than prices rise, both movements proceed faster than the increase in the amount of money. For when people expect a further rise in price they are willing to pay rather higher prices at once for the sake of spending their money as soon as possible. Wages and salaries are paid out at more frequent intervals, and, finally, people resort to barter or use foreign money as the medium of exchange. In these ways the effective velocity of circulation of legal tender is enormously increased, and the volume of work which money has to perform is reduced. How far the discrepancy between changes in the quantity of money and changes in its value can develop, is shown by the example of the German mark. In November 1922, the total volume of money in circulation was worth in gold at the current rate only 1-38th of what it had been worth in 1919. In terms of the comparison worked out above, one would have to say that the rapid increase in the volume of water caused the cylinder to contract. The depth of water increased therefore more than in proportion to its volume.

(c) In the final stages of the German inflation the situation changed once more. A ' flight to goods ' became general, and the rise in prices caught up with the depreciation of the exchange. By 1923 when the inflation reached its height the discrepancy was no longer very large : both movements were proceeding at the same lightning speed. The increase in the quantity of money had meanwhile been left far behind.

(d) This last fact very much simplified the problem of stabilising the currency. Once confidence has been restored the velocity of circulation falls to its normal rate, and the supply of foreign currency increases. This means that if the central bank were to establish a gold-parity corresponding in equilibrium to the amount of money in circulation just before stabilisation, then the exchange would immediately appreciate and prices would have to fall. In that case, however, the bank would be unable to accumulate a gold reserve. Most of the post-war stabilisations were therefore carried out at a parity, somewhat higher indeed than the actual rate of exchange, but lower than would correspond in equilibrium to the ruling price-level. This allowed the central bank to accumulate a gold reserve and at the same time to increase the quantity of money in circulation. Such was the experience of Austria, Germany, France, and various other countries. The possibility or rather the necessity of increasing the quantity of money and raising prices if the exchange is to be kept stable has indeed the effect of facilitating stabilisation; but, on the other hand, it is liable to produce an inflationary boom, with a consequent depression later on.

§ 3. DEPRECIATION AS INTERPRETED BY THE BALANCE-OF-PAYMENTS THEORY AND THE CLASSICAL THEORY RESPECTIVELY.

It must be emphasised that the preceding analysis only supplements the classical theory without in any way contradicting it.

The classical theory may usefully be contrasted with the balance-of-payments theory, by quoting a passage from Helfferich, which criticises the former from the point of view of the latter, and refers particularly to the time-lag, analysed above, between changes in exchange-rate, price-level and quantity of money.

" . . . In considering the monetary conditions in Germany, the view widely held, especially abroad, is based on the pure quantity theory, and accordingly regards the increase in the circulation of paper-currency in Germany as the cause of the rise in the level of Germany prices and of the depreciation of the currency. On closer examination, however, we find that cause and effect are here interchanged, and that the increase in the amount of paper money circulating in Germany is not in fact the cause but the result of the fall of the German exchanges and of the consequential rise in wages and prices.

" . . . Thus in the twenty months which followed the acceptance of the London Ultimatum . . . the note issue of the Reichsbank (was multiplied) 23 times, the wholesale index number for home products 226 times, . . . and the dollar-rate 346 times.

" If ' inflation ' had been the cause, and the depreciation of the German exchanges the effect, then, in accordance with the theory of the classical English economists, events would have developed on the following lines: an increase in the paper circulation causes a corresponding rise in the level of prices at home. These higher prices encourage imports and make export more difficult. They tend, therefore, to make the trade balance, and with it the balance of international indebtedness, unfavourable. When the latter balance is passive, the demand for foreign currency increases and the rates of foreign exchange are forced up. A glance at the figures given above shows, however, that this chain of reasoning does not apply; in fact, it is immediately obvious that in the case of Germany the increase in the note circulation did not precede the rise in prices, and also that the depreciation of the currency followed it but slowly and at some distance of time. The twenty-three-fold increase of the note circulation cannot possibly be the cause of the 10 times greater rise in prices at home and of the 15 times greater rise . . . of the dollar rate. A conception of the general and comprehensive outline of the interplay of causes in these developments can, in fact, be obtained only if foreign exchange is made the starting-point.

" For the following, if for no other reason, the collapse of the German exchanges will be seen to be in no way related to the increase of the note circulation. At a dollar rate of 21,546, the rate quoted on the 25th January 1923, a gold mark was worth about 5,000 paper marks. The note circulation of the Reichsbank, which at that time amounted to 1,654 milliard paper marks, thus represented a value of only 330 million gold marks. This is not much more than one-twentieth of the gold value of the German currency circulating before the outbreak of War. . . .

" The theory which attributed the collapse of the German currency to ' inflation ' is based on the *petitio principii* that the foreign value of money, which finds its expression in the rates of foreign exchange, can be determined only by the quantitative factor of the paper circulation. In the above case, however, in which it has just been shown that the increase in paper remained far behind the currency depreciation, the causes of the collapse in the foreign exchanges, which are independent of the development of the paper circulation, are quite clear. We are dealing with a country whose international indebtedness, quite apart from payments and deliveries due under the Treaty of Versailles, was passive to the extent of about 3 milliard gold marks, and the London Ultimatum added to the country's indebtedness an annual payment of ' reparations ' estimated at about 3·3 milliard gold marks. To this were added the payments imposed upon Germany for the ' clearing ' of pre-war debts and gold payments to the occupying Powers. The annual passive balance of the German balance of international indebtedness was thereby increased to more than 7 milliard gold marks. . . .

" The chain of causes and effects is, therefore :

" First came the depreciation of the German currency by the overburdening of Germany with international liabilities and by the French policy of violence. Thence followed a rise in the prices of all imported commodities. This led to a general rise in prices and wages, which in turn led to a greater demand for currency by the public and by the financial authorities of the Reich ; and, finally, the greater calls upon the Reichsbank from the public and the financial administration of the Reich led to an increase in the note issue. In contrast, therefore, to the widely held view, it is not ' inflation ' but the depreciation of the currency which is the first link in this chain of cause and effect. Inflation is not the cause of the rise in prices and of the depreciated currency, but the latter is the cause of the higher prices and of the greater volume in the issue of paper money."[3]

This passage does not show a very profound understanding of the theory which it attacks. For the classical theory is strictly

---

[3] *Cf.* Helfferich, *Money*, pp. 598-601.

static in the sense already explained; whereas the phenomena
instanced by Helfferich to refute it are clearly the very opposite
of equilibrium conditions. The whole tendency of the classical
doctrine shows that it must be interpreted as a theory of equilibria.
These phenomena of inflation, therefore, being clearly anomalies
confined to the process of transition, cannot be used in evidence
against the theory, as we have formulated it.

The classical theory asserts that in the long run—and not such
a very long run at that—the functional relations, already worked
out, between prices and exchange-rates are valid, and that an
increase in the quantity of money must lead both to a rise in
prices and to depreciation of the exchange. But it is by no means
necessary that the former should precede the latter: the order
of events may be in the reverse direction. If prices lag behind,
there is in effect a premium on exports and ' exchange-dumping '
takes place. But for this very reason equilibrium would soon be
restored if it were not continually prevented by new injections
of money. It is true that one must be cautious in the formulation.
One should not say as supporters of the theory of purchasing-power
parity are fond of doing[4]—that the rise in prices is the primary
phenomenon, and that the depreciation of the exchange is merely
an effect of this. The two changes bear a functional relation
to one another and are both effects of the same cause. This is
the increase in the quantity of money, which in its turn is the
effect of the budget-deficit.

It cannot be denied that depreciation and rising prices make
it more difficult to balance the budget, and that this leads to
further inflation, a further rise of prices, and further depreciation. But, as shown by the event, this ' vicious circle ' can be
broken; and even if it were impossible to cover the budget-deficit
—because a sound financial policy cannot be carried through, or
because the burdens placed on the national exchequer from without
(e.g., Reparations) exceed the taxable capacity of the economy—
this does not contradict the hypothetical proposition, that, if the
quantity of money is kept stable, forces are released which bring
the movements of prices and of the exchange to a standstill and
adjust prices and rates of exchange to one another, as asserted
by our modified theory of purchasing-power parity.

The fact that the increase in the quantity of money lags behind
the fall in the value of money—so that the quantity of money in
circulation, reckoned in gold, becomes smaller—is also not in

---

[4] In Ricardo, for example, there seems nowhere to be a hint that price-movements and movements of the exchange may temporarily diverge.

contradiction with the classical theory, as correctly interpreted. It is fully explained by the increased velocity of circulation and the contraction in the volume of trade, due partly to the fact that a large proportion of transactions are carried out by other means of exchange. Helfferich's attempt to refute the quantity-theory by pointing to this fact merely proves his failure to understand the theory and his inability to distinguish between equilibrium-conditions and the phenomena of transition.

§ 4. STATISTICS OF THE GERMAN INFLATION.

The qualitative analysis can be supplemented by detailed statistics. In figs. 3, 4 and 5 changes in the rate of exchange between marks and dollars are contrasted with the movement of purchasing-power parity between Germany and America. Price-levels are computed from the wholesale index of the *Statistisches Reichsamt* and of the *Bureau of Labour Statistics* respectively, the base being in each case 1913=100. Exchange rates are computed from the monthly average of quotations on New York in the Berlin money market.

In figs. 3 and 4 the dollar rate is represented by the continuous

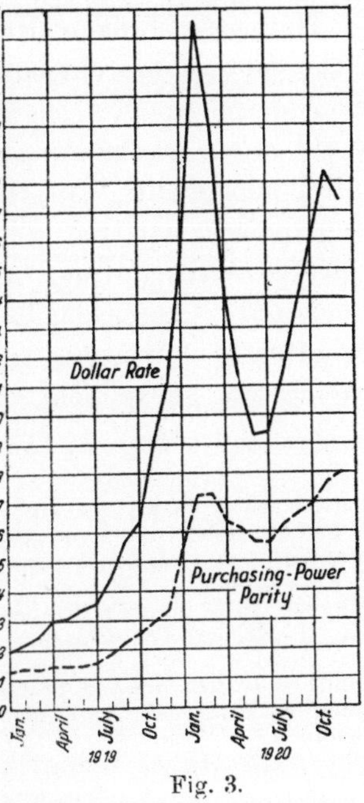

Fig. 3.

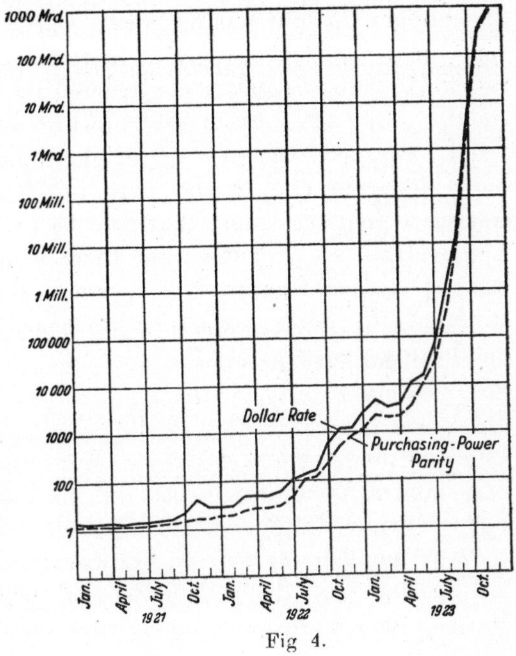

Fig 4.

Figs. 3 and 4 Movement of the Berlin dollar rate and of purchasing-power parity between Germany and America, 1919-23.

line and shifts in purchasing-power parity (German price-level

divided by American price-level) by the broken line. In fig. 3 both
curves are drawn on the ordinary arithmetical scale. But the
figures soon become too unwieldy for this method of presentation;
they are therefore drawn separately in fig. 4 on a quasi-logarithmic
scale. This is why the two curves appear closer together for
January, 1921, than for the end of 1920. It should be noted that
fig. 4 is not strictly accurate, since the logarithmic values have not
been worked out for smaller intervals than those represented by the
horizontal lines.

In fig. 5 changes in the dollar rate are expressed as a percentage

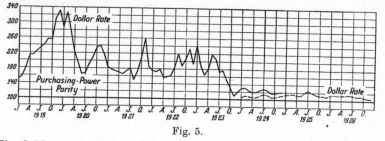

Fig. 5.

Fig. 5 Movement of the dollar rate expressed as a percentage of purchasing-power parity.

of changes in purchasing-power parity. Here the broken line
represents the same deviation in terms of the more comprehensive
index of wholesale prices constructed by the *Statistiches Reichsamt*
for the year 1924. From 1925 onwards the old index was no longer
used. For 1924 the two curves show parallel movements, but the
more accurate one is closer to purchasing power parity. The
statistical evidence must therefore be interpreted with caution. It
is, nevertheless, probable that there were not only temporary but
also permanent changes of k, since even after stabilisation the
curve of the dollar exchange remained somewhat above that of
purchasing-power parity.[5]

---

[5] The most elaborate studies of the German inflation are Graham, *Exchange,
Price and Production in Hyper-inflation* : *Germany, 1920-1923* (1930), and Bresciani-
Turroni, *Le vicende del Marco Tedesco* (1932). *Cf.* also *Zahlen zur Geldentwertung
in Deutschland* 1914-23 (published by the *Statistisches Reichsamt* in 1925).

For Austria, *cf.* Walré de Bordes, *The Austrian Crown* (1924), and for France,
E. L. Dulles, *The French Franc* 1914-28 (1929), and J. H. Rogers, *The Process of
Inflation in France* (1929).

Cf. further European Currency and Finance (published by the United States
Commission of gold and silver enquiry, 2 vols., Washington, 1925) and *Depreciated
Exchanges and International Trade* (U.S. Tariff Commission, Washington, 1922)
Cf. also Angell, *op. cit.*

CHAPTER VII.

THE TRANSFER PROBLEM.

§ 1. INTRODUCTORY.

The present chapter deals with the unilateral payment of large sums by one country to another. This is in reality only a special case of the phenomena already analysed. But it nevertheless deserves separate treatment because this case has always attracted a great deal of attention, and in discussing it a number of refinements will be added to the analysis given in previous chapters.

One must distinguish in international, as indeed also in domestic trade, between unilateral and bilateral transfers. This distinction applies equally to the transfer of money and to the transfer of goods. The prototype of a bilateral transfer is the exchange of commodities for cash, since the two sides of the exchange here confront one another directly. Clear cases of unilateral transfer are free gifts and political tribute such as reparations.

Expenditure on transport, by tourists, &c., represents a bilateral transfer, since money is exchanged for real services. The granting or the repayment of a loan occupies an intermediate position. From the point of view of the economic period within which the payment or repayment occurs, they are unilateral transfers. If, on the other hand, one extends the period sufficiently to cover both the point of time when the loan is made and the point of time when it is repaid, then it must be regarded as a bilateral transfer. Interest payments are in a sense bilateral transfers, since the use of capital is a real service. But as this item—the services of capital—does not appear in the balance of trade and services, interest payments must nevertheless be regarded as a unilateral transfer.

The question now arises why the transfer of unilateral payments should be supposed to involve any special problem not involved in the transfer of bilateral payments. Here it is convenient to draw up a double balance sheet of the economic transactions between one country and the rest of the world. On the one hand, there is the balance of real values, or in other words of goods and services exchanged. On the other hand, there is the balance of the means of payment, in the sense of money payments actually made to foreign countries and received from them. As we have already pointed out, the balance of payments in this latter sense is in the

63

long run always in equilibrium, unless payment is made out of an existing stock of foreign money or the foreign country wishes to accumulate a stock of the domestic money.[1] In such cases, however, the amounts involved are always small. They are very important from the point of view of monetary policy, as signifying ' confidence in the currency,' but quantitatively they do not count for very much in the total balance of international payments.

Now if the economic system of one country is connected with the rest of the world only by bilateral transfers (*i.e.*, by the sale and purchase of goods and services) then both the balance of payments and the balance of transfer of real values are in equilibrium. But if there are also unilateral transfers (*e.g.*, reparations) then the balance of trade and services must show a surplus, since the balance of payments cannot in the long run be out of equilibrium. In other words, unilateral transfers must be made in kind.[2] Capital movements must finally take the form of a transfer of goods and services.

In this respect, too, there is really no difference between domestic and foreign trade. The assertion is constantly made that in international trade payments must in the long run be made in goods, whereas in domestic trade payments are made in money. It is of course true that in domestic trade payments are made in the first instance in money, but, normally, the person receiving payment wishes to buy something with the money. In spite of such unilateral payments the individual balances of payment remain intact, because the individual, like a plurality of individuals or a country, cannot in the long run spend more than he receives, unless, indeed, he entrenches on a stock of cash. This, however, applies equally to international trade. Thus even in domestic trade unilateral transfers are carried out finally in goods or services. But the flow of goods goes unnoticed, because it does not pass a political boundary, and is therefore not recorded.

The assertion commonly made in textbooks that debtor countries have an active, and creditor countries a passive, balance of trade must be received with caution. In the case of capital movements over a long period the state of the balance of trade depends on the

---

[1] This played an important part during the German inflation. Foreigners speculated on a rise in the mark and allowed Germany to export marks and to make, as a result of the depreciation, considerable profits.

[2] Unless, indeed, the payment is small enough to be made out of existing stocks of foreign means of payment. Unilateral transfers which can be made out of stocks of money present for that very reason no problem. But, clearly, payments of the magnitude of German reparations can only be transferred in the form of an export surplus. The annual payments provided for in the Young Plan amounted to about 2000 million marks. Germany's whole stock of gold and foreign money would therefore have been exhausted in two years, if the amount had not kept returning in payment for an export surplus.

phase reached by the process of indebtedness. If a country whose balance of trade is in equilibrium starts to import capital at a uniform rate, her balance of trade becomes passive. But sooner or later payments for interest and amortisation become larger than the amount of new capital imported. The balance of trade then becomes active. The same holds, *mutatis mutandis*, for creditor countries. The existence of an active or a passive balance of trade is therefore no sufficient criterion for distinguishing between debtor and creditor countries. In the post-war period up to 1929 Germany had a passive balance of trade because she was contracting more foreign debts than she was repaying. In 1929, when the stream of capital dried up, the balance of trade became active. Before the War the United States was a debtor country and had an active balance. The surplus of exports over imports paid for interest and amortisation to the European creditors. During the War the United States became almost overnight a creditor country, and after 1919 her balance of trade remained active because the export of capital continued to exceed receipts for interest and amortisation.

§ 2. RAISING AND TRANSFERRING PAYMENTS. CREATION OF THE EXPORT SURPLUS.

The problem of making unilateral payments from one country to another has two aspects. First, a sum of money has to be raised at home. In the case of reparations this is a problem for the national exchequer; when private capital is exported, it is a problem for the individual concerned. Secondly, however, the sum of domestic money thus raised must be changed into money of the country receiving payment. The transfer can only be regarded as successful if a corresponding export surplus is created, and that, moreover, without a collapse or a permanent depreciation of the exchange.

The question how the export surplus is created has already in effect been answered. This is merely a special case of the operation of the mechanism, already described in detail, which keeps the balance of payments in equilibrium. Applied to German Reparations, the process is in essentials as follows. If the sums intended for export are raised by taxation, then the money income or purchasing power of the German nation is reduced, the quantity of money in circulation contracts and prices fall. Conversely, in the countries receiving reparations national income increases, the quantity of money expands and prices rise. In this way a gap is created between prices in Germany and prices elsewhere; Germany's exports are stimulated, her imports are restricted, and the export surplus is created. It is therefore not the case, as the still popular balance of payments theory supposes, that the possibility of transfer depends on an already existing active balance of trade or payments. It is not necessary to wait till the gods present one with an export surplus. On the contrary, the export surplus arises automatically when the mechanism of payment is set in motion.

If the pressure on German prices is insufficient to produce the necessary export surplus at once, and if payment is nevertheless continued, then the foreign exchanges will rise above the gold point, and the gold and foreign exchange reserve of the German Reichsbank will decrease. This will cause the Bank to put up its rate of discount, with the double effect, explained in Chapter V, § 4, of increasing the pressure on prices and of encouraging an inflow of short-term credit from abroad.

The importance of reparations and international war debts for economic policy ever since the War, has caused the mechanism of transfer to be widely discussed once more. But the greater part of the relevant literature[3] has reached only a low level of scientific attainment. In many cases the political bias was too strong for a really scientific treatment of the problem and not many of the participants in this discussion have realized that the solution of their problem was already contained in the writings of Thornton, Ricardo, Senior, Mill and Cairnes. In the following pages only the few scientific contributions to the transfer discussion will be considered.[4] These concern mainly the rôle of price-movements in the mechanism of transfer.

§ 3. The Rôle of Price-Changes in the Mechanism of Transfer.

(a) *The Problem Stated.* Here two schools of thought can be clearly distinguished. The first is inclined to minimise the importance of price-movements in the mechanism of transfer, and indeed to contest the necessity, for the transfer of unilateral payments, of any price-movement at all. The other school lays great stress on the necessity of opposite price-movements in the two countries concerned. It considers that under unfavourable circumstances

---

[3] For an exhaustive bibliography, cf. H. Sveistrup, *Die Schuldenlast des Welt-krieges, Quellen und Literatur,* 2 vols. (Berlin, 1929 and 1931), and Moulton and Pasvolsky, *War Debts and World Prosperity* (1932).
[4] Unfortunately Ragnar Nurkse's *Internationale Kapitalbewegungen* (1935), which carried the analysis a big step forward, appeared too late for me to make use of it. The same is true of the book of Iversen; see next footnote.

these price-movements would have to be so large that serious difficulties might arise, rendering transfer, in extreme cases, absolutely impossible.

The former opinion has been vigorously maintained of recent years by Professor Ohlin, while the most prominent champion of the latter has been Mr. Keynes.[5] The discussion between them has revealed much more clearly than before the inner workings of the transfer mechanism. By considering it more closely, we shall therefore be enabled in certain points to extend and modify our previous analysis.

(b) *The Controversy between Mr. Keynes and Professor Ohlin, and its Precursors.* It is convenient to start with Mr. Keynes's argument, which is the more closely in line with our previous exposition. According to Mr. Keynes, Germany must increase her exports in order to achieve an export surplus. For this purpose she must lower the prices of her export goods. How large the reduction of price must be, in order to create an export surplus of a given value, depends on the conditions of the foreign demand for German export goods and services. An increase in the volume of exports only yields an export surplus if the elasticity of demand for German exports is greater than unity.[6] If the elasticity of demand is equal to, still more if it is less than, unity no increase in exports, however great, could produce a surplus in terms of value, since prices would fall as fast as, or even faster than, the volume of exports increased.[7]

---

[5] *Cf.* (a) Ohlin, " The Reparations Problem," in *Index*, Nos. 27 and 28, March-April 1928; " Is the Young Plan Feasible? " in *Index*, No. 50 (1930), published by the Svenska Handelsbanken; " Transfer Difficulties, Real and Imagined," in *Economic Journal*, June 1929, p. 172, and Sept. 1929, p. 400 (*cf.* now also *Inter-regional and International Trade* (1933) which appeared after the present chapter had been written); Rueff, *Une Erreur Economique: l'Organisation des Transferts* (1928); " Les Idées de M. Keynes sur le Problème des Transferts," in *Revue d'Economie Politique* 43ieme année July-August 1929, pp. 1067 *et seq.;* " Mr. Keynes' Views on the Transfer Problem," *Economic Journal*, Sept. 1929, pp. 389-390. (b) Keynes, " The German Transfer Problem," *Economic Journal*, vol. 39, 1929, pp. 1 *et seq.*, further pp. 179 and 404; *Treatise on Money*, chap. xxi; Pigou, " Disturbances of Equilibrium in International Trade," *Economic Journal*, vol. 39, 1929, p. 344. Reprinted in Pigou and Robertson, *Economic Essays and Addresses* (1931). For a critical review of the whole literature see Carl Iversen, *Aspects of the Theory of Capital Movements* (1935). Compare also R. Wilson, *Capital Imports and the Terms of Trade. Examined in the Light of Sixty Years of Australian Borrowings* (1931) and H. D. White, *The French International Accounts* 1880-1913 (1933). The two last-mentioned works came into my hands only after the present chapter had been written.

[6] Or more precisely the weighted average of the elasticities of demand for the various export goods. An appropriate hypothesis must also be made as to the existence of potential export goods. Compare also § § 4 and 5 of chap. xi where it is shown that the complex Marshallian demand-and-supply curves take the existence of potential export and import goods into consideration.

[7] If elasticity were less than unity, an export surplus could be produced by an increase of price and by the restriction of exports, since in that case the volume of exports decreases more slowly than prices fall. But under free competition this could hardly occur.

Now Mr. Keynes is of the opinion that in Germany's case the conditions of demand are such that only a large fall in price could produce an export surplus to the magnitude of the payments required. This implies for Germany an extra loss over and above the direct burden. For German exports of a given total value now contain, because of the fall in prices, a larger volume of goods than before. This is expressed by saying that the ' real ratio of exchange ' or the ' barter terms of international trade ' have moved against Germany.[8] The terms of trade become still more unfavourable if the prices of German imports rise. Germany has therefore to bear a double burden. In the first place, 2 milliard gold marks are paid to foreign countries. In the second place, a larger quantity of German goods is required to command 2 milliard gold marks, and also to command any given quantity of imports, than before.

The monetary mechanism produces this result ' on the commodity side ' as follows. First of all, the reparation taxes are collected in Germany. This is the primary burden. If the necessary export surplus is not produced, then the cash reserves of the Reichsbank fall, gold and foreign money flow out, and credit must be restricted. This makes prices and incomes fall still further (secondary burden). It might be objected that, apart from temporary losses due to labour disputes and so forth, this does not represent an extra burden since incomes and prices have both fallen. But this objection is not valid since only domestic prices fall. The price of imports is unaffected and real wages have therefore diminished. Thus the contraction of credit does involve an extra burden.

Professor Machlup has shown that under a gold or gold-exchange standard, or where the central bank has so large a gold reserve that it need not restrict credit when gold flows out, the same result is produced automatically by the deflationary influence of the payments themselves. If the first instalment does not depress prices sufficiently to create the necessary export surplus, then its influence is reinforced by the second instalment. Tariffs and other obstacles to the export trade can be surmounted in the same way, though of course at each step an extra burden is placed on the country paying reparations.[9]

This ' secondary burden ' is the ' transfer loss.' It is therefore appropriate to speak of transfer difficulties when an outflow of

---

[8] On the significance of this magnitude and on the possibility of measuring it, cf. chap. xi, § 6, also Taussig, *International Trade*, chap. xxi.
[9] " Transfer u. Preisbewegung " in *Zeitschrift für Nationalökonomie*, vol. 1, 1930.

gold is caused by this extra burden.[10] Transfer difficulties need not always take the form that on the date when payment falls due, the foreign exchange required is not forthcoming. They may show themselves in an inability to carry out the adjustments required by the contraction of credit, in labour disputes or in widespread unemployment. Under these circumstances it is also difficult for the State to raise by taxation the money required. Transfer difficulties then take the form of a budget deficit.

If the necessary financial measures are not or cannot be carried out, then gold will flow out and transfer difficulties in the sense of a shortage of foreign means of payment will arise. This happens if the deflationary influence of the payments is neutralised by a liberal credit policy, if the gold which flows out is replaced by newly created bank money, or if the necessity of restricting credit due either to the payments themselves or to other reasons is disregarded.[1] But the term ' transfer difficulties ' has, in this case, no very precise significance. A policy of credit expansion always leads to an outflow of gold whether unilateral payments are being made or not.

It cannot therefore always be said whether in a particular case difficulties of this kind are due to the primary burden, to the secondary burden, or to other causes. It is true there is no rigid economic law to the effect that the transfer must be followed by a policy of expansion, or by a failure to deflate sufficiently. Hence it could be argued that the source of the difficulties is really the monetary policy adopted and not the obligation to transfer large sums abroad. But if account is taken of the psychological and political factors, it must be conceded that such a monetary policy, and hence the difficulties which it produces, may inevitably follow from the obligation to transfer. Changes in the terms of trade are generally a good symptom of whether there has been a secondary burden or not. It must however be remembered that the statistical evidence is not in itself conclusive, since the terms of trade may have altered for other reasons. The terms of trade moved, for example, very much in Germany's favour between 1928 and 1931, because the price of raw materials, which constitute the greater part of Germany's imports, fell more sharply than the price of manufactured goods, which Germany exports.[2] Clearly this was not a result of reparations, although, as will be shown in a moment, such a connection is not quite inconceivable.

---

[10] This point is brought out with special clarity by Professor Pigou, *cf. op. cit.* p. 347.

[1] For details, *cf.* §§ 5 and 6 of the present chapter.

[2] For the statistical evidence, *cf.* chap. xi, § 7.

Mr. Keynes's line of thought has been criticised by Professor Ohlin on the ground that it ignores changes on the demand side. Professor Ohlin urges that the payment of reparations by Germany involves *ipso facto* a transfer of purchasing power to the countries receiving payment. This means that their demand increases and Germany's demand diminishes. " We can therefore least of all argue on the basis of unaltered demand. The decisive point for the machinery of capital movements is, on the contrary, that demand has undergone a radical change. . . . There is thus a market in A for more of B's goods than formerly. On the other hand, the market in B for A's goods is not as big as it was before. The local distribution of demand has changed. . . . Prior to the beginning of the movement of capital the two countries were buying so much of all kinds of goods that their value equalled that of the goods produced at home. On the other hand, after the capital movement started, A buys more and B less of their combined production than before," and, it may be added in accordance with Professor Ohlin's argument, the two groups together purchase the same amount as before.[3] M. Jacques Rueff calls this the principle of the conservation of purchasing power. It " simply states that never in the course of the various economic transformations that occur is purchasing power lost or created, but that it always remains constant." The loss of one party is exactly balanced by the gain of the other party.[4] This means in our particular case that the country paying reparations can never lose more purchasing power than the amount of the payments themselves.[5] There is therefore, according to this view, no secondary burden.[6]

---

[3] *Cf. Index*, April 1928, pp. 4-5.

[4] In parenthesis it may be remarked that a rigid assumption to the effect that the effective quantity of money remains constant, may be necessary in a preliminary stage of the analysis; but if strictly adhered to, it will completely block the way to the solution of a number of extremely important problems. For recent analysis in business cycle and monetary theory makes it more and more evident that—as the aggregate result of the actions of private individuals, abstracting altogether from any conscious regulation by the monetary authorities—the effective quantity of money (MV) is a much more variable magnitude than traditional theory has assumed. Recognition of this fact and a careful study of the factors which are likely to determine these variations (changes set up by the transfer of large sums are certainly among them) are indispensable for an understanding of the vagaries of industrial fluctuations. This has been made quite clear by Dr. Thomas Balogh in his paper " Some Theoretical Aspects of the Central European Credit and Transfer Crisis," in *International Affairs: Journal of the Royal Institute of International Affairs*, vol. 11, May 1932. This remarkable paper which contains a penetrating and realistic analysis of many generally neglected aspects of the problem has not received all the attention which it deserves.

[5] *Cf. Economic Journal*, vol. 39, 1929, pp. 389-90.

[6] Prof. Ohlin has been accused by Mr. Keynes, amongst others, of a *petitio principii* on the ground that there is no shift of purchasing power until the sum paid has actually been transferred. " Germany can only acquire such bills if she has already sold the necessary exports " (*Economic Journal*, 1929, pp. 407-8).

Mr. Keynes's view that unilateral transfers necessitate price changes and a shift in the terms of trade can be traced back as far as Thornton, who propounded it eight years before the publication of Ricardo's *High Price of Bullion*. " At the time of a very unfavourable balance (produced, for example, through a failure of the harvest) a country has occasion for large supplies of corn from abroad : but either it has not the means of supplying at the instant a sufficient quantity of goods in return, or . . . the goods which (it) is able to furnish as means of cancelling its debt, are not in such demand abroad as to afford the prospect of a tempting or even of a tolerable price. . . . In order, then, to induce the country having the favourable balance to take all its payment in goods, and no part of it in gold, it would be requisite not only to prevent goods from being very dear but even to render them excessively cheap. It would be necessary, therefore, that the bank should not only increase its paper, but that it should, perhaps, very greatly diminish it . . ." (*Paper Credit*, &c., pp. 131-2).

This doctrine was afterwards taken over and extended by John Stuart Mill, and it has come to be regarded as *the* classical doctrine. But it is incorrect to attribute this variant to Ricardo, as is often done.[7] On the contrary, Ricardo lent his authority to the other version, maintaining that the shift in purchasing power was sufficient to restore equilibrium without gold movements and without a shift of prices. He criticised the passage from Thornton quoted above as follows : " Mr. Thornton has not explained to us why any unwillingness should exist in the foreign country to receive our goods for their corn ; and it would be necessary for him to show, that if such an unwillingness were to exist, we should agree to indulge it so far as to consent to part with our coin."[8] In contrast to Thornton, Ricardo asserted that the export of coins was caused by their ' cheapness,' *i.e.*, by the high level of prices. It was therefore not the effect but the cause of an unfavourable balance.[9] In the following passage he formulated the same idea even more clearly. " If . . . we agreed to pay a subsidy to a foreign power, money would not be exported

---

This criticism is however invalid since it is only reasonable to assume that every Central Bank possesses a certain stock of international means of payment, out of which the first instalment can be paid. If the Bank has no cash reserves or if the country receiving payment does not react to the inflow of gold by expanding the circulation, then part of the mechanism is put out of action (*cf.* § 5 of the present chapter).

[7] This has been pointed out notably by Professor Viner, *Canada's Balance of International Indebtedness*, chap. ix, pp. 191 *et seq.*, and *Wirtschaftstheorie der Gegenwart*, vol. 4, p. 108-9.

[8] *Cf. High Price of Bullion; Works*, p. 268.

[9] *Op. cit.* p. 268. It would be more accurate to say ' criterion ' or ' symptom ' rather than ' cause.'

whilst there were any goods which could more cheaply discharge the payment. The interest of the individuals would render the exportation of the money unnecessary " (*op. cit.*, p. 269).

The export surplus arises therefore automatically, without having to be preceded by a movement of gold. " Thus, then, specie will be sent abroad to discharge a debt only when it is superabundant; only when it is the cheapest exportable commodity " (*op. cit.*, p. 269). But Ricardo denied that a failure of the harvest or the granting of a subsidy could produce a redundancy of money.[1]

Malthus sided, apart from small differences, with Thornton. In his review of the *High Price of Bullion*[2] he maintained that Ricardo had not shown why the country receiving a subsidy should immediately increase its demand at the old price for goods of the country paying the subsidy. He agreed with Thornton that demand could not be expected to increase until gold had flowed out and prices had fallen.

Malthus considered that the export of specie occurred not only when it was present in superabundance but also " it is owing precisely to the cause mentioned by Mr. Thornton—the unwillingness of the creditor nation to receive a great additional quantity of goods . . . without being bribed to it by excessive cheapness; and its willingness to receive bullion—the currency of the commercial world— without any such bribe . . . whatever variations between the quantity of currency and commodities may be stated to take place subsequent to the commencement of these transactions, it cannot be for the moment doubted, that the cause of them is to be found in the wants and desires of one of the two nations, and not in any original redundancy or deficiency of currency in either of them " (*op. cit.*, p. 345).

Among more recent writers one of the few to adopt the Ricardian version was Bastable. In 1889 he expounded his view in practically the same words as Professor Ohlin. " It is . . . doubtful whether Mill is correct in asserting that the quantity of money will be increased in the creditor and reduced in the debtor country. The sum of money incomes will no doubt be higher in the former; but that increased amount may be expended in purchasing imported articles. . . . Nor does it follow that the scale of prices will be higher in the creditor than in the debtor country. The inhabitants of the former, having larger money incomes, will purchase more at the same price, and thus bring about the necessary excess of imports over exports."[3]

(c) *The Problem Solved.* A tentative answer to the question, what part price-movements play in the mechanism of transfer, can now be proposed.[4] The truth lies in this case midway between the

---

[1] Ricardo granted, indeed, that in the case of a failure of the harvest there had to be an export of gold. This was not however in order to change prices and thus create an export surplus, but because the failure of the harvest meant a decrease in the volume of trade and hence in the amount of money required. " England in consequence of a bad harvest, would come under the case . . . of a country having been deprived of a part of its commodities and therefore requiring a diminished amount of circulating medium. The currency, which was before equal to her payments, would now become superabundant and relatively cheap " (" Appendix " to *The High Price of Bullion; Works*, p. 293).

[2] *Edinburgh Review*, vol. 17, pp. 342 to 345, Feb. 1811, quoted by Viner, op. cit., p. 193.

[3] " On some Applications of the Theory of International Trade," *Quarterly Journal of Economics*, vol. iv, p. 16 (Oct. 1889).

[4] *Cf.* Haberler, " Transfer und Preisbewegung," *Zeitschrift für Nationalökonomie*, Bd. 1, pp. 548 *et seq.*, and Bd. 2, pp. 100 *et seq.*; Lösch, " Eine Auseinandersetzung über das Transferproblem," *Schmollers Jahrbuch*, jg. 54, pp. 109 *et seq.*; Machlup, " Transfer und Preisbewegung," *Zeitschrift für Nationalökonomie*, Bd. 1, 1930; Wilson, *Capital Imports and the Terms of Trade* (1931).

two conflicting theories, both of which are one-sided and give an over-simplified picture of the facts. For in reality one can conceive both cases in which transfer involves changes in the general price level and cases in which it does not involve them. The terms of trade may remain unaffected, they may move against the country paying reparations, or, on the other hand, they may move in favour of it. Transfer may therefore involve a loss, but, on the other hand, it may even involve a gain.[5]

Professor Ohlin is undoubtedly correct in maintaining that Mr. Keynes ignores the shifts on the demand side produced by the payments themselves. One cannot operate with unchanged demand curves of given elasticity, since the demand curves of the countries receiving payment will have shifted to the right. This means that owing to the increase in money incomes a larger amount than before will be bought even at the old price. In the limiting case it is even possible for the transfer to be made without any fall in the price of German exports. This happens if the fall in Germany's demand, due to the reduction of the national income by a reparation tax, is offset by an increase in foreign demand for the same goods. It makes no difference whether these are German goods, the export of which now increases, or whether they are goods previously imported into Germany, which are now imported in smaller quantities than before.

Normally, however, the fall in demand and the rise in demand affect different goods and there must, in consequence, be a shift of prices and of production. Professor Ohlin admits that the fall in demand will affect primarily goods produced in the country paying reparations and the rise in demand goods produced in the country receiving them. But he contends that production of the former will be restricted and means of production will be released for use in the export industries.[6] The same argument applies of course also to the goods for which demand has increased. Their production will expand at the expense of exports, and the balance of trade will consequently be affected.

No one disputes that the final result must be an increase in the exports of the country paying reparations and/or a decrease in the exports of the country receiving them, since the export surplus cannot be produced in any other way. But the question is, what price changes are brought about by this shift of production? Here it is important to distinguish two kinds of price change

---

5 This last possibility has not been considered by either party.
6 Cf. Zeitschrift für Nationalökonomie, vol. 1, p. 764.

which are apt to be confused with one another.[7] These are, on the one hand, temporary price discrepancies in the transition from the old to the new equilibrium, and, on the other hand, permanent shifts of the terms of trade as between the new and the old equilibrium. A single harvest failure or the payment of a single lump sum may give rise to a price discrepancy by which exports are encouraged, imports reduced, and equilibrium thus restored. But differences of price greater than the cost of transport from one country to the other are incompatible with equilibrium and cannot, therefore, persist very long. In a frictionless market the adjustment would be instantaneous, and while price changes might very well occur, price discrepancies would be impossible. If, therefore, one operates with this assumption, or if one skips the transitional period and concentrates entirely on the new equilibrium which will finally be reached, it is only logical to deny the possibility of price discrepancies. The Ricardian[8] variety of transfer theory is static in this sense.[9] Its procedure is not unreasonable in the case of recurring payments such as reparations.

The fact that a price-discrepancy cannot persist very long by no means implies that the terms of trade must remain unchanged.[1] The prices of German exports may have to fall and those of German imports may have to rise. But this does not contradict the rule that prices in different countries tend to equality, since the price of German export articles falls both in Germany and elsewhere; the same argument applies to imports. This shift of prices is to be expected in the normal case where the direct influence of changes in demand on the balance of trade is insufficient to create the necessary export surplus, because foreign countries spend only a small part of their receipts for reparations on the purchase of German exports.[2]

---

[7] This has been pointed out in an unpublished memorandum by Dr. Koopmans. In this respect there is perhaps a difference of degree between movements of capital and shifts of demand in international and in domestic trade respectively. In domestic trade one can assume the existence of a homogeneous market, whereas in international trade there are separate markets, between which price equilibrium is then restored by arbitrage. But, of course, there are exceptions and each case must be examined on its merits.

[8] It is, of course, not intended to imply that writers of the opposite school always identify temporary price discrepancies with changes in the terms of trade. That would clearly be a misinterpretation, e.g., of Professor Taussig, who does not speak of price differences in general but of differences in *supply* price.

[9] This has become quite clear since Mr. Keynes has returned in the *Treatise on Money* to his controversy with Prof. Ohlin. In chap. xxi he distinguishes explicitly between the new equilibrium and the period of transition. He now regards the transfer difficulties as concerning almost exclusively the process of transition.

[1] It is true that a price-discrepancy always implies a change in the terms of trade, but this proposition is not reversible : changes in the terms of trade usually do not take the form of price-discrepancies.

[2] This is very probable since it may reasonably be assumed that foreign countries divide the extra income between domestic goods, export goods and import

By how much the price of German exports must fall depends, first, on the elasticity of demand abroad.[3] In contrast to Mr. Keynes, I am of opinion that demand is as a rule very elastic, since the world market is, after all, large compared with the volume of exports from any single country. Moreover, the fact that Germany has no monopoly but competes with other countries also works in the same direction. A fall of prices does not only stimulate demand as a whole but will also drive some foreign competitors out of the market. This is rendered easier by the fact that in the country receiving reparations demand for domestic goods has risen, and, in consequence, the necessary adjustment there is already under way.

The extent of the fall in price depends, secondly, on the conditions of supply in Germany and also, *mutatis mutandis*, in the competing industries abroad. If, for example, the output of German exports could be expanded under diminishing costs per unit, Germany's difficulties would obviously be reduced. If the law of constant costs prevails in the industries concerned, no shift of prices will occur.

It is not easy to predict on theoretical grounds how these factors will work out. Moreover, the result depends on how long one allows for supply to adjust itself. In general it holds true that the longer one allows, the smaller will be the necessary price changes.[4] For, once the obstacles to an expansion of exports have been swept aside by energetic under-cutting, exports can afterwards be maintained in the channels thus opened even at a rather higher price than before.

An accurate summary of all these interdependences is hardly possible without mathematical symbols.[5] But it should be mentioned that it is theoretically possible for the terms of trade to change in favour of Germany so that the prices of German exports rise and the prices of German imports fall. This leads to the rather paradoxical result that gold flows into Germany, and the transfer mechanism thus eases the situation of the country paying reparations! This is not a very probable case, but it

---

goods in about the same proportion as the old income and because in almost all countries the volume of export and import is small compared with total production.

[3] It is a question of the elasticity of the demand curve after the payment had been made and the curve has therefore shifted. Elasticity will probably not be the same as before. The elasticity of the German demand for German export goods is also relevant.

[4] *Cf.* Eucken, *Das Reparationsproblem* (*Verhandlungen der F. List-Gesellschaft*, Berlin, 1929).

[5] *Cf.*, *e.g.*, Yntema, *A Mathematical Reformulation of the General Theory of International Trade* (1932), chap. v, pp. 61 *et seq.*, and Wilson, *Capital Imports and the Terms of Trade* (1931).

would arise if the increase of foreign demand were for German exports, and the fall in Germany's demand related to imports.[6]

These considerations are, however, of theoretical rather than of practical interest, since the relevant factors and their possible repercussions are in concrete examples so complex that the price changes involved by transfer can hardly be worked out. But in any case, as pointed out by Professor Ohlin, it is an oversimplification to say that prices fall in the country paying reparations and rise in the country receiving them. The analysis must be in terms not of general but of sectional price levels.[7]

§ 4. Unilateral Payments and International Movements of Capital.

The influence of unilateral payments, such as reparations, on imports and exports of commodities and services and on the price level is normally obscured for a longer or shorter period by their profound influence on the international movement of capital.

A country making large unilateral payments will tend to import capital in one form or another. In this way the direct effect of these payments on the balance of trade and services will be suspended or at least weakened. Payment will be made in the first instance not out of current production but by the foreign creditors. Transfer is postponed and, provided that the new credits are actually repaid, is made finally in instalments over a period of years.

The form in which these transfer credits are granted and the mechanism connecting them with the unilateral payments may vary considerably. A direct and obvious connection exists where the loan is made to the debtor himself, as the Dawes Loan and the Young Loan were made to the German Government. The transfer of titles to durable property has similar effects. Thus the surrender of Germany's mercantile marine and of German property abroad affected the balance of trade not immediately but over the period during which this property would have yielded income.

But the view that transfer would have been impossible without capital imports refers not so much to direct loans as to the indirect effects of the payments, in inducing persons other than the debtor himself to import capital.

The payments actually made, the raising of the sums required,

---

[6] Prof. Pigou now supports the view that this is possible. *Cf.* " Reparations and the Ratio of International Exchange," *Economic Journal*, vol. 42, Dec. 1932.

[7] The analysis has been carried forward by R. Nurkse, *Internationale Kapital-bewegungen* (1935).

and the restriction of credit necessary to ensure transfer,[8] all impose a relative stringency on the money and capital markets; the rate of interest rises compared with the rate in foreign markets. As shown in chapter v, § 4, this attracts short-term capital, or in the case of a capital-exporting country less capital is exported than before. If, as in the case of Germany, the payments are large enough seriously to restrict the accumulation of capital, then not only short-term but also long-term capital is imported. That is to say, debentures and shares are sold to foreigners, new issues are floated abroad, &c., &c.[9]

The French war indemnity to Germany in 1871 was paid chiefly by the sale of securities in French hands to foreigners. It is common knowledge that German Reparations were accompanied well into 1929 by large capital imports into Germany. But clearly the transfer problem is not thereby solved but only postponed. If transfer does finally take place, it must be in accordance with the principles worked out above. Postponement may indeed lead to cancellation, if the ' transfer credits ' become valueless owing to the bankruptcy of the debtors. But it should be noted that the creditors who lose their money, e.g., American purchasers of German stocks, need not be nationals of the country receiving unilateral payments, e.g., France.

It is important, however, to avoid the *post hoc propter hoc* fallacy which has vitiated to a large extent the discussion of German Reparations especially in the German literature. The fact that between 1924 and 1929 Germany took up credits abroad to the value of so many milliard marks by no means implies that the whole of this amount was due to the payment of reparations. Germany would in any case have imported capital even if no political tribute had been imposed. Its economic system had been weakened by the ravages of war and inflation; but the stage was set for a rapid recovery. The potential labour force and the spirit of enterprise were practically intact and the confidence of foreign lenders in Germany's economic future was unimpaired. The conditions were therefore extremely favourable for the import of capital on a large scale.

Only a part, therefore, of the capital imports which took place can be attributed to the influence of reparations; how large a part, it is difficult to say. That depends on whether the German repara-

---

[8] Credit policy need be restrictive only in a relative sense. In a period of boom it need only be less ' expansive ' than that of other countries. *Cf.* the following section.
[9] This point is stressed notably in Hansen, *Economic Stabilization in an Unbalanced World* (1932).

tion taxes led chiefly to reduced consumption or to reduced accumulation of capital. Many other factors, such as the existence and the magnitude of any transfer loss in the sense already explained and the degree of credit restriction, also affect the result.

If one assumes, for example, that the payment of reparations to the amount of two milliards per year resulted in the import of one milliard over and above what would have been imported in any case, then ignoring any transfer loss there was an effective transfer of one milliard in the sense that the supply of goods in Germany was decreased by this amount, whereas the transfer of the other half was postponed. The milliard actually transferred did not indeed constitute an export surplus, but the import surplus was smaller than it would otherwise have been by that amount. Half the reparation payments may therefore be regarded as coming out of the fund of goods of the country from which they were due, although this fund was larger than it would have been, had no capital been imported.

But even on the assumption that there was in this sense an effective transfer of one milliard, it must nevertheless be emphasised that the import of capital for commercial purposes was a necessary condition. For without the assistance of foreign capital production in Germany could not have expanded sufficiently to enable the very large sums required to be raised.[1]

§ 5. The Limits of Possible Transfer.

No description, however detailed, of the mechanism of transfer is sufficient in itself to show whether in any particular case transfer is possible or not. Apart from the fact that it abstracts from the problem of raising the necessary sum, such a description can only say what price-movements would be necessary to effect the transfer. Whether these price-movements can be brought about in a concrete case depends on a number of factors not yet mentioned, about which something must be said in this section. It will be assumed, on the one hand, that the money has already been raised and, on the other hand, that there is the minimum degree of flexibility without which no transfer would be possible at all. The prices of factors of production, particularly wages, must not be completely rigid.

Whether the necessary adjustments are or are not made depends to a very great extent on credit policy in the countries involved. As shown above, the country paying reparations must restrict

---

[1] This has been stressed notably by Prof. J. H. Williams.

credit. Given the willingness to pay and to effect the transfer, any reluctance on the part of the central bank will be overcome sooner or later by the shrinkage of its gold reserves. In practice, however, the decisive question is generally whether the receiving country obeys or disobeys the ' Rules of the Gold Standard.' To produce deliberately the effects which would follow of themselves under an automatic gold standard, it must increase the monetary circulation by at least the whole amount of the gold which flows in. If the circulation is not increased by this amount, then that part of the transfer mechanism which consists in raising incomes and prices in the creditor country is put out of action. The whole burden of the adjustment then falls on the debtor country, where prices and wages must fall more sharply than would otherwise be necessary. Obviously the prospect of a smooth functioning of the mechanism is not thereby improved.[2]

In assessing the practical importance of this circumstance one must however bear in mind that if the circulation is increased by the whole amount of the additional reserves, the proportion of reserves to circulation goes up. This minimum degree of expansion in the creditor country may therefore be expected. If the bank does not wish to increase its reserve ratio, then the quantity of money must be increased by more than the sum transferred. The same holds true *mutatis mutandis* for contraction in the country making payment. It must also be remembered that the price discrepancy has only to be created once. Later, when the process of transfer has already begun, it can even be reduced. There is no need for progressive contraction to pay each annual instalment.

The likelihood of a policy favourable to transfer varies, of course, with the phase of the trade cycle through which the countries concerned are passing. When credit is being expanded, the necessary adjustments require only that expansion shall be accelerated in the country receiving payment and retarded in the country making it. But in the depression the latter country must aggravate the process of deflation which always characterises this phase of the trade cycle; moreover, there is small prospect of assistance from the monetary authorities of the former country.

The difficulties of transfer are, of course, greatly enhanced by the erection of obstacles to trade. If at the existing level of tariffs the volume of international trade is nevertheless considerable, then

---

[2] The writers who stress the difficulties of transfer generally rely on the assertion that an automatic expansion of the circulation is nowadays improbable. Attention is drawn particularly to the policy of the United States and of the Banque de France, who preferred to accumulate large gold reserves rather than to let the transfer mechanism operate freely. *Cf.* notably *Treatise on Money*, chap. xxi, and the *Macmillan Report* (Cmd. 3897) drawn up under Mr. Keynes's influence.

the transfer of unilateral payments should not prove very difficult. For, tariffs notwithstanding, the price of many commodities will be only just above the export point and that of many others only just above the import point; and only a small effort will be needed to increase exports and reduce imports. Tariffs already in existence are therefore not a very serious obstacle to the transfer of any but impossibly large amounts. Moreover, as stressed particularly by Mr. Hawtrey, even if tariffs render impossible a further increase of exports, it is still possible to reduce imports. But if tariffs are progressively increased, as during the last few years, then prices must fall progressively in the country making payment.[3] If the very countries which insist on payment being made at the same time restrict imports by every possible device to ' improve the balance of trade ' and to ' protect themselves from foreign competition ' then their policy can only be described as sadistic. It makes no difference whether the import restrictions are directed impartially against all countries or whether the country making payment has preferential treatment. For, as already pointed out, the transfer of payments in commodity form is often carried out not directly but indirectly, by means of triangular trade. The European countries, for example, pay their debts to the United States by exporting manufactured goods to South America, while South America exports to the United States raw materials and food stuffs, on which tariffs in the latter country are low or non-existent. Dr. Benjamin Anderson has characterised the policy of the United States as follows: " The debts of the outside world to us are ropes about the necks of our debtors, by means of which we pull them towards us. Our trade restrictions are pitchforks pressed against their bodies, by means of which we hold them off. This situation can obviously involve a very painful strain for the foreign debtor."[4] The same holds true to an even greater extent of certain European countries.

§ 6. THE TRANSFER MECHANISM IN TIMES OF CRISIS.

The reader will already have asked himself how much of the transfer mechanism remains operative in times of acute financial crisis, such as swept over the world in 1931. It has already been stressed that under such circumstances international lending—and

---

[3] Cf. Machlup, " Währung und Auslandsverschuldung " in Mitteilungen des Verbandes der österreichischen Banken und Bankiers, Jahrgang 10 Nr. 7-8, pp. 194 et seq., 1928.

[4] Cf. Chase Economic Bulletin, published by the Chase National Bank, 14th March 1930; further, Hansen, Economic Stabilization in an Unbalanced World (1932), chap. v.

with it the possibility of regulating short-term capital movements by discount policy—disappears altogether. If the creditors of a country lose faith in its solvency and in the stability of its currency, they will follow the cry ' every man for himself.' Clearly in that case no rise in the bank rate, however large, can ' attract ' capital. But this is not all. The collapse may very well spread from the international capital market to the currency itself. For the joint stock banks try to safeguard their position by discounting at the central bank bills to replace the foreign credits which have been withdrawn. The central bank then finds its cash reserve melting away and the exchange threatening to depreciate. It is thus lured into restricting international payments and perhaps fails nevertheless to maintain parity. At first sight one might suppose that, in contradiction to our theory, it is after all not purchasing power parity but the passive balance of payments induced by the withdrawal of foreign credit which determines the rate of exchange. But more careful analysis shows that these phenomena in no way contradict our theory. On the contrary, their full significance cannot be grasped except with its help.

The deeper cause of a financial crisis may be cyclical or it may be a special circumstance such as the outbreak of war. However that may be, the crisis is usually precipitated by a sudden drying up of the stream of credit. It makes no essential difference whether an expansion of credit at home is brought to a halt or whether credit is withheld by foreign lenders.[5] In both cases the numerous persons who depend directly or indirectly on the stream of capital get into difficulties. In the cyclical change-over from boom to slump the industries producing capital goods, in which investment was heaviest during the credit expansion, have to bear the brunt. Pressure is soon transmitted to the banks which finance these industries, and the former seek to protect themselves by rediscounting an increased volume of bills at the central bank. As soon as important bankruptcies occur panic may easily become general, manifesting itself in a run on the whole banking system. Not knowing how far the collapse will spread, everyone tries to put his money in a safe place. If the panic attains large dimensions, even the soundest bank will be compelled to close its doors. For every credit system presupposes a certain minimum of confidence, and no bank is able to meet all its obligations simultaneously in cash.

It is usual in such cases for the central bank to intervene,

---

[5] As when capital exports from America ceased in 1929 after the collapse of the boom.

D

if the joint stock banks cannot maintain their position by mutual support. The history of financial crises provides many examples, and if it is really a question of temporary illiquidity due to panic withdrawals of money, the intervention of the central bank is without doubt calculated to restore confidence.

If the withdrawal of credit is *from abroad*,[6] if there is in addition a flight of domestic capital,[7] and if the central bank cannot obtain sufficiently large credits from abroad, it can intervene only at the expense of reserves. But since a fall in the reserve proportion diminishes confidence still further and accelerates the withdrawal of credit, the scope of this policy is very restricted.

The central bank must then decide whether to withdraw support from the banks in difficulties or whether to strain its credit and thus jeopardise the exchange. The choice between these two alternatives involves very weighty problems, which cannot be adequately discussed here. It is possible that a drastic application of the first policy would compel foreign creditors to cease withdrawing capital for fear of driving their debtors into bankruptcy. It is moreover arguable that mistrust of the currency is really due either to the liberal credit policy of the central bank or to the expectation, based on past experience and on knowledge of the views prevailing, that such a policy will probably be followed. On the other hand, there are sometimes strong arguments for the second alternative.

However that may be, our theory of the gold standard mechanism remains unaffected. No monetary system can work unless its rules are observed. These demand that the central bank shall refuse to increase the effective circulation by granting extra credit. The currency is then in no danger. For it is almost inconceivable that 20 or 30% of the notes in circulation will be presented simultaneously for conversion into gold, for the purpose of repaying foreign credits. This would constitute an enormous deflation, and prices could not help falling. Long before withdrawals reached this magnitude the debtors would be bankrupt, and payment would automatically come to an end.

If there is a 40 to 50% gold backing, the exchange is in no danger unless the public begins to use foreign money instead of domestic money as the normal means of payment. But there is

---

[6] *Cf.* notably Machlup, " Theorie der Kapitalflucht," in *Weltwirtschaftliches Archiv*, Bd. 36 (1932), Heft 2, pp. 512 *et seq.;* Th. Balogh, " Some Theoretical Aspects of the Central European Credit and Transfer Crises " in *International Affairs*, vol. 11, 1932; Marco Fanno, *I Trasferimenti Anormati di Capitali e le Crisi*, Torino (1935).

[7] Whether by the transfer of deposits to foreign banks, or by their withdrawal to purchase foreign bills.

no reason to expect a flight from the currency so long as the central
bank eschews dangerous experiments. Experience shows that a
panic of this kind occurs only where the public has learned by
bitter experience to expect a currency inflation.[8] A run on the
banks, signifying that the public prefers not foreign to domestic
money but cash to deposits, may lead to bank failures,[9] but the
currency will not be endangered.

The object of this analysis is to show that such abnormal cases
neither contradict our theory nor prove the ' inadequacy ' of the
gold standard mechanism. It is not intended to gloss over their
extreme gravity or to deny that a temporary suspension of the
gold standard may perhaps be the lesser of two evils.[10]

§ 7. Exchange Control.[1]

To round off our account of the monetary mechanism, something must be said of the attempts to replace it by state regulation
excluding the free play of economic forces from the foreign
exchange market. The endless ramifications of exchange control
in different countries cannot be examined in this context, but only
the fundamental principles according to which the point—or point-
lessness—of any particular device can readily be grasped. These
are themselves easily deducible from the results already obtained.
For it is by no means the case that under exchange control the
market mechanism ceases to function altogether or that the laws
governing it can be ignored.

The primary function of exchange control is to maintain without
the loss of gold a rate of foreign exchange higher than that which

---

[8] This represents a sudden contraction of the ' cylinder ' (cf. p. 41). A catastrophic fall in the volume of production would have similar effects.

[9] As in America during 1931 and 1933. The number of bank failures was very
large because the law prohibiting banks from having more than one branch led to
extreme decentralisation.

[10] But as the reader will see for himself England can indulge more safely in this
policy than countries where the public is prone to panic and where inflation has
undermined faith in the currency.

[1] There is no systematic exposition of this subject, the relevant literature
being small in quantity and confined to periodicals, many of them weekly papers.
Cf. Machlup, " Die Theorie der Kapitalflucht," Weltwirtschaftliches Archiv, Bd.
36, Heft 2, pp. 512 et seq.; article " Devisenbewirtschaftung " in Handwörterbuch
des Bankwesens (1935) (with Bibliography); Whittlesey, " Exchange Control," in
American Economic Review, vol. 22 (1932), pp. 585-604; Basch, " Probleme der
Devisenkontrolle," in Mitteilungen des Verbandes osterr, Banken und Bankiers, 14
Jg. Nr. 9/10, Oct. 1932; Gross, " Zielsetzung der Devisenzwangswirtschaft in
Deutschland und im Ausland," in Bank-Archiv, 15th Feb. 1933; " Ausgangspunkte,
Formen und Wirkungen der Devisenzwangswirtschaft," in Archiv für Sozialwissenschaft, vol. 69, April 1933, pp. 49 et seq. Enquiry into Clearing Agreements,
League of Nations Publication (1935). The official regulations in all countries are
published in extenso at intervals by the Bank of International Settlements. Cf.
further Das Devisenrecht der Welt herausgegeben von der Korrespondenz, Industrie
und Handel, Berlin, Eildienst-verlag. For the legal principles involved, cf. Koppe
and Blau, Das gesamte Devisenrecht (1932).

would rule in a free market. It is also desired in some cases to ensure a sufficiency of foreign bills for payments regarded as particularly pressing, or to prevent import prices from rising. Another very important aim is to discourage the withdrawal of money for the sole purpose of converting it into foreign currency, and thus to prevent bank failures. But exchange control often comes to be used also for protectionist ends,[2] although this is seldom admitted to be its real object.

As a means of manipulating the exchange rates and preventing the outflow of gold the attempt is made to influence both the supply of foreign money and the demand for it. But this almost always involves the further step of providing that all monetary transactions with foreign countries, or certain types of transaction, shall require the assent of a central authority.[3]

To influence *supply* the authorities may sell bills out of an exchange fund. But this can hardly be called exchange control since it is practised by central banks under the ordinary gold standard mechanism. A more drastic device is to impound all current receipts from abroad. Exporters of goods and services and recipients of interest and amortisation payments are not allowed to invest the proceeds abroad but must change them into domestic money at a fixed rate. A further step is the mobilisation of credits or even securities and titles to property already held in foreign countries.

To reduce the *demand* for foreign bills certain types of payment to foreign countries are prohibited. Payments for imports obtain preference over purely financial transactions and interest payments over repayments of capital; a distinction is drawn between ' necessary ' and ' superfluous ' imports. Foreign travel is prohibited or travellers are allowed to take only a certain sum of money with them. By transfer moratoria debtors are prevented from transferring money to their foreign creditors. In the same way a general moratorium provides for the optional or compulsory renewal of credits falling due for repayment. Effects similar to those of a transfer moratorium are secured by negotiation under standstill agreements.[4] Thus in 1931 and 1932 Germany's creditors agreed to let their short-term claims remain outstanding or to call in and withdraw only an agreed percentage.

Exchange control is much more likely to be effective in some

---

[2] See below chap. xix, § 6.
[3] *Cf.* what was said on p. 25 about the 16th century bullion system.
[4] On this subject, too, the literature is confined to periodicals. *Cf., e.g.,* Friedheim, " Der Sinn der Stillhaltung," in the monthly *Währung und Wirtschaft* (Feb. 1933) and articles in *The Economist, Bank-Archiv, Die Bank, Deutscher Volkswirt,* &c.

circumstances than in others. Two main cases must be distinguished:

(a) The weakness of the exchange, the outflow of gold and the ' crisis of the balance of payments ' may be due simply to the *flight of foreign and of domestic capital*. This differs from ' export of capital ' in being determined not by the ' profit ' but by the ' risk ' factor.[5] Capital flows as it were up-stream not into countries with a high rate of interest, but into countries where risk is small and where the rate of interest is generally low. The capital balance may be upset in this way by a momentary panic as in America (February to March, 1933) or, as in Germany from the autumn of 1930 onwards, disequilibrium may persist for a long time.

(b) The weakness of the exchange and the outflow of gold may be due also to the much more serious fact that the *balance of payments on income account is chronically passive* at the given exchange rate. If prices and incomes are above the equilibrium point relatively to other countries,[6] then imports—including services, interest payments, normal repayments of capital and normal movements of capital seeking the point of maximum profit —will show a surplus over exports. This can be rectified only by restoring equilibrium between domestic and foreign prices': either the exchange must be allowed to depreciate or prices must be forced down.

These two cases seldom occur separately and each has a tendency to produce the other. As already shown, flight of capital can easily lead to credit inflation and, on the other hand, a long-continued outflow of gold, resulting from the refusal to adjust prices downwards, ends by destroying confidence and producing a flight of capital. But nevertheless the two cases must be kept separate for purposes of analysis.

In the former there is a flight of capital but the balance of payments on income account remains in equilibrium. Prices are not therefore above the long-run equilibrium position, but they are nevertheless too high, having regard to the temporary flight of capital. To effect the transfer either there must be a painful contraction of the circulating medium or, if the capital is replaced by credits granted by the bank of issue, the exchange must fall. The object of exchange control is to avoid the dilemma by preventing flight of capital.

---

[5] *Cf.* Machlup, " Theorie der Kapitalflucht," in *Weltwirtschaftliches Archiv*, vol. xxxvi, 1932.

[6] Either because of inflation or, as already pointed out, because of the refusal to keep step with falling prices abroad. In recent years a number of countries have been forced off the gold standard for this reason.

This represents fairly accurately the situation in 1931-32 of Germany, where the flight of capital was as a matter of fact successfully reduced to manageable proportions. For commercial purposes and for the service of foreign loans bills were in principle assigned up to 100% of the demand. Moreover, the value of the mark was maintained even abroad, and there was no appreciable development of black markets with lower rates of exchange.

Thus German experience has shown that within certain limits the flight of capital can be prevented without crippling the normal business of payments on income account. But these limits and the conditions which render such a policy possible at all must be noted carefully. It is imperative that measures should simultaneously be taken to restore confidence: in particular the currency must be stabilised. If the balance of payments on income account is passive, then prices and incomes must be lowered by credit restriction. Indeed, a surplus must be created on income account to provide for such export of capital as eludes even the most rigid exchange control. Otherwise gold must flow out or the exchange will fall, and in either case the tendency to a flight of capital will be strengthened.

It should also be noted that the best means of stopping the foreign creditors from withdrawing their money is to facilitate repayment as much as possible. For just as with a run on the banks, money will no longer be withdrawn if the creditors feel sure of obtaining it whenever they so desire.

The comparative success of exchange control in Germany must be attributed to the fact that credit was adequately restricted. The volume of bills discounted at the Reichsbank fell between February 1932, and February 1933, from 3295 to 2351 million marks. Deflation was of course greatly facilitated by the drastic cuts in money incomes initiated by Brüning's emergency decrees.

Any attempt to discriminate between ' flight of capital ' and ' legitimate international payments ' must encounter serious technical difficulties. If the tendency to a flight of capital persists for long, then transfer moratoria, standstill agreements for short-term liabilities and embargoes on the export of notes must be reinforced by other devices. For the export of capital can take many different forms. Thus current receipts from abroad on account of commodity exports[7] are not changed into domestic money but are invested abroad. If the flight of capital is to be successfully prevented, it must therefore be made compulsory for all

---

[7] Including services. Hotels, for example, arrange with their foreign guests for bills to be paid into an account at a foreign bank.

foreign bills received in payment to be handed over. Evasion is of course very difficult to prevent entirely, and further compulsion and control become necessary, to the great detriment of international trade. Moreover, import and export invoices must be checked to prevent capital being smuggled out under the cloak of fictitiously high import prices or low export prices.

Once the causes producing flight of capital are removed, control could be relaxed without a fall in the exchange. But as a rule the first type of exchange control degenerates gradually into the second. How this happens can be illustrated by the classic example of Germany from 1933 onwards.

Early in 1933, or even before, the policy of restoring international price equilibrium by deflating incomes was definitely given up. Simultaneously the attempt was made to ' stimulate business ' by public works, which involved a large expansion of credit. The question whether this radical change of policy was a good or a bad thing is not relevant to the present discussion, but only the fact that for various reasons the Government did not dare to change the official gold rate of the mark. Gold prices, therefore, rose in Germany, while they were falling steadily in the gold-standard countries and countries with depreciated currencies. The balance of payments thus became increasingly passive, the demand for foreign money exceeded its supply, imports increased and exports diminished. In this situation it was the task of exchange control by one means or another to equate supply and demand.

To increase supply was impossible since depreciation of the exchange and a lowering of prices and incomes were both ruled out. It was therefore necessary to restrict demand and to discriminate between buyers. Amortisation payments to foreign creditors were suspended, interest payments were restricted more and more, and their transfer was prohibited; foreign travel and commodity imports were restricted; payment for current imports was suspended, &c., &c.

There are endless devices for preventing or postponing payment and directly or indirectly restricting imports;[8] but the general principle is clear enough. In place of the price mechanism demand must be adjusted to supply in some other way. Either general rules of one kind or another are evolved or it must be decided arbitrarily from case to case which imports shall and which imports

---

[8] This policy involves to some extent a vicious circle. Import restrictions raise the price of important raw materials, and, notably in the textile industry, these are replaced to some extent by expensive and inferior substitutes; moreover, foreign countries are goaded into reprisals. Thus exports are curtailed and the import surplus is not removed.

shall not be paid for. Any number of different arrangements are conceivable and in fact the regulations were revised every month or two according to a ' new plan.' A detailed study of all this would be superfluous. Nor need we examine the official pronouncements explaining the reason of the various regulations, since for political reasons they ignored almost everything of real significance. Instead of pointing out that the mark was overvalued—chiefly owing to the policy of expansion—they emphasised the passive balance of payments, for which the unneighbourly refusal of foreign countries to accept payment in German goods was made responsible. Similarly, instead of high costs they talked about the ' Exportmüdigkeit ' of German industry!

If a country is prepared to export only those commodities in which she has the greatest comparative advantage, then obviously the exchange can be maintained at a much higher rate than if the international division of labour is fully utilised. For instance, if imports were drastically restricted, *some* German goods could still be exported even at an exchange rate of 3 marks to the pound, without a deflationary fall of prices in Germany, though the standard of living would of course have to be considerably reduced.

Interesting material for observation is provided by *clearing agreements*,[9] under which two countries regulate the making of payments between them. In both countries importers pay into a central account the purchase price of the goods imported; these sums are then utilised to pay exporters. In most but not in all cases the clearing system covers also amongst other things payment for interest and amortisation on debts already contracted. Frequently it was the creditor countries who instituted a clearing system in order to exact payments due to them. Suppose, for example, that Germany has an export surplus with Great Britain, which she uses not to pay her British creditors but to purchase goods from other countries. Then it is understandable that Great Britain will try to impound this surplus by a clearing system.

Obviously a creditor country cannot exact payment in this way unless she has an ' unfavourable ' balance of trade with her debtor. If Great Britain had an export surplus with Germany, she could not obtain payment even for the whole of her exports out of imports, still less could she satisfy those of her nationals who had lent money to Germany. The United States have a ' favourable ' balance of trade with Germany and are therefore from this point of view in an ' unfavourable ' bargaining position.

---

[9] *Cf. Enquiry into Clearing Agreements* published by the League of Nations (Geneva, 1935).

If a clearing agreement is reached between Germany, where prices are above the equilibrium point, and Switzerland, with whom she normally has a favourable balance of trade, then imports from Switzerland will rise and the export surplus will decrease; similarly, imports from United States must fall because there will not be enough money to go round. In this way Germany's clearing agreements with Switzerland, Holland, Great Britain, France, &c., have considerably altered the channels of international trade.[1]

Clearing agreements have again and again been made between countries whose balance of trade with one another cannot be equalised. Where the country with the over-valued currency has an excess of imports, ' clearing surpluses ' accumulate, paid in by importers and waiting to be paid out to exporters. In such cases the clearing is said to be ' blocked up.' Foreign exporters and other ' clearing creditors ' must wait for their money, which is equivalent to a forced loan from one country to the other.

The clearing agreements were an attempt to get out of the *impasse* into which the independent exchange control of different countries had led. But the mistake was made of trying to reopen the channels of payment without restoring the mechanism of adjustment—which consists as already shown in the flexibility either of prices or of exchange rates.

In spite of the complexity in detail of exchange control it is really not difficult to grasp the general situation and to point the way out of this tangle of restrictions, prohibitions and regulations, if one understands in principle the workings of the international monetary mechanism. Most of the ' practical ' men who introduced and administered exchange control entirely lacked this knowledge. They had to discover step by step through bitter experience the principles of international trade—a wearisome process very costly to the economic system. Since 1931 exchange control had decimated the volume of international trade. Bilateral forms of exchange control, represented most strikingly by clearing agreements,[2] which tend to equalise the balance of payments between pairs of countries, have been particularly injurious to ' triangular trade.'[3]

---

[1] *Cf.* F. Hilgerdt, " The Approach to Bilateralism—a Change in the Structure of World Trade " in *Index*, Stockholm, 1935, and J. B. Condliffe in *World Economic Survey* (1934-35) (published by the League of Nations, 1935), p. 156 *et seq.*

[2] Multilateral clearing agreements have been much discussed, but not as yet put into practice. For the present, Governments have their work cut out administering bilateral agreements!

[3] *Cf.* the statistical computations in the *Review of World Trade*, 1934 (League of Nations, Geneva, 1935), p. 67, and *Enquiry into Clearing Agreements* (League of Nations, Geneva, 1935).

The only way of escape from this pernicious system is to give up trying to maintain an artificial rate and to let the exchange depreciate in accordance with purchasing-power parity. In recent years Austria and some of the South American countries have in this way reached a new equilibrium permitting exchange control to be relaxed or abolished. In most cases the exchange is not depreciated openly and all at once but step by step. At first 'emergency taxes' and 'license charges' are levied on foreign money allotted to importers, and the proceeds are handed over to exporters as premiums on the bills which they pay in. The extra charges are generally graded, 'necessary' imports being given preference over 'luxury' imports. Then they are gradually extended and unified until sooner or later depreciation is made definitive.[4] In this way during 1932 and 1933 exchange control was almost entirely abolished in Austria. Hungary, Germany, and Rumania are still (summer 1935) at an early stage of the process. Even at the cost of endless difficulties and disadvantages they have postponed adjusting the exchange rate, partly from stupidity and partly from weakness. For it is a sign of weakness that the necessary adjustments of the exchange rate is considered likely to cause panic in a country which has experience of inflation.

The working of exchange control in Germany and in other countries during recent years has been by no means uninteresting. But the results which it has yielded were easily deducible from the theory of international trade, and were, indeed, for the most part actually predicted beforehand.

---

[4] A new form of veiled devaluation has recently (1935) been introduced in Germany. It consists of a more or less general and uniform export premium. Reliable information on the details of this scheme is not available, but the premium is believed to amount on the average to 25 per cent. of the export value. While under an open devaluation the exporter (seller of foreign currencies) receives his subsidy from the proceeds of a premium or surtax on the official rate of exchange payable by the importer (buyer of foreign currencies), under this system the sums required for the payment of export bounties are raised by a special levy imposed on industry as a whole; hence the necessary check on imports is not an automatic one but has to be provided—as is actually the case in Germany at present—by administrative control and selection of imports through a comprehensive licensing system.

CHAPTER VIII.

HISTORICAL ILLUSTRATIONS OF UNILATERAL TRANSFER.

§ 1. General Remarks.

In economics hypotheses reached by deduction can seldom be verified completely by statistics. There is almost always room for doubt whether the observed result can only have been produced in accordance with the theoretical construction by a certain force operating in a certain way. For it is usually impossible to observe the effects of one force in isolation from the effects of other forces working in the same or in the opposite direction.

The attempt to find statistical examples for the functioning of the transfer mechanism involves two distinct problems. In many cases it is comparatively easy to trace the influence of unilateral transfers on the balance of payments. But it is not so easy to trace the price-changes involved in the restoration of equilibrium.

(a) The first of these two problems is to verify the conclusion that when a country makes unilateral payments its balance of trade (in goods and services, including the precious metals) tends to improve. This means either that an export-surplus is created, or that an existing export-surplus becomes larger, or that an existing import-surplus becomes smaller; when transfer ceases there should be a movement in the opposite direction. If the shifts to be expected on theoretical grounds cannot be detected statistically, one is justified in assuming that the balance of payments is kept in equilibrium by invisible items such as the granting of credits or the transfer of titles to property, bankruptcies, &c., which sometimes elude statistical enquiry. But if the unilateral payments are on a large scale, as when capital is imported steadily over a long period, then equilibrium must be reached by the movement of goods. For in the long period commodity imports and exports are the flexible items in the balance of payments.

To show how equilibrium is reached, one must take into account all the trade connections of a country and not merely its balance of trade with the particular country to which it makes the unilateral payments. For the adjustment almost always involves the

91

'triangular trade,' particularly where a direct adjustment is made impossible by tariff barriers. In this case the adjustment will also be made largely by means of services on which there are no duties. For instance, the United States will receive payment in the form of tourist traffic and shipping services.

(b) The second problem is to verify statistically the shifts of price asserted by economic theory to result from unilateral transfers. But attempts to do so have not hitherto been very fruitful. Apart from the Canadian example, where the conditions were especially favourable,[1] the observed price-changes are mostly insignificant, they often contradict expectations, and in all cases they can be attributed to other causes without doing violence to the facts. The reason is first of all that there is no theoretical necessity for prices in the country making payments to fall relatively to prices in the country receiving them: as shown above the opposite is conceivable. Secondly, there are always other forces at work which influence prices. Apart from inflation and deflation, boom and depression, there are secular changes of all kinds due to technical progress in production and transport, to shifts in demand, to the introduction or abolition of tariffs, &c., &c. It should be noted in this connection that at certain stages of the trade cycle the export prices of countries producing raw materials move in the opposite direction to those of countries producing manufactured goods. All these influences on price-levels obscure the effects due to unilateral payments—which are moreover in themselves complex. It is therefore hardly surprising that statisticians have not been able to discover many striking examples of recurrent price-changes.

This negative result is however by no means valueless. For it justifies the conclusion that the shifts of price necessitated by unilateral payments are of a lower and not of a higher order of magnitude than other influences on the price-level. In particular the shifts of price which occur during a normal trade cycle are undoubtedly much larger than those due to transfer.

§ 2. THE FRENCH INDEMNITY OF 1871.

Few episodes in modern financial history have excited so much astonishment as the successful discharge of the French War-indemnity to Germany in 1871. Particularly surprising were, on the one hand, the ease and rapidity with which France raised the 5 milliard francs required—a very large sum in those days. The

---

[1] Cf. § 3 below.

Indemnity was not spread like German Reparations under the Dawes and Young Plans over a large number of annual instalments, but had, in accordance with the Treaty of Frankfort, to be transferred in a few lump sums by 2nd March 1874. To the astonishment of the whole of Europe the final instalment was paid on 15th September 1873—a unique example of the prompt unilateral transfer of capital. The second point of interest is the comparatively small disturbance to European trade caused by the transfer of this sum within so short a period of time.

In the following paragraphs a short summary is given of (a) the actual transfer, (b) the raising by France of the sums required, (c) the uses to which the proceeds were put by Germany.

(a) The sum to be paid was fixed by the Treaty of Frankfort at 5,315 million francs. From this amount 325 million francs were subtracted on account of the railways in Alsace-Lorraine belonging to the Chemin de Fer de l'Est, whose shareholders were to be compensated by the French Government: 125 million francs were accepted in notes of the Banque de France, but the remaining 4,865 million francs had to be transferred in gold or in foreign bills. There were to be no payments in kind.

Only a very small proportion of the 4,865 million francs were paid over in cash. This part was made up as follows:—

In German coins, which for the most part had been brought into France by the German troops and were called in by the French Government, - - - -	105 million francs
In gold bullion, - - - - - -	273 ,, ,,
In silver, - - - - - - -	239 ,, ,,
	617 million francs

The whole of the remainder, that is to say much the greater part of the whole indemnity, was transferred in bills of exchange.

(b) Clearly this large sum could not be raised all at once by taxation but only by borrowing; moreover it could not all be saved out of current income. Recourse had therefore to be made on a large scale to the liquidation of capital already existing in French hands. The success of the 1871 and of the 1872 loans was due to two circumstances. On the one hand, the national credit had remained intact in spite of war and defeat; and, on the other hand, France's foreign investments had by 1870 reached a very large figure. From the middle of the nineteenth century onwards France was a typical creditor country, investing much of her savings abroad and living to a considerable extent on the interest and dividends. The reason why her balance of payments remained for decades, with only short interruptions, passive was that the annual receipts from foreign investments exceeded the annual exports of new capital.

Now everything depended on whether the French Government could succeed in mobilising these foreign investments. In 1871 and 1872 two large loans were issued amounting altogether to 5,792 million francs. The second loan in particular was amazingly successful, being ten times over-subscribed. The money came from the following sources: —

(1) About 2,250 million francs were subscribed from abroad, an appreciable part from Germany.

(2) About 2,000 million francs were taken up by French nationals, who sold foreign investments for the purpose. This meant the transfer of capital on a very large scale. The French Government, as it were, indirectly borrowed the foreign investments in private hands, thus obtaining the francs necessary to buy foreign bills. In some cases the Government accepted payment for its stock directly in foreign scrip, which it could then sell abroad.

(3) According to Moulton and McGuire one cannot be sure where the remaining 1,500 million francs came from. Presumably they were provided in part out of current savings in France.

In any case practically the whole sum required was raised by borrowing. Of course the amount of the indemnity had to be reflected sooner or later in reduced consumption in France. But the burden on the French taxpayer was distributed over a long period of time. The annual interest-service on the new debt amounted altogether to 374.6 million francs. The volume of taxation increased from 1869 to 1873 as follows: —

FRENCH TAXATION.
In millions of francs.

Year.	Direct Taxes.	Indirect Taxes.	Total.
1869	576	1,229	1,805
1870	586	1,083	1,669
1871	581	1,239	1,820
1872	605	1,524	2,129
1873	673	1,698	2,371

France succeeded in paying the actual indemnity surprisingly fast. But the ensuing burden on the national exchequer was not entirely removed even by 1914, although the rate of interest was reduced by conversion operations towards the end of the century.

The influence of the indemnity on France's international trade
is brought out clearly by the following table:—

FRANCE'S BALANCE OF TRADE.

In millions of francs.

Year.	Imports.	Exports.	Surplus.
1867	3,202	3,085	− 117
1868	3,415	2,974	− 441
1869	3,269	3,257	− 12
1870	2,935	2,915	− 20
1871	3,599	2,925	− 674
1872	3,603	3,814	+ 211
1873	3,651	3,925	+ 274
1874	3,574	3,806	+ 232
1875	3,585	3,968	+ 383
1876	4,046	3,689	− 357
1877	3,737	3,552	− 185
1878	4,246	3,297	− 949

The balance of trade was passive the whole time except from 1872
to 1875 when it promptly became active. The outflow of goods
began shortly after the first transfers of capital, continued for
several years, and was then reversed. This is, so far as it goes,
exactly what one would expect on theoretical grounds. The further
question, what proportion of the additional exports found its way
to Germany cannot be answered with confidence, since the statistics
of Germany's foreign trade were at that time still rather unreliable.
It is nevertheless significant that *direct* commodity exports from
France to Germany, which averaged in 1868-9 only 260 million
francs rose in 1872-3 to 436 million francs. That the increase of
direct transfer from France to Germany should not have played a
major part is quite in accordance with the predictions of economic
theory. Although transfer is normally made in the form of commodities, only part of these are transferred direct from the country
making payments to the country receiving them.[2] But in the
present example by no means the whole transfer was made in kind.
For, on the one hand, it is fairly certain that Germany's increase
of imports was much smaller than one would expect from the large
amount of capital which had been transferred; and, on the other
hand, the French balance of trade showed an export surplus once
more as early as 1876. If an amount corresponding to the whole
indemnity had been transferred in goods, the export surplus would
have had to persist much longer.

(c) The fact that less goods were exported from France than

---

[2] In the Canadian example (*cf.* § 3) imports rose almost to the full extent of
the loans contracted abroad, but only a small proportion of the commodities came
from England, where most of the capital had been raised.

might have been expected can be adequately explained by the peculiarities of the German situation after 1871. Part of the money was employed for special purposes—notably for the introduction of the gold standard—and was therefore not spent on imports. In the absence of detailed statistics the following rough summary must suffice : —

(1) The relatively small sum of 150 million francs (=120 million marks) was deposited at the Fortress of Spandau in gold.

(2) A large sum, estimated at 750 million francs, was spent on introducing the gold standard. One of Germany's chief benefits from the indemnity was that gold could be purchased without the unpleasant necessity of raising loans or taxes.

(3) A further sum, which cannot be estimated precisely, was expended by the national exchequer on pensions, repayment of debt, and on military works.

It would be interesting to trace the effects of the whole transaction on the economic position in France and in Germany. The flow of payments into Germany, by facilitating credit-expansion, undoubtedly helped to produce the boom which led up to the crisis of 1873. There is no space here for a detailed analysis and, particularly as regards the exact course of price-movements, statistics are lacking.

§ 3. Canadian Imports of Capital 1900-1914.

Canada's economic relations with other countries from 1900 to 1914 provide one of the very few cases where adequate verification is possible. Here it can be shown inductively whether the effects attributed by theory to large capital movements followed in this case the taking up of loans by Canada, or not. For the loans were so large as to overshadow any change, during the relevant period, in other factors influencing Canada's balance of payments. The very striking changes which occurred in the latter can therefore be imputed almost wholly to the import of capital.[3]

During the last few decades of the nineteenth century the annual increase in Canada's international indebtedness was only small: it was exceeded by the annual interest payments on debts already contracted. The balance of trade was therefore predominantly active. After 1900, however, when the western provinces

---

[3] Cf. the detailed analysis in Viner, *Canada's Balance of International Indebtedness* (1924).

began to develop, Canada borrowed from abroad amounts very large compared with the size of her population—which in 1901 was only 5·3 millions.

Loans were subscribed to the following amounts, and by the following countries[4] :—

CANADA'S IMPORTS OF CAPITAL.		COUNTRIES EXPORTING CAPITAL TO CANADA.		
Year.	In thousands of dollars.		In thousands of dollars.	per cent.
1900-1904, - -	227,792	Great Britain, -	1,753,118	68·8
1905-1909, - -	788,425	United States, -	629,794	24·7
1910-1913, - -	1,529,410	Other Countries,	162,715	6·5
Total,	2,545,627		2,545,627	

At the outbreak of war this large movement of capital came abruptly to an end.

In the following paragraphs the principal changes to be expected, according to the classical theory, are compared briefly with the observed facts.

(a) *Balance of Trade.* **Hypothesis.** On theoretical grounds one would expect Canada's balance of trade to become passive shortly after the inflow of foreign credits, with import surpluses to about the amount borrowed. For geographical reasons equilibrium should probably be reached not by the direct purchase of goods in England, but indirectly.

Verification. Canada's balance of trade in commodities is represented in the following table by quinquennial totals from 1881 onwards[5] :—

CANADA'S BALANCE OF TRADE.

Year.	Imports.	Exports.	Export Surplus.
	In millions of dollars.		
1881-1885	581	478	− 103
1886-1890	565	451	− 114
1891-1895	610	563	− 74
1896-1900	730	774	+ 44
1901-1905	1,169	1,051	− 118
1906-1910	1,627	1,305	− 322
1911-1914	2,374	1,484	− 890
			−1,330

As one would expect, the import surplus grew rapidly. It should be noted that the import surplus from 1900 to 1913 was smaller than the amount of capital imported; but the difference can be

[4] *Cf.* Viner, *op. cit.*, p. 139.
[5] Calculated from the exhaustive compilation in Viner, *op. cit.*, p. 282.

accounted for by other items in the balance of payments, notably interest payments.

The following table shows how important triangular trade was in producing the new equilibrium of imports and exports:—

CANADA'S TRADE-BALANCE AND CAPITAL-BALANCE.

Year.	Export Surplus with G.B.	British Investments in Canada.	In millions of dollars. Import Surplus with U.S.	U.S. Investments in Canada.	Import Surplus with other Countries.	Investments of other Countries in Canada.
1900	+ 51·9	10·1	− 47·2	17·9	− 11·5	3·7
1905	+ 46.6	76·4	− 78·8	32·4	− 17·8	3·7
1910	+ 29·8	218·5	− 161·5	72·7	− 26·9	22·1
1913	+ 72·3	375·8	− 258·8	135·0	− 35·0	36·0
1900-13	+670·0	1,753·1	− 1,722·8	629·8	− 302·1	162·7

Throughout the period Canada had actually an export surplus to Great Britain, the country which provided most of the credits. For while these were spent on commodities, the latter were purchased not in Great Britain but in other countries, for the most part in the United States.[6] This was due partly to financial reasons—American investors exercising a much more rigid control than the English lenders over their Canadian investments—but partly also to geographical and other advantages which American exporters had over their British competitors.[7] This is quite in accordance with the fact, as shown by the following table, that Canadian exports were considerably larger to Great Britain than to the United States:—

CANADIAN EXPORTS TO GREAT BRITAIN AND TO THE UNITED STATES.

Year.	To Great Britain.		To the United States.	
	In millions of dollars.	As a per cent. of total exports.	In millions of dollars.	As a per cent. of total exports.
1900,	96·6	59·1	52·5	32·1
1905,	97·1	50·1	70·4	36·9
1910,	132·2	48·2	104·1	38·0
1913,	215·3	50·0	163·4	37·0

The fact that capital imports were balanced by commodity imports not directly but ' triangularly ' renders possible a verification of the theory in other particulars. For theory asserts that the intermediate stages (outflow of gold, shift of prices, &c.), while superfluous where equilibrium is reached directly by purchases in the lending country, must necessarily occur where the adjustment

---

[6] Of course the Americans also loaned money to Canada. But Canada's surplus of imports from the United States exceeded her imports of capital from that country by about 1,000 million dollars.

[7] For further details cf. Viner, op. cit., pp. 284 et seq.

is indirect.[8]   In the present case one expects therefore the whole mechanism of adjustment to be called into play.   That this was actually the case can be demonstrated point by point.   In contrast to the indemnity of 1871 it is possible here to observe statistically not only the first and the last link in the chain of causation, *i.e.*, the movement of capital and the change in the balance of trade in commodities, but also the intermediate links.

(*b*) *Gold Movements and Volume of Circulation*.   **Hypothesis.** On theoretical grounds one would expect considerable imports of gold into Canada shortly after the loans had been made.

Verification.   That this was so is shown by the following table :—

CHANGES IN CANADA'S VOLUME OF COINED GOLD.

Year.	In thousands of dollars.	Year.	In thousands of dollars.
1900	+ 432	1907	+ 350
1901	− 64	1908	+ 1,806
1902	+ 449	1909	+ 568
1903	+ 923	1910	+ 999
1904	+ 654	1911	+ 2,349
1905	− 26	1912	− 112
1906	+ 423	1913	+ 1,622

The total volume of bank credit, represented by the note issue and by short-term credit held at Canadian banks, rose during the same period from about 350 million dollars in 1900 to over 1,100 million dollars in 1913.   As already noted[9] the increase in the volume of currency and of credit preceded by a short interval the corresponding inflow of gold.   But this is only a slight modification of the theory, according to which the inflow of gold normally precedes the expansion of credit based on it.   Such modifications always have to be made where the transfer and utilisation of loans is in the hands of a complicated banking organisation.   In many cases the Canadian banks made advances to their customers as soon as it was known that the latter had been successful in raising a loan in London.   The sum in question either remained in London or— more frequently—was credited, in the first instance, at New York to the Canadian banks, which had already expanded credit by increasing the supply of liquid resources.   The funds remained in New York until the Canadian banks called them in, to adjust their cash reserves to the increased volume of credit.   The gold did not actually flow into Canada until this happened.   As one would expect, the selling rate on New York was low and the selling rate on Canada in New York was high during the whole of this period.

---

[8] *Cf.* p. 73 and Taussig, *International Trade* (1927), pp. 124 *et seq.*
[9] *Cf.* p. 52.

That this state of affairs persisted for years, giving rise to a steady inflow of gold from New York into Canada, can only be explained by the continued use of this method of raising foreign loans, which went on until 1914.

(c) *Prices.* This is perhaps the most interesting aspect. The predictions of theory can be verified with surprising accuracy.

(1) *Changes in General Price-Levels.* **Hypothesis.** One would expect a rise of Canadian prices and perhaps a fall of British prices compared with the 'world price-level.' Since world prices rose between 1900 and 1913 one would expect, therefore, a rise in Canadian prices larger than and in British prices smaller than the rise in world prices.

Verification. As shown by the following table, the development was therefore exactly as one would expect:—

GENERAL PRICE LEVELS.[1]

Year.	Canada.		World.	Great Britain.
	Unweighted.	Weighted.	Unweighted.	Weighted.
1900	100.0	100.0	100.0	100.0
1901	98.8	100.2	99.8	96.7
1902	100.7	103.6	102.0	96.4
1903	102.1	103.7	102.3	96.9
1904	102.0	104.5	100.9	98.2
1905	105.1	107.6	104.6	97.6
1906	110.9	113.5	108.7	100.8
1907	116.6	122.1	113.8	106.0
1908	111.6	118.2	109.4	103.0
1909	112.0	119.4	110.0	104.1
1910	114.7	121.0	112.8	108.8
1911	116.8	123.9	116.3	109.4
1912	124.2	136.0	122.6	114.9
1913	124.8	131.9	121.2	116.5

It is particularly interesting to compare the movement of prices in Canada with that in the United States. In the period under review the United States also imported capital, but to a smaller extent than Canada. One would therefore expect prices to rise there more than in Great Britain or in the world as a whole but rather less than in Canada:—

WHOLESALE PRICES IN THE UNITED STATES.

Year.	Unweighted.	Weighted.	Year.	Unweighted.	Weighted.
1900	100.0	100.0	1907	117.2	117.3
1901	98.2	98.8	1908	111.1	113.6
1902	102.1	106.2	1909	114.5	121.0
1903	102.8	106.2	1910	119.1	124.7
1904	102.2	107.4	1911	116.9	118.5
1905	104.9	106.2	1912	120.9	125.9
1906	110.8	109.9	1913	122.3	124.7

[1] Selected from Viner, *loc. cit.* Prices in 1900, when the capital movements began, equal 100.

It is particularly significant that price movements in Canada and in the United States respectively, after keeping fairly close together for the greater part of the period, diverged during the last three years, when Canadian imports of capital were particularly large. Prices now rose in Canada considerably faster than in the United States.

(2) *Changes in Sectional Price-Levels*. **Hypothesis.** One would expect that, compared with world prices, the price of imports would fall, that of domestic goods would rise, and that of exports would also rise, but to a smaller extent. For domestic prices are affected only by conditions at home, exports also by conditions elsewhere, and imports for the most part only by the latter. Since world prices rose one would expect domestic prices to rise most, those of exports to rise less, and of imports still less.

Verification. The anticipated results are confirmed so accurately by the following table as to require no further comment:—

DOMESTIC, EXPORT AND IMPORT PRICES IN CANADA.

Year.	Domestic Goods.	Exports.	Imports.
1900	100·0	100·0	100·0
1901	111·5	101·7	94·8
1902	118·5	102·8	92·5
1903	119·1	103·3	97·7
1904	119·1	104·0	94·0
1905	120·9	107·9	98·3
1906	122·8	115·3	107·3
1907	135·6	124·4	114·2
1908	133·6	119·9	99·5
1909	141·0	123·6	102·2
1910	145·7	125·7	105·0
1911	151·4	129·0	103·8
1912	161·8	138·8	113·1
1913	161·7	133·9	114·1

§ 4. GERMAN REPARATIONS.[2]

(a) *Introductory*. There can be no doubt that German Reparations form the largest unilateral transfer in economic history. The

[2] *Bibliographical Note*. The literature on Reparations is very extensive and only a few of the more important works can be mentioned here. Most of them deal also with Inter-Allied Debts, but the latter problem has been discussed—apart from official publications on the various agreements, &c.—chiefly in periodicals of one kind or another. Moulton and Pasvolski, *War Debts and World Prosperity* (1932). *Das Reparationsproblem; Verhandlungen und Gutachten der Konferenzen von Pyrmontund Berlin*, Berlin, 1929 (*Veröffentlichung der Friedrich List-Gesellschaft*, 2 Bde.). Moulton, *The Reparation Plan* (1923). Moulton and McGuire, *Germany's Capacity to Pay* (1933). Bergmann, *The History of Reparations* (1927). Auld, *The Dawes Plan and the New Economics* (1927). M. J. Bonn, *Der Neue Plan als Grundlage der Deutschen Wirtschaftspolitik* (1930).

time is not yet ripe for a sober and exhaustive examination *sine ira et studio* of this unique phenomenon. For the post-war period is not yet at an end and its passions have still to die down. Moreover, in this case the problem is far more complicated than in the Canadian example. The whole series of events took place in an economic system already shaken to its very foundations. The War and the Peace Treaties had produced revolutionary changes and disturbances in the social order, and a new equilibrium had not yet been reached. Simultaneously the drama of inflation was being played out. Whereas the Canadian example approximates to the conditions of a laboratory experiment, in this case the complex of intersecting movements makes it almost impossible to disentangle the different strands of causal connection.

Here moreover—once more in contrast to the Canadian example—there existed the problem of raising the sums to be transferred. Theoretical analysis has shown that the difficulties due to this cause are in part similar to the difficulties of transfer, and that they are in any case so closely bound up with the latter that it is almost impossible to disentangle them. It should not be supposed, merely because the actual mechanism of transfer is the same in both cases, that capital imports and political payments have similar economic consequences.

Reparations, which poisoned international politics and wrought untold mischief, have not survived the unparalleled economic crisis of the last few years. The conclusion is often drawn that the transfer of such enormous sums is outside the bounds of possibility altogether. The prevalence of this idea may be welcomed on political grounds, as a guarantee that the attempt will not be repeated; but in view of the many complicating and disturbing factors at work, the conclusion itself is nevertheless premature. It must be repeated that the time is not yet ripe for a final judgment. We give therefore only a short historical summary, followed by a very tentative analysis.

(b) *Historical Summary. From the Treaty of Versailles to the London Ultimatum.* The Treaty of Versailles did not fix the amount of Reparations to be paid by Germany but merely laid down that the sum-total should be determined within two years of the Treaty being signed. For this purpose the signatories appointed the Reparations Commission, whose terms of reference were to assess the total losses suffered by the Allies and the consequent total of liabilities incurred by Germany under Article 231 of the Treaty, having regard to Germany's capacity to pay.

The years up till 1921 were occupied by Inter-Allied conferences, to determine what sum was to be extracted from Germany, and how it was to be divided. At first, opinion was very much divided on both points, the powers being united only in fantastically over-estimating Germany's capacity to pay. Germany was at first excluded from discussions on the sum-total to be paid. The Allies negotiated with Germany only over the provisional settlement of particular questions. Thus in June 1920 the first monthly requisi-tions of coal were settled at Spa.

At the conference of Boulogne in June 1920 the Allies reached agreement on the sum-total of Reparations. This agreement was elaborated and in part revised in January 1921 at Paris, where the following scheme of payments was drawn up:—

(1) 226 milliard gold marks in 42 annual instalments rising gradually to 6 milliard marks per year.

(2) 12% of the annual value of German exports.

(3) The cost, to be determined later, of the military occupa-tions, of Inter-Allied commissions, &c., &c.

The Paris Agreement, which was denounced by some allied statesmen as too lenient, showed what order of magnitude the final demands of the victorious powers would assume. Germany fought desperately for revision. Thus Herr Simon, the German Foreign Minister, made a counter-offer of 50 milliard gold marks, less the amount already transferred, calculated at 20 milliards. But the Allies rejected this offer and applied sanctions. They occupied Duisburg, Düsseldorf and Ruhrort, put tariffs on imports from Germany, and erected a customs-barrier in the Rhineland between the occupied area and the rest of Germany.

On 27th April 1921, more than two years after the Armistice, the sum-total of German Reparations was definitely fixed by the Reparations Commissions at 132 milliard gold marks, and on this basis at the Reparations Conference which met in London on 1st May 1921 an agreement was reached with the following provi-sions:—

(1) 132 milliard gold marks, less the amounts already paid.

(2) Responsibility for the debt, of about 6 milliards contracted by Belgium during the war to her allies.

(3) The whole amount to be paid in annual instalments of 2 milliards plus 26% of the value of German imports, starting from 1st May 1921; 1 milliard to be transferred within a month.

These demands were coupled in the London Ultimatum, with the threat to apply sanctions by occupying the Ruhr. Germany's political impotence finally compelled acceptance on 11th May 1921.

From the London Ultimatum to the Dawes Agreement. During the next eighteen months various matters of detail were negotiated between Germany and the Allies. Thus, at Wiesbaden in October 1921, Rathenau and Loucheur settled provisionally what payments were to be made in kind for reconstruction of the French devastated areas; and this settlement was modified soon after in an arrangement with the Reparations Commission allowing reparations in kind to be transferred without restriction. But the main provisions of the London Agreement very soon proved unworkable, since Germany was unable to raise the necessary volume of foreign bills. Application was therefore made in December 1921 for a moratorium, and at the conference of Cannes (January 1922) the annual payments were reduced provisionally to 1,450 million gold marks in kind and only 720 millions in cash. But as early as April 1922 Germany was compelled to ask for further postponement, and, finally, in September a short breathing space was allowed her to balance her budget and to stabilise the mark.

In November 1922 an international committee of experts reported that stabilisation would be impossible without a longer moratorium. Germany therefore applied towards the end of 1922 for a year's moratorium and continued thereafter to press for revision on that ground.

But by this time France had conceived the policy of ensuring reparation payments by a kind of mortgage, no longer merely on public revenue but also on industrial concerns. A pretext offered itself late in 1922 when the Reparations Commission decided, against the vote of the English representative, that Germany had defaulted on the payments in kind.[3] An 'Industrial Ruhr Commission' was therefore despatched early in 1923 to supervise the Ruhr Coal Syndicate as a means of exacting payment in kind; and on 11th January 1923 60,000 French and Belgian troops marched into the Ruhr to enforce its decisions.

Germany thereupon suspended all reparation payments to France and Belgium and attempted passive resistance. As a result the civil and military organs of occupation could only carry through their measures in many cases by force.

In the autumn of 1923 Germany had to give up passive resistance under pressure of the financial and economic chaos resulting from the inflation by which it had been financed. She now urged

[3] 145,000 telegraph poles had not been delivered and the amounts of wood and coal were slightly below specification.

with redoubled vehemence a scaling-down of Reparations and in particular an enquiry into her capacity to pay. Moreover, while recognising in principle the French demand for guarantees, she pointed out that a mortgage, *e.g.*, on the State Railways would be just as valuable to the Allies as the seizure of German industrial concerns.

Those Allied powers which had not joined in the occupation of the Ruhr were favourable to this solution. After some delay France also gave her consent and on 30th November 1923, by a resolution of the Reparations Commission, two expert committees were appointed under General Dawes and Mr. M'Kenna. They presented their report on 19th April 1924.

It is not for us to say how long the Allies seriously believed in the 132 milliards of the London Ultimatum, but at any rate by the end of 1923 the necessity of revision was almost universally recognised. Nominally the Dawes Committee was concerned only with methods of balancing the German budget and stabilising the mark, and the M'Kenna Committee with the extent of the flight of German capital and with possible ways of forcing it to return. But at a time when the belief in the indissoluble connection between stabilisation and Reparations had become general, the question of the sum-total to be paid would clearly not be passed over in silence. Although the London Agreement was not officially abrogated, nevertheless the acceptance of the Dawes recommendations was in effect a first step towards revision.

The Dawes Agreement. The political basis of the Dawes Agreement, which attempted only a provisional settlement, was still the Treaty of Versailles. Germany must pay Reparations to her utmost capacity; but for this very reason her economic and monetary system should not be subjected to too great a strain. For this dual purpose a complicated system of mortgages and of international supervision was devised by the Dawes Agreement, of which the main provisions were as follows :—

(1) *Germany's Liability.* After a complete two years' moratorium in the interests of German financial recovery, Reparations were to be paid in annuities rising by 1929-30 to 2,500 million marks and remaining thereafter at that amount. In addition there were to be supplementary annuities, varying in accordance with a complicated index of national prosperity.[4]

---

[4] More recent calculations have shown that this provision would probably have meant an additional burden rather than a safeguard in bad times. For the index included factors regarded as ' symptomatic,' such as the volume of trade and the consumption of coal; but these factors tend in the long run to rise faster than the standard of living. *Cf.* Soltau, " Der Wohlstandsindex—die Bedeutung seines Fortfalls " in *Deutchlands Reparationslast*, 1930, pp. 50 *seq.*

Of the 2,500 million marks 960 millions were to be paid annually for thirty-seven years, while annuities consisting of the remaining 1,540 millions and of the surplus already mentioned were to be continued indefinitely. This meant in effect the payment of tribute for ever. The sums mentioned were to cover all obligations including the cost of the military occupation, &c. A 'gold clause' provided that the nominal amounts to be paid should vary with changes in the purchasing power of gold.

(2) *Restrictions on Transfer*. In contrast both with the previous settlement and with the Young Plan, Germany's obligation was in this case limited to handing over the annuities in marks to the Reparations Agent, a trustee who was to be responsible for actually changing the marks into foreign money and handing over the proceeds to the Governments receiving Reparations. If the German exchange threatened to depreciate, transfer was to be suspended. In that case the sums paid over in marks should accumulate up to 5 milliard marks. If this limit was reached further contributions were to be reduced in amount.

(3) *Obligations Laid on the German Economic System*. The fixed period annuities of 960 million marks were to be raised not by the national exchequer but by the State Railways and by German industry. The railways were to be responsible for a total of 11 milliards, industry for a total of 5 milliards.[5]

(4) *Methods of Guaranteeing Stability*. The Reichsbank was put under international control and its independence of the German Government was laid down in international law. A board of fourteen directors—seven Germans, seven foreigners—was to examine the reports of the Bank and a foreign commissioner was to supervise the note-issue and the reserve-proportion. Any attempt to use inflation in the struggle against Reparations was rendered impossible by these very drastic provisions.

(5) *Loan to Germany*. Finally, it was decided to issue an international loan, with the proceeds of which Germany was to pay the first Dawes annuity.

The Young Plan. The Dawes Agreement was regarded from

---

[5] It was hoped by the creation of marketable securities to commercialise this part of Reparations. But the hope was vain so long as restrictions on transfer were maintained. For foreigners purchasing these debentures could not be certain of receiving payment in foreign money; which meant, at a time when the memory of inflation in 1923 was still fresh, that only part of the 16 milliards could be floated.

the beginning only as a provisional settlement. Not only was this clear from the Agreement itself, which in particular fixed no limit, as regards the greater part of Reparations, to the number of annuities: it was also stressed repeatedly both by the original committee of experts and later in the reports of the Reparations Agent. By the end of 1928 various circumstances pointed to the necessity of a speedy and final settlement.

The Dawes Plan was intended above all to show by experiment the extent of Germany's capacity to pay.[6] But all it proved was that during the four experimental years the sum envisaged could be transferred in the first instance without serious difficulty. It did not prove very much about Germany's capacity to pay; for Reparations were financed out of the enormous foreign loans raised concurrently by the Reich, the states and private industry. The Reparations Agent did not wish Germany's foreign debt to increase indefinitely, but he feared that without foreign credits the Dawes annuities could not be transferred. He therefore pressed for revision.

The transfer restrictions which had at first been welcomed even in Germany, came to be regarded as a comparatively ineffective guarantee of stability. On the other hand, they clearly had the disadvantage, already mentioned, of hampering the commercialisation of Reparations; by which it had been hoped to turn Reparations from a political into a quasi-commercial problem.

A conference of experts met at Paris in February 1929 under the chairmanship of Owen Young and presented its report on 7th June. On this basis the new Young Plan was elaborated by two political conferences held at The Hague in August 1929 and in January 1930, and formulated, along with various political provisions (including the evacuation of the Rhineland) in a number of agreements and protocols. This settlement was regarded as final.

The main provisions concerning Reparations were as follows:—

(1) The Dawes annuities, definitely fixed neither in number nor in size, were replaced by 59 annuities averaging 1,989 million marks and coming to an end in 1988. Further, in accordance with the separate agreement of July 1929, Belgium was to receive between 9.3 and 26 million marks annually until 1966, on account of paper marks issued in Belgium during the German occupation. Finally, there were to be annuities representing the cost of the American Army of Occupation and claims to compensation of American

---

6 *Cf.* Bonn, *Der neue Plan* (1930), p. 28.

nationals. Of the Young annuities proper 660 million marks were to be raised and transferred unconditionally. But Germany could apply to the new Bank of International Settlements, set up to receive these payments, for a two years' transfer moratorium on the remainder, and twelve months after this had been granted also for a moratorium on payment, both up to half the current amounts. The assent of the creditors was not to be required but only a *bona fide* declaration by Germany that her economic and monetary stability would be endangered by the transfer of the whole postponable annuity. A sub-committee of the Bank of International Settlements would then examine the position and, if necessary, recommend revision. There were no other safeguards. Once more, Germany had to procure the foreign money herself.

(2) The mobilisation of the unconditional annuities was begun by the issue of ' Young Loan ' to the value of 200 million dollars,[7] the proceeds being handed over to the Powers receiving Reparations, and Germany accepting responsibility for interest and amortisation. At the same time Germany was granted a loan of 100 million dollars to assist the State Railways and the Post Office. These two operations were combined in a single issue of 300 million dollars—under the somewhat misleading title of ' International $5\frac{1}{2}$% Loan of the German Reich '—to be repaid or repurchased within thirty-five years. It was offered for subscription in a number of countries. The equivalent in marks of the total issue was 1,473·5 million marks, of which Germany received one-third or 491·17 millions. Interest and amortisation on this portion, as opposed to the other two-thirds, did not constitute true reparation payments.

(3) The index of prosperity and the gold-clause were abolished.

(4) The whole burden was laid once more on the national exchequer. Private industry was freed from all liability, and the debentures—including those of the State Railways—already issued were cancelled. The railways had however to pay a special reparations-tax of 660 million marks.

(5) International control was abolished, and with it the foreign Commissioners and Representatives on Boards of Directors, the Reparations Agent and, finally, the Reparations Commission itself.

---

[7] The rest of the unconditional annuities were never commercialized.

(6) The Bank of International Settlements, founded by the seven countries concerned including Germany, was charged with the technical management of reparation payments.

From the Young Plan to the Treaty of Lausanne. Although Reparations raised important economic problems both for theory and for practice, the main problem, that of the sum-total to be paid, was essentially political. But this obvious truth was obscured between 1923 and 1931 by attempts to commercialise Reparations and by the efforts of one expert committee after another to determine ' by scientific methods ' Germany's capacity to pay. People were slow to realise that one could not pass judgments having scientific validity about the future capacity to pay tribute of two whole generations. Thus the Young Plan, which—in contrast to the Dawes Agreement—was to settle the total amount definitely, lacked scientific foundation, just like any other conceivable settlement extending over more than a very few years. There can be no doubt that the virtual cancelling of Reparations at Lausanne was due primarily not to any new assessment of Germany's capacity to pay but to the new political situation.

It could be determined with fair certainty whether or not payment was possible in the immediate future. The world-wide depression which began in 1929 was particularly severe in Germany and by the summer of 1931 it became very questionable whether the Young annuities could any longer be paid. The Young Plan was kept nominally intact by President Hoover's proposal for a moratorium—from July 1931 till June 1932—on all political war-debts. The Hoover Plan affected Germany as follows. By the London Protocol of August 1931 and the Berlin Supplementary Protocol of June 1932 the conditional annuity was postponed, and while the unconditional annuity, which France would not allow to be formally postponed, was paid over, an equivalent sum was lent to the German State Railways. When soon after the Hoover Declaration, Germany's bank-crisis began, the Government demanded that —as provided for in the Young Plan—the advisory committee of the Bank of International Settlements should meet to consider what was to be done on the expiry of the Hoover Year.

Germany's strenuous and successful defence of the mark put her in a strong bargaining position. The committee reported on 23rd September 1931 that—in accordance with the Young Plan and in view of the serious position which still persisted despite the measures taken—Germany was justified in declaring payment of the next conditional annuity to be impossible. The committee reported further that the Young Plan was based on assumptions which, under the abnormal conditions prevailing throughout the world; were unlikely to be realised again for some time. The Allied Governments should therefore take the necessary steps without delay.

In view of this report no one was surprised when in. January 1932 Dr. Brüning announced that the payment of Reparations could not be resumed after the moratorium, and that he would be satisfied only with total cancellation. But, while the necessity of postponement was universally recognised, it was still felt in some quarters abroad that Germany might be capable of further payments after a period of convalescence.

The Lausanne Agreement. By the agreement reached on 9th July 1932 Reparations were reduced to 3 milliard marks, to be paid by the German Government to the Bank of International Settlements in 5% redeemable bonds. The scrip was not to be issued for three years, it was to be redeemable at any time up to 37 years, and the conditions of issue were carefully laid down. Germany's other liabilities were all cancelled except the service of the Dawes Loan and of the 1930 Young Loan. Since, as already mentioned, two-thirds of the service of the latter represented reparation-payments for which Germany got no compensation, a reparations-burden was in effect maintained to this amount. On the other hand, it was only a small part of the total, since not only did the whole of the conditional annuities disappear but also that part of the unconditional annuities the commercialisation of which was provided for but never carried out.

This arrangement was to take effect immediately on ratification. But it subsequently came out that the Allies had reached a separate 'gentleman's agreement' providing that ratification of the agreement with Germany should be conditional on a satisfactory arrangement being reached between themselves and their own creditors. Otherwise 'the legal position of all the interested parties would revert to that obtaining before the Hoover Moratorium.' Thus the connection between Reparations and Inter-Allied Debts, denied by Germany and ignored in the Lausanne Agreement itself, was asserted in this special agreement. The whole settlement therefore had provisionally no very firm legal foundation. But for the time being Germany was relieved of all reparation payments. For the London Protocol and the Berlin Supplementary Protocol of June 1932, implementing the Hoover Moratorium, were prolonged till either the Lausanne Agreement should come into force or one of the main signatories should refuse to ratify it.

(c) *Reparations, Balance of Trade and International Indebtedness.* For the years preceding 1924, when the Dawes Agreement came into force, not even a rough picture of the connection between reparation payments, the balance of trade, and the balance of indebtedness can be obtained. For it is almost impossible to determine how much was actually paid. The contradictory and often fantastic estimates of the sums involved include the value of State property in the ceded territories, unpaid claims on Germany's allies, the value of military equipment surrendered, &c., &c. Since these estimates[8] do not confine themselves to effective transfers, they are useless for studying the influence of Reparations on foreign trade. No definitive classification and computation of the amount actually transferred exists. Moreover in the period in question everything else was overshadowed by the effects of inflation.

Reparations can be transferred either by raising credits abroad or by creating an export surplus. In this connection the purchase of gold or foreign currency by the central bank must be regarded as export and their sale as import. The four magnitudes, trade in commodities, movements of gold and currency between the central banks, short- and long-term capital movements and Reparations formed the main items in the German balance of payments between 1924 and 1931. Reparations were purely debit-items, whereas the other three items appeared both on the debit and on the credit side. One would expect the volume of Reparations roughly to balance the surplus on the first three magnitudes combined, since the remaining items in the balance of payments (*i.e.*, any surplus or deficit on services and on interest) were comparatively small. As imports of capital exceeded exports of capital for each year from 1924 to 1930, there was a surplus throughout, represented in the statistics of the balance of payments by positive magnitudes. The crucial item was therefore the balance of trade, including gold-movements, &c. According as it was active or passive, the following equations should hold approximately:—

With an active balance of trade.	With a passive balance of trade.
Reparations = Export Surplus. + Capital Imports.	Reparations + Import Surplus. = Capital Imports.

The symbol ' = ' represents not exact equality of the annual magnitudes but roughly parallel movements from year to year.

In each year except 1924 and 1931 movements of gold and currency were comparatively small and exports and imports in the

---

8 *Cf.*, *e.g.*, Lujo Brentano, *Was Deutschland gezahlt hat* (1922); Moulton and McGuire, *Germany's Capacity to Pay* (1923); Benedikt Kautsky, *Reparationen und Rüstungen* (1931).

above equations can be adequately represented, as in the following table, by the statistics of trade in commodities :—

REPARATIONS, TRADE BALANCE AND CAPITAL BALANCE.

Year.	Reparations.	In milliards of marks. Import Surplus.	1+2.	Capital Imports.	Export Surplus.	4+5.
	1	2	3	4	5	6
1924	0.3	1.8	2.1	2.5	—	2.5
1925	1.0	2.5	3.5	1.4	—	1.4
1926	1.2	—	1.2	1.5	0.8	2.3
1927	1.6	3.0	4.6	3.5	—	3.5
1928	2.0	1.3	3.3	3.1	—	3.1
1929	2.5	—	2.5	1.7	—	1.7
1930	1.7	—	1.7	1.1	1.6	2.7
1931	1.0	—	1.0	0.6	2.8	3.4

In 1925 there appears to have been no asset to balance the large liability of 3,500 million marks consisting of reparation payments and the import surplus. But it is almost certain that in that year capital imports were appreciably larger than appeared in the statistics of the balance of payments. The item ' unclassified capital movements ' reached the considerable sum of +1,700 million marks. If the whole of this remainder is added to capital imports, the total (3,100 million marks) approximately balances the deficit mentioned. Similarly for 1929, when the balance of trade showed neither an import nor an export surplus, there must be added to the surplus of capital imports (1,700 million marks) unclassified capital imports of 1,000 million marks. The total surplus of capital imports (2,700 millions) is then approximately equal to the amount paid in Reparations.

In 1930 there was an apparent discrepancy in the other direction, capital imports plus export surplus being far in excess of Reparations. The explanation is that in that year there was a large passive balance of interest payments. If this liability of 1,000 millions is added to Reparations, then total liabilities exactly equal total assets at 2,700 million marks.

With these reservations the figures show approximately parallel changes in columns 3 and 6 respectively, thus confirming the equations set out above.

For 1931, on the contrary, corresponding movements cannot be established. Reparations, at about 1,000 million marks, were considerably exceeded by the export surplus of 2,800 million marks. But the capital balance was not passive, as one would expect both on general grounds and also from the historical situation: on the contrary, it showed net capital imports of 600 million marks. Rediscount credits and short-term foreign loans showed a surplus of 486 millions over repayments, and the movement of long-term capital still showed a small import surplus, chiefly owing to the release of German property abroad. On the debit side there were indeed net payments of 1,300 millions, but these were more than compensated by the large exports of gold and currency. There must therefore have been some item or other unaccounted for, and the assumption is plausible that a large proportion of the withdrawals of capital which undoubtedly took place in 1931 were not represented in the official statistics. In fact no less than 2,923 million marks were included on the debit side as ' unclassified capital movements,' and the ' Statistisches Reichsamt '[9] commented that the greater part of the unexplained surplus was probably due to a decrease in short-term foreign debts, particularly withdrawals of credit not negotiated through banks.

§ 5. INTER-ALLIED WAR-DEBTS.

This problem is closely connected with the Reparations question. The idea of linking the Inter-Allied War-Debts with the payment of German Reparations was conceived as early as 1922. During the next few years ' funding agreements ' were reached between the various Allies, fixing definitely the amounts to be paid and the methods of payment. By the time of the Young Report— on which a definitive arrangement about German Reparations was to be based—the complex of Inter-Allied debts and claims was in the main already settled. The Allies now proceeded—in a supplementary memorandum, which though not forming part of the Young Report itself, was signed simultaneously with it at the Hague—to couple German Reparations with the settlement of Inter-Allied indebtedness on a permanent basis.

This memorandum was based on the principle that all the net liabilities of the Allies between 1931 and 1988, as provided in the funding agreement, should be covered by German Reparations. The German annuities from 1967 to 1988 were to be only to this amount, whereas from 1931 to 1966 they were to yield a surplus or ' indemnité nette.'

The United States was in effect to be the final recipient of all the Inter-Allied debt-payments. For each of the Allied Powers in Europe owed the United States a sum larger than its net receipts, if any, from the other Allies.

The following table is divided into two parts. The first shows the total net liabilities of the Allies, which extended from 1923

---

[9] *Wirtschaft und Statistik* (1932), No. 10.

E

ASSETS AND LIABILITIES OF THE ALLIES ACCORDING TO THE PRESENT FUNDING AGREEMENTS.

In millions of marks.

Rates of exchange—£1 = 20·429 marks; $1 = 4·198 marks; 1 Greek franc = 0·81 marks; 1 French franc = 0·16 marks; 1 lira = 0·221 marks.

	Great Britain.	France.	Italy.	Belgium.	Rumania.	Jugo-slavia.	Greece.	Portugal.	Total.	U.S.A.
1923-1990.										
Receipts from Allies,	24,266	733	508	—	—	—	—	—	25,507	89,529
Payments to Allies (including U.S.A.),	47,075	45,079	15,761	3,055	1,758	1,238	580	490	115,036	—
Net indebtedness, -	− 22,809	− 44,346	− 15,253	− 3,055	− 1,758	− 1,238	− 580	− 490	− 89,529	+ 89,529
1931-1988.										
Receipts from Allies,	23,242	729	497	—	—	—	—	—	24,468	84,104
Payments to Allies (including U.S.A.),	42,342	43,982	15,299	2,974	1,738	1,209	562	466	108,572	—
Net indebtedness, ·	− 19,100	− 43,253	− 14,802	− 2,974	− 1,738	− 1,209	− 562	− 466	− 84,104	+ 84,104

to 1990. In the second the net liabilities from 1931 to 1988, which were to be covered by German Reparations, are calculated separately[1]

According to this table, for the period from 1931 to 1988 a total of 84,104 million marks was to be covered. But in accordance with a supplementary agreement Germany had in addition to pay Italy a series of annuities (Golddepotzahlung) amounting to 443 to 454 million marks from 1931 to 1988. The total sum to be covered represented therefore 84,547 million marks.[2]

Of this total 50,737 millions belonged to the years 1931-1966, the remaining 33,810 millions to the years 1967-1988. German Reparations, which in accordance with the Young Plan totalled 110,736 million marks for the whole period from 1931 to 1988, were graded to cover exactly the 33,810 million marks of 1967 to 1988 and to yield a total surplus of 26,189 millions in the period from 1931 to 1966. Thus over the first thirty-five years 65·96% of the German payments were to be paid out again by the countries receiving Reparations, and 34·04% were to be retained by them.

The following summary shows what proportion of German payments the different countries were to retain as an ' indemnité nette ' and what proportion they were to pay out again in settlement of their net funded liabilities : —

ULTIMATE DESTINATION OF REPARATIONS.

	1931-1966.		1967-1988.	
	Required for payment of foreign debts.	Available surplus.	Required for payment of foreign debts.	Available surplus.
	per cent.	per cent.	per cent.	per cent.
France, - - -	61·53	38·47	99·93	0·07
Great Britain, -	86·72	13·28	100·02	−0·02
Italy, - - -	81·79	18·21	100·01	−0·01
Belgium, - -	39·71	60·29	100·00	—
Roumania, - -	82·57	17·43	101·41	−1·41
Jugoslavia, -	21·29	78·71	99·80	0·20
Greece, - - -	122·94	−22·94	99·48	0·52
Portugal, - -	54·99	45·01	99·67	0·33
Total, -	65·96	34·04	100·00	0·00

The net payments required by the funding agreements represented a definite annual charge on the national exchequer. It was therefore only natural that the attitude of the various Allies to

---

[1] The figures are taken from *Die interalliierten Schulden*, Einzelschriften zur Statistik des Deutschen Reiches (1930), pp. 72 *et seq.*

[2] The division of this total between countries represents the Young Plan not in its original form but as revised slightly by later agreements. In the case of Greece no arrangements were ever made to cover the whole net payments by German Reparations. These discrepancies cancel out in the total of 84,547 million marks.

the cancelling of Reparations should be greatly influenced by the extent to which each required the Young annuities to cover such fixed charges. As already noted, Greece's obligations were higher than her Young annuities. Of the other countries Great Britain, Roumania, and Italy had to pay away the largest proportion of their receipts from Reparations between 1931 and 1966. In the case of France this proportion was appreciably smaller, though it should not be forgotten that, as shown by the table on p. 114, France's absolute ' net liability ' was considerably larger than that of Great Britain or Italy. The country with the largest relative surplus of receipts over payments was Jugoslavia.

From 1967 to 1988 the whole of the German annuities, with small discrepancies each way which in the total cancelled out, were to be passed on in settlement of the debts to America.

The Order of Magnitude of Inter-Allied Debts. There is a tendency to exaggerate the size of the European War-Debts to America. In Great Britain and in other European countries it has become almost an article of faith that War-Debts block the path to economic recovery.

The burden on the national exchequer involved by the raising of the necessary sums is a separate problem which cannot be examined here: we are concerned only to throw light on the question whether transfer was possible. For this purpose the amounts of the annuities will be compared with the volume of international trade—the main item in the balance of payments—done by the countries concerned, in order to show how exaggerated is the idea that they are so enormously large.

For the years 1931-35—to select for comparison the liabilities of the present and the immediate future—net receipts or liabilities, as the case may be, amount in millions of marks to the following:—

NET RECEIPTS OR LIABILITIES.

Year.	United States. (Net Receipts).	Great Britain. (Net Liabilities).	France. (Net Liabilities).
		In millions of marks.	
1931	959.9	313.3	479.8
1932	937.2	308.8	418.7
1933	937.6	311.3	459.9
1934	1,128.6	407.0	501.7
1935	1,191.2	402.3	564.3
Total,	5,154.5	1,742.7	2,424.4
Annual average,	1,030.9	348.5	484.9

The average annual receipts of the United States may be compared with the volume of American exports for 1929, 1930 and 1931, and the average liabilities of Great Britain and France with their annual volume of imports in the same years. The figures of foreign trade, as calculated in the *Vierteljahrsheft fur Konjunktur-forschung* (VII/2/B, pp. 137 *et seq.*) in terms of marks, were as follows:—

TOTAL EXPORTS OR IMPORTS.

Year.	American Exports.	British Imports. In millions of marks.	French Imports.
1929	26,660.0	22,662.0	9,576.0
1930	15,849.8	19,506.0	8,638.8
1931	10,008.0	15,218.4	6,966.0

It will be seen that the average annual receipts of the United States according to the present arrangement represent only a small addition to the receipts from exports in the past few years. In the same way the average annual liabilities of Great Britain and France do not form any very considerable addition to the debit-side of the balance of payments. Moreover, as shown by the following table, even the annual surpluses of exports or imports, as the case may be, are of a much greater order of magnitude than the average debt-payments given above:—

EXPORT OR IMPORT SURPLUSES.

Year.	United States.	Great Britain. In millions of marks.	France.
1929	+3,535.2	−7,785.6	−1,329.6
1930	+3,279.6	−7,874.4	−1,591.2
1931	+1,406.4	−7,797.6	−1,944.0

It should be noted that even changes from year to year in the figures of international trade are often considerably larger than the debt-annuities. These are also of a much lesser order of magnitude than other main items in the balance of payments, such as movements of capital.

These comparisons show that the quantitative importance of Inter-Allied Debts has been much exaggerated. If any connection is to be established between War-Debts and the economic crisis or its liquidation, this can only be in terms of complicated chains of indirect cause and effect.

PART I.

B—THE PURE THEORY
OF INTERNATIONAL TRADE.

CHAPTER IX.

INTRODUCTION.

§ 1. The Problem Stated.

Up to the present we have simply taken it for granted that international trade is carried on. We have supposed that a whole range of goods are normally exported and imported in large quantities and that, moreover, international payments must also be made for other reasons. Upon these assumptions we have reached a number of important results. We have explained the forces which determine rates of exchange, and the relation between the prices and price-levels of different countries. We have learned that exports are connected with imports and that, taking account of the ' invisible items ' in the balance of payments, the two must be equal. We have analysed the mechanism which equalises the two sides of the balance of payments and makes possible the transfer of unilateral payments. The fact that this equalisation must take place, and that in the long run it can come about only through appropriate changes in the balance of trade in the wider sense, that is through changes in the imports and exports of goods and services, has been proved. We must now show how it comes about, in the sense of showing which goods will be exported and imported and what conditions are necessary for an exchange of goods between countries to take place at all.

These questions can scarcely be separated in a presentation of the pure theory of international trade, to which they belong, from the question of what advantages international trade brings to the various countries which engage in it. For the question, " why does an exchange of goods between two countries take place? " is usually answered by, " because the international division of labour makes it profitable," and the question, " which goods will a country export? " by " those which it is especially suited to produce." This question of the advantages of international trade is especially to the fore in the classical theory of the subject. But this in no way robs that theory of its scientific character. The classical theorists were indeed concerned mainly with the bearing of their analysis upon questions of trade policy; they used it as a weapon to attack Protection, and this even influenced the

121

form in which they presented it.[1] But the correctness of their theory does not depend upon the value judgments they drew from it; and the political standpoint plays no part in the *content* of their analysis. In a later chapter[2] we shall discuss more fully the relations between value judgments and theory in the sphere of trade policy, and the meaning of the statement that every dictum as to trade policy implies a value judgment. But it would be pedantic, besides hampering the exposition, to refrain from drawing at once certain obvious conclusions as to trade policy from the theoretical analysis of the next three chapters.

§ 2. The Available Theoretical Systems.

There are four theories available for us to utilise in explaining why export and import take place at all and in what circumstances certain goods will be exported and certain others imported. These four theories more or less supplement one another, but they have been propounded by different writers and have never been combined into a synthesis.

(1) We have, in the first place, the Theory of Comparative Costs, to which we have already made frequent reference. This theory developed out of the classical Labour Theory of Value. We probably owe it to Col. Robert Torrens,[3] but to-day it is linked with the name of Ricardo, who gave it its classical formulation in the famous chapter VII of his *Principles*.[4] John Stuart Mill made important additions to it, and it was taken over and amplified by Cairnes and Bastable. Its latest and most detailed exposition is to be found in the classic work by Professor Taussig entitled *International Trade*.[5] The theory is fairly generally accepted to-day in England and America. It has not met with a sympathetic reception in Germany and France, owing to its close association

---

[1] Viner even believes that their choice of analytical tools, namely of ' real cost ' theories, was dictated by their politico-economic aim. *Cf.* " The Doctrine of Comparative Cost," *Weltwirtschaftliches Archiv* (Oct. 1932), vol. 36, pp. 401 *et seq.*

[2] Chap. xiv.

[3] *The Economists Refuted* (1808).

[4] Upon the question of priority, see the discussion between E. Seligmann and Professor J. Hollander, " Ricardo and Torrens," *Economic Journal* (1911), vol. 21, p. 448. Seligmann ascribes the development of the fundamental principle to Torrens; Professor Hollander believes that it was formulated for the first time by Ricardo. *Cf.* also *A Letter on the True Principles of Advantageous Exportation* (1818). This is a work by an unknown author who develops and applies the principle of comparative cost with astonishing clarity. It was rescued from oblivion and published in *Economica* (Feb. 1933), by Professor Arnold Plant.

[5] *Cf.* also Graham, " The Theory of International Values Re-examined," *Quarterly Journal of Economics* (Nov. 1923), vol. 38, pp. 54-86, and especially J. Viner, " The Doctrine of Comparative Cost," *Weltwirtschaftliches Archiv* (Oct. 1932), vol. 36.

with the Labour Theory of Value, but most Italian economists accept it.[6]

(2) Another theoretical apparatus for solving certain problems of international trade is due to Alfred Marshall.[7] We shall become more closely acquainted with it in chapter XI. Marshall employs so-called reciprocal supply-and-demand curves. This theory forms an essential supplement to the theory of comparative costs; indeed, the latter, if carried through to its logical conclusion, merges into the former. Marshall also quite explicitly bases himself upon Ricardo[8] and especially upon J. S. Mill's Theory of International Values.

(3) We have already observed that the Theory of International Trade must be regarded as a special case of general economic theory. Hence it must be possible to apply the general theory of economic equilibrium to this special case. This has in fact been done by Pareto.[9]

(4) The doctrines of Richard Schüller[1] and Enrico Barone[2] constitute a fourth type of international trade theory. These two writers both deal with the same subject-matter, but they employ different techniques: Schüller uses arithmetical examples while Barone works with curves. Both apply the method of partial equilibrium, which is involved in the familiar supply-and-demand curves for a particular commodity, to the international exchange of goods. Hence they do not give us a complete model, but always show only particular sections of the whole structure.

These four theories are not mutually exclusive; on the contrary, they supplement one another. Hence a systematic exposition can very well make use of all four. We shall begin with the theory

---

[6] *Cf.*, *e.g.*, Professor Cabiati, *Scambi Internazionali e Politica Bancaria in Regime di Moneta Sana ed Avariata* (1929).

[7] *Cf.* his pamphlet, *The Pure Theory of Foreign Trade*. This was first privately printed in 1878-9. It was used extensively by Pantaleoni in his *Pure Economics* in 1898, and was reproduced with considerable alterations and additions, in Marshall's last work, *Money, Credit and Commerce* (1923). The original pamphlet was reprinted, together with *The Pure Theory of Domestic Values*, by the London School of Economics as No. 1 of its *Series of Reprints of Scarce Tracts in Economic and Political Science*. *Cf.* also Edgeworth, *The Pure Theory of International Values* in *Papers Relating to Political Economy* (1925), vol. 2, who makes a truly ingenious use of the Marshallian curves. Auspitz and Lieben in their *Untersuchungen über die Theorie der Preise* (1889) employ similar curves.

[8] *Cf.* especially appendix H in *Money, Credit and Commerce*.

[9] *Cf.* his *Cours d'Économie Politique* (1896), vol. 2, and his " Teoria matematica dei Cambi Forestieri " in *Giornale degli Economisti*, Serie 2 (1894), vol. 8, pp. 142 *et seq.* See also Yntema, *A Mathematical Reformulation of the General Theory of International Trade* (1932).

[1] *Schutzzoll und Freihandel* (1905).

[2] *Grundzüge der theoretischen Nationalökonomie:* German translation by Hans Staehle, with an introduction by J. Schumpeter (1927. New edition 1935). The same curves as those used by Barone are used also by Cunyngham, *Geometrical Political Economy* (1904).

of comparative costs, since this makes the most drastic hypotheses and thereby achieves the greatest simplification. We shall then pass on to the Marshallian theory, and finally we shall apply the all-embracing theory of economic equilibrium to our problem. We shall have to make an extensive use of the theory of partial equilibrium—particularly in many special problems—in Part II, which deals with Applied Theory.

But there is little point in saying any more about the reciprocal relations of these four theories before we have become better acquainted with them.

CHAPTER X.

THE THEORY OF COMPARATIVE COST.[1]

§ 1. The International Division of Labour and the Difference in Production Costs.

To the question which goods a country will import and which it will export, the classical theory gives the following answer. Each country will produce those goods for the production of which it is especially suited on account of its climate, of the qualities of its soil, of its other natural resources, of the innate and acquired capacities of its people, and—this must be given special emphasis —of the real capital[2] which it possesses as a heritage from its past, such as buildings, plant and equipment, and means of transport. It will concentrate upon the production of such goods, producing more of them than it requires for its own needs and exchanging the surplus with other countries against goods which it is less suited to produce or which it cannot produce at all.

Supposing for the moment that there are only two countries, each will supply its own needs for goods whose conditions of production are about the same in both countries, or which cannot be transported, or whose transport costs more than offset the gain from specialisation. But in the production of other goods a division of labour will come about, under unrestricted trade, between the countries concerned. This division of labour will clearly represent a gain to the world as a whole in so far as it enables more of each good to be produced than would otherwise be the case. We shall consider, in the course of our discussion, how this total gain is distributed among the participating countries and whether there may be particular exceptions to the general rule that *every* country gains by this international division of labour.

In order to discuss the international division of labour more precisely, we must turn to the Doctrine of Cost Differences, of which the Theory of Comparative Cost is a special case. Whether one

---

[1] *Cf.* the works of Ricardo, Mill, Cairnes, Bastable, Taussig, already cited. An excellent and very precise presentation is that of Viner, " The Doctrine of Comparative Cost," *Weltwirtschaftliches Archiv* (Oct. 1932), vol. 36; *cf.* Harrod, *International Economics* (1933).

[2] Especially stressed by Mises, " Das festangelegte Kapital " in *Economische Opstellen*, Festschrift für C. A. Verijn Stuart (1931), pp. 214 *et seq.*, reprinted in Mises, *Grundprobleme der Nationalökonomie* (1933).

country is better suited than another to produce a given commodity and, if so, by what extent, is exactly expressed by the difference between the two countries in the cost of producing a unit of that commodity. That country is better suited for the production of a particular good which can produce it more cheaply, that is to say at less expense per unit.

It is common knowledge that the classical economists used the Labour (Cost) Theory of Value. This theory asserts that goods are exchanged against one another according to the relative amounts of labour embodied in them. Quantities of goods which have equal prices embody equal amounts of labour. Adam Smith gives the following well-known illustration. If with the same expenditure of labour one can kill either one beaver or two deer, then one beaver will always exchange in the market against two deer. If this ratio were different, for example one beaver against three deer, deer would no longer be hunted, for everybody would turn to killing beaver in order to exchange them in the market against deer. The supply of beaver would increase and the supply of deer would diminish until the 'normal' exchange-ratio was again established. Thus exchange-ratios or prices are determined sole' by relative labour costs, through their influence upon supply and demand.

This doctrine simplifies reality too much to be adequate. Broadly speaking, it is valid under the assumptions that all labour is of the same quality, of the same irksomeness, that every occupation is open to all, that labour is the only mobile factor of production, and that there is free competition between the workers. In reality, some of these assumptions are never true and some are not always true, so that the Labour Theory of Value, at least in its simplest form, breaks down. In particular, the element of time, which gives rise to interest, is a difficulty which it cannot surmount.

In spite of the defectiveness of this theory, we shall adopt it as our provisional point of departure. It will greatly facilitate the analysis, and, fortunately, we shall be able to show that the deductions obtained with its aid do not depend for their validity upon its assumptions. We shall end by discarding the theory, with all its assumptions, without having to discard the results obtained from it: these will remain, just as a building remains after the scaffolding, having served its purpose, is removed. Since we shall use the Labour Theory of Value only as a provisional hypothesis to help the analysis, we need neither state all its assumptions exactly nor concern ourselves with the supplementary hypotheses which have been suggested to make it correspond more closely to reality. We shall only remark that account must also be taken of the previously performed labour stored up in the form of instruments of production. One can, of course, substitute for Labour ' real cost ' or, in Pigou's phrase, ' resources in general.' Thus some writers speak of the available productive resources of a countr·, measured in units of ' a typical combination of labour and capital,' being directed into this or that channel. I am well aware that these concepts, which certain Cambridge economists in particular like to employ, are not entirely satisfactory, but we can admit them in our provisional hypothesis. I must beg the reader to bear with the sweeping simplifications with which we must begin. As we continue, we shall abandon these assumptions one by one, in order to reach an approximation to reality. But the only possible method is to proceed from the simple to the more complex.

§ 2. Absolute and Comparative Differences in Production Costs.

The classical doctrine assumes that labour is completely mobile within a country and therefore distributes itself among the different branches of production in such a way that its marginal productivity is everywhere equal to its wage. This rule does not apply to international trade, since labour is not mobile between countries. It cannot move from one industry to another if the two industries are in different countries, and hence Labour Cost cannot regulate Supply.

This immobility of factors between two countries clearly will not matter if the distribution of labour between them happens to be the same as that which would come about under complete mobility. In such circumstances an exchange of goods will take place only if each of the two countries can produce one commodity at an *absolutely lower production cost* than the other country. Suppose, for example, that country I can produce a unit of commodity A with 10 and a unit of commodity B with 20 labour-units, and that in country II the production of a unit of A costs 20 and a unit of B 10 labour-units. Then country I will confine itself to the production of A and country II to the production of B. Exactly the same would happen if I and II were parts of one country; given an appropriate distribution of labour between I and II, there is no economic reason for migration. We speak of an *absolute* difference in costs because each country can produce one commodity at an absolutely lower cost than the other country. It is self-evident that in such a case a division of labour between them must lead to an increase in total output.

A large part of world trade rests upon absolute differences in cost. One thinks at once of the trade between the temperate zones and the tropics. However one may interpret the concept of ' real cost,' tropical products, if they can be grown at all in the temperate zones, can be grown there only at much greater cost. (One recalls the well-known remark of Adam Smith that grapes could be grown even in Scotland—under glass.) The same applies to the exchange of goods between agricultural countries with fertile land and industrial countries with deposits of coal and iron.

Ricardo starts from another state of affairs, apparently less favourable to Free Trade, which he considers typical. He assumes that one of the two countries can produce *both* goods with a smaller expenditure of labour (cost) than the other country. In chapter VII of his *Principles* he gives the following celebrated example :

In England a unit of cloth costs 100 and a unit of wine 120 hours of labour; in Portugal a unit of cloth costs 90 and a unit of wine 80 hours of labour. Were such a cost-constellation to exist between two districts within a country, all goods would be produced only in that district where costs were lower. If the conditions of production were more favourable south of the Thames than north of the Thames, workers would migrate from the north bank to the south. But in international trade it is usually not possible for factors of production to move from one country to another. The great achievement of the classical economists was to prove that, nevertheless, an international division of labour would take place. They showed, moreover, that this would benefit both the more favoured country and also the country whose conditions of production were less favourable in every branch of industry.

Let us return to our arithmetical example. Portugal has an absolute superiority in both branches of production. This superiority, however, is greater in wine than in cloth; she has a *comparative* advantage in the production of wine, since here her cost-difference is relatively greater than in the case of cloth. For $\frac{80}{120}$ is less than $\frac{90}{100}$.

The exact meaning of ' comparative advantage ' should be noted. There must be at least two countries and two goods, and we have to compare *the ratio[3] of the*

---

[3] Or the difference, in this case 120−80. But it facilitates the computation to operate with ratios rather than differences.

costs of production of one good in both countries $\left(\frac{80}{120}\right)$ with the ratio of the costs of production of the other good in both countries $\left(\frac{90}{100}\right)$. Expressed in words: Portugal has a comparative advantage over England in wine relatively to cloth. Conversely, the disadvantage of England is greater in wine than in cloth. Stated in another way, England has an *absolute* disadvantage in cloth, but at the same time she has a *comparative* advantage in cloth. The above inequality $\left(\frac{80}{120} < \frac{90}{100}\right)$ states the position exactly; and the position assumed in our previous example of reciprocal absolute differences in cost can be stated in the same form, namely $\left(\frac{10}{20} < \frac{20}{10}\right)$.

The theorem can be expressed algebraically. Let us call the labour cost of good A in country I a_1 and in country II a_2, and the labour cost of good B in country I b_1 and in country II b_2. Then there is an absolute difference in costs if $\frac{a_1}{a_2} < I < \frac{b_1}{b_2}$. Country I has an absolute advantage over country II in A, and country II has an absolute advantage over country I in B. There is a comparative difference in costs if $\frac{a_1}{a_2} < \frac{b_1}{b_2} < I$. This means that country I has an absolute superiority over country II in both goods but that its superiority is greater in A than in B.

The conclusions which we shall draw from cases of comparative differences in costs will apply equally to cases of absolute differences. We have hitherto distinguished between the two only because the advantage of international exchange is self-evident in cases of the latter type but requires a brief demonstration in cases of the former type.

Let us return to the illustration given by Ricardo. Suppose there were no commodity trade between the two countries. Then, in accordance with the relative costs, an exchange-ratio will be established in England of 1 unit of wine against 1.2 units of cloth, and in Portugal of 9 units of wine against 8 of cloth, that is to say of 1 unit of wine against 0.88 units of cloth. We must emphasise at once that the main task of the labour-cost hypothesis is to determine these exchange-ratios or *relative* prices—in distinction to the *absolute* money-prices, to determine which an assumption must be made concerning the quantity of money.[4]

Suppose now that trade takes place. It is clearly advantageous to Portugal to send wine to England, where a unit of it commands 1.2 units of cloth. Under our provisional assumption that within each country labour is completely mobile between the various industries, Portugal will take to producing wine instead of cloth. England, on the other hand, can obtain wine at much less expense by specialising upon the manufacture of cloth and exchanging the cloth with Portugal against wine. For Portugal there is a sufficient inducement to engage in international trade if 1 unit of wine commands a little more than 0.88 units of cloth; for England,

---

[4] It will be necessary to bear in mind this function of the simplifying assumptions of the Labour Theory of Value when we later discard them.

if a little less than 1.2 of cloth must be given for 1 of wine. Hence any exchange-ratio between 0.88 and 1.2 cloth against 1 wine represents a gain to both countries. Let us suppose that the exchange-ratio which becomes established is 1 to 1. Then for every 100 labour-units which England sends to Portugal, embodied in the form of cloth, she receives 1 unit of wine which, in the absence of international division of labour, would have cost her 120 labour-units to produce for herself; and Portugal obtains cloth at a cost of 80 per unit whereas to produce it for herself would cost 90.

The consequence is that each country specialises upon that branch of production in which it enjoys a comparative advantage, thereby obtaining a greater total product from its given factors of production.

It has often been pointed out that the same principle of comparative advantage applies to the division of labour between particular persons. All gain if the better qualified persons concentrate upon the more difficult tasks although they themselves could perform the less difficult tasks better than those who do in fact perform them. Thus the business manager will employ a book-keeper even if he himself is better at book-keeping than the man he employs.[5] It pays him to concentrate upon the task or tasks in which his superiority, and therefore his comparative advantage, is greatest. The arithmetical examples which we have used to illustrate the international division of labour can be applied equally well here.

But the division of labour between persons is rather different from that between countries or districts. (a) The former often consists in different persons performing different processes in the production of a common product, as in a factory, so that their individual products are not exchanged against one another. The division of labour between *occupations* corresponds much more closely to the international division of labour, since the products of the farmer, baker, tailor, and so on, are exchanged against one another. (b) The other, and more important, distinction is that specialisation by persons increases the capacity of each to perform the task on which he specialises : practice makes perfect. We do not think of this circumstance, or at any rate not primarily, when we speak of the advantage of division of labour between countries. This is because that advantage would remain even if a country were large enough to permit of complete *personal* division of labour without having any intercourse with the rest of the world. Such a country could enjoy even in isolation all the advantages of specialisation by persons; the advantages of international division of labour, of specialisation by national areas, would be an additional and independent influence.[6]

The economic relations between two countries may provide an analogy to the increase in personal capacities resulting from the division of labour between persons in that one country alone may constitute too small a market to permit a plant of optimum size to be set up in some particular branch of industry. This applies to many small countries, such as Austria and Switzerland and Czechoslovakia.

---

[5] *Cf.* especially John D. Black, *Introduction to Production Economics* (1926), pp. 129 *et seq.*, and J. D. Black and A. G. Black, *Production Organisation* (1929), which contain numerous illustrations.

[6] This was recognised, for example, by Cairnes, who distinguished between two advantages of international division of labour : (a) that resulting from the Principle of Comparative Costs and (b) the improvement in personal skill through specialisation upon particular tasks (*cf. Some Leading Principles of Political Economy*).

Technical developments have increased the optimum size of the plant in many industries, and the home market of a small country could not absorb sufficient sales to make it profitable to set up a plant of optimum size if that size were very large. But this point takes us out of the realm of free competition, to which we are for the present restricting ourselves. For if there is not room in an economy for a number of works of optimum size, this must lead to a monopolistic situation.[7]

§ 3. THE ORDER OF TREATMENT TO BE FOLLOWED.

We must at once begin to make our highly simplified model a more accurate representation of reality. The present section recapitulates our simplifying assumptions and states the order in which they will be discarded to be replaced by more realistic ones. All these simplifications constantly give rise to annoying misunderstandings. Somebody or other is always trying to show that the Law of Comparative Cost is valid only under the simple assumptions upon which it was originally formulated. But we shall demonstrate that this is not so and that the simplifications merely help the exposition without affecting the essentials of the matter.

(1) Our first modification must be the *introduction of money*. In an economy which practises division of labour, goods are not exchanged directly against other goods, but goods are bought with money. People do not think of the exchange-relations between goods *in natura* but of money-prices. The flow of international trade is determined directly by absolute differences in money-price and not by comparative differences in labour-cost. Our first task will be to explain the mechanism by which the latter are transformed into the former.[8]

(2) We must next enlarge our model so that it applies to more than two goods and to more than two countries.[9]

(3) We have provisionally abstracted from transport costs, supposing that goods could be transported without cost. This assumption also must be dropped if we wish to paint a realistic picture.

(4) Hitherto we have tacitly assumed constant costs. We have supposed that the production of wine and of cloth could be expanded without altering the cost of production per unit. But

---

[7] This is discussed more fully in chap. xii, § 4.

[8] Even some qualified economists have overlooked the fact that this transformation can be effected at once. *Cf.* Angell, *loc. cit.*, p. 372, and my criticism " The Theory of Comparative Cost Once More " in *Quarterly Journal of Economics* (1928-29), vol. 43, pp. 376 *et seq.*

[9] It has also been said—by an economist of the rank of Professor Ohlin—that the Theory of Comparative Cost loses its meaning when more than two goods are traded between two countries. *Cf.* also Professor del Vecchio in the *Giornale degli Economisti* (1932).

we must take account of the possibility that costs may either rise .or fall as production increases.

(5) The Theory of Comparative Cost fixes the limits within which the exchange-ratio must settle under international trade. (In our example these limits were 0·88 and 1·2 units of cloth per unit of wine.) We must show how the exact point within these two limits is determined.[1] This will lead us beyond the field of cost-analysis.

(6) Closely connected with the hypothesis of constant costs is the assumption that there is only one mobile factor of production, homogeneous labour, and that the labour can move freely from one branch of production to another. If we wish our theories to apply to reality, we must discard this assumption, upon which the strict Labour Theory of Value[2] is based, that there is one sole factor of production. We must assume that there are many different qualities of labour and that other factors of production besides labour are available. We must also assume that many means of production are specific, that is, are confined to one particular use and cannot be transferred to another. But these assumptions are inconsistent with the labour theory of value—which must therefore be discarded.[3]

§ 4. Comparative Costs expressed in Money.

The translation of comparative differences in cost into absolute differences in price is very simple and, as will be seen, in no way alters the real exchange-relations between commodities which lie behind the money-prices. We can best explain how this translation comes about with the aid of a brief arithmetical example borrowed from Professor Taussig.[4]

In the United States

        10 days labour produce 20 units of wheat

        10   ,,   ,,   ,, 20 ,, ,, linen.

In Germany

        10 days labour produce 10 units of wheat

        10   ,,   ,,   ,, 15 ,, ,, linen.

Thus the United States has an absolute superiority in both

---

[1] This problem is discussed in the next chapter.

[2] Mason, " The Doctrine of Comparative Cost " in *Quarterly Journal of Economics* (1926-27), vol. 41, especially stresses the point that the Theory of Comparative Cost is based upon an obsolete theory of value.

[3] See chap. xii, § 1.

[4] *International Trade*, p. 45. It will be observed that this time figures of yield (product per unit of cost) are used instead of, as before, figures of costs (cost per unit of product)

branches of production and a comparative advantage in wheat. Hence the United States will specialise in wheat and Germany in linen. The position in terms of money is as follows:

Country.	Daily Wage. $	Total $	Product of 10 Days Labour	Money Cost = (Supply) Price per Unit $.
United States	1.50	15.00	20 Units of wheat	0.75
„ „	1.50	15.00	20 „ „ linen	0.75
Germany . .	1.00	10.00	10 „ „ wheat	1.00
„ . .	1.00	10.00	15 „ „ linen	0.66

The price of wheat is lower in the United States than in Germany, so that wheat will be exported from the United States to Germany; and conversely with linen. This result is in harmony with the Theory of Comparative Cost. It is true that we have arbitrarily chosen the money wages. But that is not an objection, for it can be shown that, under our assumptions, the ratio of money wages between the two countries must lie between an upper and a lower limit. It is only the choice of one or other of the ratios within these limits which is arbitrary.

Let us suppose that the daily wage in Germany is $1.00. Then the daily wage in the United States cannot exceed $2.00: it cannot be more than double the German wage. This upper limit is fixed by the cost-advantage of the United States in wheat, namely 20 to 10. If the American wage were to rise to $2.00, the American price per unit of both wheat and linen would be $1.00. The export of wheat would become unprofitable, yet linen would continue to be imported, so that the American balance of payments would become passive, gold would flow out, and prices and wages would have to fall again.[5]

In the same way it can be shown that the daily wage in the United States cannot be lower than $1.33: it cannot be less than four-thirds of the German wage. This lower limit is fixed by the cost-advantage of the United States in linen, namely 20 to 15. If the American wage were to fall below $1.33, the German wage being, by hypothesis, $1.00, the German balance of trade would become passive, gold would flow out from Germany, and prices and wages would rise in the United States and would fall in Germany.

---

5 We consider the problem of rigid wages in chap. xvii, § 3.

We cannot say from the cost-data alone exactly where within these limits the ratio of wages, and therefore the ratio at which (American) wheat is exchanged for (German) linen, will settle. This depends upon the conditions of demand. One might assume, for example, that if wheat is $0.75 per unit Germany will import 8 million units, making a total value of $6 million; and that if linen is 0.66 per unit the United States will import 9 million units, making the same total value of $6 million. This would then be an equilibrium position. If, in equilibrium, the price of wheat were lower, relatively to the price of linen, than in the above illustration, Germany would import a greater quantity of wheat and would export a smaller quantity of linen. The exact ratio is determined, given the conditions of demand, by the fact that (supposing the other credits and debits to balance) the total value of each country's exports must equal the total value of its imports. This important addition to the Theory of Comparative Cost was made by J. S. Mill, who introduced the principle of ' the equation of reciprocal demand,' showing that the two sides of the balance of payments must be equal.

We shall discuss all this in detail in the next chapter; for the present it will be sufficient to know the upper and lower limits, which are determined solely by the relative costs.

The Theory of Comparative Cost in no way implies that the division of labour must always be complete, in the sense that each country produces only one good or, more generally, that no good is simultaneously produced in both countries. Even if we assume no transport costs and constant returns, it is quite possible that only one country will specialise completely, producing only one good, while the other country produces both goods. This will happen if the former country cannot itself meet the total demand of both countries for the good in which it specialises. This will be especially likely when it is a small country and the other is a large one.

We can derive from our illustration the general rule that in the country which enjoys the more favourable conditions of production, wages or, more generally, incomes must be higher than in the other.[6] There is nothing strange in this; it is what we should expect. Nevertheless this almost self-evident fact is constantly overlooked. Nobody denies it in so many words, but one of the most potent arguments for tariffs[7] is based upon an

---

[6] Under our simplifying assumptions, the ratio of money wages between the two countries is the same as that of real wages, since in the absence of transport costs the prices of goods must be the same in both countries.

[7] It may be objected that at this stage of the analysis we are working with

implicit denial of it. I refer to the propaganda which is carried on especially in the United States (but also in certain other countries, including Great Britain) against imports from countries which have lower real wages and therefore a lower standard of living. The general public is quite convinced by the argument that only high Protection can enable American industries to compete with European industries which pay much lower wages and that a high standard of living can be maintained only behind a high tariff wall. The truth is that the high standard of living is a *consequence* of the favourable conditions of production and in no way rules out an advantageous trade with the rest of the world.[8]

Whilst the United States fears competition from the ' sweated labour ' of Europe, Protectionist propaganda in Europe lays much stress upon the favourable conditions of production enjoyed by the American economy. The statement that conditions of production are more favourable in the United States is undoubtedly correct. The main reasons for this are :

(1) Her much sparser population. She has only 15 inhabitants per square kilometre, as against 185 in Great Britain, 134 in Germany, 74 in France, and so on. This affects mainly her agriculture. Only first-grade and possibly second-grade land is worked, whereas in Europe land of the third, fourth, and fifth grade is brought under the plough. (2) In Europe the existing distribution of the population is the result of a long historical development. The United States was peopled during the industrial era, and its population is therefore probably distributed, from an economic standpoint, in a much more rational manner. (3) Her great wealth of natural resources of all kinds. (4) She constitutes a great Free Trade area, within which the exchange of goods can take place without having to overcome any tariff obstacles. This makes possible an extensive division of labour and the development of large establishments and mass production.

These and other circumstances make labour in the United States more productive than in the Old World, so that her ' real ' costs of production are lower than in Europe. But, as our illustration shows, it is quite wrong to conclude that trade between the two continents should be restricted on that account. On the contrary, such a trade makes possible a division of labour by which both parties gain.

---

such great simplifications that no conclusions can be drawn about practical problems. The answer is that the argument for tariffs which we are discussing makes the same simplifications.

[8] Cf. esp. Taussig, *How the Tariff Affects Wages*. Reprinted in *Free Trade, the Tariff and Reciprocity* (1920), pp. 48 *seq.*

We may conclude with a word about so-called '*proportional costs.*'[9] Costs are proportional when the superiority of one country over another[1] is the same in every branch of production. For example :

	Wheat.	Linen.
United States,	20	18
Germany,	10	9

The costs are proportional, since $20 : 10 = 18 : 9$.

In such a case—which is of course exceptional—no exchange will take place between the two countries, since there will be no difference in prices. Both in the United States and in Germany the ratio between the price of wheat and the price of linen will be 10 to 9. Thus the only possibility is that *both* the money-prices may be lower in one country than in the other. But such a situation would be promptly corrected by the operation of the monetary mechanism. The necessary condition for an exchange of goods is that the price of one good should be higher in one country and of the other good in the other country, and this is excluded, in the long run, by our assumptions.

§ 5. The Theory of Comparative Cost applied to more than Two Goods.

Our theory can be applied to the case in which not merely two but any number of goods are produced in the two countries. We need only take the two goods which we have hitherto discussed as representative and regard the figures of costs, which we have laid down for them, as averages derived from a whole range of goods with similar cost-ratios. The theorem can then be formulated as follows : *Country I enjoys a comparative advantage over country II in all its export commodities relatively to all its import commodities.* The same applies, of course, to country II.[2]

This is easy to prove. Let us denote the number of units of labour-cost needed to produce a unit of the goods A, B, C . . . in country I by a_1, b_1, c_1 . . . and in country II by a_2, b_2, c_2 . . . Let the (money) supply-prices (that is, the money cost per unit) of A, B, C . . . be $p_{a_1}, p_{b_1}, p_{c_1},$ . . . in country I and $p_{a_2}, p_{b_2}, p_{c_2}$ . . . in country II. Let the money wage (per unit of labour) in country I be W_1 and in country II W_2. We have then the equations $p_{a_1} = a_1 W_1$, $p_{a_1} = b_1 W_1$, $p_{b_1} = c_1 W_1$, . . . and $p_{c_2} = a_2 W_2$, $p_{a_2} = b_2 W_2$, $p_{b_2} = c_2 W_2$. . . . We can also say that the *relative* prices in each country are fixed by the labour-costs: $p_{a_1} : p_{b_1} : p_{c_1}$ . . . $= a_1 : b_1 : c_1$ . . . and $p_{a_2} : p_{b_2} : p_{c_2} = a_2 : b_2 . c_2$ . . . In order to determine the *absolute* height of the *money*

---

[9] In order to avoid misunderstanding, it should be pointed out that 'proportional costs' in the sense in which we are using the term here have nothing to do with the proportional (total) costs (=constant average costs) referred to, in distinction to increasing and decreasing costs, in the theory of costs.

[1] Of course, this superiority may be nil, which means that costs are the same in both countries.

[2] Under the assumption of constant costs and abstracting from costs of transport, only 'border-line' goods can be produced simultaneously in both countries (see p. 138).

prices we must include in our data the quantity of money. This is done by making assumptions as to the absolute rates of money wages which {prevail. It is important to recognise that the sole function of the Labour Theory of Value is to detemine the *relative* prices.

[margin note: not absolute money prices]

Let us go a step further. Let R denote the rate of exchange, that is to say, the number of units of currency of country II which exchange for one unit of the currency of country I. Then we can say that the relation $a_1 \times W_1 \times R < a_2\, W_2$ applies to any commodity A which country I exports, for a good will be exported only if its supply price, that is, its money cost, is lower than in the foreign country. In the same way, the relation $b_1 \times W_1 \times R > b_2\, W_2$ applies to any commodity B imported by country I. It follows that $\dfrac{a_1}{a_2} < \dfrac{W_2}{W_1 \times R}$ and $\dfrac{b_1}{b_2} > \dfrac{W_2}{W_1 \times R}$,[3] and thence that $\dfrac{a_1}{a_2} < \dfrac{b_1}{b_2}$. But that as we have seen above, is simply the expression of the fact that country I enjoys a comparative advantage over country II in the production of commodity A, that is of all its export commodities, relatively to all its import commodities.

We can arrange the various goods in the order of the comparative advantage of country I over country II,[4] so that if we call them A, B, C, D, E, . . . $\dfrac{a_1}{a_2} < \dfrac{b_1}{b_2} < \dfrac{c_1}{c_2} < \dfrac{d_1}{d_2} < \dfrac{e_1}{e_2}$. If we then draw a line dividing the commodities which country I exports from those which it imports, all the former will be on one side of the line, and all the latter on the other side, without our having to change the order in which they are arranged. For example, it will not be possible for country I to export A and C and to import B.

So long as our assumptions continue to cover only the cost-data, we can *not* determine the exact position of this dividing line.[5] We can say only that it must be drawn in such a manner that country I enjoys a comparative advantage in every commodity it exports relatively to every commodity it imports. If we wish to determine its exact position—whether between B and C or between C and D and so on—we must introduce the further condition that the credit side and the debit side of the balance of payments must be equal.

---

[3] $\dfrac{W_2}{W_1 \times R}$ is the ratio of the money wages. In our previous arithmetical example we expressed them in the same currency units. This time we explicitly introduce the rate of exchange, R.

[4] *Cf.* the similar scheme in Appendix H to Marshall, *Money, Credit and Commerce.*

[5] Clearly it must be this circumstance which has led Ohlin to declare that the Theory of Comparative Cost breaks down when there are more than two goods.

Let us assume that we have the following cost-data:

Kinds of Goods.		A	B	C	D	E	F	G	H	I	J
'Real Cost' per unit, expressed in hours of labour.	In country I[6] $(a_1, b_1, c_1, \ldots)$,	20	20	20	20	20	20	20	20	20	20
	In country II $(a_2, b_2, c_2, \ldots)$,	40	36	32	30	25	20	18	16	14	12

The quotient $\dfrac{W_2}{W_1 \times R}$ determines the position of the dividing line between the goods which country I exports and those which it imports. If money wages are the same in both countries $\left(\dfrac{W_2}{W_1 \times R} = 1\right)$, then the money cost of all those goods which country I can produce with a smaller absolute 'real cost,' that is of A to E inclusive, is lower in country I than in country II: it will export these goods and import all goods denoted by G or a succeeding letter. The commodity F lies on the boundary and will be produced simultaneously in both countries.

If money wages in country I are 10 per cent. lower than in country II $\left(\dfrac{W_2}{W_1 \times R} = 1\cdot1\right)$, then country I has a lower *money* cost than country II even when its real cost is 10 per cent. higher. In other words, unfavourable conditions of production will be offset by lower wages.

Let us assume that money wages are the same in both countries. Then we know exactly which goods will be exported and which imported, and at what money-prices. Country I will export A to E at a price of 20 per unit, and country II will export G at a price of 18 per unit, H at a price of 16 per unit, I at a price of 14 per unit, J at a price of 12 per unit, and so on. It depends upon the reciprocal demand of the two countries whether or not this situation maintains equilibrium in the balance of payments.

Let us suppose that it does not, and that the balance of payments of country I is passive, or, alternatively, that the existing equilibrium is disturbed,[7] so that the balance of payments of I becomes passive. The monetary mechanism comes into play; gold flows from I to II; prices and wages rise in II and fall in I;

---

[6] We choose the units of quantity of the various commodities in such a way that the cost per unit of every commodity in country I is the same. Hence this equality (all costing 20) is not a simplifying assumption.

[7] Because, say, country I has to pay reparations, or makes a loan to country II, or because its demand for the products of country II increases.

W_1 becomes smaller and W_2 greater; the quotient $\dfrac{W_2}{W_1 \cdot R}$ increases; the dividing line is shifted; and F moves into the group of commodities exported by I. The balance of payments is brought into equilibrium, since (1) F is now exported (2) the other export commodities (A to E) of country I become cheaper and (3) the export commodities of country II become dearer. If, however, this is not enough to produce equilibrium, the outflow of gold from I must continue, the dividing line must move still further, country I may export G instead of importing it, and this movement will continue until equilibrium is attained.

It is clear that the complications we have just introduced do not disturb our presumption—at this stage of the analysis it cannot be called more than a presumption—that the unrestricted exchange of goods between the countries is economically advantageous. The examples we gave upon the assumption of only two goods showed plainly that *both* countries could increase their total output by each specialising upon the good in which it had a comparative advantage. We can reach the same conclusion upon the assumption of numerous export and import commodities. We can ' pair off ' any export commodity with any import commodity. It is clear that whichever of these pairs we consider, each country has an advantage in the commodity it exports relatively to the commodity it imports. Thus the division of labour between the two countries increases their total output. The division of this gain between the two countries depends upon the exact position of the dividing line between export and import commodities.

The process of correcting the passive balance of payments of country I turns the terms of trade against it : its export prices fall relatively to its import prices. This must be so if (either spontaneously or as the result of, for example, a reparations payment or loan made by I) the demand in I shifts towards the export goods of II or the demand in II shifts away from the export goods of I. But we have seen[8] that a unilateral payment may lead to the opposite result, turning the terms of trade in favour of the paying country. This will occur if the fall in demand in the paying country hits the goods it imports from the receiving country and the increased demand in the receiving country is directed towards the goods of the paying country. The result, in the terms of our analysis, will be that W_1 increases, W_2 decreases, the dividing line moves in the opposite direction, and country I imports commodity E instead of exporting it. How, then, does the export surplus come about? It comes about by country I exporting greater quantities of commodities A to D at higher prices and importing small quantities of commodities F to J . . . at lower prices.[9] For country I produces goods A to E for its home demand as well as

---

[8] *Cf.* chap. vii, § 3.

[9] But it is very unlikely that the whole amount of the payment can be transferred in this way. As a rule, the fall in demand in I will affect predominantly its domestic goods (since in nearly all countries imports are small relatively to home

for export, and the payment it has to make will lead to a fall in its home demand for, and therefore consumption of, these goods : hence it can export more without needing to increase its production. Leaving aside the rare case in which the decreased demand in I and the increased demand in II both affect exactly the same goods and so offset one another, the monetary mechanism *must* act in one of the two following ways : either (a) *the rate of exchange* will remain stable and equilibrium will be achieved through a rise in wages in one country or a fall in wages in the other country or a combination of the two; or (b) the *money-wages* in both countries may remain stable and equilibrium will be achieved through a shift in the rate of exchange.   However the mechanism may act, under the influence of the monetary systems and banking policies of the two countries, the result will always be a change in the *ratio* of money wages between the two countries: that is, in $\dfrac{W_2}{W_1 \times R}$ Thus our analysis does not depend for its validity upon a frictionless working of the gold standard; it applies equally to paper currencies and to any form of managed currency.[1]

This discussion has demonstrated the falsity of the view that " international capital movements have never found a place in the Theory of Comparative Cost."[2] Of course, the theory does not explain why capital movements take place, but it does explain *how* payments are made and equilibrium re-established.

How the capital will be transferred depends not only upon the way in which the loan-money is spent, but also upon the relative comparative costs of the different commodities. A loan for the purpose of building a railway will not necessarily be transferred in the form of railway material. When industrial countries lend to agricultural countries to enable them to develop their industries, the export surplus may well consist of machines and similar products. But when one industrial country lends to another or when—as may happen—an agricultural country lends to an industrial one, it may well be that the goods which immediately follow those which it already exports in the comparative-cost series are foodstuffs or luxury goods. For example, the capital for constructing an underground railway may enter the country in the form of cosmetics and perfumes, and factors of production which had previously been employed in producing these luxuries in the borrowing country will be set free. This will bring about a reshuffle, permitting factors to be diverted to the task of directly or indirectly assisting the construction of the railway. If the loan is granted upon the condition that part or all of it must be spent in certain ways, this of course somewhat changes the situation.

§ 6. Costs of Transport.

Our conclusion that a given good can be suddenly transformed from an export commodity into an import commodity, or, conversely, may seem unreal. This is because it flows, quite logically, from our assumption that there are no costs of transport[3]; and this assumption is an unreal one. The introduction of transport

production). The terms of trade must then turn against it, although possibly only to a very slight extent. We can regard cases in which they do turn against it as normal and others as exceptional. See Nurkse, *Internationale Kapital-bewegungen* (1935), chap. iii.

[1] The attempt to keep both the rate of exchange and the wage level stable disturbs the equilibrium and leads to congestion of the market and unemployment.

[2] Eulenburg, *Grossraumwirtschaft und Autarkie* (1932), p. 62.

[3] And also from our assumption of constant costs, which we discard in the following section.

costs gives us a third class of goods, namely those which enter only into domestic trade, in addition to export goods and import goods. A commodity does not pass directly from the export class into the import class; it must first enter this third class and be produced simultaneously by both countries for their home markets. This can be expressed in terms of our algebra as follows. Let $_at_{12}$ represent the real cost (expressed in units of labour or in the same units of ' productive resources ' as a_1, b_1, c_1, and so on) of transporting commodity A from country I to country II, and let $_at_{21}$ represent its real cost of transport in the opposite direction. Let us further suppose, to simplify the discussion, that the country of supply always pays the cost of transport. We can then say that the commodity will be exported by I if $\dfrac{a_1 + _at_{12}}{a_2} < \dfrac{W_2}{W_1 \times R}$ and will be imported by I if $\dfrac{W_2}{W_1 \times R} < \dfrac{a_1}{a_2 + _at_{21}}$ But $\dfrac{a_1}{a_2 + _at_{21}} < \dfrac{a_1 + _at_{12}}{a_2}$ and hence the commodity will be neither exported nor imported if the numerical value of $\dfrac{W_2}{W_2 \times R}$ lies between these two values, so that $\dfrac{a_2}{a_2 + _at_{21}} < \dfrac{W_2}{W_1 \times R} < \dfrac{a_1 + _at_{12}}{a_2}$. We thus have two expressions relating to any good A, namely : $\dfrac{a}{a_2 + _at_{21}}$ and $\dfrac{a_1 + _at_{12}}{a_2}$. In other words a good will not be exported or imported unless the difference in its cost of production between the two countries exceeds the cost of transporting it from one to the other. The order in which the various goods must be arranged, as on p.138, to show which good would next become an export commodity of I if I increased its export, and so on, will of course be changed when we take account of transport costs. The export capacity of a country does not depend, as we previously assumed, solely upon its comparative costs of production; it depends also upon the costs of transport. We may illustrate from our table on page 138. If the quotient $\dfrac{W_2}{W_1 \times R}$ becomes smaller (because gold flows from II to I or because the rate of exchange, R, rises), moving the dividing-line in the direction of A, the good D ceases to be exported as soon as the value of this quotient falls below $\dfrac{d_1 + _dt_{12}}{d_2}$. But D does not become an import commodity until the value of this quotient has fallen further and has become less than $\dfrac{d_1}{d_2 + _dt_{2 1}}$;

This complication in no way changes the presumption that international division of labour benefits *every* country. It is true that division of labour will not be carried so far as under the assumption that commodities can be transported without cost. The necessity of paying transport charges makes the world poorer than it would be if all goods could be produced in the relatively most suitable places and thence transported without any cost. But in so far as international trade takes place despite the existence of transport costs, it must be advantageous, since it will be undertaken only if the gain from division of labour exceeds the costs of transport.

§ 7. VARIABLE COSTS OF PRODUCTION.

We have hitherto assumed that the Law of Constant Unit Costs prevails (within both countries) in every branch of production, so that additional quantities of any good can be produced with the same expenditure of labour, per unit, as before. Thus, to revert to the example given on page 132, if Germany gradually gives up the cultivation of wheat and instead produces linen, then for every 10 units of wheat which she ceases to produce she will produce 15 additional units of linen. Similarly, there will be a constant substitution-ratio between the two commodities in the United States, namely 1 to 1.

We must now abandon this assumption. There is no doubt that constant costs, or—to use another expression for the same phenomenon—constant returns, are an exceptional case. The rule is *increasing costs*, or diminishing returns. Beyond a certain output, which—at any rate, under competition—is in practice always exceeded, additional quantities can be produced only at an increasing cost per unit.

It is not difficult to see how this fact can be brought into our scheme. If we assume that in Germany and the United States alike both branches of production are in the stage of diminishing returns, the figures of returns given in our example must be taken as figures of *marginal returns*. Before international trade begins, the last increase in the quantity of wheat produced in Germany costs 10 units of labour for each 10 units of wheat and, similarly, the marginal cost of linen is 10 per 15 units.

When Germany is constrained by the pressure of foreign competition to produce more linen and less wheat, her marginal cost of producing linen must rise. Less suitable land will be brought under flax, and more labour and capital will be expended upon land already under flax. On the other hand, her marginal cost of producing wheat must fall. The least suitable land will be withdrawn from wheat-growing and less labour and capital than before will be expended upon land which remains under wheat.

Consequently in Germany the ratio of marginal costs will shift in favour of wheat, while in the United States it will shift in favour of linen, since she will produce more wheat and less linen than before. Thus, as Germany substitutes linen-production for wheat-production and the United States does the opposite, the difference in the comparative-cost ratio between the two countries will be progressively reduced from four directions, and this must sooner or later bring this process of substitution to an end. The division of labour will remain incomplete in the sense that Germany will not completely abandon her production of wheat but will only restrict it to land which can successfully meet American competition, whilst in the same way the United States will only restrict, and not abandon, her production of linen. How far the division of labour will be carried or, in other words, how long the comparative advantage of the United States in wheat and of Germany in linen will continue at the margins, as the margins move owing to the progressive substitution of wheat-production for linen-production in the United States and conversely in Germany, will depend partly upon the rapidity with which costs rise as production expands, or fall as production contracts.

We can include increasing costs in our scheme as follows. We have hitherto assigned only *one* cost of production in each country (a_1 in I and a_2 in II) to any commodity A. We must now assign a whole *series* of costs to each commodity—a_1', a_1'', a_1''', . . . in I and a_2', a_2'', a_2''', . . . in II; and similarly for B, C, D, . . . These terms represent the different marginal costs of producing different quantities of the commodity.

This complication, like the others already discussed, makes no essential difference. The division of labour will, indeed, be carried less far than under constant costs, since, as it is extended, the comparative disadvantage of a country (at the margin) diminishes and finally disappears. Thus the comparative disadvantage of a country is less if we regard the cost-data as relating to (increasing) marginal costs and not to constant costs; and it is not profitable to carry the division of labour beyond the point at which increasing costs wipe out the cost-differences between the two countries. But it *is* profitable to carry it up to that point. Our presumption that Free Trade is the best economic policy therefore remains intact.[4]

---

[4] This is not realised by Dr. Kellenberger, who argues ("Zur Theorie von Freihandel und Schutzzoll" in *Weltwirtschaftliches Archiv* (1916), vol. 7, pp. 5-7) as follows : If Portugal specialises upon the production of wine and if this is subject to diminishing returns, or increasing costs, then the new vineyards she will create in consequence of the international division of labour will yield a smaller return than those which she cultivated before engaging in international trade. Hence under increasing costs the international division of labour leads

The case of *decreasing costs*, or increasing returns, is as difficult as that of increasing costs is easy. We must postpone a detailed discussion of it (to chapter XII, § 4), confining ourselves for the present to the following remarks:

I cannot share the view of those distinguished writers, such as Professors Schumpeter, Mises, and—although he holds it only with qualifications—Knight, who deny the very possibility of increasing returns. I believe they can exist in exceptional cases and that these exceptional cases are of importance. Let me hasten to add that a reduction in costs due to progress in technique and organisation (the possibility of which is of course not disputed by the writers in question) does not constitute a true case of decreasing costs even if it is associated historically with an increase in production. Such progress is a change in the economic data and is to be represented graphically by a downward shifting of the whole cost curve and not by a cost curve which slopes downwards to the right. When people speak of the Law of Decreasing Costs they frequently have in mind mainly these ' historical ' reductions in costs; but our theory is not invalidated by such cases.

Decreasing costs in the proper sense are the consequence of an expansion of production, and not merely phenomena which happen to take place at the same time as such an expansion. They come about (under certain assumptions, which will be stated at a later stage) through an increase in the size of the works. They are due, fundamentally, to the fact that many factors of production are not completely divisible, so that a large output is needed for a plant to be of the technical optimum size and yet to utilise fully all its factors. When a market is large enough to absorb the total output of a number of works of optimum size, the ' law ' of decreasing costs no longer applies and we are again in the region of increasing costs.

If the optimum size of a plant is so great, relatively to the extent of the market, that it can be attained only by very few or only by one plant, decreasing costs lead directly to a monopolistic situation. If we find something approaching free competition in any branch of production, we can conclude that it is subject to increasing costs.

These remarks reflect, in broad outline, the present state of the Theory of Costs. They show that we are not committing too grave an error by provisionally working with the assumption of increasing costs.

---

to a fall in productivity and a diminution in output. Only under falling or constant costs does it yield a gain. . . . The fallacy of this argument is too obvious to warrant a detailed refutation.

CHAPTER XI.

SUPPLY AND DEMAND IN INTERNATIONAL TRADE.

§ 1. Introductory.

This chapter deals with an important extension of the Theory of Comparative Cost. We have several times had occasion to remark that the exact point of equilibrium is determined by the supply-and-demand situation. If each of the two countries exports only one commodity, the comparative costs determine the limits within which the terms of trade must lie, but their exact position within these limits depends upon the demand of each country for the commodity exported by the other. If a country produces numerous goods, we cannot tell from the cost-data alone exactly which goods it will export and which it will import; the dividing-line between the two is determined by Supply and Demand.

The extension of the Theory of Comparative Cost which covers these points was first made by John Stuart Mill.[1] It was later developed and generalised by Alfred Marshall. Marshall also introduced a diagrammatic apparatus for dealing with these problems. We shall examine the theories of Mill and Marshall; and we shall consider the different meanings of ' the real ratio of inter-national exchange '—or, more briefly, ' the terms of trade '—and the methods of measuring it.

§ 2. Mill's Theory of International Values.[2]

Let us return to the illustration in § 4 of the foregoing chapter, retaining all the simplifying assumptions which we made at the time. Before trade takes place between the two countries, let the ratio of exchange between linen and wheat be 1 to 1 in the United States and 1.5 to 1 in Germany. When trade between them takes place, the United States will specialise in wheat and Germany

---

[1] *Principles of Political Economy*, bk. 3, chap. xviii.
[2] *Cf.* Bastable, *Theory of International Trade*, chap. 2; the criticisms of the classical theory by Graham, " International Values Re-examined " in *Quarterly Journal of Economics* (Nov. 1923), pp. 54 *et seq.*; its defence by Mering, " Ist die Theorie der internationalen Werte widerlegt? " in *Archiv für Sozialwissenschaft* (April 1931), vol. 65, p. 251; and Graham's reply, " The Theory of International Values " in *Quarterly Journal of Economics* (Aug. 1932); Colm, " Das Gesetz der komparativen Kosten—das Gesetz der komparativen Kaufkraft " in *Weltwirt-schaftliches Archiv* (1930), vol. 32, pp. 371 *et seq.* See also Mangoldt, *Grundriss der Volkswirtschaftslehre*, especially the 1st edn. (1863), and Edgeworth's exposition of Mangoldt's theory *loc. cit.*, pp. 52 *et seq.*

in linen. Any ratio of exchange between 1.5 linen to 1 wheat and 1.0 linen to 1 wheat will produce this result.

Let us begin with an exchange-ratio of rather less than 1.5, say 1.4, linen to 1 wheat. If we assume German wages to be $1, this ratio corresponds to an America wage of nearly $2 (to be exact, $1.87).[3] The price of wheat (both its domestic price and its export price, in the United States, equalling its cost of production) is then $93.4, and the price of linen $66⅔. Let us suppose that, in this price-situation, the United States imports 900 units of linen from Germany. The German balance of payments will become favourable and the monetary mechanism will begin to operate. Let us simplify by supposing that wages in Germany are kept stable, so that the price-adjustments leading to equilibrium take place on the American side. This means that the price of wheat, and American wages, must fall. This will stimulate the imports and check the exports of Germany until equilibrium is reached at an exchange-ratio of, say, 1.3 linen to 1 wheat.

The table on page 147 shows the result of the whole process.

Columns 1 to 5 give the 'international demand,' expressed in goods, of both countries. Columns 6 to 10 show the results of each wheat-linen ratio, given these demand schedules, in terms of money, upon the assumption that German wages are kept stable. If this simplifying assumption were dropped and we were to suppose the monetary mechanism to act in some other way, the absolute money figures would be changed, but (a) the ratio of money wages and hence (b) the ratio of money prices and hence (c) supply-and-demand schedules expressed in goods, would remain unaltered. It is true that in actual fact these 'real' relations will not always be exactly the same if the monetary mechanism acts in one way as if it acts in another. But we are constrained to assume, as a first approximation, that they will not be affected by the particular way in which the monetary mechanism works; this assumption underlies not only the whole theory of international trade but also the greater part of general economic theory.[4]

Since we have sufficiently established the connection between money prices and the real exchange-relations, we may perhaps be permitted to use briefer expressions, such as 'Germany's demand for wheat.' But to prevent misunderstanding we must emphasise that the concept 'the demand of one country for the export commodities of another' in the Theory of International Values

---

[3] The method of computing this is stated in note 6 to the table on page 147.

[4] It is a function of monetary theory, provided that it is not tied down to a strict Quantity Theory approach, to consider deviations from this hypothesis.

must not be confused with the concept of demand in terms of money for some particular good.[5]

Whether the one country or the other reaps the greater gain depends on whether the real exchange-ratio settles near the one or the other of its two possible limits. If it approaches the upper limit—the ratio of 1.5 linen to 1 wheat existing in Germany before international trade began—the United States gets the lion's share of the difference and gains more than Germany. For it now gets 1.5 instead of 1.0 linen for 1 wheat. A glance at the table will show how its money wages and real wages are affected. If the ratio approaches its lower limit of 1 to 1—the American ratio before the commencement of international trade—the gain accrues mainly to Germany.

International Exchange-Ratio (Units of Linen per 1 Wheat between the Price of Wheat and the Price of Linen).	Germany's Supply-and-Demand Schedule.		America's Supply-and-Demand Schedule.		Ratio of Money Wages in Germany (=1) to Money Wages in U.S.A.	Price (=Money Cost) of Wheat in U.S.A.	Price (=Money Cost) of Linen in Germany.	Value of	
	Demand for Wheat (=Sales of Wheat in Germany)	Supply of Linen.	Demand for Linen (=Sales of Linen in U.S.A.)	Supply of Wheat.				Wheat Exports from U.S.A.	Linen Exports from Germany.
						in $	in $	in $	in $
	In Units of Quantity.								
(1)	(2)	(3)	(4)	(5)	(6)	(7)	(8)	(9)	(10)
or 1 W.	(800)*	—	1800	1200	1:2	1·000†	0·66⅔	—	1200·1
,, 1 W.	900	1260	1540	1100	1:1·87	0·934	0·66⅔	840·6	1026·7
,, 1 W.	1000	1300	1300	1000	1:1·73	0·867	0·66⅔	867·1	867·1
,, 1 W.	1100	1320	1080	900	1:1·60	0·800	0·66⅔	880·0	720·0
,, 1 W.	1300	1430	880	800	1:1·47	0·733	0·66⅔	952·9	586·7
,, 1 W.	1500	1500	(800)*	—	1:1·33	0·667	0·66⅔‡	1000·5	—

* At this exchange-ratio no export takes place. The quantity sold, shown in brackets, would be produced at home.

† This is equal to the supply-price of wheat in Germany; hence there will be no export.

‡ This is equal to the supply-price of linen in U.S.A.; hence there will be no export.

---

[5] The relations between the two are discussed below, in § 4.

(1) The limits of 1.5 linen for 1 wheat and 1 linen for 1 wheat, between which the international exchange-ratio must lie, are determined by the comparative costs. The intermediate ratios have been chosen arbitrarily.

(2) Arbitrarily assumed. The figures (read downwards) could increase at a different rate or could decrease instead of increasing. The latter case would be one of inelastic demand, discussed in § 5 of this chapter.

(3) Calculated, by multiplying (2) by (1).

(4) Arbitrarily assumed. The remarks on (2) apply here also.

(5) Calculated, by dividing (4) by (1).

(6) Money wages in Germany are assumed to be stable. Money wages in U.S.A. are calculated under the assumption that in Germany 10 days' labour produces 15 units of linen and in U.S.A. 10 days' labour produces 20 units of wheat. The calculation rests upon the fact that the exchanged quantities have always equal money costs. Thus, if we call the labour-time needed to produce 1 unit of linen in Germany a_L, the labour-time needed to produce 1 unit of wheat in U.S.A. a_W, the exchanged quantities of linen and wheat respectively q_L and q_W, and wages in Germany w_G and wages in U.S.A. w_A it must be true that $a_L \, w_G \, q_L = a_W \, w_A \, q_W$. The absolute height of money wages cannot be calculated from this equation, but the ratio of money wages in Germany to money wages in U.S.A. can be calculated. Thus if we take the former as I, we have $a_L . q_L = a_W . x . q_W$ where x is the ratio of American to German money wages. For example, at an exchange-ratio of 1.4 units of linen for 1 unit of wheat, it follows from the given comparative-cost ratios that $\frac{10}{15} \times 1 \cdot 4 = \frac{10}{20} x$, i.e. that $x = 1.87$.

(7) Calculated, by multiplying money wages per day in the U.S.A. by the number of day's labour ($\frac{1}{2}$) needed to produce 1 unit of wheat.

(8) Calculated, by multiplying money wages per day in Germany by the number of day's labour $\frac{1}{1 \cdot 5}$ needed to produce 1 unit of linen.

(9) $= (7) \times (2)$.

(10) $= (8) \times (4)$.

Which ratio will, in fact, be established clearly depends upon the demand (-and-supply) schedules of the two countries. We can distinguish two aspects of these schedules, each of which affects the final result: (*a*) the size of the amount demanded (and therefore of the amount supplied) at any given ratio—depending upon the capacity of each country as a market and as a producer, and (*b*) the elasticity of the demand—the extent to which it increases in response to an improvement in the ratio (that is, to a fall in relative price).

When the absorptive capacity of one country is large relatively to that of the other, this will tend to make the ratio favourable for the latter. If, in our example, the United States were very large compared with Germany, the figures in columns 4 and 5 would be larger. This would shift the ratio downwards, in favour of Germany. If, for example, at a ratio of 1.1 linen to 1 wheat the American demand were 1650 and the American supply therefore 1500, Germany would not be able to supply the whole of the American demand for linen. Hence there would be only a *partial* change-over in American production, sufficient to supply the German demand for wheat. The United States, although importing linen, would continue to produce it, but would produce less of it than before, while Germany would specialise completely upon the production of linen. The international exchange-ratio would be the same as that prevailing in the United States, namely 1 linen to 1 wheat, and the whole of the gain from the international division of labour would accrue to Germany.

The same result would come about if the sole export commodity of the United States were something like pepper for which the demand is so small that the total amount of money expended upon it by consumers could not approach their expenditure upon the commodity (linen) which Germany exports. For then the United States would be compelled to produce linen to supplement its imports of linen, whilst Germany could obtain all her pepper from the United States and specialise completely upon linen.

We can also lay down the rule that, other circumstances remaining the same, the ratio will be more favourable to a country the less elastic is its demand for the export commodity of the other and the more elastic is the demand of the other for the commodity exported by the country in question. When the figures in column 2 rise only slowly, the amount of wheat imported by Germany increases relatively little in response to a fall in its (relative) price and the ratio is pushed down towards 1:1. The same result occurs if the American demand for linen increases rapidly in response to a fall in its (relative) price: that is to say, if the figures in column 4 increase rapidly from bottom to top.

There is no point, however, in prolonging this discussion upon the simplifying assumptions that costs are constant and that there are only two commodities to be exchanged. For under these assumptions it is highly probable, as Graham has shown, that—unless we choose illustrative figures relating to two countries of about the same size and to two commodities of about the same importance—the exchange-ratio will be very near one of its two possible limits.[6]

But Graham goes further, and concludes from this that the conditions of demand have no influence at all upon the real international exchange-ratio. He points out[7] that if there are many actual and potential export-goods and import-goods, it will require

---

[6] This can be shown much more easily by curves than by arithmetical examples.
[7] "The Theory of International Values," *Quarterly Journal of Economics* (Aug. 1932, pp. 583, 585, &c.

only a slight alteration in the exchange-ratio, and therefore in the relative wage-levels of the two countries, to bring a good whose price was just above the export-point into the export category or to take a good whose price was just above the import-point out of the import category. This is indeed correct; and it follows that the real exchange-ratio (together with its monetary parallel, the ratio between the wage-levels) will be more stable when the number of commodities exported and imported is large. But to conclude from this that the nature of the demand schedules does not affect the exchange-ratio is about as logical as to deny that demand, in the usual sense, influences price, on the ground that when there are numerous actual and potential sources of supply, every increase in price will call forth a greater supply.

§ 3. Marshall's Generalisation of the Theory of International Values.

When each country has a whole range of export-goods and import-goods and the dividing-line between the two categories is not given to begin with but has to be determined, it is no longer so easy to find a simple way of expressing the supply and demand of each country, since the assortment of goods in each category is not constant. Marshall tried to overcome this difficulty by measuring all the export-goods of a country in terms of one common unit. He expressed the exports of Germany in ' representative bales of German goods.' This unit of a ' bale ' is defined by stating that it embodies a *constant quantity of German labour (of different qualities) and German capital.* Thus its ' real cost ' remains constant, whilst the individual goods which compose it may vary. We can readily follow Marshall so long as we keep to the Labour Theory of Value, with its assumption that homogeneous labour is the sole factor of production. Instead of ' a representative bale ' we can say simply ' the product of a constant quantity of the labour of the country in question.' When, in the next chapter, we give up the hypothesis of the Labour Theory of Value, it will be necessary for us to resort to averaging and to speak of a representative export-good, to be defined as the product of a constant quantity of *means of production in general.*

Marshall then takes by way of illustration the following reciprocal demand schedules of Germany and England[8]:

---

[8] See *Money, Credit and Commerce*, Bk. 3, chap. vi, p. 162, and Appendix J, pp. 330 *et seq.*

Terms of Trade (Number of G-bales per 100 E-bales). (1)	E's Demand for G-bales (Sales of G-bales in E at the "price" shown in (1)). (2)	E's Supply of E-bales (= total receipts from the sale of (2) in E at the ratio shown in (1)). (3)	Price (in G-bales per 100 E-bales) at which the E-bales shown in (3) can be sold in G. (4)	G's Supply of G-bales in exchange for (3) (= total receipts from the sale of (3) in G at the ratio shown in (1)). (5)
10	1,000	10,000	230	23,000
20	4,000	20,000	175	35,000
30	9,000	30,000	143	42,900
35	14,000	40,000	122	48,800
40	20,000	50,000	108	54,000
46	27,600	60,000	95	57,000
55	28,500	70,000	86	60,200
68	54,400	80,000	$82\frac{1}{2}$	66,000
78	70,200	90,000	78	70,200
83	83,000	100,000	76	76,000
86	94,600	110,000	$74\frac{1}{2}$	81,950
$88\frac{1}{2}$	106,200	120,000	$73\frac{3}{4}$	88,500

Note to Table.—(1) assumed; (2) assumed; (3) calculated from (1) and (2); (4) assumed; (5) calculated from (4) and (3).

A portion of the demand schedule of England is shown by columns 1 to 3 and of Germany by columns 3 to 5. Before we embark upon a discussion of the figures and of their diagrammatic representation, we must show how they are derived and how they are connected with the Theory of Comparative Cost.

Let us return to the arithmetical example which we gave in chapter X, § 5 (p. 138).

Kinds of Goods.		A	B	C	D	E	F	G	H	I	J	K	L	M	N	··· ··
l cost,' per unit quantity, ex- ⸱essed in hours labour.	In England	20	20	20	20	20	20	20	20	20	20	20	20	20	20	...
	In Germany	40	36	30	25	20	18	16	15	14	13	12	11	10	9	

We must now choose an arbitrary starting-point. Let us say that both countries have the same money wages, of $1 per day, and let us choose the product of one day's labour as our unit or 'bale.' We know that under these conditions England will export the goods A to D and will import the goods F to N···. The money prices and the money incomes are fixed by the assumption of equal money wages; and it follows that a quite definite quantity of the goods F to N··· can be imported into England and sold there. How great this quantity is will depend upon England's demand for German products at the given ratio between English and German prices. Let us assume that the total value of the imports into England will be $140,000. This means that, at an exchange-ratio of 1 to 1, England will demand 140,000 German bales and hence will be prepared to supply 140,000 English bales. Next let us suppose that wages in Germany fall by 10 per cent. The prices of the goods F to N···, and hence the price of a German bale, will fall. A greater quantity of these goods can now be sold in England; and in addition Germany can now export the good E. In other words, the number of German bales demanded by England will be greater, increasing to, say, 150,000. The money receipts from this larger quantity will be, say, $145,000. But a dollar still represents one English bale, since English wages have not altered. Therefore England will offer 145,000 of her bales in exchange for the 150,000 German bales. In this manner, we can derive step by step the whole of the English demand schedule, and we can do the same *mutatis mutandis* for Germany.

Thus a table drawn up in this way shows the demand of each country for the bales of the other, and the supply of its own, which would be associated with each exchange-ratio (between German bales and English bales, corresponding to the ratio between the money wages in the two countries). That exchange-ratio will be established at which the supply and demand of the two countries coincide; in Marshall's table this equilibrium ratio is 78 German bales for 100 English bales.

Thus Marshall's table shows the *final result* of a complicated process, namely of the whole mechanism of international trade. Each step in the table should be thought of as bound up with a multitude of changes in prices and production. Edgeworth has compared the curves which represent graphically the data of such a table to the hands of a clock, whose movement is the result of a complicated mechanism.[9]

We can best continue the discussion with the aid of a diagram. We measure (fig. 6) along the X axis the number of E-bales supplied by E (column 3) and along the Y axis the corresponding demand of E for G-bales (column 2) thus obtaining the curve OE —the Supply-Demand curve of England.[1] The curve OG, the

---

[9] Graham's objection "that reciprocal demand is for individual commodities and not for any such uniform aggregate of labour and capital" (as the Marshallian bales) (*loc. cit.*, p. 583) thus springs from a misunderstanding. The demand for products is a derived demand for the means of production embodied in them.

[1] For the sake of simplicity, we shall henceforward speak simply of demand curves. E's demand for G-bales implies, however, a certain supply of E-bales offered in exchange, just as the demand for a good, in the ordinary sense, implies a certain supply of money offered in exchange for it.

demand curve of Germany, is the graphic representation of columns 3 and 5.

The point P', for example, shows that P'M' G-bales can be exchanged in E against OM' E-bales. The exchange-ratio is

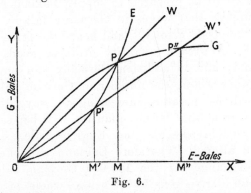

Fig. 6.

$\dfrac{P'M'}{OM'}$, best shown by the slope of the straight line OW' relatively to the X axis.[2] But at this exchange-ratio OM" E-bales will be sold in G. This means that the demand of G for E-bales is greater than E's supply; G's balance of payments will become unfavourable or ' passive '; the monetary mechanism will push prices and wages down in G and up in E. E will be induced thereby to take more G-bales. Sooner or later an equilibrium will be reached at the point P, at which the demand and supply of E equals the supply and demand of G.

The E curve is convex towards the X axis, showing that greater quantities of G-bales can be sold in E only under less favourable conditions. The same applies *mutatis mutandis* to the G curve. The greater the angle between the straight line OW and the X axis, the higher will be the position of P on the curve OE, and therefore the more favourable will be the exchange-ratio to E and the less favourable to G. A movement of the point P outwards along OE corresponds to a movement of the quotient $\dfrac{W_2}{W_1 \times R}$ towards the left and *vice versa*.[3] The higher are incomes in E relatively to incomes in G, the greater will be its demand for imports and supply of exports. But before proceeding further we must explain, in order to prevent misunderstandings, the relation between the demand of a country in the Marshallian sense and demand in the usual sense.

---

[2] Provided we abstract from transport costs, this slope equals the quotient, which we have often mentioned, $\dfrac{W_2}{W_1 \times R}$ = the ratio of money wages.

[3] See the table on pp. 138 and 151.

§ 4. The Relation between the Marshallian Curves and the Usual Supply and Demand Curves.

The demand or supply of a country in the sense developed in the preceding section is often confused with demand in the usual sense. There are definite relations between the Marshallian demand curve of a country and an ' ordinary ' demand curve, but the two are not identical. The latter shows the relation between the *money* price and the quantity demanded of *one* good, and slopes downward from left to right. At a lower price, a greater

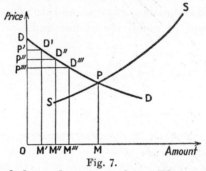

Fig. 7.

amount is demanded, and conversely. The supply curve (SS) shows the relation between the money price and the quantity supplied of a good, and hence slopes upward from left to right.

The Marshallian curves differ from these curves both formally and materially. They differ *formally* in that their ordinates measure not the price per unit of the good in question but the *total receipts* from the sale of the quantity shown upon the horizontal axis.[4] Thus their successive ordinates correspond to the areas of rectangles inscribed in the ordinary demand curves.

The *material* difference between the two types of curves is that the Marshallian curves give *a complete* picture, showing the final result of the whole international-trade mechanism, and relate to *representative bales*, while the ordinary curves relate to the *money prices* of an *individual* commodity, upon the assumption that other things remain equal and in particular that all other prices remain the same, so that they can give only a partial picture.[5]

---

[4] Of course, the data shown in the Marshallian curves could equally well be shown by making the ordinate measure the price per unit of E-bales expressed in G-bales or conversely, that is by making it measure the exchange-ratio. (Such curves have been constructed : for example, by Viner, " The Doctrine of Comparative Cost " in *Weltwirtschaftliches Archiv* (Oct. 1932), vol. 36). Conversely, it is possible to present the data of an ordinary demand curve by measuring along the ordinate not the money price per unit but the total money receipts from the quantity shown on the horizontal axis. Such total demand curves, which superficially resemble the Marshallian curves, are used, *e.g.*, by Auspitz and Lieben, *Untersuchungen über die Theorie des Preises*.

[5] The use of these curves in dealing with problems of international trade is discussed in § 8 of this chapter.

§ 5. The Elasticity of Demand.

We are now sufficiently equipped to lay down a number of rules as to the effect of various circumstances upon the terms of trade. But we have not the space to consider these matters in detail: we must refer the reader to Marshall.[6] Moreover, as Marshall himself points out, his curves are so complex that in practice their applicability to these questions is very restricted. Hence we shall confine ourselves mainly to explaining the concept of elasticity of demand, in the sense in which it is used in connection with these Marshallian curves, and to showing its relation to the usual concept of elasticity of demand.[7]

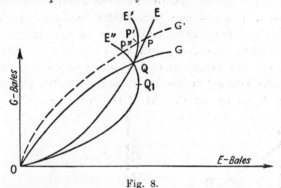

Fig. 8.

Let us take the curve OE, in fig. 8, as given. Then the more urgent is the demand of G, the more favourable to E will be the terms of trade. If the demand of G becomes stronger—owing, for example, to an increase in her population or to an improvement in her productive efficiency, increasing her purchasing power, or to a reduction in transport costs—so that her curve moves from OG to OG′, this will place E in a better position. But if this curve were to move—in consequence, for example, of the imposition of a tariff by G—in the opposite direction, let us say from an initial position OG′ to OG, this would have an adverse effect upon E.[8]

The extent to which a given upward shift in the G-curve turns the terms of trade in favour of E depends upon the shape of the E-curve, that is to say upon the elasticity of E's demand. The

---

[6] *Cf. Money, Credit and Commerce*, Bk. 3, chaps. vii and viii, and especially Appendix J. See Edgeworth, *loc. cit.*
[7] This problem should really be treated mathematically. Such a treatment is to be found in Yntema, *A Mathematical Reformulation of the General Theory of International Trade*, chap. 4.
[8] It does not follow that G would benefit by imposing a tariff. Although she enjoys better terms of trade at the point Q than at P, her general economic position may be better at P.

greater is the curvature of the E-curve—that is, the more inelastic
is E's demand—over the relevant portion, the more favourable to
E will be the new terms of trade. P″ is more favourable to E
than P′ and P′ is more favourable to it than P.

What is the exact meaning, in this context, of ' elastic ' and
' inelastic ' demand, and what is the relation between elasticity
in this sense and the elasticity of ordinary supply and demand
curves? An ordinary demand curve is elastic, over the relevant
(small) portion, if a fall of, say, 1 per cent. in price would be
followed by an increase of more than 1 per cent. in the amount
demanded, causing the total receipts to become greater. More
exactly, the elasticity of demand in such a case is greater than 1.
It is less than 1 when the percentage increase in the amount
demanded is less than the (small) percentage fall in price, so
that total receipts diminish; and it is equal to 1 when the two
percentages are the same, so that total receipts remain constant.

In fig. 9 the demand is elastic or, more exactly, has an elasticity
greater than 1, as far as P. At P the total receipts, represented

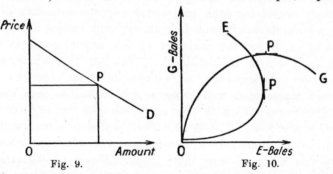

Fig. 9.   Fig. 10.

by the inscribed rectangle, are at a maximum, and the elasticity
is equal to 1. Beyond P the demand is inelastic or, more exactly,
has an elasticity less than 1. The corresponding Marshallian
curves, shown in fig. 10, are elastic from O to P and thereafter
are inelastic. The E-curve becomes inelastic when it turns to
the left and the G-curve when it turns downward. At the turning
point, P, the elasticity is equal to 1.[9] The curve OE″ in fig. 8
is inelastic from Q_1 onwards. In other words, beyond a certain
point (Q_1 in fig. 8), as greater quantities of G-bales are thrown
upon the market in E, their price (the real exchange-ratio or terms

---

[9] The percentage increase in quantity divided by the percentage fall in price
gives a precise measurement of the elasticity of demand. But total receipts remain
constant when these two percentage changes are equal only if the latter are
infinitesimal. Hence we should really distinguish between point-elasticity, to
which our discussion refers, and arc-elasticity. Upon this distinction see Schultz,
Statistical Laws of Demand and Supply, p. 8.

of trade) falls by a greater percentage than the quantity sold increases, so that the total receipts of E-bales diminish. In fig. 8, E obtains a greater quantity of G-bales for a smaller quantity of E-bales at the point P″ than at the point Q.

There is nothing exceptional about an inelastic demand in terms of money for a particular commodity. But it is most unlikely that the elasticity of demand of a country, as shown on a Marshallian curve, will in practice be less than unity. Marshall himself considers such a case to be quite exceptional and interesting more as a *curiosum* than on account of its importance in practice.[1] This view is based upon the following considerations.

We have seen that a movement along the E-curve implies that wages in G have fallen relatively to wages in E. The question is whether the increased quantity of G-bales sold in E, in consequence of this change in the terms of trade in favour of E, will yield greater or smaller total receipts (of E-bales) to G than she obtained before the change. This depends upon several circumstances. It depends upon (a) *the nature of E's demand*, in the ordinary sense, for each individual export-commodity of G. The case which Marshall considers exceptional cannot arise unless the demand of E for the majority of G's export-goods is inelastic.[2] This in itself is improbable.[3] Even so, this alone would not suffice to produce such an exceptional case, for the relatively reduced wages of G will bring *new* commodities into the category of her exports. Thus the issue depends also upon (b) *G's range of possible products*. The greater the number of actual and potential export-goods included in this range—the more many-sided, that is, is G's economy—the more improbable is an inelastic demand for her exports. (c) Let us now drop the assumption of constant costs. Then E will herself produce most or all of the goods which she also imports from G. The change in the terms of trade will cause E merely to contract her output of these goods, and not suddenly to cease producing them at all, while the production of them in G will expand. The issue will then depend also upon the cost-conditions or *the elasticity of supply* of these goods in both countries. If a small rise in money costs leads to a marked

---

[1] The consequences of such a case—some of them quite remarkable—are developed by Marshall, *loc. cit.*, Appendix J. They were in part foreshadowed by J. S. Mill.

[2] To be exact, the weighted average of the individual elasticities must be less than unity.

[3] If G does not represent the rest of the world but is only one country among many countries trading with E, it is extremely improbable. E's demand for, say, wheat may be inelastic, but her demand for wheat from any *one* source, such as G, will be very elastic.

contraction of their output in E,[4] and a small fall in money costs leads to a marked expansion of their output in G, E's elasticity of demand, in the Marshallian sense, will be greater than if the average elasticity of the individual supply curves of the various commodities is relatively small.[5]

These considerations, taken together, make it very unlikely that a country will have an inelastic demand. If we think of G as trading with a number of countries, and not only with E, it is practically certain that the demand of the rest of the world for G's products will not be inelastic. Such a situation would be conceivable only if G produced and exported only one commodity, or a very small number of commodities, in which she had something approaching a monopoly.

Our discussion has shown that the conditions which determine the elasticity of demand of one country for the products of another are very complex. Hence it requires some courage to hazard an estimate of this elasticity in any concrete case. But such estimates have been made. Robertson, for example, believes that the present depression is partly due to the demand of industrial countries for foodstuffs and raw materials being inelastic. He thinks this partly explains the sharp fall in the import-prices of industrial countries relatively to their export-prices and the accompanying depression in their export industries.[6]

Robertson also applies the Marshallian concept of the elasticity of demand of a country to the analysis of the transfer problem,

---

[4] According to Schüller and others this is the case in, for example, the textile industry, the difference between the production costs of different countries being slight, so that the supply of any one country is very elastic. In agriculture the contrary is usually true.

[5] A detailed account of the exact mathematical relation between the elasticity of the Marshallian curves and that of the individual supply-and-demand curves of the particular commodities will be found in Yntema, loc. cit.

[6] Cf. his Economic Fragments (1931), p. 3, his Study of Industrial Fluctuation, pp. 131 and 203-5, his Banking Policy and the Price Level (1926), and his essay on The Terms of Trade in Economic Essays and Addresses (1931) by Pigou and Robertson. In the last-named essay he says : " She [England] is potentially richer than before, for she finds herself with a surplus of productive power, no longer required for obtaining imports but theoretically divertible into other uses. But in so far as that surplus is stereotyped in the form of cotton-stocks, cotton-mills and cotton operatives, those stocks will accumulate, those mills be idle, and those operatives unemployed : there will occur all the recognised symptoms of trade depression." Hicks, in his review of the book (Zeitschrift für Nationalökonomie (1932), vol. 3, p. 634), makes the important objection that if consumers respond to a fall in import-prices by spending a smaller total sum of money upon imports, they will spend more than before upon other goods, and this will facilitate the transfer of factors from the export industries into other employments. It would seem that Mr. Robertson's theory can be upheld against this criticism, if certain monetary assumptions are inserted, namely that the breakdown in the export industries sets up a vicious spiral of credit contraction. We must here observe that in cases of this kind one usually speaks of the elasticity of demand of a country, in the complex Marshallian sense, only after factors of production temporarily set free have been reabsorbed and a new equilibrium has been reached.

and in particular to the question of whether the terms of trade must move against the paying country.[7] He considers how the Marshallian curves would be shifted by Reparations payments and how this would affect the terms of trade. But it is much more difficult to estimate this shift than to estimate the shift in an ordinary demand curve. If we knew the position and shape of the Marshallian curves both originally and after the transfer-payments had been completed, it would be a simple matter to read off the result. But these curves show the final result of the whole mechanism of international trade. In order to form an opinion upon their position and shape after such a transfer, we must try to reconstruct the whole process step by step, and to build them up out of their elements. But this means that we must work with the ordinary supply-and-demand curves, in order to analyse the transfer of purchasing power and the shifting of demand, as Ohlin does and as we have tried to do in chapter VII, § 3. There is no method of attaining this object more directly. One can make a rough estimate of the nature of the money demand for some particular good, but it is almost impossible to estimate the elasticity of the Marshallian demand curve of a country. Guessing the shape of these curves and then reading off the result means simply jumping to the final outcome of a complicated process without analysing it. By assuming Marshall's curves as given we really assume the result. The most we can hope is that *after the event* we can establish *statistically* how the terms of trade have moved, that is to say, what has been the result of a certain shifting of the curves. To this question we now turn.

§ 6. THE TERMS OF TRADE AND THEIR STATISTICAL MEASUREMENT.

We must begin by considering more closely the meaning of this concept, ' the terms of trade,'[8] which plays such a large part in the classical and neo-classical doctrines of English and American writers.

In our simple illustration of Germany and the United States exchanging linen and wheat, with no costs of transport and with

---

[7] He says quite rightly that when we consider discussions of this question we must be careful to make sure which type of demand curve a writer has in mind. Writers, such as Pigou and Taussig, who uphold the view that the paying country suffers an additional transfer-loss in that the payment turns the terms of trade against it, think as a rule of the Marshallian curves, whilst their opponents think of ordinary demand curves and hence, like Ohlin, speak of a shifting of *these* curves.

[8] This is the term now usually applied to this concept. It was employed by Marshall (*Money, Credit and Commerce*, Bk. 3, chap. vi), who suggested (p. 161) ' rate of interchange ' as a possible alternative. Taussig (*International Trade*, chap. 2, p. 8) speaks of ' the barter terms of trade,' and Pigou (*Essays in Applied Economics* (1930), 2nd edn., pp. 149 *et seq.*) of ' the real ratio of interchange.'

constant costs of production, the whole matter is perfectly clear. The terms of trade are equal to the ratio in which linen and wheat are exchanged against one another. It will be remembered that in our illustration they lay between 1 wheat to 1 linen and 1 wheat to 1.5 linen. Under our assumption that each unit of both linen and wheat represents the same expenditure of labour, this ratio is also the ratio at which German labour exchanges against American labour. Hence, thinking of the goods or of the labour lying behind the façade of money prices, we can properly term it a ' real ' ratio. In this simplified case, the real terms of trade and their variations can be measured by either (1) the ratio of money wages[9] or (2) the ratio between the quantity of wheat and the quantity of linen exchanged against one another or (3) the ratio between the money prices (per unit) of the two goods.

If we suppose that many commodities are exported and imported, although still under constant returns and with no costs of transport, we can no longer use physical units of quantity, such as bushels of wheat and yards of linen. But we can use as a measure the ratio between an index[1] of export-prices and an index of import-prices; and under our simplifying assumptions this ratio will coincide with the ratio between money wages in the two countries. We have already seen that this ratio is represented upon the Marshallian demand curve of a country by the slope of a straight line from O to the relevant point upon the curve (being, for example, $\frac{PM}{OM}$ at the point P in fig. 6).

If we suppose, for example, that import-prices rise by 10 per cent. relatively[2] to export-prices, we can conclude that the product of a unit of foreign labour will exchange against the product of 10 per cent. more domestic labour that before, the reason being, say, an increased demand for foreign goods.

Let us now drop all simplifying assumptions, taking account of transport costs and assuming increasing costs in every branch of production. The relations between the above two ratios are now more complicated, and we can no longer use the one as a measure of the other without further investigation.[3]

---

[9] So long as we abstract from transport costs, a comparison of *money* wages between the two countries is the same as a comparison of *real* wages.

[1] Under our assumption of constant costs, all export commodities would have parallel price-movements, and so would all import commodities. Hence there would be no need to compute an average of export-prices or of import-prices : the price of any individual export good would serve as an index of export-prices and the price of any individual import good as an index of import-prices.

[2] The *absolute* prices may, of course, fall.

[3] A systematic analysis of this subject is lacking. See, however, the interesting study of Wilson, *Capital Imports and the Terms of Trade Examined in the Light of Sixty Years of Australian Borrowings* (1931).

The measure which is the simplest and the most frequently used is the ratio between export-prices and import-prices. Since costs are not constant, the prices of different export-goods (or import-goods) will not show parallel movements, so that we must use *averages* of export-prices (and import-prices). Such averages, or indexes, are computed regularly for England by the Board of Trade. Taussig, in his *International Trade* (pp. 411 seq.), gives computations of this kind relating to England, Canada, and the United States. If we represent the prices of the year 1900 by the index-number 100, the ratio of import-prices to export-prices has moved in the following way:

England			Canada		
1880	- -	124	1900	- -	100
1885	- -	123	1905	- -	91.1
1890	- -	113	1910	- -	83.5
1895	- -	111	1913	- -	85.2
1900	- -	100			
1905	- -	107			
1910	- -	112			

These figures show that from 1880 to 1900 there was a continuous improvement in England's terms of trade, the prices of the manufactured goods which formed the bulk of her exports continuously rising relatively to the prices of the foodstuffs and raw materials which formed the bulk of her imports. During the first decade of the present century her terms of trade rapidly worsened, whilst the opposite occurred in the case of Canada.

Nevertheless, we must show caution in interpreting such figures. They measure the exchange-ratio in terms of *goods* but they do *not* coincide (as they do in our simplified example) with the exchange-ratio between G-bales and E-bales in the sense of Marshall, for this latter ratio is measured in terms of *labour*.[4] A difference between these two exchange-ratios may exist[5] for either of two reasons. (1) It may arise from technical improvements which reduce the costs of the export-goods of one country. (2) It may arise from the marked effects of the Law of Diminishing Returns in the countries from which England is drawing an increasing quantity of imports.

The worsening of England's (commodity) terms of trade between 1900 and 1910 was probably due mainly to the former reason.

---

[4] It will be remembered that each G-bale is defined as embodying a *constant* quantity of German labour and capital, and similarly with E-bales.
[5] Robertson points out in his review of Taussig (*Economic Journal* (1928), p. 277) that the latter does not mention this difference between the two ratios.

M

If so; it is much less alarming than it appears at first sight. It means simply that during this period the English export industries made greater technical progress than that made by her foreign suppliers in the production of foodstuffs and raw materials.[6] In such a case, the terms of trade in the second and more fundamental (Marshallian) sense do not worsen.[7] The fall in the ratio at which export-goods exchange for import-goods is not accompanied by a parallel fall in English wages relatively to foreign wages. For the technical progress enables a greater quantity of export-goods to be produced with the same labour as before.

If the two ratios—the commodity terms of trade and the labour terms of trade—were to move in different ways for the second reason, this would place England in a far more unfavourable position. For then the relative rise in the prices of her imports would be due to an increased demand for goods of this kind, coupled with the fact that greater quantities of them could be produced only at increasing costs. The increased demand for such goods might come from other countries, or from the consumers of the countries which produced them: it need not necessarily come, even in part, from England. But it would mean that England would have to pay dearer than before for her imports. In such a case, the worsening in England's commodity terms of trade would represent a still greater worsening in her labour terms of trade, since the higher prices of her imports would embody an increased proportion of rent accruing to foreign landowners.

It is obvious that direct statistical investigation and measurement can be applied only to the commodity terms of trade. We can only conjecture, with the help of indirect indications, how the labour terms of trade have moved.

Taussig has introduced yet another distinction—between the 'net' and the 'gross' barter terms of trade.[8] His net barter terms of trade are the ratio between import-prices and export-prices, which we have called simply the commodity terms of trade. According to him, this ratio is appropriate only when the balance

---

[6] The opposite was the case in the last quarter of the nineteenth century—owing to such changes as the opening-up of the American Middle West to wheat production—and again in the post-War period. This partly explains the fall in the prices of foodstuffs and raw materials relatively to the prices of industrial products.

[7] But, of course, it is true that the position of the country in question would be still better if the reduction in the costs of producing her exports was not accompanied by a fall in her *commodity* terms of trade. Such a situation might arise if there happened to be a simultaneous increase in the foreign demand for her goods or a simultaneous decrease in her own demand for foreign goods.

[8] *International Trade*, p. 113. *Cf.* his article, " The Change in Great Britain's Trade Terms after 1900 " in *Economic Journal* (1925), vol. 35, and the criticism by Viner, " Theorie des auswärtigen Handels " in *Die Wirtschaftstheorie der Gegenwart* (1928), vol. 4.

of payments of the country in question includes nothing but payments for goods and services. If it includes unilateral payments, so that there is an excess of either exports or imports, we should consider the gross and not the net barter terms of trade in forming a judgment upon the gain which the country derives from its international trade. The *gross* terms relate to the *total money value* of exports as compared with the *total money value* of imports, but both totals are obtained by correcting the crude figures by the relevant price-index, in order to eliminate changes due merely to a change in the price-level of exports or imports.

This procedure enables us to compare the total (corrected) value of the goods which a country parts with and the total (corrected) value of the goods which she receives. According to Taussig, when a country has an export surplus (because she is making Reparations payments, or paying interest, or repaying or granting a loan), the net terms of trade cover only that part of her exports which represents payment for her current imports and hence give too favourable a picture of her position.[9] Conversely, when a country has an import surplus, the net terms give too unfavourable a result. The following table[1] makes clear the relations between the net and the gross commodity terms of trade and the method of computing them.

England's Net and Gross Terms of Trade.

Index of		Net Terms of Trade $\dfrac{A}{B}$	Value in £ Millions.		Value after correcting for Price-Changes.		Corrected Values expressed as Relatives. (1900 = 100).		Gross Terms of Trade $\left(\dfrac{I}{H}\right)$
Import-Prices. (1900 = 100).	Export-Prices.		Imports.	Exports.	Imports. $\dfrac{D}{A}$	Exports. $\dfrac{E}{B}$	Imports.	Exports.	
(A)	(B)	(C)	(D)	(E)	(F)	(G)	(H)	(I)	(J)
107	95	113	356	263	333	278	72·4	98·6	136
100	100	100	460	291	460	291	100	100	100
110	98	112	575	430	525	438	114·1	150·3	132

[9] In contrast to the customary but superficial mercantilist view, Taussig regards an export surplus as a loss or, at least, as a temporary sacrifice. But, of course, in certain circumstances it may be a symptom of a favourable position.
[1] *International Trade*, pp. 251 and 412.

The actual value as recorded in the trade statistics of, for example, imports in 1890 was £356 (million), but column A shows that import-prices were 7 per cent. higher in 1890 than in the base year, 1900; we accordingly divide the crude figure of 356 by 1.07, obtaining 333 (column F). The rest of the table is self-explanatory.

From 1890 to 1900 the net terms of trade improved, import-prices falling relatively to export-prices. From 1900 to 1910 the movement was in the opposite direction. The gross terms of trade show a much greater improvement than the net terms, over the former period. This arises from the increase in the import surplus, which in turn is due to the fact that the export of capital was much smaller in 1900 than in 1890. In 1910 the export of capital was considerably greater; and hence the excess of imports was *relatively* smaller and the gross terms of trade more unfavourable.[2]

Certain comments may be made upon this proposal of Taussig to substitute the gross terms of trade for the net terms. To draw up a balance-sheet of the 'real' values exported and imported is certainly interesting and illuminating. Nevertheless, it is quite essential to know the reason for the surplus of imports or exports. It is obviously not a matter of indifference whether an export surplus arises from the payment of Reparations, as with Germany from 1930 to 1931, or from the granting of foreign loans, as with the United States in the post-War period, or from the payment of interest upon foreign loans and the repayment of such loans, as with Germany in 1932. It will not do to lump together in one category these different kinds of payments.[3] Nor is it at all clear why the values which leave a country as tribute payments or as foreign loans should be introduced into the national balance-sheet in this complicated way. It would be much simpler to state the amount of such sums directly.

It is misleading to regard an export surplus arising from the grant of a credit to a solvent debtor as an unfavourable symptom and to treat it in the same way as a payment of tribute. It is true that one could try to correct this by taking a period of time long enough to include the repayment of such credits, as well as the granting of them. But this course is not open if the export of capital goes on continuously. And even if we manage to find a period of time which is complete in the sense that all foreign loans made during the period are repaid within the period, and that it includes no repayments of loans granted earlier, the picture

[2] Of course, in any concrete case it is necessary, as Taussig points out, to study the figures over a long series of years, in order to get a more accurate picture.
[3] Taussig himself makes this point in another part of his book, pp. 117 *et seq.*

is still misleading. It is misleading because of the unilateral *interest-payments*, which give the creditor country a surplus of imports over the period as a whole. This gives the impression that the creditor country obtains a one-sided advantage. But we must remember that the capital which it lent abroad could have been profitably used at home. Hence, as Viner observes, when drawing up a balance-sheet of the values which a country parts with and receives, we should include something for the services of the capital it exports as a *contra* to the interest-payments it receives. Viner also points out that it is dangerous to make a sharp distinction between ' services ' (such as shipping services) and the services of capital, since the former always include some interest on capital. To illustrate this, he constructs the following case : " An American oil company uses the services of an English fleet of oil-tankers which cost £1,000,000 to construct, and for this ' shipping service ' pays £200,000 yearly. Of this £200,000, £50,000 is in fact interest on the English capital invested in the ships, another £50,000 represents amortisation to cover the wearing-out of the ships, which is equivalent to a yearly export of ships, and not more than £100,000 represents pure shipping services. Let us suppose that in another case an English fleet of oil-tankers is sold to an American company for £1,000,000, payable over twenty years at a rate of interest of 5 per cent. Let us further suppose that the operation of this fleet is entrusted to an English shipping company, which receives £100,000 a year for its services. The exports of England now include as before £200,000 yearly, of which £50,000 without question represents the export of ships, another £50,000 interest paid for the use of English capital, and £100,000 payment for shipping services. There is no fundamental economic difference between these two cases. Yet Taussig, in the first case, would include under the export of shipping services two items of £50,000 yearly, one of which would appear in the second case, on his method of reckoning, as an export of ships, while the other would not appear at all."[4]

Apart from all these difficulties, we must beware of treating a balance-sheet of this kind, which sets the ' real values ' which a country exports against those which it imports, as a measure of the gain or loss which a country derives from its international economic transactions.[5] It is clear that, for example, Reparations payments should be counted as a loss; it is equally clear that this loss cannot be ascribed to international trade. The part played

---

[4] *Loc. cit.*, p. 123.
[5] Taussig, of course, does *not* do this.

by the terms of trade in the computation of gain and loss was originally a different one. The concept was used to show how the total gain, namely the increase in total production, was *distributed* between the two countries. The bulk of the gain would accrue to the one country or to the other according as the terms of trade were near the one or the other of their two possible limits. It is fundamentally impossible to discover from the terms of trade, in any of the above senses, what is the absolute ' gain ' which a country derives from the international division of labour. We can discover from them only favourable or unfavourable *changes* due to shifts in demand, and, possibly, the existence of what we have termed[6] the *secondary* burden arising from unilateral payments. But we have seen above that the bald statistical findings, taken by themselves, are open to various possible interpretations, on account of the continuous changes in the data arising from such causes as technical progress.

Taussig has pointed out[7] that we cannot speak of a loss when the terms of trade are turned against a country by an increase in its demand[8] for foreign products. For such a change in demand is a *voluntary* act, and when a person decides to purchase different goods from those he purchased formerly, and does purchase them although their prices rise, we must conclude that he thinks he gains by changing his habits.[9] But, when stating that the terms of trade have become more or less favourable, we should be clear as to what we are comparing. In the above case, for example, we can say that the situation which results from the change in demand is more unfavourable than it would have been had the foreign supply been so elastic that *despite* the increased demand the terms of trade worsened only slightly or not at all.

But these discussions about the ' gain ' from international trade and from changes in the international economic situation of a country ignore such important factors as changes in distribution and gains or losses due to the fact that a cumulative process of expansion or contraction might be started or interrupted, retarded or accelerated. Therefore these considerations have such an unreal air that there is little point in pursuing them further.

---

[6] Chap. vii, p. 68.
[7] *Loc. cit.*, pp. 117 and 118.
[8] Clearly he is thinking of demand in the ordinary sense. But such a change also produces a similar shift in the Marshallian curve.
[9] But we should ask whether such a shift in demand arises from a change in tastes or from a rise in the prices of *other* goods.

§ 7. Statistical Illustrations.

The following chart illustrates the above remarks. It shows the terms of trade of *Great Britain* for the years 1920 to 1932. It is a continuation (leaving out the war years) of the computation made by Taussig for the period 1880 to 1913. The figures have been calculated for each quarter by his methods. The continuous line shows what we have called the commodity terms of trade and what he calls the net barter terms of trade, obtained by dividing the index of import-prices by the index of export-prices. The dotted line shows what he calls the gross barter terms of trade, obtained by dividing the total value of exports, measured at the export-prices of 1924, by the total value of imports, measured at the import-prices of 1924; the average of the year 1924 is taken as 100. The right-hand scale relates only to the broken line, which shows for each quarter the actual value, in £ million, of the excess of imports.

This chart, like that of Taussig, shows that the net terms and the gross terms tend to move in the same direction, but that the fluctuations of the latter are much more marked. Again, the

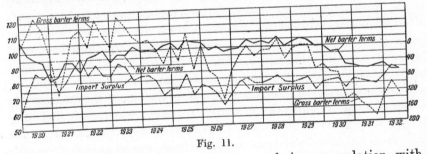

Fig. 11.

movement of the gross terms shows an obvious correlation with the movement of the import surplus, both rising from 1923 to 1926 and falling from 1926 to 1929. After 1929, however, there is a discrepancy: the import surplus does not increase—indeed, after 1931 (when Great Britain went off gold) it falls somewhat—but, nevertheless, there is an improvement in the gross terms of trade. There are two reasons for this. The first is the marked fall in the prices of foodstuffs and raw materials, which enabled Great Britain to keep her total volume of imports at a comparatively high level. The second is the sharp diminution since 1929 in the absolute total value of both imports and exports. This second reason calls for a little explanation.

The present depression, like others, has been marked by a fall in production and in prices and a growth of Protection, which have brought about a heavy decrease in the total value of the foreign trade of nearly every country in the world. The general rule, when this happens, is that a creditor country, with an ' unfavourable ' or ' passive ' balance of trade, finds that the proportionate fall in the total value of its exports is greater than the proportionate fall in the total value of its imports (whilst a debtor country, with a ' favourable ' balance of trade, finds the opposite). This is because the *absolute amount* of certain items in the balance of payments, and notably of external interest-payments, is fixed, whilst—in addition—the export of capital (from creditor countries) tends to diminish. Hence the absolute amount of the import surplus of a creditor country diminishes comparatively little, if at all. But with a falling volume of trade, this implies an increasingly ' unfavourable ' ratio between its total imports and its total exports.

These considerations show how misguided it is, in such a situation, for creditor countries to frown upon their (relatively) growing surplus of imports and to look with envy at the (relative) growth in the export surplus of their debtors. If they try to reduce their ' unfavourable ' balance of trade by restricting their imports, they will only make the supposed evil still greater. This end, which they desire so keenly, will be attained only when the efforts of the Protectionists, quite probably in the debtor as well as in the creditor countries, have so injured the former that they can no longer pay the interest and capital which they owe.

One other feature of the chart deserves mention, namely, the deep trough formed in the second half of 1926 by the line depicting the gross barter terms of trade. This has its origin in the brief General Strike and the prolonged coal stoppage of that year, which caused exports of coal and other products to diminish, while imports increased. Since there was little change in the ratio of export-prices to import-prices, this of course made the British balance of trade especially ' unfavourable ' and caused the gross barter terms of trade to show a marked ' improvement.' This should be a sufficient warning not to treat an ' improvement ' in the gross barter terms of trade, without further investigation, as a favourable sign.

As a further illustration, we show the movement in the commodity terms of trade (or the ' net barter ' terms of trade) of *Germany* from 1924 to 1932. Unfortunately, no index of either import-prices or export-prices is computed for Germany. As a substitute for the former, we employ the official price-index of raw materials and semi-finished goods, and for the latter the

official price-index of finished goods. This procedure opens up
a possible source of error, since imports do not consist exclusively
of raw materials and semi-finished goods nor exports exclusively
of finished products. But the error is perhaps not so large as to
make the result useless, for goods of the former category have
formed about half of the commodity imports and finished products
have formed over two-thirds of the commodity exports. The official
price-index of raw materials and semi-finished goods (which we take
as representative of import-prices) and the official price-index of
finished products (which we take as representative of export-prices)
are both computed monthly (with 1913 = 100), but to make the chart
easier to read we have taken three-monthly averages and have called
the figure for the middle of 1928, 100. Hence the following curve
may be taken to show quarterly movements in the commodity terms
of trade.

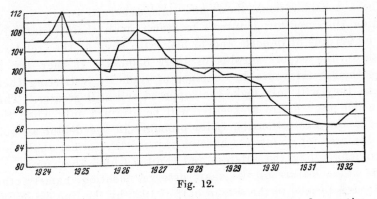

Fig. 12.

It will be seen that the commodity terms of trade continuously
improved after the beginning of 1927. The swing in Germany's
balance of trade which took place in 1929 did not halt this improvement. But it was checked towards the end of 1931 and thereafter
the terms of trade began to worsen. This coincided with the
marked increase in Germany's export surplus following that
summer of 1931—so disastrous to the German economy.

§ 8. THE DIRECT EFFECT OF INTERNATIONAL TRADE UPON PRICE AND SALES.

This is the appropriate place to consider the use of a most
powerful analytical tool, namely the ordinary supply and demand
curves. As we have already remarked, these give only a partial
view of the whole situation, but, nevertheless, they are quite
indispensable to a study of the *direct* effects of international trade

and of measures of trade policy, such as tariffs. and their use is an essential preliminary to a more far-reaching analysis.

These curves are used, of course, to explain the price and sales of a particular commodity in a single market, but they can equally well be used for the same purpose when there is international trade, and therefore two or more different markets for the commodity. This method has been systematically applied by Richard Schüller[1] and Enrico Barone[2] and forms the basis of countless other treatments of problems of international trade.[3]

The mechanism of the market fixes the price of any good at the level which equates the amount supplied and the amount demanded—in the language of diagrams, at the point where the supply curve and the demand curve intersect. If the price were above this equilibrium point, it would be forced down to it by competition among sellers, and if it were below it, it would be pushed up by competition among buyers.

Fig. 13 shows the conditions of supply and demand relating to a given commodity A in each of two countries.

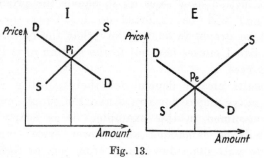

Fig. 13.

Before trade takes place between these two markets, the price of A is P_i in country I and P_e in country E. Suppose now that trade takes place. The commodity will be exported by E, since in that market its price is lower than in I. Its price will rise in E and fall in I; the amount produced (or supplied) will rise in E and fall in I; the amount consumed (or demanded) will fall in E and rise in I. If we provisionally abstract from transport costs, and consider the two countries as together forming one market, throughout which there is a uniform price, we can say that the new equilibrium price will be that which equates the total supply and the total demand of the two countries taken together.

[1] *Schutzzoll und Freihandel*, especially pp. 58 *et seq.* and 101 *et seq.*
[2] *Grundzüge der Theoritischen Nationalökonomie*, 2nd edn. (1935), pt. 3, pp. 101 *et seq.*
[3] *Cf.* Colm, " Das Gesetz der komparativen Kosten—das Gesetz der komparativen Kaufkraft " in *Weltwirtschaftliches Archiv* (1930), vol. 32, pp. 371 *et seq.;* Carver, *Principles of National Economy* (1921).

This result can best be demonstrated by supposing the left-hand
diagram in fig. 13 to be turned round and placed back-to-back
against the right-hand diagram, as in fig. 14.

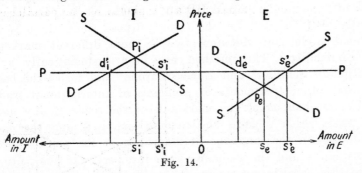

Fig. 14.

The new price (in both countries) is P. The total supply
(or production) s'_i s'_e is equal to the total demand (or consumption)
d'_i d_e. In E, owing to the rise in price, production has increased
(from Os_e to Os'_e), demand has fallen (from Os_e to Od'_e), and the
excess of production over sales d'_e s'_e equals the production deficit
d'_i s'_i in I and will be exported to I. Thus the new price-
line P must be drawn in such a way that the section of it lying
between the two I curves is equal to the section of it lying between
the two E curves.

These results clearly depend for their validity upon whether
the demand curve slopes downward and the supply curve upward,[4]
as we have assumed in this example. It is nearly always true
that more will be demanded at a lower price—that is, that a
demand curve will slope downwards from left to right; and when
costs are increasing, as they are in the great majority of cases,[5]
the supply curve must slope upward. Hence our results are usually,
although not universally, valid.

The direct effects of transport costs and of other obstacles to
trade, such as tariffs and prohibitions, can be readily shown with
the aid of such a diagram. An import prohibition means simply
a return to the situation which prevailed before trade took place.
A tariff, provided it is not prohibitive, exerts a weaker influence
in the same direction.

The producers in the exporting country E regard the imposition
of an import duty by the importing country I, or of an export
duty by E, as equivalent to a reduction, by the amount of the
duty, in the price which they can obtain by selling in I. This

---

[4] Unless, of course, we reverse them, as we reversed the curves of I in fig. 14.
[5] The possibility of exceptions to the general rule of increasing costs is discussed in § 4 of the following chapter.

is shown in fig. 15 by lowering the whole curve-system of I, relatively to that of E, by the amount of the duty T. (The same procedure would apply, of course, if T represented transport costs.) Thus in I the curves SS and DD are replaced by the parallel curves S′S′ and D′D′.

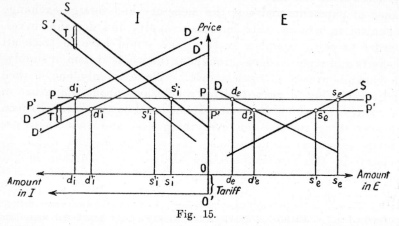

Fig. 15.

In the new equilibrium, the price-line P′P′ must be such that the portion of it between the two E-curves equals the portion of it between the two *new* I-curves: $d'_e s'_e = d'_i s'_i$. It must, therefore, lie below the old price-line PP. The price in E falls from P to P′ and the price in I rises by the difference between the amount of the duty and PP′. For the difference between the price in I and the price in E must equal the duty, so long as the duty is not prohibitive. (The price in I must be reckoned from the sunken axis, OO′ equalling T.) The quantity produced falls in E from Os_e to Os'_e. Those units of the commodity which now cannot cover their costs are no longer produced, and in the new equilibrium the marginal costs of the reduced output are sufficiently below the old marginal costs to make production profitable despite the tariff. Exports are contracted from $d_e s_e$ to $d'_e s'_e$, but consumption (in E) is increased from Od_e to Od'_e. Production in I has expanded, in response to the rise in price, from Os_i to Os'_i and consumption in I has contracted from Od_i to Od'_i.

The effects of a duty, and in particular its incidence as between the two countries, are discussed more fully in chapter XV, § 1. But before leaving this subject, it may be well to say a little about the limitations of the supply-and-demand approach or, as it is sometimes termed, ' the method of partial equilibrium.'

This method can be applied only to some *one* commodity, taken by itself; and, even so, it rests upon the assumption that other things remain equal: if any change occurs in any of these other data, it may cause a shift in the supply-curve or demand-curve of the commodity in question. Thus we can use it to study, for example, the effects of a particular duty only if we can assume that the indirect effects may be neglected. A full analysis must take account of the fact that the imposition of a duty affects the balance of payments and sets the monetary and foreign-exchange mechanism in motion, shifting other supply- and demand-curves. In order to get a complete picture, one would have to trace all the effects and repercussions throughout the whole system of supply- and demand-curves—a hopeless task.[6] There is only one method which enables us to draw fruitful conclusions about *the situation as a whole,* and which does not restrict itself to the barren truism that everything depends on everything else and that there are as many equations as unknowns. This is the method which we developed in the last chapter and shall develop further in the next, namely, the Theory of Comparative Cost.

We must emphasise, however, that the doctrine of supply and demand, if carried right through to its logical conclusion, merges in the Theory of Comparative Cost. But for this it is necessary to make assumptions not only about the shape and position of supply- and demand-curves but also about *the way in which they shift* when the monetary mechanism comes into play. Let us suppose that a duty is placed upon the commodity A. Less of it will be imported, the balance of payments will become favourable, the quantity of money will expand, supply- and demand-curves will be shifted upwards, and the consequence will be that the import of certain commodities will expand and the export of others contract, whilst some new commodities may now be imported and the export of some others may now cease—exactly as the Theory of Comparative Cost declares.

It is purely a question of exposition whether one begins, as we have done, with the labour cost or (as will be explained in the next chapter) with the substitution cost and comes back later to the ordinary supply- and demand-curves or whether, conversely, one begins with the latter and goes on from them to the labour-cost or substitution-cost relations. But if the later course is chosen, and one wishes to get a general view of the whole situation, some simplifying assumptions must be made about *the way in which the curves shift.* For example, Yntema, who employs this method,[7] assumes that each curve moves to a position parallel to its old one and that all the curves are shifted to the same extent.[8] Despite this sweeping simplification, his mathematical solutions are very complicated.

If one does not make this simplification—which underlies also the Theory of Comparative Cost[9]—and takes account of the possibility that the working of the

---

[6] We know, from our study of the monetary mechanism, that the exports of the country imposing the duty must diminish unless the duty merely results in additional imports of other commodities equal to the diminution in the imports of the commodity subject to the duty (*e.g.,* flour instead of wheat or tea instead of coffee).

[7] *A Mathematical Reformulation of the General Theory of International Trade* (1932).

[8] Similarly, Colm, *loc. cit.*

[9] We have assumed that when money flows in, the money costs (the price of labour) and hence the money prices of all commodities rise to the same extent. This, together with the further assumption that the real costs (the expenditure of labour per unit of product, or the coefficients of production)—whether they are constant or variable as output increases—remain as they were before, unchanged by the new situation, implies that every supply-curve moves to a parallel position.

monetary mechanism may *not* shift all the curves to the same extent, and that with this shifting they may simultaneously change their shape (instead of moving to a parallel position), it is quite impossible to get a general view of the result. This, however, it not because the method is inadequate but because the conditions of the real world, or rather the conceivable possibilities, are so complex.

CHAPTER XII.

INTERNATIONAL TRADE AND GENERAL EQUILIBRIUM.

§ 1. THE LABOUR THEORY OF VALUE DISCARDED.

The present chapter tries to display the Theory of International Trade as a constituent part of the modern doctrine of economic equilibrium, which is associated with such names as Menger, Böhm-Bawerk, Wicksteed, Marshall, Walras, Pareto, Schumpeter, Knight, &c.,[1] and which finds its most exact expression in the system of equations of the mathematical economists.

Our first step towards this end must be to show that our theory remains valid even if we drop the assumptions of the Labour Theory of Value. This latter doctrine holds good, as a special case of the general theory, if there is only one factor of production: homogeneous labour. But in reality any country has a great number of different factors of production—a whole range of different qualities of labour, of land and other natural resources, and of produced means of production, such as buildings, plant and equipment, and raw materials. It is technically impossible to measure all these diverse factors of production in terms of any one common unit of quantity; they certainly cannot all be resolved into simple unskilled labour. A further point is that many of these factors of production are specific[2]: either they can be used only for one particular purpose, or they would yield so much less if transferred to another use (machinery, for example, being used as scrap-iron) that in fact they are not transferred. This specificity may arise from obstacles to movement, such as the legal prohibition of migration or prohibitive transportation cost, or from the technical unsuitability of the factor for a different use; and it may be permanent or it may be overcome, in time, as when workers are trained for a different employment.

We saw in chapter X that the sole purpose for which we introduced the Labour Theory of Value was to determine the relative prices in each of the two countries. As Ricardo explained,

---

[1] It is true that these writers differ on various points of detail and of exposition, but here we are speaking of the fundamental principles which they all hold in common.

[2] The distinction between specific and non-specific factors of production, the latter being capable of employment in a number of different uses, was first introduced by Wieser.

labour cost fixes the prices through its influence upon supply. This can be shown diagrammatically in the following way:

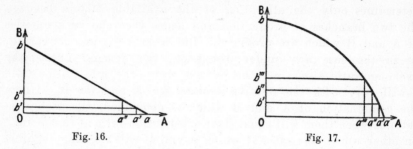

Fig. 16.   Fig. 17.

Let us assume constant costs, each unit of commodity A requiring the expenditure of one, and each unit of commodity B of two, units of labour. In fig. 16, quantities of A are measured along the X axis and quantities of B up the Y axis, so that any point in the area between the two axes represents a certain combination of A and B. If the whole of the available supply of labour is employed in producing A, it can produce the quantity Oa. For every two units of A whose production is forgone, one unit of B can be produced. Thus the available labour can produce, instead of Oa of A and no B, Oa' of A plus Ob' of B, or Oa" of A plus Ob" of B, and so on; or it can produce Ob of B and no A. Thus all the possible combinations of A and B which can be produced by utilising all the available labour lie upon the straight line ab. The exchange-ratio between A and B will equal the constant ratio—of two units of A to one unit of B—at which A and B can be substituted for one another.

When we assume increasing labour costs for both A and B, the substitution-curve takes the form shown in fig. 17. It is possible, as before, to produce Oa of A and no B. If it is wished to produce Ob' of B, the quantity aa' of A must be forgone. A further equal quantity b'b" of B can be obtained only at the cost of giving up a greater quantity of A (a'a" > aa'), and so on; the more the production of B is substituted for that of A, the greater is the cost of producing B and the smaller is the cost of producing A, and the greater is the amount of A which must be forgone in order to obtain an additional unit of B. The same applies, *mutatis mutandis*, if we start from the point b: an increasingly greater quantity of B must be forgone in order to produce an additional unit of A. Hence the substitution-curve ab is concave towards the origin, O.[3]

---

[3] The exceptional case of decreasing costs is discussed in § 4 of this chapter. It is represented, on a diagram of this kind, by a curve which is convex towards

How is the exchange-ratio determined in such a case? Under constant costs, it is determined solely by the costs : the demand determines only the allocation of the available factors between the two branches of production and hence the relative quantities of A and B which are produced. But when costs are increasing, as in the case now under discussion, the demand affects the exchange-ratio also, since the relative costs—the substitution-ratio —will vary with the relative demand for A and for B. Given the combination of A and B which is demanded, the exchange-ratio between them will equal their substitution-ratio at that point.[4] In other words, the ratio at which A and B will exchange against one another in the market will be equal to the ratio of their marginal costs. Any other situation would be one of disequilibrium : there would be an incentive to produce more A and less B, or conversely.

It is now obvious that we have no further need of the Labour Theory of Value. We can derive the conditions of substitution between the two commodities, and express them in the form of a substitution-curve, when many different factors of production are available just as well as when there is only homogeneous labour. However many factors there may be, the relative prices of the two commodities will be determined (given the demand) by their costs—but we must now follow the Austrian school in measuring costs not by the absolute amount of labour required but by the alternatives forgone. Thus the marginal cost of a given quantity x of commodity A must be regarded as that quantity of commodity B which must be forgone in order that x, instead of $x-1$, units of A can be produced.[5] The exchange-ratio on the market between A and B must equal their costs in this sense of the term.

The proportions in which the various factors of production are combined, in each of the two fields, will of course vary with the relative quantities of A and B which are produced. Thus if more B and less A is produced, more use will be made of those factors of production which can be employed only in the production of B, or which are especially suitable for producing B and com-

---

0. See Lerner, " The Diagrammatical Representation of Cost Conditions in International Trade " in *Economica*, No. 37 (Aug. 1932), pp. 346 *et seq.* Mr. Lerner, in Paretian terminology, calls our ' substitution-curve ' a ' production indifference curve.' He shows how the curves of two countries can be added together and how the point of equilibrium is the point where a consumption indifference curve touches such a curve without cutting it.

[4] Geometrically, the exchange-ratio equals the slope of the tangent to the substitution-curve at the point in question. *Cf.* Lerner, *loc. cit.*

[5] American writers introduced the term ' opportunity cost.' See especially Green, " Pain Cost and Opportunity Cost," *Quarterly Journal of Economics*, vol. 8 (1894), p. 218, and Davenport, *Value and Distribution* (1908), chap. 7, and Knight (see footnote 7).

paratively unsuitable for producing A. If a factor is completely specific to the production of one commodity it will have no value at all unless the amount of that commodity produced is sufficient to enable all the available units of the factor to be employed.[6] But we shall consider this point more fully in § 3.

The rest of this section will be devoted to the further elucidation of the proposition that the exchange-ratio between two commodities will be determined by their substitution costs. In particular, we must prove that it applies to a modern monetary economy.[7] We begin by discussing what determines the form of the substitution-curve.

The greater the proportion of the available factors which can be employed in producing either the one or the other commodity, the flatter will be the curve, and the smaller will be the change in the relative prices of the two commodities associated with a change in the combination of them which is produced. If, however, most of the available factors are specific to the production of either A or B, the curve will have more of a bulge, and there will be a marked change in relative prices if an alteration in demand causes a shift in production. An extreme example of this is shown in fig. 18. We can think of A as an agricultural

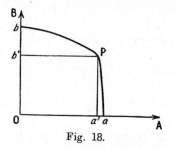

Fig. 18.

product and of B as an industrial product. The only factor of production which is common to both A and B is labour, and— at any rate in the short run—the mobility of labour between the

[6] The Labour Theory of Value may be regarded as presenting a special case, although a highly improbable one, of the general solution given here. For it makes the simplifying assumption that all the available factors are equally suitable for the production of either A or B, none of the factors being in the least specific.

[7] The best and most exact formulation of the general theory under discussion in non-mathematical terms will be found in the writings of F. H. Knight. See especially his two essays, " A Suggestion for Simplifying the Statement of the General Theory of Price," *Journal of Political Economy*, vol. 36 (June 1928), pp. 356 *et seq.*, and " Fisher's Interest Theory," *Journal of Political Economy*, vol. 39 (April 1931), pp. 181 *et seq.* See also his *Risk, Uncertainty and Profit* (1921), chaps. 3 and 4. Recently he has introduced a number of qualifications (see his two essays, " Bemerkungen über Nurtzen und Kosten " in *Zeitschrift für Nationalökonomie*, vol. vi, 1935) which are partly identical with those discussed in § 3, point 3, of the present chapter.

two branches is quite small.   Hence the curve has the kind of
shape shown in the diagram.   The sharp kink at P indicates that
the production of B cannot be expanded much, even if the production of A is greatly contracted or quite abandoned, and
conversely.

The shape of the curve reflects the fact that only a small part
of the available factors can be transferred from one branch of
production to the other.   If no factors whatever could be transferred, the curve would become the L-shaped line b'Pa', indicating
that it is impossible to bring about even the smallest increase
in the output of one commodity by contracting the output of the
other.[8]   The reason why a change in demand leads to a comparatively great change in relative prices, in such cases, is that production cannot adapt itself to the new demand-situation.

The shape of any substitution-curve will vary according to the
length of time which is supposed to elapse between the old situation,
represented by one point on the curve, and the new situation, represented by another.   The longer the time allowed for production to
adapt itself, the flatter will be the curve.   In the short run, most
means of production, such as plant and equipment and even labour,
are specific.   In the long run, plant and equipment wear out or
become obsolete, and labour can be trained for other jobs, while in
the very long run a new generation of workers replaces the old.
Thus labour and capital can be diverted, in time, to other branches
of production.[9]   But it will be noted that our doctrine is by no
means a purely static one.   It does not relate only to a hypothetical
final equilibrium, in which there is no incentive for further movements of factors between industries.   It applies also to short
periods.[1]   For even in the short run some movement of factors can

---

[8] A hair-splitter might object to calling this a substitution-curve, since by
hypothesis no substitution can take place, but this purely verbal objection need not
detain us.
[9] See Knight, *Fisher's Interest Theory*, loc. cit., p. 189. But I cannot
altogether agree with his statement (p. 196), " There can be no question that, if
sufficient time for adjustment is allowed, productive capacity can be transferred
from nearly any use to nearly any other without serious diminution in its relative
efficacy in the expanding industry. That is, the general rule for the long run . . .
is approximately constant cost; the amount of one commodity which must be given
up in order to produce an additional unit of another is generally not much affected
by the relative amount produced." He at once qualifies this by adding, " given time
for readjustment, and speaking of important industries and of changes within a
range which does not take either of those (industries) affected out of that class."
Even so, it seems to me definitely an exaggeration. Nevertheless, it is true that
the adaptability of a modern economy is much greater than is usually supposed.
In particular, physical capital goods are more mobile and less specific than is
commonly believed. (See the interesting article by Seltzer, " The Mobility of
Capital," *Quarterly Journal of Economics*, vol. 46 (May 1932), pp. 496 *et seq.*)
[1] The twofold division into short run and long run is an over-simplification.
As Marshall has suggested, we should assume a whole series of ' runs ' of different
lengths.

take place : for example, whenever a particular capital good wears out or is discarded, the capital which it represents (provided that sufficient provision has been made for its amortisation) again becomes ' free capital,' which need not be reinvested in the same form as before.

We have seen that the curve will be less flat in the short run than in the long run. This implies that a change in demand will at first produce a relatively marked change in prices. In the industry towards which demand has turned, time will be required for establishments to attain their optimal capacity, for additional workers to learn their new tasks properly, and so on. In the industry from which demand has turned away, output will not at once diminish by the full amount appropriate to the new situation. Many of its means of production will be either completely specific or capable of employment elsewhere only at a heavy loss. Provided that prime costs can be covered, these will continue to be used, although, of course, their value will be written down. Hence output will remain comparatively large and, owing to the decrease in demand, there will be a comparatively great fall in the prices of the products. As time goes on, the situation will alter. On the one hand, new firms and factors will enter the expanding industry, and its output will increase. On the other hand, in the contracting industry, machinery and other appliances of production will in time wear out and will not be replaced, and hence its output will diminish. Thus the fall in the prices of its products, relatively to the prices of the products of the expanding industry, will become less than it was at first.

This sequence of events can be observed after the imposition or increase of import duties, which divert demand away from the foreign suppliers, and after a time away from the export industries of the country in question, and towards the protected industries.

We must now show the application of this reasoning to a modern money economy. Of course we cannot state directly the substitution-ratio between two commodities, saying, for example, that a certain change in the relative prices of wheat and motor cars will cause one additional motor car to be produced in place of so many bushels of wheat. Nevertheless our doctrine can be applied in its essentials, given certain conditions, to a modern economy.

The substitution-relations between the commodities are no longer direct, but are indirect, operating through the medium of money costs. All the various substitution curves are brought, so to speak, under one common denominator, being split up into the money cost-curves of the individual commodities. Hence by ' costs ' we shall in future mean money costs, unless otherwise stated, and not labour-cost or opportunity-cost.

Our proposition remains valid in a monetary economy under the following assumptions: (1) The price of every product equals its marginal (money) cost, this being the sum of the prices of the additional factors required to produce x units instead of $x-1$ units; (2) the units of any factor of production, provided that they are mobile and substitutable for one another, have the same price in all uses; (3) the price of every factor of production, including immobile and specific factors, equals its marginal productivity. This—the value of the addition to the physical product due to the addition of one unit of the factor—is the same in all uses, provided that the factor-units are similar and substitutable for one another.

These conditions, as is well known, are brought about by competition. Workers[2] and landowners and, in general, owners of means of production, try to get as much as possible for the services of their labour or land or other factors. The entrepreneurs who hire these services endeavour (given such circumstances as the state of technical knowledge) to combine them and utilise them in the most productive ways and, in general, to conduct their businesses in such a manner as to maximise their own incomes. It follows that if the marginal productivity of any factor in some given establishment is less than its general marginal productivity (which equals its price) the entrepreneur in question will reduce his costs more than his receipts by dismissing some units of that factor. These will then go elsewhere, into other establishments and possibly other uses, in which their marginal productivity is higher. If, on the other hand, the marginal productivity of any factor in any establishment is higher than its price, the entrepreneur in question will hire more units of that factor, since by so doing he will increase his receipts more than his costs. In this way, competition equalises marginal productivity and price in every branch of production.[3]

---

[2] If we divide workers into groups, so that each group contains workers of the same grade and efficiency, it is sufficient if there is competition among the members of each group. See § 3 below, *passim*.

[3] These propositions form a generally-accepted part of economic theory, and it would be out of place to discuss them here at any length. They are perhaps best formulated by Knight, *Risk, Uncertainty and Profit*, chap. iv See also Wicksteed, *Co-ordination of the Laws of Distribution* (reprinted by the London School of Economics, 1932) and *The Common Sense of Political Economy* (1910; new edition 1933-4). J. B. Clark's exposition in his *Distribution of Wealth* is oversimplified and suffers from a hazy concept of capital and from his endeavour to find a moral significance in the law of marginal productivity. The subject is treated much better by Böhm-Bawerk, *Positive Theorie des Kapitals*—see especially Exkursus 7 in the 3rd edn., or the 4th edn. *Cf.* also Wicksell (1893), *Ueber Wert, Kapital und Rente* (reprinted by the London School of Economics, 1933), and *Lectures on Political Economy*, vol. 1, part 1. Schumpeter, "Das Grundprinzip der Verteilungstheorie," *Archiv für Sozialwissenschaft*, vol. 42 (1916-17); Landauer, *Probleme der funktionellen Verteilung des*

Let us now recapitulate our assumptions. The price of every factor equals the value of its marginal product. Hence a (small) quantity of any factor can be substituted at the margin[4] for a (small) quantity, having the same value, of any other factor. (The substitution may be direct or may take place through a general reshuffling of the distribution of factors among industries.) On the other hand, the price of any product equals the sum of the prices of the factors required to produce the marginal unit of it. Since two things both equal to a third are equal to one another, it follows from these assumptions that a unit of commodity A will exchange against that quantity of commodity B which requires (at the margin) an equally valuable collection of factors to produce it. In other words, the exchange-ratio between two commodities will equal their (indirect) substitution-ratio or opportunity-cost (in terms of one another)—which is the proposition we set out to prove.

§ 2. THE THEORY OF COMPARATIVE COST RESTATED, WITH SPECIAL REFERENCE TO SPECIFIC FACTORS.

It should now be clear that, if the exchange-ratios between commodities are equal to their substitution-ratios, the doctrine of comparative advantage is perfectly valid even if we discard all the simplifying assumptions of the Labour Theory of Value. The same applies, of course, to the presumption, derived from this doctrine, that unrestricted international exchange will be advantageous to all parties.

In order to show this, we should have to set out, instead of a series of absolute labour-costs (like that on page 138), a series of relative prices or exchange-ratios, using any one commodity as a *numeraire* with which to measure prices. This series would equally represent the substitution-ratios, since these are the same as the exchange-ratios. Each country would specialise in those branches of production in which it had a comparative advantage or, in other words, would produce those goods whose costs were relatively lowest. For example, if in country I one unit of A exchanged against one-and-a-half units of B, and in country II one unit of A exchanged against one of B, country I would plainly have a comparative advantage in the production of B. The rest of the argument, and the proof that specialisation would increase the total

---

wirtschaftlichen Wertes (1922); Mayer, article on " Zurechnung " in *Handwörterbuch der Staatswissenschaften*, 4th edn., and the references there given; Hicks, *Theory of Wages* (1932).

[4] If the quantities of factors substituted for one another are not relatively small, so that more than a marginal change occurs, the substitution-ratio will be shifted. But this does not invalidate our doctrine.

output, would be exactly the same as in chapter X, where we assumed the Labour Theory of Value. But one new problem would emerge: that of the change in the distribution of the total product among the various factors of production. This problem is discussed in § 3.

The point which gives rise to most misunderstanding is the influence of international trade upon the prices and employment of immobile and specific means of production. It is constantly urged that the Theory of International Trade, as we have presented it, assumes the complete mobility of all factors, or means of production, within a country, and that a country can carry out the adaptations required by international trade without loss only if this condition is fulfilled. It is contended that when immobile and specific factors exist, every adaptation must involve severe loss, even if it is in the direction indicated by the principle of comparative advantage. When, for example, an import duty is removed, a shift in production will be required. It is urged that this must reduce the value of those means of production—land, buildings, machinery, intermediate products, and so on—which are employed by the industries from which protection has been removed and which cannot be transferred to other uses, and that the owners of these specific factors will thereby suffer a reduction in their incomes. This argument is always employed against every proposal for a customs union or for the removal or reduction of a tariff. For instance, a Pan-European, or even an Austro-German, customs union would necessitate great adjustments in all spheres of production. It is maintained that these adjustments would involve such a vast destruction of capital that it might well be asked whether the expected but distant increase in output might not be purchased too dearly.[5] How would the present generation profit from advantages reaped only after all the adjustments and adaptations have been made? As Mr. Keynes once remarked, in the long run we are all dead.

But this argument, which is always making its appearance in one or other of its various forms, contains a serious error. For the loss of capital does not imply any loss of national income. It reflects only an altered distribution of that income. The actual loss arising from the frictions of adaptation is much less than the loss of capital, with which this argument wrongly identifies it.

---

[5] See, e.g., P. Kaufmann, " Paneuropäische Wirtschaftsfragen " in *Der österreiche Volkswirt*, Jg. 18 (1925-26), p. 372, or Eulenburg, " Gegen die Idee einer europäischen Zollunion " in *Europäische Zollunion* (1926), pp. 109 *et seq*. Both these contain the fallacy discussed below in our text.

The proof of this is implied in our previous analysis.[6] But, since it is desirable to bring it out as clearly as possible, we shall consider at some length a concrete arithmetical example.[6a]

Let us suppose that a country has a field of iron ore, upon which an iron and steel industry is based, and let us trace the consequence of an increase in foreign competition which causes the price of iron and steel to fall until in the end some or all of the works are compelled to close down. The fall in the price of foreign iron and steel may be due to any of several causes. The country in question may have lowered its import duties or there may have been a reduction in transport costs. The foreign industry may have made some improvements in technique not open to the home industry or may have been granted a subsidy by its Government. Again, the reduction in foreign costs might be general, arising from the working of the monetary mechanism: for example, the foreign country might be making unilateral payments. In any event, let us assume for the sake of simplicity that the fall in price is a permanent one.

The receipts and expenditure of a concern in the home iron and steel industry may be as follows[7]:

Receipts.

Gross receipts from sales of products,   -   -   -   100

Expenditure.

(1) Current expenses for wages and salaries, materials, &c., including interest upon this outlay, *i.e.*, upon the circulating capital,   - - - - - 50

(2) Interest and depreciation upon the fixed capital invested in buildings, machinery, &c.,   - - 20

(3) Rent of land, including the iron-ore deposits owned by the concern,   - - - - - - - 30

  100

(1) 50 represents the payments for the mobile and non-specific factors of production, which at any moment can find employment elsewhere in other uses. (2) 20 represents the 'costs' of the fixed capital. This is specific to the industry; broadly speaking, it will

---

[6] The presence of specific means of production is expressed in the shape of the substitution-curve (which it makes more like an L and less like a straight line), so that our analysis has already taken it into account.

[6a] The following analysis is static in the sense that it abstracts from processes of deflation which may, and probably will, be started by such changes as are produced by the formation of a customs union. This does not, however, rob it of its importance, since the transition to the new equilibrium can be made smooth—the deflation may be avoided—by appropriate measures.

[7] The figures are quite arbitrary; the reader may vary them as he wishes.

become ' free ' and therefore transferable only after a relatively long period, after it has been worn out and amortised. This item is what Marshall terms quasi-rent. (3) 30 is the income of the completely specific factors, which cannot be employed for any other purpose. It is rent in the strict theoretical sense of the term.[8]

Now suppose that the price of iron and steel falls, reducing the receipts by 30. This represents an enormous loss to our entrepreneur, but he will not diminish his production in the slightest. The value of the specific factors must perforce be written down, and all the rent is wiped out, but so long as interest can be earned upon the circulating and the fixed capital, production will continue. The loss of the producers of iron and steel is balanced by an equal gain, measured in money, to the consumers. The national income is not diminished,[9] since the volume of production remains constant. Suppose now that the price of iron and steel falls still lower, reducing the receipts by a further 10 or 15. This increases the loss to the producers, but so long as the circulating capital needed for current expenses, under (1), continues to reproduce itself and to earn interest, production will go on. The value of the specific factors—the fixed capital—will be written down to the value (as scrap) of the material in them; if any of such factors are not completely specific, but can be used elsewhere, their value will be written down to what they are worth elsewhere. This loss of capital has occurred and must be accepted; an entrepreneur would rather recognise it in his books, and continue producing, than abandon the enterprise and lose everything. The quasi-rent disappears. But the outlay under (1) cannot be reduced, for it consists of payments to non-specific factors, which would leave the concern and go elsewhere if they did not receive their full market price.

Up to this point, we have recorded losses only to particular persons and not to the community as a whole, since the consumers

---

[8] Opinion may vary as to the allocation of particular items of expenditure among these three groups; but that does not affect the issue. For example, the value of the iron ore would be included under (1) if our concern bought its ore from another firm, and in that case the rent of the ore deposits would not appear under (3). We have not space to discuss fully all such variations, which do not affect the main argument. We assume, for example, that the high cost of transporting ore causes each iron and steel works to have its own adjacent ore mines; hence, from the standpoint of our entrepreneur, the rent of his iron ore deposits is a residual income.

[9] If the consumers live outside the territory of the national or other community under consideration, this community may of course suffer a loss. But there will be no loss from a cosmopolitan standpoint. This does not mean, however, that Free Trade is to be advocated, in such a case, only from an altruistic cosmopolitan standpoint. For if the industry of one country is displaced by the industry of another from some third market, the country which is injured is powerless to alter the situation by imposing or increasing import duties.

of iron and steel gain as much as the producers lose. Let us
now go a step further, and suppose either that the price of iron
and steel falls still lower or that part of the fixed capital wears
out and must be replaced if the concern is to continue producing.
Now, at last, the concern will be compelled to close down, since it
can no longer pay the market price for its non-specific factors.
But this implies that these factors can produce sufficient elsewhere
to earn their market price.[1] Hence the closing of the concern
represents no loss to the community. On the contrary, such a
loss would be caused if these factors were artificially retained,
by means of a duty or some form[2] of public subsidy, in their present
employment, where they are now of less utility than they would
be in other employments.

As a rule, an industry comprises numerous concerns, including
marginal ones which, unlike the one in our example, earn no rent
to serve as a buffer against shocks. Moreover, it is probable
that at any moment one or other of these concerns will be about
to replace some of its fixed capital. Under these conditions,
every fall in the price of the product will probably cause some
contraction of the industry by compelling a concern on the margin
to close down. But in principle the process remains the same.[3]

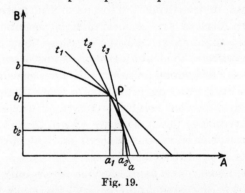

Fig. 19.

The lower the price falls—the more cheaply, that is to say, foreign
countries can supply—the greater will be the gain of the home
country from the international division of labour. We should

---

[1] If their productivity elsewhere were less, their price would be less.
[2] For example, the industry might be granted public contracts upon favourable
terms.
[3] If the marginal concern does earn a rent and can therefore survive a moderate
fall in price, this is to be represented diagrammatically as in fig. 19. The substitution-curve contains a kink at the point P, instead of being continuously
smooth. The two straight lines t_1 and t_2 are both tangents to the curve at P.
If the price-ratio were originally in the neighbourhood of that represented by the
slope of t_1, it could fall to the level represented by the slope of t_2 without
causing any shift in production. But if the price-ratio were to fall to t_3, the combination $a_2 b_2$ would be produced instead of the combination $a_1 b_1$.

add, however, that to prevent a fall in price by imposing a duty will not necessarily diminish the national income in those exceptional cases in which the marginal concern earns a rent and would therefore maintain its output, at any rate for a time, despite the fall in price. For under these conditions a duty would not cause any misdirection of factors : production would be the same as it would be without a duty, ignoring indirect influences, the duty would cause only an alteration in the distribution of the national income.

The whole of the above analysis rests upon the important assumption that competition ensures flexible prices and, in particular, that the prices of specific factors will fall, if necessary, to zero before their owners cease to use them. This will probably be true of material means of production : the owner of, say, a plot of land or a building would rather obtain something from it, either by hiring it out or by utilising it himself, than leave it idle. Indeed, we are always witnessing entrepreneurs working ' at a loss ' instead of closing down.[4] But our assumption does not apply to one most important factor, namely, labour. Here the working of the price-mechanism is partly stultified, since workers often respond even to quite small reductions in wages by withholding their labour. This involves a true loss from friction, in the form of strikes and unemployment.[5] But clearly such a loss, accompanying a period of transition, is different in nature from a fall in the value of certain fixed capital, for the latter could not be avoided even if the price-mechanism worked perfectly smoothly. We may perhaps add that these frictional losses due to the imperfect flexibility of wage-rates are less serious than one might at first suppose, since of all factors labour, apart from a few exceptional cases, is the least specific.[6]

One important practical conclusion to be drawn from our discussion is that, despite the contrary view expressed, for example, by Schüller,[7] the existence of unutilised means of production is no argument whatever for tariffs. Schüller sets out from the indisputable premise that " In no country are the natural resources of fertile land, water-power, and deposits of coal, iron, and other minerals fully utilised. They remain available for the expansion of whatever branches of production may require them." But from

---

[4] It is also possible that during a period of transition a concern may continue to operate even if it cannot cover its prime costs; this will happen if the entrepreneur thinks that the situation will soon improve again, and that it will be less costly to continue producing in the meantime than to close down and then reopen.

[5] We discuss this matter in detail in chap. xvii, § 3, p. 260.

[6] This point is expanded in § 3 of the present chapter.

[7] *Schutzzoll und Freihandel*, p. 78, and the translation in *Selected Readings, &c.*. ed. by Taussig.

this he concludes[8] that tariffs can bring about the utilisation of such idle means of production and thereby, under certain conditions, lead to an increase in the total production of the economy.[9] We have seen that this argument, at least in so far as it relates to material means of production, rests upon a fallacy. It is in no way surprising or abnormal that not all means of production are utilised; on the contrary, there are good economic reasons for it. As Röpke has pertinently remarked,[1] economic forces tend to bring about not a maximal but an optimal utilisation. One can scarcely conceive a situation in which all the means of production are utilised, every scrap of land being tilled, all plant and equipment, however old or obsolete, being employed, and every deposit of coal, however poor, being mined. An approach to such a situation, such as perhaps exists in, say, China or India, would be a sign of great poverty and not, as Schüller's theory implies, a symptom of abounding wealth.[2] Nor does it make the slightest difference whether the unutilised means of production are due to Nature, like land and mineral deposits, or have been made by man, like factories and machinery, although the layman is far more impressed by the idleness of man-made means of production. In reality, the non-utilised means of production (provided that the value of their products would not cover the costs of the other factors which must be combined with them, since the latter can produce more elsewhere) represent neither a destruction of capital nor a loss to the economy as a whole. They are milestones upon the road of economic progress along which the economy is moving under the influence of technical progress or of the international division of labour.[3] The losses, which seem so obvious and impressive, may indeed be real losses from the standpoint of the owners of the idle factors, but they are outweighed by greater gains to other persons. To the community as a whole, the net result is a gain and not a

---

[8] Schüller adduces other circumstances, in addition to this premise, in support of his claim that tariffs may enable a better use to be made of existing means of production. But this does not affect the discussion in our text.

[9] See the trenchant criticism of G. Mackenroth in his interesting article " Zollpolitik und Produktionsmittelversorgung," *Weltwirtschaftliches Archiv*, vol. 29, 1 (1929), pp. 89 *et seq.* See also Haberler, " Die Theorie der komparativen Kosten und ihre Auswertung für die Begründung des Freihandels," *Weltwirtschaftliches Archiv*, vol. 32 (1930), and Mises, " Das festangelegte Kapital " in *Economische Opstellen*, Festschrift für Verrijn Stuart (Haarlem, 1931), reprinted in *Grundprobleme der Nationalökonomie*, p. 201 *et seq.* (1933).

[1] " Die neue Wirtschaftsstruktur Deutschlands als Grundlage seiner künftigen Handelspolitik." *Schriften des Vereins für Sozialpolitik*, vol. 171, 1 (1925), p. 9.

[2] Another interpretation of Schüller's theory is possible. He might have in mind certain resources, such as water-power, which are not utilised owing to a shortage of capital. In that case it is true that their idleness is a symptom of poverty. But it in no way follows that tariffs would lead to a net import of capital. We discuss this point in chap. xvii, § 4, pp. 273 *et seq.*

[3] Unutilised labour-power—unemployment—is in a different category. See chap. xvii, § 3, p. 259.

loss. When, for instance, a factory is closed down for the reasons given above, before the capital invested in it has been amortised, it may be said with truth that the original investment (owing either to miscalculation or to subsequent unforeseen changes) has turned out to have been a misdirection of capital. But in economic affairs bygones are bygones; and, in the circumstances which we are assuming, the best utilisation of the community's resources in the future involves closing down the factory.[4]

§ 3. The Influence of International Trade upon the Distribution of the National Income.

1. The Treatment of the Problem in Classical and Neo-Classical Doctrine.—The foregoing discussion has shown what a powerful influence international trade may have upon the personal and functional distribution[5] of the national income, since every change in international economic relations may alter the relative prices of different means of production.

In classical and neo-classical doctrine, this very important topic is considered under two different heads. The first of these is the analysis of how international trade affects wages, rent, and interest (or profits),[6] relatively to one another. The second is the doctrine of ' non-competing groups ' of workers.[7]

Under the first head, it is shown that the importation of agricultural products by an industrial country tends to reduce the

---

[4] We are not here supposing that the mal-investments occurred during a general boom. In that case, the loss and writing-down of capital during the subsequent depression would represent a net loss to the economy, since it would not be offset by gains elsewhere. But the loss occurred when the investments were made; the subsequent writing-down of capital-values merely recognises an accomplished fact. The loss would be increased, and not lessened, by any form of intervention which prevented full account being taken of it and thereby hindered such transfers of capital as might be possible to adapt the economy to the new situation. See Schiff, *Kapitalbildung und Kapitalaufzehrung im Konjunkturverlauf* (1933), pp. 73 *et seq.* The preceding considerations are not intended to deny that indirectly such a loss of ' private ' capital may have very serious consequences and lead to losses for the economy as a whole—losses which, from the point of view of static theory, are due to frictions, but, nevertheless, very real and painful losses. *E.g.*, a cumulative process of deflation may be set in motion by a breakdown in any particular industry or the maintenance of the capital stock may be endangered because of a change in the ratio of saving and spending due to the change in distribution. The latter case is touched on in Pigou, *Economics of Welfare*, 4th edn., and Hayek, " The Maintenance of Capital," *Economica*, vol. 2 (new series), No. 7 (August 1935), pp. 241 *et seq.*

[5] Upon the concept of ' personal ' and ' functional ' distribution, see especially Clark, *The Distribution of Wealth*, and Landauer, *Grundprobleme der funktionellan Verteilung des wirtschaftlichen Wertes* (1924).

[6] See, *e.g.*, Bastable, *Theory of International Trade*, chap. 6, " Influence of Foreign Trade on the Internal Distribution of Wealth," pp. 97 to 109.

[7] The concept of ' non-competing groups ' is due to Cairnes, *Some Leading Principles of Political Economy* (1875). The most detailed treatment of the question is that given in Taussig's *International Trade*, chap. 6.

incomes of its landowners, by bringing down rents, but has a favourable influence upon wages and incomes from capital. Real wages increase, since the imported foodstuffs are cheaper. In the exporting agricultural countries, the effect is the opposite. There rents tend to rise, since the margin of cultivation is extended.[8]

This analysis is undoubtedly pertinent. At the same time, it is inadequate in that the threefold division of factors into land, labour, and capital, and the corresponding threefold classification of incomes, is too great an over-simplification of reality. As Knight drastically puts it, a threefold division of factors of production into animal, vegetable, and mineral, would be just as satisfactory from the theoretical standpoint as the traditional classification.[9] We shall endeavour later to bring the main conclusions of the classical theory under a more general formulation.

The doctrine of ' non-competing ' or, more briefly, ' closed ' groups of workers is based upon the fact that there are many different kinds of labour. The movement of workers from one of these closed groups to another cannot take place, owing to some obstacle or other, but within any one group there is free competition and hence a uniform rate of wages. When labour is thus regarded not as one homogeneous factor but as a number of different factors, the assumption of one uniform wage-level for all workers of course disappears.

The effect of this phenomenon upon the price-system is treated differently by different writers. Cairnes, who introduced the concept, regards the number and nature of the various closed groups as definitely fixed and given. He points out that under the classical theory of international trade, which assumes that factors are immobile between countries, the homogeneous labour-supply of each different country is in effect a different non-competing group. He concludes that if there are non-competing groups within a particular country, the economic relations between them can be explained by applying the Theory of International Values. The reciprocal demand of these groups, within the same country, for one another's products will determine the level of wages in each group.

Taussig's analysis goes much deeper than that of Cairnes. He points out that it is not correct to take the number and composition of these groups as something which is given once and for all. We should not, at least when taking a long view, regard

---

[8] S. N. Patten adduces this circumstance as an argument for tariffs. See his *Economic Basis of Protection* (1890).

[9] Bastable, *loc. cit.*, calls attention to the limits of this classification and emphasises that it is only a first approximation, although a very useful one.

the demand for a particular kind of labour (derived from the demand for its products) as the sole force determining the level of wages in that particular group. We should take account also of the conditions of supply of the labour in question. Indeed, it is even conceivable that the demand may have no influence whatever upon the relative levels of wages as between the different groups. Marshall has constructed the following case to illustrate this possibility.

" . . . suppose that society is divided into a number of horizontal grades, each of which is recruited from the children of its own members; and each of which has its own standard of comfort, and increases in numbers rapidly when the earnings to be got in it rise above, and shrinks rapidly when they fall below that standard. Let us suppose, then, that parents can bring up their children to any trade in their own grade, but cannot easily raise them above it and will not consent to sink them below it. . . .

" On these assumptions the normal wage in any trade is that which is sufficient to enable a labourer, who has normal regularity of employment, to support himself and a family of normal size according to the standard of comfort that is normal in the grade to which his trade belongs; it is not dependent on demand except to this extent, that if there were no demand for the labour of the trade at that wage the trade would not exist. In other words the normal wage represents the expenses of production of the labour. . . ."[10]

In the language of pure economics, these sociological assumptions about induced changes in population mean that the various kinds of labour are supplied at constant cost: they have a horizontal supply-curve. When this is so, a change in demand would have no influence, in the long run, upon their price, but only upon the amount supplied.

We thus have two extreme cases. Cairnes assumes that the supply of labour within these closed groups is completely inelastic. Marshall, in the case quoted above, assumes that it is completely elastic.[1]

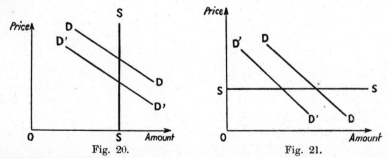

Fig. 20.   Fig. 21.

[10] *Principles of Economics*, 2nd edn., pp. 557-8. Taussig quotes from the second edition because the formulation is more precise there than in the later editions.

[1] The two cases are shown in the following supply-and-demand diagrams, relating to one of these closed groups. The quantity of labour, supplied and demanded, is measured along the abscissa and the price—that is, the wage—up the ordinate.

The supply curve, according to Cairnes, is completely inelastic, or vertical, as in fig. 20. According to Marshall, it is completely elastic, or horizontal as in fig. 21. In the former case, a shift of the demand-curve from DD to D'D' affects only the price; in the latter case it affects only the quantity supplied. The Ricardian doctrine that the different kinds of labour can be brought under a common denominator by taking their different exchange-values as they appear in the market, can be interpreted along the lines of this Marshallian construction.

One's conclusion as to the influence of international trade upon the comparative position of the various groups will differ according to which of these two limiting cases one regards as the more likely. Suppose that in a given country there is a closed group of the type assumed by Cairnes. Suppose that some change in conditions abroad gives this country a greater comparative disadvantage than before in the products of this group, which must therefore face more intense competition from imports. The wages of the members of this group must fall, as, for example, they fell in Europe a agriculture under the pressure of increased imports of grain from overseas. But if their wages fall sharply, workers will leave this group as time goes on, and will not be replaced by new ones. Thus the case of Cairnes is to be regarded rather as a short-run construction, whilst that of Marshall is essentially of a long-run character.

If, on the contrary, the country enjoys a comparative advantage in, and therefore exports, the products of the closed group, international trade will raise their wages. It is quite possible that the trade union of this group may be sufficiently powerful to keep out would-be new entrants, and thus keep the group a closed one, even if its wages are much higher than wages in other groups. But if one thinks that the hypothesis of an elastic supply tallies more with the facts, one must conclude that in the long run international trade has no influence upon the relative wages of the different groups of workers. Taussig seems to hold this view, for he says:

" The lines of social and industrial stratification in a country are determined chiefly by the conditions that prevail within its own limits—by the numbers in the several groups and their demands for each other's services, and in some uncertain degree *by their different standards of living.*[2] An added impact of demand from a foreign country will rarely change the relative rates of wages which have come about from the domestic factors. The social stratification that results from the domestic conditions is well established and seems to be deeply rooted; and it is not likely that international trade will impinge on it with such special effect on a particular grade as to warp it noticeably.[3]

If we regard such a situation as a modified version of the Marshallian case, there is no contradiction when Taussig, despite his denial that international trade has any great influence upon the relative position of the various groups of workers, not only concedes

---

[2] My italics.
[3] *International Trade*, pp. 56-7.

but stresses the influence exerted by the supplies of different types of labour on the nature of international trade. Indeed, it is clear that the latter will be strongly influenced by the presence in one country of social strata and of closed groups of workers not present in other countries, if this results in an abundant and cheap supply of certain kinds of labour. Taussig gives as an example Germany's export of chemicals and especially of coal-tar products, which is largely due to the presence of an abundant supply of qualified chemists and trained assistants. (The presence of a large supply of a certain kind of labour has the same consequences as the presence of a large quantity of any other means of production—for example, of fertile land, which makes a country especially suitable for agriculture. To be accurate, we should consider the available quantity of the means of production in relation to the demand. If the home demand for the products of any particular factor is especially strong, those products may not be exported, despite the large quantity of that factor which is present.)

In many respects Taussig's exposition is most ingenious and persuasive, combining acuteness of analysis with a wide knowledge of the relevant facts. Nevertheless, the treatment of non-competing groups in the classical theory, even as he presents it, cannot be termed theoretically complete and systematic. It is somewhat of a patchwork, and can be replaced with advantage by a more complete and elegant solution, provided that we substitute our general theory for the simplifying assumptions of the Labour Theory of Value. This we shall now endeavour to do.

2. A SYSTEMATIC ANALYSIS OF THE PROBLEM.—' Closed groups of workers' are obviously only special cases, in our terminology, of more or less specific factors, limited for technical or other reasons to certain employments. The following propositions can be stated as to the influence of international trade upon the relative scarcity, the marginal productivity, and hence the relative prices of the various specific and non-specific means of production: (1) When international exchange of commodities begins to take place, it will cause a rise in the prices of those factors which are specific to the export industries of a country, being employed there in relatively greater quantities than in other industries; (2) it will cause a fall in the prices of whatever factors are specific to those industries in which the country has a comparative disadvantage, and which must therefore contract or be abandoned; (3) it will cause a rise in the prices of non-specific factors, capable of many different employments, since it will increase the total output, but this rise will be

less than the rise under (1). In other words, the incomes[4] of owners of factors of type (2) will fall, those of owners of factors of type (1) will rise, and those of owners of factors of type (3) will rise also, but to a less extent.

We must distinguish between material means of production and labour. In the long run, material means of production which are highly specific are found mainly in agriculture and consist of land of various qualities and of natural resources of all kinds, although, of course, not all these gifts of nature are specific.[5] In other spheres, such as manufacturing and commerce and transport, highly specific material factors play only a minor part in the long run. But the situation is very different if we take a short view, for a large part of the buildings, plant and equipment, means of transport, and intermediate products which exist at any time will be specific. Hence a change in the intensity of foreign competition, an increase or reduction in tariffs, or any other alteration in international economic relations, may bring large losses or gains to the owners of means of production affected by the change.

We turn now to labour. In the long run, and apart from certain exceptions, this is the least specific and most adaptable factor of all. But, in the short run, it is more specific and less mobile. Whenever the appropriate response to a change in economic conditions involves more employment of labour in one industry, or even in one firm, and less in another, this will mean a temporary or permanent diminution in wages and other unpleasant effects for some workers, and will therefore arouse opposition. Moreover, it is beyond dispute that various modern developments have tended, and still do tend, to lessen the mobility and adaptability of labour. On the one hand, the strength of organised labour, including the influence of trade unions, and State intervention in labour questions, especially in connection with unemployment insurance and unemployment relief, have both increased greatly. On the other hand, the rapid growth of population, which in the past made possible a great redistribution of labour between industries by the diversion of new entrants towards the expanding industries, has now been replaced by an approach to stationary populations, so that a redistribution now involves an actual movement of workers out of the contracting industries and into the expanding ones.

---

[4] To be accurate, we should speak of real incomes and of real prices or, better, of relative prices, since it is quite possible that there would be a general rise or fall in all money prices.

[5] Strictly speaking, we should distinguish different degrees of specificity. For our purpose, the relevant consideration is whether a factor is used predominantly in the export industries or only in the industries which must face competition from imports.

We may conclude that in the long run the working-class as a whole has nothing to fear from international trade, since, in the long run, labour is the least specific of all factors. It will gain by the general increase in productivity due to the international division of labour, and is not likely to lose at all seriously by a change in the functional distribution of the national income. Hence the political representatives of labour lean as a rule towards Free Trade. But, in the short run, specialised and immobile groups of workers, like the owners of specific material factors, may suffer heavy reductions in income when for one reason or another they are faced with more intense foreign competition. They are rendered more vulnerable by the fact, already mentioned, that wages are less flexible than most prices. The price of a material factor must sink to zero before it ceases to be used, but workers, especially when they have strong trade unions and are supported directly or indirectly by State intervention, will withhold their labour if wages fall below a certain limit. The consequence may be chronic unemployment in the industries affected by the change in conditions.[6]

This solution is sufficiently accurate for all long-run purposes. Nevertheless, some refinements may be added, since under certain conditions the general rules given above may be modified.

One possibility which must be considered is that a country may have a comparative disadvantage in those industries where labour is used comparatively intensively, so that international trade diverts demand towards industries which employ comparatively little labour relatively to other factors. The international division of labour will then lower the marginal productivity of labour relatively to that of other factors. Some writers, such as Wicksell, believe that this occurs in agricultural countries, since in agriculture the proportion of land is greater and of labour smaller than in other branches of production. Wicksell thinks it conceivable that for this reason tariffs on industrial products may raise the absolute real income of labour in agricultural countries, and not merely raise it relatively to the real incomes of other factors.[7]

Exactly the same analysis applies to this problem as to the problem of the influence of technical progress upon the share of labour in the national income, since there is a complete analogy between technical progress and an increase in the international division of labour due to reductions in tariffs or transport costs or to other causes. The latter problem has been examined, notably by Pigou[8] and by Hicks.[9] We cannot here reproduce their complex theoretical analysis. They

6 We discuss this deviation from full equilibrium, and the argument for tariffs based upon it, in chap. 17, § 3, pp. 259 *et seq.*

7 *Finanztheoretische Untersuchungen* (1896), pp. 63-6. Similarly, Carver, *Principles of National Economy* (1921), p. 458. Carver at first held the view that the loss in wages might be greater than the gain in rent, so that a tariff might increase the national income. See " Some Theoretical Possibilities of a Protective Tariff " (14th annual meeting of the American Economic Association). E. H. Johnson has shown that this is not possible in " The Effect of a Tariff on Production," *Quarterly Journal of Economics*, vol. 18 (1903), pp. 135-7.

8 *Economics of Welfare*, 3rd edn. (1929), part 4, chap. 4, pp. 669-70.

9 *The Theory of Wages* (1932), chap. 6, pp. 112 *et seq.* For a different view see, *e.g.*, Lederer, *Technischer Fortschritt und Arbeitslosigkeit* (1931). N. Kaldor gives a convincing criticism of Lederer in " A Case against Technical Progress," *Economica* (May 1932). See also Wicksell, *Lectures*, vol. 1, pp. 195 *et seq.*

conclude that it is extremely unlikely that the *absolute* real income of the working-class will be unfavourably influenced, and that whilst the possibility that its *relative share* in the national income may be reduced is greater, this also is on the whole improbable. These conclusions apply equally to our present problem, and there is no doubt that they are fully confirmed by experience.

3. DIFFERENCES IN WAGE-LEVELS AND THE GAIN FROM INTERNATIONAL TRADE. We have considered the influence of international trade on the distribution of income and how the presence of non-competing groups affects international trade. We shall now consider how the proposition that the free exchange of goods with foreign countries will increase the national income as a whole is affected when we discard the assumption of a uniform wage-level. In other words, we shall enquire whether differences in wages, within a country, provide a valid argument for Protection. For this purpose we must distinguish the various possible reasons for differences in wages.[1]

(1) One important reason is that which we have hitherto assumed to be the sole one : differences in the quality of the labour supplied by the different groups. If there is a given fixed supply of each different kind of labour, each kind will earn a different wage, just as different kinds of land and of other material means of production have different prices. When differences in wages are due to this cause (or, if weekly wages are considered, the differences in the amount of labour performed per week), our conclusions need no modification.[2]

(2) The same applies when differences in wages arise from artificial obstacles to entry into certain occupations, imposed by law or custom or the power of trade unions. Suppose that a group of workers succeed, by keeping out would-be new entrants, in raising their marginal productivity above that of equally qualified workers outside the group. International trade will have the same results as in case (1). If the industry employing the monopolistic labour group has a comparative advantage, their wages will rise, and in the opposite case they will fall, but in any event the national income will be increased. It is true that the national income would be increased also, with or without international trade, if such monopolistic groups were broken up. But this is a different question, and does not affect the fact that, given these monopolies, international trade will increase it.

(3) Differences in wages may be so-called ' equalising ' differences.[3] A worker takes into account not only the money wage attached to a particular occupation or employment, but also such conditions as the agreeableness or disagreeableness of the work itself and of the conditions under which it must be performed and of the neighbourhood in which he must live. Other things, and in particular money wages, being equal, most workers prefer an interesting employment to a dull one, a regular job to an irregular one, and so on. Hence differences in money wages

---

[1] See Taussig, *loc. cit.*; Ohlin, " Protection and Non-Competing Groups," *Weltwirtschaftliches Archiv*, vol. 33 (Jan. 1931), pp. 30 *et seq.*; Viner, " The Doctrine of Comparative Costs," *Weltwirtschaftliches Archiv*, vol. 36 (Oct. 1932), p. 405, and his review of M. Manoïlesco's *The Theory of Protection and International Trade* (1931), in *Journal of Political Economy* (1932), pp. 121-5. Manoïlesco tries to base an argument for tariffs upon the existence of permanent differences in wages between different industries and employments, which are due, in his opinion, to differences in the marginal productivity of labour.

[2] It is noteworthy that Viner (*loc. cit.*, p. 405-7) does not mention this important case. It falls outside the scope of the real-cost theory, to which Viner adheres—apparently from reverence for tradition; or at least it can be included only under quite definite assumptions. But it falls quite readily under our opportunity-cost doctrine. Hence Viner's statement (*Weltwirtschaftliches Archiv*, *loc. cit.*, p. 413) that the latter doctrine carries one no further than the old-fashioned labour-cost theory is incorrect. But I do not dispute that both doctrines march parallel for a good part of the way, and that certain situations suggested by Viner form exceptions to both of them. See cases (3) and (4) below.

[3] See Taussig, *loc. cit.*, and also Viner, *loc. cit.*, p. 405.

may merely equalise the ' net advantages ' of different occupations; workers able to enter either a relatively attractive or a relatively unattractive occupation will require the compensation of higher money wages to induce them to enter the latter.

When differences in wages are of this ' equalising ' nature, the international division of labour may cause a diminution in the national income, provided that we take no account of the attractiveness or otherwise of different occupations, apart from the actual money wage, in computing the national income.[4] Suppose that a country has a comparative advantage, and therefore specialises upon, those industries in which money wages are low. If its comparative advantage over foreign countries in these industries is smaller than the difference in money wages between these industries and other industries, international trade, by expanding the former and contracting the latter, may diminish the national income.[5] But if we take into account the advantages and disadvantages of different occupations other than the money wages, which is obviously the correct procedure, the result will appear as a gain and not as a loss.[6]

(4) Higher wages in certain occupations may be due to the monopoly power of trade unions or may be prescribed by law, without being payments for a superior or scarcer quality of labour, as in (1), or compensation for the comparative unattractiveness of the occupation, as in (3). This case differs from (2) in that here there are no obstacles to movement from the worse-paid to the better-paid groups, provided that the higher wages in the latter are maintained, whereas in case (2) the number of workers in each closed group is fixed, the wage adapting itself to the conditions of demand, whilst the supply of labour is given. Thus in (2) an increase in the demand for the product would raise wages, whilst in the present case it would not alter the wage but would increase the number of workers in the group.[7]

Such a situation forms a theoretically important exception to our general conclusions, since under these conditions the price-ratio is not the same as the substitution-ratio. Thus a fundamental proposition of our analysis does not apply : as the following example shows, the exchange-ratio is not determined exclusively by the ' opportunity costs.'

Suppose that one unit of commodity A and commodity B alike requires the expenditure of one unit of labour,[8] but that the labour employed for B is organised and obtains double the wage of the labour employed for A.

Hence the ratio of the price of A to the price of B is - - - 1 : 2
In other words, the exchange-ratio between them is - - - - 1 : $\frac{1}{2}$
But the substitution-ratio between them is - - - - - 1 : 1
Let us further suppose that abroad the ratio of the price of A to the
price of B is - - - - - - - - - - - 1 : $1\frac{1}{2}$
that is, the exchange-ratio between them is - - - - 1 : $\frac{2}{3}$

It follows that the country in question will specialise upon A. Its output of B will contract and it will import B in exchange for A. For the sake of simplicity let us take ' abroad ' to represent the world-market : this makes no essential difference

---

[4] One could say alternatively, to bring out the fact that a value-judgment is involved, " provided that one considers a higher money income preferable to a lower one, whatever the other circumstances may be."

[5] A numerical illustration is given below under (4).

[6] See Robbins, " Certain Aspects of the Theory of Costs," *Economic Journal* (Mar. 1934), where it is shown how this and similar cases can be dealt with by the opportunity-cost doctrine.

[7] As a rule, we find in practice mixed forms, neither the numbers in the group being absolutely constant as in (2), nor the wages, as in the present case.

[8] To suppose that other means of production co-operate with labour would merely complicate the discussion without making any essential difference to the argument.

to the argument, but it enables us to ignore the complication that unilateral action by our country may alter international exchange-ratios.

If the exchange-ratio of $1 : \frac{1}{2}$ were the same as the substitution-ratio, international trade would yield a clear gain; 2 units of A could be produced instead of 1 of B and could be exchanged, by hypothesis, against $1\frac{1}{3}$ units of B, showing a gain of $\frac{1}{3}$ B.

But in our present case the substitution-ratio of $1 : 1$ is not the same as the exchange-ratio. If the production of B contracts, only one unit of A will be produced in place of each unit of B which is no longer produced. But, by hypothesis, 1 unit of A can be exchanged internationally against only $\frac{2}{3}$ units of B, showing a loss of $\frac{1}{3}$ B. Hence in this case a tariff which prevented our country from specialising upon A would undoubtedly benefit it.[9]

Such a state of affairs, however, is very improbable. It can exist only if the monopolistic groups of workers are strong enough to maintain their wage-rates after they are faced with foreign competition—only, that is, if they prefer a reduction, and quite possibly a heavy reduction, in the amount of employment available in these highly-paid occupations, to a reduction in wages. If international trade does bring about a reduction in their wages, the situation forms no exception to our general conclusions : international trade will merely be a means of breaking the monopoly power of such groups and thus of ending their exploitation of the rest of the community.

We should not have treated these matters in such detail were it not for the widespread interest which has been aroused by the Protectionist theory[10] of M. Manoïlesco, formerly Minister of Commerce in Roumania. His theory is based upon the existence of differences in wages or, as he puts it, in ' the productivity of capital and labour,' between different branches of production. Himself an industrialist in an agricultural country, he declares that capital and labour are always more productive in industry than in agriculture and that therefore agricultural countries can benefit by imposing tariffs upon industrial products. There is a grain of truth implied in this theory, but, as Viner remarks in his admirable review of the book, M. Manoïlesco does not reveal but conceals it, for he is unaware of the numerous qualifications which limit his doctrine.[1]

§ 4. Decreasing Costs and International Trade.

1. The Problem Stated.—Hitherto[2] we have ruled out the case of decreasing costs (or increasing returns), supposing increasing, or in limiting cases constant, costs to prevail in every branch of production. The hypothesis that decreasing costs prevail in important branches of industry leads, as we have frequently observed, to difficult complications. It has been developed by Professor Frank

---

[9] Conversely, if our country has a price advantage, relatively to other countries, in those branches of production where wages are maintained above the competitive level, it would reap an extra gain from the international division of labour, since this would permit more of its workers to move into these better-paid groups.

[10] *The Theory of Protection* (1931), *cf.* the reviews, already mentioned, by Ohlin and by Viner.

[1] The above analysis could well be expanded by distinguishing further cases in addition to the four discussed. Thus, for example, it could be assumed that the superior qualification of the better paid workers depends on a certain training or education involving cost which will be incurred only if a higher wage-level obtains. If this skill has once been acquired, it may persist or it may be lost, if wages fall again. Thus developed, the argument approaches the infant-industry argument. See below, chap. xvii, § 5, p. 278.

[2] See chap x, § 7, pp. 142 *et seq.*

D. Graham[3] into a detailed criticism of the classical theory. He calls into question not so much the doctrine of comparative cost as the conclusion, derived from it, that international division of labour along the lines indicated by comparative cost must lead to an increase in the volume of production of every participating country. He tries to show by means of an arithmetical example that, assuming a certain constellation of costs, the international division of labour between two countries must involve one of them in considerable loss, measured by the diminution in its volume of production. He completely abstracts from losses due to friction and from undesired changes in the distribution of income.

His argument relates to the case in which a country is induced by the comparative-cost situation to specialise in those industries where costs are increasing and to give up those industries where costs are decreasing. According to him, agricultural countries are as a rule in this position, which applied, for example, to the United States until the end of last century and to Continental Europe, in its relations with England, during at least the first half of that century. The industrial countries, on the contrary, are in the pleasant position of being able to introduce or expand branches of production in which decreasing costs prevail.[4]

Graham illustrates his theory by the following example.[5] Let wheat represent agricultural products and watches industrial products. Before international trade begins, let the exchange-ratio be 40 units of wheat to 40 watches in England and 40 units of wheat to 37 watches in the United States. Thus the United States has a comparative advantage in the production of wheat, and by degrees will specialise more in that, whilst England will specialise more on watches. In the United States increasing costs prevail in agriculture and decreasing costs in manufacturing. In England industrial output can be expanded without any significant change in average or marginal costs, and the same applies to a contraction of her agricultural output—Graham makes this assumption in order

3 Graham, " Some Aspects of Protection Further Considered," *Quarterly Journal of Economy*, vol. 37 (Feb. 1923), pp. 199 *et seq.* See also the criticism by Knight, " Some Fallacies in the Interpretation of Social Cost," *Quarterly Journal of Economy*, vol. 38 (Aug. 1924), pp. 582 *et seq.* (now reprinted in *Ethics of Competition* [1935]), and Graham's reply and Knight's rejoinder, *Quarterly Journal of Economy*, vol. 39, pp. 324 *et seq.*, Viner, " The Doctrine of Comparative Costs," *Weltwirtschaftliches Archiv, loc. cit.,* pp. 390 *et seq.*

4 The bearing of this problem upon economic policy is considered later. Here we are concerned only with its theoretical aspects.

5 I reproduce this example, formulated by Graham, in order to be proof against the criticism which Knight had raised against his earlier exposition, from his reply to Knight, *Quarterly Journal of Economy*, vol. 39, p. 326. His original presentation contained certain errors which I do not discuss because they are not pertinent to the present issue.

to simplify the discussion.[6] Let us further suppose that the international exchange-ratio is as favourable to the United States as, under the given conditions, it can be—namely, 40 wheat to 40 watches. Under these assumptions it is profitable for American entrepreneurs to attract labour and capital away from industry and into agriculture. For so long as more than 37 units of wheat can be produced with the same quantity of labour and capital that formerly produced 37 watches, the wheat industry can offer higher wages and higher interest than the watch industry.

Suppose that the production of watches is contracted by 37,000 units and that the factors thus set free produce an additional 37,500 units of wheat, this latter figure being less than 40,000 on account of increasing costs in agriculture. By hypothesis, these 37,500 units of wheat can be exchanged against 37,500 English watches. "But the reduction in the output of watches in the United States raises the unit cost of watches . . . , so that only 36 watches are now obtainable for the same cost as were 37 before the transfer. The movement into wheat production will continue so long as more than 36 units of wheat can be obtained with the labour and capital which are necessary to produce 36 watches. Suppose that the total wheat supply is augmented by 36,200 units as a result of a transfer of labor and capital which diminishes the total output of watches by 36,000. These 36,200 units of wheat will exchange for 36,200 English watches. The result of the whole trade is thus to secure 37,500 plus 36,200 (that is 73,700) watches, for the same effort as was originally producing 37,000 plus 37,000 (that is, 74,000) watches—a loss of 300 watches . . ."[7] This process can and will go further, and the loss become still greater,[8] until the American watch industry is completely displaced by the English.

The point is, of course, that the consequence of international division of labour to any country in the unfortunate position of the United States in this illustration will be a general increase in its costs. Costs will increase in the expanding industries, since they

---

[6] Graham asserts that this assumption is not necessary to his argument, which could equally well assume variable costs, either rising or falling, in England. This is not correct, but since the situation which he does assume is a conceivable one, we can waive this point. See, however, footnote 8 below.

[7] *Loc. cit.*, p. 327.

[8] At this point, it becomes clear that the assumption we make about cost conditions in England is not a matter of indifference. Were we to assume, for example, constant or increasing costs in her agriculture and decreasing costs in her manufacturing (or that her cost of producing watches falls faster with an expansion in their output than her cost of producing wheat falls with a contraction in its output), the international exchange-ratio must become more favourable to the United States, and her loss may be transformed into a gain.

are subject to increasing costs, and they will increase also in the contracting industries, since these are subject to decreasing costs.[9]

It must be conceded that Graham's conclusion follows, provided that one accepts his assumptions, and in particular that one considers it possible for costs to decrease continuously as production expands and conversely to increase continuously as production contracts. But in fact his assumptions are highly precarious. It is not enough simply to ' assume ' decreasing costs, in the above sense. Instead, we should study the Theory of Costs, in order to discover in what circumstances given assumptions are probable or improbable. The difficult subject of decreasing costs has received special attention during recent years. We shall presently reconsider Graham's argument in the light of modern cost-doctrine. It will then be seen that little or nothing of it remains.[1]

2. ' HISTORICAL ' REDUCTIONS IN COSTS.—An industry is subject to the ' law '[2] of decreasing costs if an expansion of its output would lead to a fall in average or marginal costs.[3] Some writers contend that decreasing costs in this sense are impossible, and that there is no place for the concept in static theory. For costs can fall, they urge, only if new technical methods are employed, and this implies a dynamic change in the economic data. The only way in which a larger scale of output can reduce costs is by permitting the application of different technical methods. This argument could be used equally well against the law of increasing costs. When a field is cultivated more intensively by an increased application of capital and labour and the return per dose of capital

---

[9] The home exchange-ratio between wheat and watches can remain constant under such conditions. For costs are changing in the same direction in both these industries, and it is conceivable that the percentage rise in marginal costs may be the same in both, so that the old cost-ratio between them is maintained.

[1] Knight, *loc. cit.*, has shown that Graham merely applies a general theorem stated by Pigou in his *Economics of Welfare* which declares that the volume of production can be increased by granting some kind of subsidy to industries which obey the law of decreasing costs. On the problems of decreasing costs, see especially : Morgenstern, " Offene Probleme der Kosten- und Ertragstheorie," *Zeitschrift für Nationalökonomie*, vol. 2 (1931), p. 481; Viner, " Cost Curves and Supply Curves," *Zeitschrift für Nationalökonomie*, vol. 3 (1931), pp. 23 *et seq.*; Harrod, " Notes on Supply," *Economic Journal*, vol. 40 (June 1930), pp. 238 *et seq.*, and " The Law of Decreasing Costs," *Economic Journal*, vol. 41 (Dec. 1931), p. 566. See also Weiss, Art. " Abnehmender Ertrag " in *Handwörterbuch der Staatswissenschaften*, 4th edn.; Schüller, *Schutzzoll und Freihandel*, Absch. 1; Marshall, *Principles of Economics;* Carver, *Distribution of Wealth.* The exposition of these problems is particularly good in Garver and Hansen, *Principles of Economics* (1928). Robinson, *The Economics of Imperfect Competition* (1933).

[2] It would be better to speak of the fact, rather than of the ' law,' of decreasing costs, but we here follow the traditional terminology. See Edgeworth, " Laws of Increasing and Diminishing Returns " in his *Papers* (1925), vol. 1, pp. 61 *et seq.*

[3] Marginal costs may be falling while average costs are still rising, but in most relevant cases both will be falling, so that our discussion relates to both. A fall in total costs is ruled out, since if a larger output has a lower total cost than a smaller one, the larger output will be produced even if only the smaller one is required.

and labour employed falls, or when worse land is taken into cultivation and the costs rise, then as a rule different technical methods will be employed.

In my view, this argument is not valid. For we do not assume in static theory that the technical methods employed remain constant but only that technical knowledge and technical ability remain constant. A distinction must be drawn between a change in the technique employed which is due to an increase in demand and one due to an enlargement of our technical knowledge. In the former case, the newly-employed technical methods were already known and tested[4]: the only reason why they were not used before was that the volume of production was too small for them to be profitable. In the latter case, the new methods were previously unknown or at least had not been tested in practice: they represent a real increase in knowledge. The latter case does indeed constitute a historical and dynamic phenomenon, involving a change in the economic data; and, as we have already observed, when it leads to a reduction in costs it does not fall under the law of decreasing costs, in the theoretical sense. It is not to be regarded as an example of the working of that law even if it happens to be accompanied, as a matter of historical fact, by an expansion of output. A reduction in costs of this dynamic and ' historical ' nature has no place in our analysis, since it represents a change of data not to be explained by economic theory. It may indeed cause far-reaching alterations, under certain conditions, in comparative costs and in international trade, but such reductions in costs are not themselves dependent upon the existence or extent of the international exchange of goods.[5] Graham also does not have such ' historical ' reductions in costs in mind in stating his theory.

3. THE LAW OF DECREASING COSTS IN THE PURE THEORETICAL SENSE.—We have seen that decreasing costs in the strict theoretical sense are the consequence of an expansion of output due to an increase of demand. They may come about through either internal economies or external economies.[6] The former are economies due to an increase in the size of the individual firm or plant. The latter are economies associated with an increase in the size of the industry as a whole, possibly through the entry of new firms; every firm, even if it does not increase in size, benefits from the improved

---

[4] This meets an objection of Schumpeter, who always emphasises that technical knowledge in the laboratory is one thing and practical application of the knowledge is another thing. See his *Theory of Economic Development* (1934), chap. 2.

[5] Inventions may be induced by an expansion of output. But this is by no means certain and cannot be stated in the form of a law.

[6] It is common knowledge that we owe this distinction to Marshall's *Principles of Economics*.

conditions of production. Those economists who, like Schumpeter, deny the possibility of decreasing costs, if technical knowledge remains constant, clearly have in mind—leaving aside the confusion, criticised above, of constant technical knowledge with constant technical methods—the following considerations. The expansion of an industry, in consequence of an increased demand for its product, must raise the price of those original factors which are employed there to a greater extent than in those industries where demand has relatively declined.[7] For example, if the demand for agricultural products increases, the prices of land and of agricultural labour will rise.[8]

This rise in the price of some of the factors employed is a continuous force making for increasing money costs as the production of a good expands. This tendency is simply the monetary expression of the fact, already pointed out,[9] that the substitution curve is concave towards O, so that when the demand for good A increases, constantly increasing quantities of other goods must be forgone in order that an additional units of A can be produced.[1]

This argument is correct as far as it goes. But it is beyond question that the tendency towards increasing costs can be temporarily or permanently offset or more than offset by the internal and external economies which we discuss in detail below. When it is more than offset, we have the phenomenon of decreasing costs.

(a) DECREASING COSTS DUE TO INTERNAL ECONOMIES.—Over a wide range, and more especially in industry rather than in agriculture, an increase in the size of an establishment permits a reduction in costs. The reason for this is that many means of production are not perfectly divisible. Some, such as a conveyor-system for, say, the manufacture of motor cars, or a linotype machine, must be a certain minimum size in order to be worth using at all. Thus the establishment must have a certain minimum output before they can be profitably installed. Once installed, however, they may make possible greater specialisation among the co-operating factors, since the methods of production will be different from formerly. Others, again, are available in different sizes and, up to a point, the larger they are the less is their cost per unit of output. For example, an electric motor costs not

---

[7] Cf. F. Benham, " Taxation and the Relative Prices of Factors of Production," *Economica* (May 1935), p. 198.

[8] Agricultural labour is to a large extent a specific factor in that there are great difficulties in attracting workers from other occupations into agriculture.

[9] Cf. p. 176.

[1] The reason is that the proportions in which the factors are combined in the various industries must be changed. Thus factors specific to the expanding industry, like land in our example, must be combined in less and less favourable proportions with others. In other words when (say) land is worked more intensively, its marginal productivity will rise.

double, but only some 30 per cent. more than one of half its capacity. A larger output may permit the fuller utilisation of certain existing factors: for example, of the office staff and equipment. Hence certain items of expenditure may increase by a smaller proportion than output increases, so that their cost per unit of output will fall when output expands. All this is familiar ground; the advantages of relatively large establishments, in certain industries, are obvious; and we may refer the reader to the literature on this subject for further details.[2]

The following aspects of the matter are relevant to the present discussion. If it is possible, in a given industry at a given time, to reduce costs of production by increasing the size of establishments, free competition will bring about that result. For it will be to the interest of each entrepreneur to reduce his own costs by increasing the size of his establishment; and he will do so, in the hope of undercutting his rivals. This process of increasing the size of establishments will cease only when either (a) the limit is reached beyond which a further increase in size would involve technical or administrative difficulties which would cause costs to rise instead of to fall,[3] or (b) free competition comes to an end, the optimal size of the establishment being so large relatively to the extent of the market that only a very few firms remain. In that case, these few firms will combine or come to a mutual understanding, so that the situation will become monopolistic.

It follows that decreasing costs due to internal economies are inconsistent, in the long run, with free competition. This important fact removes the foundations of Graham's argument, for his theory rests upon the assumption of free competition. He supposes that the American watch industry, operating under decreasing costs, gradually contracts under the pressure of English competition; and this supposition depends upon the assumed existence of free competition in the American industry. But this is an impossible assumption: if the industry is really subject to decreasing costs it would long ago have been monopolised.

It remains to enquire whether a similar argument to that of Graham can apply if, owing to decreasing costs, the industry is already under a monopolist, such as a trust or cartel. The monopolist is in no way compelled to expand output whenever this would reduce his (marginal) costs.[4] He will do so only if the demand is

---

[2] Marshall, *Principles of Economics* and *Industry and Trade*. Robinson, *The Structure of Competitive Industry* (1931).

[3] This limit is reached quickly, as a rule, in agriculture.

[4] For a fuller discussion, see, *e.g.*, Schneider, *Reine Theorie monopolistischer Wirtschaftsformen* (1932); Robinson, *The Economics of Imperfect Competition*, and Chamberlain, *The Theory of Monopolistic Competition*.

sufficiently elastic to increase his total receipts more than his total costs. Suppose now that this industry is confronted with increased foreign competition. Will this lead to the unfavourable results predicted by Graham? Not at all. The fall in price, due to the foreign competition, will reduce the profits of the monopoly. But this in itself represents only a change, and perhaps not an undesired one, in the distribution of the national income. We must consider what will happen to production. The monopolist—unlike the numerous competitive entrepreneurs imagined by Graham—will be able to survey the situation as a whole and to decide what output is most profitable under the changed conditions, instead of being driven blindly, step by step, from one position to another. It may be that, if decreasing costs still prevail, it will pay him to increase his output, thereby reducing his marginal costs, and to expand his sales both at home and abroad by bringing down the price still lower. This, however, would involve no loss to the community as a whole, unless we count the unavoidable fall in profits on his foreign sales. If it does not pay him to undercut the price set by foreign suppliers, he must accept it. If, in these circumstances, the total money receipts of the industry do not cover the total money costs, we have simply the case discussed in § 2 of this chapter. The rents and quasi-rents of the factors specific to the industry will fall; and if, even so, receipts do not cover payments to the co-operating non-specific factors, the industry will close down. The effects of this upon the size of the national income will be the same as those explained in § 2.[5] But in no event can there be a gradual contraction of production, accompanied by continuously increasing costs, as visualised by Graham.

We may take this opportunity to point out that the wide prevalence of decreasing costs due to an increase in the size of establishments is not only no argument against the unrestricted international exchange of goods, but is, on the contrary, one of the most important arguments in favour of it. For one of the main advantages of international trade is that it widens the extent of the market and thereby permits the fuller utilisation of the advantages of large-scale establishments. At the same time, widening the extent of the market prevents, or renders more difficult, the exploitation of consumers by a monopoly. The importance of this consideration, especially for small countries, in view of the modern tendency towards large-scale establishment and mass-production and monopoly, needs no emphasis.[6]

---

[5] The case in which the foreign producers are organised in a monopoly, and the foreign market is protected against imports by a tariff—the case, that is, of Dumping—requires a special discussion. See chap. xviii below, *passim*.

[6] This is discussed more fully in chap. xiv, § 2.

(b) Decreasing Costs due to External Economies.[7]—
Marshall has shown that there may be a double connection between
the cost of production of a commodity and the quantity produced.
On the one hand, costs may vary, as we have just seen, with the size
of the establishments composing the industry: an increase in the
output of any given establishment may make possible internal
economies and so reduce its costs. On the other hand, the costs of
every establishment in the industry may be reduced by an
expansion of the industry as a whole. Thus the costs of a particular establishment may be a function not only of the quantity
which it produces but also of the quantity which the industry as
a whole produces. Each individual plant or firm may be operating
under increasing costs, so that if its output were larger its average
costs would be higher; but an expansion of the industry as a whole
might lower, so to speak, the whole upward-sloping cost-curve of
each individual establishment.[8]

An example of an external economy is the development of a
larger and more reliable supply of skilled labour in consequence of
the growth of an industry, through the entry of new firms. Another
example, often cited, is the improvement of the various means of
transport and communication—such as railways, roads, telephones,
and telegraphs—which serve the industry, when it becomes larger.
In general, the expansion of an industry may reduce the prices of
the machinery and other means of production which it employs,
by enabling them to be produced in greater quantities and therefore, possibly, more cheaply.

It is theoretically conceivable that in these and other ways the
cost and price of a commodity may fall in the long run—for this is
definitely a long-run phenomenon—if, in response to an increased
demand, the industry expands owing to the entry of new establishments, although each individual establishment would increase its
costs if it expanded its output.

We must now point out a fundamental distinction between
internal and external economies. The gain from internal economies,
arising from an increase in the size of an individual establishment,
enters fully into the calculations of the entrepreneurs; and hence
the realisation of these economies can be left to private initiative.

---

[7] See Marshall, *loc. cit.*; Taussig, *Principles of Economics*, vol. 1, chap. 14;
Viner, " Cost Curves and Supply Curves," *Zeitschrift für Nationalökonomie*, vol.
3 (1931); Shove, " Increasing Returns and the Representative Firm," *Economic
Journal* (March 1930).

[8] See the diagrammatic exposition in Viner's article, cited in the preceding
footnote. An expansion of the industry lowers the supply curves and cost curves
of the individual establishments, but these curves continue to slope upwards from
left to right. The collective supply curve, however, slopes downward from left
to right.

But external economies, on the contrary, benefit all the entrepreneurs in the industry, and not only those who, by erecting new works or enlarging existing works, enable them to be realised. They are somewhat vague and indeterminate in nature; it is difficult to estimate their extent or value. Moreover, they partly relate to factors which cannot be appropriated by the entrepreneur, such as the capacities of a skilled labouring population. Hence an entrepreneur will hesitate to spend money on such purposes, since he has no guarantee that the fruits of his investment may not accrue to his competitors or workers rather than to himself. It has been urged that for this reason we cannot leave it to private inititiative to bring external economies into realisation.[9]

The relevance of all this to our present problem is as follows. It may happen that an industry is already benefiting from external economies, and could obtain increased benefits by a further expansion, which is impeded by competition. The further expansion will not now take place, since each individual entrepreneur is working under increasing costs and therefore has no incentive to expand his output. On the contrary, the output of the industry may even contract under the pressure of increasing foreign competition, and this contraction, by depriving it of external economies previously enjoyed,[10] will raise the costs of those undertakings which remain in it. The vicious circle described by Graham makes its appearance. But the industry could survive, and could obtain further benefits from external economies by expanding, if it were temporarily protected by a tariff.

This argument for a tariff is clearly an exact parallel to the infant-industry argument.[1] But it is really not practicable to base a policy of Protection upon phenomena so vague and difficult to estimate as external economies. From a theoretical standpoint, it can be said only that they are conceivable, and even this statement must at once be limited by the following qualifications: (a)

---

[9] The presence of elements of cost which do not enter into the calculations of entrepreneurs gives rise to cases (such as that of Professor Graham, if interpreted in this way) similar to the case discussed on page 197, where the price-ratio is not the same as the substitution-ratio or, in other words, where prices do not equal marginal costs, so that there is a divergence between what Professor Pigou calls the " social " and the " private marginal net product." It can easily be proved that such a divergence must always cause international trade to divert production away from the optimum, not only if costs are decreasing but also if they are increasing. Indeed, even if there is no international trade, the distribution of factors among different branches of production will diverge from the optimum in such cases. (I am indebted to Mr. N. Kaldor for drawing my attention to the possibility of thus generalising the point made in the text.)

[10] It should, however, be noticed that frequently external economies are of such a sort that they do not disappear, once they have been acquired, even if output contracts. Therefore, as Marshall has shown, the downward-sloping supply curve is not reversible.

[1] See chap. xvii, § 5.

It must be remembered that the expansion of an industry may give rise to external diseconomies, which raise the costs of every establishment. Thus means of communication may become congested and the increased demand for means of production used by the industry will raise their price if they are produced under increasing costs. (*b*) Every economy external to industry A which is at the same time an internal economy to industry B falls outside the scope of the present argument. If, for example, the machines used by industry A could be produced more cheaply if they were produced in larger-scale establishments, entrepreneurs in the machine-making industry should be aware of this possibility and will not need the impetus of an expansion of industry A to induce them to utilise it. If, bearing these points in mind, one can still assert that numerous actual and potential external economies exist, it must be remembered (*c*) that most of them, like the improved organisation of the labour market, benefit not only one individual industry, but many industries simultaneously or possibly manufacturing as a whole relatively to agriculture. This consideration is very important for the framing and appraisal of tariff policy.

If due weight is given to all these considerations, one will be constrained to the conclusion that decreasing costs, in the true theoretical sense, are phenomena which occur only seldom and in exceptional cases. It is very improbable that external economies will outweigh, over any length of time, the permanent tendency to increasing costs which we have demonstrated to exist. Hence we shall commit no grave error by continuing to assume, in general, that costs are increasing.[2]

---

[2] Knight is of the same opinion. See his rejoinder to Graham's reply. Marshall held a different view. The question at issue is a question of fact, which can be answered only by empirical research. Materials for forming a judgment upon it are to be found mainly in writings upon questions of industrial organisation and upon cartels and trusts. See, *e.g.*, Marshall, *Principles of Economics* and *Industry and Trade;* Beckerath, *Modern Industrial Organisation;* MacGregor, *Industrial Combination* (1906), reprinted by the London School of Economics (1935); Robinson, *The Structure of Competitive Industry* (1931).

PART II.

TRADE POLICY.

A—INTRODUCTION.

CHAPTER XIII.

THE SCIENTIFIC TREATMENT OF THE SUBJECT OF TRADE POLICY.

§ 1. The Order of Treatment which will be Followed.

In this Part we shall try, basing ourselves upon the conclusions of Part I, to examine the principles and problems of external trade policy. This requires three stages. We must, *first*, study the *technique* of trade policy. We must, *secondly*, make clear the standpoint from which the various measures of trade policy are to be judged or criticised. We must, that is, try to discover the *axiological standpoint* from which it is most possible to reach the conclusion that this or that measure is ' good,' ' advisable,' ' correct ' or ' desirable.' Of course, it is impossible scientifically to prove such value-judgments. We can only point out what men consciously accept as the highest ethical values and then demonstrate that a particular value-judgment follows from them.

We must, *thirdly*, amplify the theoretical frame-work of Part I by making more concrete assumptions. This is necessary in order to discuss prevailing views at all justly and to decide whether, and, if so, in what circumstances any particular measure is desirable from this or that axiological standpoint. In particular, we must consider whether the theory developed in Part I does not make so many simplifying assumptions that it fails to apply to any case in which these simplifying assumptions are not true, and whether, therefore, the views there expressed as to the advantage of Free Trade may not be false. Such simplifying assumptions might be : the existence of free competition, the absence of frictions, and an absence of phenomena arising from the economic development of the community.[1] The most important serious arguments for Protection revolve around these three assumptions, which are alleged to be untrue of the real world and yet always assumed in the theory of international trade.

We shall proceed as follows. The detailed discussion of the technique of trade policy is postponed to section C, since it seems undesirable to obscure the fundamental points by a mass of technical

---

[1] This is synonymous in essentials with the assumption of a given fixed and unalterable quantity of original means of production.

detail.   A very general account of different systems of trade
policy will be a sufficient preliminary to the greater part of the
discussion in section B : indeed, for this purpose a division between
policies of Free Trade and policies of Protection (see below) will
suffice.   § 2 of this chapter contains a discussion of the most appropriate axiological standpoint.   Section B discusses various economic
arguments for Free Trade or Protection.

We understand by commercial policy or trade policy all measures
regulating the external economic relations of a country : that is,
measures taken by a territorial Government which has the power
of assisting or hindering the export or import of goods and services.
These consist primarily of *duties, bounties* and *prohibitions* upon
imports or exports.   But the international exchange of goods can
be prevented or hindered or stimulated by other measures also,
such as veterinary regulations, the regulation of freight rates, an
insistence upon an expensive packing for certain imported goods,
and a host of other chicaneries to which international trade may
be subjected, together with concealed subsidies and bounties to
promote export.

In our discussion of the main principles, however, we shall
speak always (unless otherwise stated) of *import duties*, including
those so high as to be prohibitive.   For duties are the most important and most rational weapons of trade policy ; once an insight
into the working and results of duties has been attained this can
readily be applied to other similar measures.

We shall begin with the view, stated and proved in Part I,
that the international movement of goods and capital, unrestricted
by any governmental measures, is economically advantageous.   The
opposing arguments in favour of State intervention will then be
reviewed.   We shall thus set against the pure Free Trade principle
the numerous arguments, often incompatible with one another, for
tariffs.

We must not, however, let this lead us into the conscious or
unconscious exaggeration of calling everyone who considers that
tariffs or other interferences may be useful in certain circumstances
(which may very rarely occur) a Protectionist, and reserving the
designation of ' Free Trader ' for those very few authors who
believe that circumstances in which tariffs may be advantageous
are inconceivable.   This is, of course, a purely terminological
matter.   Nevertheless, it is not merely terminological to point out
that a twofold division into Free Traders and Protectionists is
scientifically insufficient.   It would be more appropriate to construct a scale, with absolute Free Traders at one extreme and
' autarchists,' the advocates of complete national self-sufficiency,

at the other, and other writers ranged between them, the position of each depending upon the amount of protection which he advocates. At which point on the scale we should draw the line between Free Traders and Protectionists depends upon the customary political uses of these terms and will not be further considered here.

§ 2. VALUE-JUDGMENTS UPON INTERNATIONAL TRADE AND UPON MEASURES OF TRADE POLICY.

How is it possible, while remaining within the realm of science, to assert that particular measures are ' desirable ' or ' correct '? To put the matter more accurately, what are the criteria for a value-judgment which declares that the situation resulting from some particular measure is preferable to the situation which would have come about if that measure had not been taken? In answering this question, we start from the principle, developed with great clarity by Max Weber, of the *Wertfreiheit* (freedom from value-judgments) of science.[2] It is not the task of science to make value-judgments, nor is it in a position to do so. It cannot, for example, demonstrate that Free Trade is the ' correct ' trade policy. It can only try to show what would be the consequences for a country of Free Trade or of Protection. But it follows from this that science is in a position to decide which means should be adopted to achieve a given end (or an end assumed to be given for purposes of discussion) and whether a *given* means is appropriate to a *given* end. *If* the national income is to be as great as possible, then this or that trade policy is the most suitable. Special cases of such decisions are the demonstration (a) that a given end cannot be attained; (b) that the attainment of one end A (for example, the greatest possible independence of other countries) inevitably works against some other end B (for example, the maximisation of the national income) which is also desired, so that A and B cannot both be attained simultaneously. The solution of this conflict by laying down a scale to show what weight must be given to A and B respectively involves a new value-judgment and is, therefore, of a non-scientific nature. (c) Frequently means to given ends (intermediate aims) are assumed to have absolute (and not merely instrumental) value, so that they become regarded as ends in themselves, and the ultimate ends tend to be forgotten. This creates the wrong impression that the object of science is

---

2 See his two papers *Der Sinn der Wertfreiheit der soziologischen und ökonomischen Wissenschaften* and *Wissenschaft als Beruf*, both reprinted in *Gesammelte Aufsätze zur Wissenschaftslehre* (1922).

to postulate an end which should be striven for instead of merely discussing suitable means of achieving a *given* end.

How is our theoretical demonstration of the advantage of Free Trade compatible with this abstention of science from the making of value-judgments? And are there not continual scientific discussions as to whether Free Trade or Protection is the ' correct ' policy? The solution of these apparent contradictions should now be clear. In every such discussion an end is tacitly taken for granted or assumed to be generally accepted as desirable.

Hence arises the problem of stating clearly and explicitly what end is taken as desirable. Otherwise there is the danger of carrying on what is apparently a scientific discussion as to the most appropriate means of achieving a given end when, in fact, the parties to the discussion hold different opinions about its desirability, and of presupposing tacitly, in different circumstances, contradictory values or incompatible ends. In political discussions ends and means are often mixed up in a quite unholy manner, so that it is often difficult to be sure whether people disagree in their social philosophy as to which end is desirable or whether they disagree as to the consequences which would follow from particular measures or as to the best means of achieving a *given* end.

In the next few paragraphs we shall discuss what are the ends which trade policy should achieve. In other words, we shall set out the scale of values by which trade policy usually is or should be judged.

We have first the important distinction between *economic* and *non-economic* ends. It is comparatively easy to make a list of non-economic values or ends, by which economic events and phenomena may be judged. Such non-economic ' standpoints ' are: the standpoint of national defence; that of social justice; irrational postulates (for example, of a religious nature); the belief that a nation can fulfil its destiny only if it avoids the too close contact with other peoples which results from international trade. Such standpoints represent pure value-judgments, although not all these ends need be ultimate, in the sense that it is inconceivable that one or the other could be subordinated to, and derived from, some other and more important aim. For example, most people regard military preparedness only as a means, or intermediate end, and not as an end in itself. Be this as it may, it is clear that one and the same economic situation or measure may be judged differently according to which of these standpoints is adopted, and that any such judgment may conflict with the ' economic ' value-judgment.

More difficult and more important for us is the analysis of the ' economic ' value-judgment or statement of ends. What does it mean to say that a particular measure is to be welcomed ' from an economic standpoint ' or is ' economically right ' when from a different standpoint the conclusion might be different? Is there one specific *economic* end or ideal, which can be clearly set out by the science of economics, without making any non-economic assumptions or non-scientific value-judgments, and the attainment of which is the task of all *economic* policy? The answer is definitely in the negative. There is no ' analytical economic ideal,' despite the view of many theorists that such an ideal is implicit in the very nature of an economy and in economic principles. The science of economics can only examine the working and consequences of economic measures, such as those connected with trade policy; it can only consider what means are most appropriate to attain or promote a *given* end; it cannot of itself decide the purpose of an economy and the task of economic policy. Attempts to do this, however, have not been lacking. ' The development of productive power,' ' the increase of productivity,' ' the increase of wealth,' ' the promotion of economic welfare ' and other ends have been put forward as criteria by which to judge economic policy on the ground that they are implied in the fundamental nature of an economy.[3] But unless such terms as economic welfare are very minutely defined, and exact criteria are given for determining whether productivity or wealth has increased or diminished, such attempts merely introduce new words. A precise definition of these terms, giving the needed criteria, implies necessarily the setting out of material values or ends, which cannot be in any way scientifically proved desirable or deduced from economic principles, but must simply be accepted as given.

The division between ' economic ' and other ends is thus merely one of terminological convenience. Moreover, in ordinary speech the division is not at all clear-cut and the boundary between the two is blurred and shifting.

Probably everybody will speak of a purely economic end when the *maximisation of the national income* or of the social product is desired.[4] Instead of ' national income or dividend,' the terms ' national wealth,' ' economic welfare,' and so on, are often used. Thus any measure which increases the size of the national income

---

3 An excellent and convincing discussion of these problems is to be found in M. St. Braun, *Theorie der staatlichen Wirtschaftspolitik* (1929), and Robbins, *The Nature and Significance of Economic Science* (1932), chap. 2.

4 This does not involve a contradiction with what was just said, because it is only a statement about the general usage of words or a terminological convention.

is regarded as economically desirable, from this standpoint. But there are very great difficulties in the analysis of such concepts as the national income, the social product and the volume of production.[5] On this subject the following comments must suffice.

It is not a question only of the *absolute size* of the national income, but also of the *mode of distribution* of the social product among the various sections of the population and among the various individual persons. If one takes account only of the absolute size of the total national income (because maybe its distribution has not been significantly altered or because the effect upon its distribution cannot be accurately traced) it would be generally conceded that the yardstick is an *economic* one. But when one in addition lays down certain postulates as to its distribution, as for example that the greatest possible approach to equality is desirable or that a change in favour of certain classes is to be taken as an end, it becomes a question of taste whether we call the yardstick an economic one or one of ' social justice.' In any case there are now two yardsticks—the absolute size of the national income *and* its mode of distribution—and one may lead to a different conclusion from the other. It is, for example, conceivable that Free Trade may yield a larger national income than Protection but may at the same time lead to a distribution of that income regarded on some ground or other as undesirable.

When we speak of the distribution of the national income we must, to be accurate, distinguish five different kinds of distribution, to each of which more or less value may be attached.

(*a*) *The distribution of the total income of the territory among the several regions.* We must decide clearly within exactly what territorial boundaries income is to be maximised. This includes a choice between cosmopolitan and nationalistic aims. This is forgotten by those Free Traders who accuse Protectionists of being inconsistent when they consider tariffs upon foreign goods to be advantageous but do not want inter-regional tariffs within their own country. There *may* indeed be a contradiction when the Protectionist declares that a tariff benefits *both* the country which

---

[5] For a closer definition *cf.* Pigou, *Economics of Welfare*, pt. 1. I have tried to define the concept ' national income ' in *Der Sinn der Indexzahlen* (1927), pp. 77 *et seq.*, and in the article '' Der volkswirtschaftliche Geldwert und die Preisindexziffern '' in *Weltwirtschaftliches Archiv* (1929), vol. 30, pp. 6**. I am well aware that the concept ' national income ' cannot be quite precisely defined without having recourse to certain value judgments. (Hence it belongs to the realm of ' welfare economics.') But some generally accepted value principles can be found, from which an exact definition can be derived. The concept in question has been subjected to an illuminating, although in my opinion exaggerated and destructive criticism (destructive, because it pours out the baby with the bath water) by Myrdal, *Das politische Element in der nationalökonomischen Doktrinbildung* (1932), pp. 200 *et seq.*

imposes it and the countries against which it is directed.   But the Protectionist is not inconsistent if he admits that the foreign countries will be injured.   For, from his nationalistic standpoint, the injury to foreign countries is not taken into account; whereas, when he is considering an inter-regional tariff within his country, he weighs the loss of one region against the gain of another, and if he concludes that the former exceeds the latter, it follows that from his standpoint (which in this case now becomes according to the accepted terminology a purely economic one) the tariff is to be condemned.   Moreover, he may consider that to promote the connection between different parts of his country is desirable in itself, apart from any calculations as to the gain of one district and the loss of another.

(b) *The ' functional ' distribution among classes and occupations*, for example between rich and poor, town and country, income from work and other income, and between wages, interest, rent of land, and monopoly profits.

(c) *The distribution among individual persons* within these classes.   This can change without any change in the distribution among classes and occupations.   In this connection we should perhaps mention the wish of some compassionate people to avoid every change in production, since it would alter the distribution of income among persons and thereby reduce the income of some below the level to which they had become accustomed.

(d) *The distribution of the social product over time*.   It is often argued that a given policy, for example Free Trade, may indeed ensure a greater social product in the present, but that the social product of the future will suffer.   The advocates of ' infant industry tariffs ' seem to take this view.

(e) *Stability and security of income*.   It is not a matter of indifference whether the income is received over a given period in an even flow or whether—while still of the same average amount per unit of time—its volume is sometimes comparatively great and sometimes comparatively small.   One can, for example, well hold the opinion that a relatively small but steady income is preferable to a greater average income received irregularly, with periods of unemployment.

PART II.

B—THE CONSEQUENCES OF DIFFERENT SYSTEMS
AND MEASURES OF COMMERCIAL POLICY.
FREE TRADE AND PROTECTION.

CHAPTER XIV.

ARGUMENTS FOR FREE TRADE.

§ 1. The Presumption that Free Trade is Advantageous.

When we set out the grounds for presuming that Free Trade is economically advantageous, we took the maximisation of the social product as the criterion by which a situation or measure was to be judged. It can be proved that, at any rate under the usual assumptions of general economic theory (free competition, absence of friction, and so on), the unrestricted international exchange of goods increases the real incomes of *all* the participating countries. The price mechanism, under competition, automatically ensures that each country specialises in the production of those goods which it is relatively best suited to produce and imports those goods, and only those goods, which it can obtain more cheaply, taking account of transport costs, in this indirect manner, than by producing them itself.

In many cases it is obvious that the production of goods can be enormously increased by the international division of labour. The production of numerous raw materials such as coal, iron, other metals, and of vegetable products, such as cotton and jute, is possible only in certain parts of the world. Those countries which cannot produce such goods within their boundaries must either obtain them by exchange or go without them, although they are indispensable to a modern standard of living. The same thing applies, although to a somewhat lesser extent, to the exchange of goods all of which could be produced, if necessary, in each one of the participating countries. The tool which we used to prove this was the theory of comparative costs. This, as we have seen, is by no means valid only under the simplifying assumptions with which we started, but is also valid under the more complicated conditions of modern international trade. Moreover, the contention that international division of labour benefits all the countries concerned is true not only under the assumption that factors of production and especially labour, are mobile between countries, but also if labour, as is for the most part the case in the world of today, does not move across national boundaries. If a good is imported at a price with which the home industry cannot compete, and the latter is in consequence compelled to disappear or to shrink in size, factors of production will move into other branches of production, where they can now produce more and, therefore, earn a higher rate of remuneration. The social product must, therefore, be damaged whenever, through some interference with the free play of economic forces, such as a tariff, factors of production are retained in an employment where their marginal productivity is smaller. We first arrived at this conclusion under the simplifying assumption that there was only one mobile factor of production (labour). But the conclusion also applies (always assuming a freely-working price mechanism under competition) when, as in fact is always the case, numerous factors of production combine together, many of which are immobile or, more accurately ' specific '—factors, that is to say, which can be used only for a certain purpose or would produce much less in any other employment (for example, a machine used as scrap iron) and, therefore, are not diverted to any other use. When, under such conditions, a branch of industry becomes exposed to foreign competition, the prices of such factors as are specific to that branch must fall first, and if necessary must fall to zero. This loss of capital implies, indeed, a change in the distribution of the national dividend, but no diminution in its size. When the price of the good falls so low that, even after writing down the value of the specific factors to nil, that industry cannot afford to pay the market price for its mobile factors (their market price being what they could earn elsewhere), then the industry ceases to exist, the specific factors being abandoned and the others employed in other uses. Since the non-specific factors can now be of greater use in another branch of production, it would be uneconomic to prevent them, by means of a tariff, from moving, and to retain them in a place where their productivity is smaller.

This is *the* Free Trade argument, briefly stated. Only upon this basis, and, of course, under the assumption that the desired end is the maximisation of the social product, can a liberal trade policy be scientifically justified, although it may be that for reasons of political propaganda other arguments are placed more in the foreground.

§ 2. OTHER ARGUMENTS FOR FREE TRADE.

The most attractive argument for Free Trade is to point out that *free import lowers the prices of imported goods.* That is, of course, correct; and the extent of the price reduction affords (with certain reservations) some measure of the gain to the economy from international trade, and an approximate measure of the injury which an impediment to the import of these goods would involve. This argument has the advantage, not to be despised, that it is useful for purposes of propaganda, since everyone is a consumer and, as such, desires lower prices. Nevertheless, this is only one side of the matter, and gives only a partial view of the problem. This explains why the objection is always raised against Free Trade doctrine that it considers only the interests of consumers and ignores the question of employment and, in general, the interests of producers. The Free Trader can answer this objection by pointing out that not only will prices fall, but, in addition, there will result a movement of factors of production to other parts of the economy, where they can earn more. But this brings us back to our first and fundamental argument. Those who find a sufficient reason for free import in the consequent price reduction should logically desire export duties, since the increased difficulty of exporting would reduce the prices of exportable goods in the exporting country.

Another point is that free import and export benefit all participating countries in that they prevent, or at least make more difficult, the establishment of injurious monopolies. This fact must again be considered from the two standpoints of the increase in the social product and of the effect on its distribution.

We have already pointed out, when speaking of the law of decreasing costs, that there is a danger in small areas shut off by import duties that in many branches of industry, in which large-scale production yields a significant advantage, the optimum size of the production unit cannot be attained because the market is too small. The complement of this is the formation of a monopoly. This involves a threefold injury to the economy.

First, under Free Trade each country can specialise in a few branches of production, and the optimum size of the production unit can be attained and costs reduced everywhere.[1] Restrictions on the freedom of trade will not only lead to a loss of these advantages of international division of labour but will also— *secondly*—raise the prices of the goods, produced by the resulting monopolies, above costs of production which, owing to the relatively small output due to the restricted market, are already at a relatively high level.

Thirdly, experience shows that the restriction of free competition may lead to a less efficient conduct of economic affairs. Free Trade has an educative effect. Home producers are spurred by foreign competition to become more efficient and to adopt quickly any

---

[1] In certain circumstances this may result in the market of a country being dominated by a foreign monopoly. Of this, more later.

improvement in methods of production, no matter where it is first introduced.

Nevertheless, Free Trade does not provide a complete safeguard against the formation of monopolies. Even under Free Trade there may emerge *international monopolies*, of which more will be said later,[2] and *local monopolies*. These local monopolies owe their existence, in the absence of a tariff, to transport costs, which have much the same effects as tariffs. In those branches of production whose products can be transported only at a high cost, the lower production-costs due to a larger production-unit may be more than offset by the increased costs of marketing the greater output over a wider area. When this is the case, there will not be a single market with a uniform price, such as is described in general price theory, but a series of adjoining monopoly districts, partly overlapping one another, with competitive prices in the contested regions and monopoly prices inside each district. These monopoly prices can exceed production costs, but only to the extent of the freight charges.[3]

If a tariff wall is erected which cuts across such a network of production districts, *first*, the existing, and rational, arrangement of production units over space, determined by the freight situation of factors and products, will be disturbed, and, *secondly*, the power of the monopolies will be strengthened. Both these effects will be especially obvious in the neighbourhood of the tariff wall. For example, two monopolists who previously competed in a certain area may find that a tariff wall runs across that area and so cuts them off from each other's competition, or a producer, who previously had to face foreign competition, may now be relieved from it by the tariff wall: the result will be to raise prices by forming monopoly districts sheltered from competition from the other side of the tariff wall.

§ 3. The Aims of Free Traders.

The aim upon which the argument for Free Trade which we have developed is based, is the maximisation of the social product or national income. The income of which group of persons? In this connection, some serious misunderstandings must be avoided. We are constantly told that the Free Trader adopts a *cosmopolitan*

---

[2] Chap xix, § 7.

[3] Such a monopoly profit may also be termed 'rent of situation.' It is a differential rent, which arises not from the superior quality of the factors used or from the ability of the entrepreneur, but from a favourable (freight) situation with regard to transport facilities. Situation rents may also exist without being of a monopolistic character.

standpoint, that he takes account of the welfare of the whole world, and that in cases of conflict he is prepared to sacrifice the interests of his own country. That is not correct; a cosmopolitan aim is in no way essential to the Free Trade postulate, although it must be admitted that it is easier to explain the advantage of unrestricted exchange of goods if one takes account of the whole world rather than considers only the interests of the particular country. Moreover, there is an easily explicable *psychological affinity* between Free Trade and internationalism. But these two are not inevitably bound together; the economic case for Free Trade shows that *all* participating countries gain by it, but it does not show that the profit of one implies a loss for another. Thus a nationalist may be a convinced Free Trader just as well as a pacifist and internationalist may be one.

As to the *relations between Free Trade and economic liberalism*, on the one hand, and *socialism* or *interventionism*, on the other hand, the following may be said.[4] Free Trade is the external trade system of *liberalism*, which opposes every interference by the State with the free play of economic forces. But it by no means follows from this that it is inconsistent to advocate, on the one hand, unrestricted Free Trade and, on the other hand, certain interferences with the free play of economic forces, for example on the labour market.

The reason why a man can without inconsistency be against import duties and in favour of State intervention on behalf of workers is that Free Trade usually does nothing, at any rate in the long run, to change the functional distribution of the national income. In so far as it does have any effect on this, it tends rather to favour income from work. Thus Free Trade increases the total income and does not appreciably alter its distribution. It is, therefore, unlikely to reduce the *relative* income of labour and still more unlikely to reduce its *absolute* income. It follows that considerations as to the distribution of the national income do not modify the general presumption that Free Trade is advantageous. It is true that in so far as Free Trade doctrine is based upon the labour theory of value, which does not clearly discuss the possibility of a changed distribution of income within the labouring class, it is inadequate. But our analysis has shown that from the standpoint of modern theory also this attitude (as

---

[4] *Cf.* Röpke, " Liberale Handelspolitik " in *Archiv für Rechts- und Wirtschaftsphilosophie* (1930-31), vol. 24, pp. 345 *et seq.*, and same author, " Staatsinterventionismus " in *Ergänzungsband zum Handwörterbuch der Staatswissenschaften* (1929), pp. 878 *et seq.*

Q

to the unlikelihood of any significant change in the distribution of the national income arising from Free Trade) is not unjustified.[5]

The valuations upon which this attitude is based are so obvious that it is unnecessary to set them out.

---

[5] *Cf.* chap. xii, § 3. L. T. Hobhouse rejects, as Röpke does, the objection that advocacy of Free Trade and of measures in favour of the working class are contradictory. *Cf. Liberalism* (1911), pp. 92 *et seq.* The same view was held by Dietzel, *Sozialpolitik und Handelspolitik* (1902), *Kornzoll und Sozialreform* (1901), Hobson, *International Trade* (1904), pp. 192 *et seq.* G. Cassel holds the opposite view; see his *Theoretische Sozialökonomie* (1927), 4th edn., pp. 587 *et seq.*

CHAPTER XV.

THE EFFECTS OF TARIFFS.

§ 1. The Direct Effects of a Particular Import Duty upon the Price and Sales of the Commodity.

We have already set out, in § 8 of chapter XI, the direct effects of an import duty under competition and increasing costs. Under increasing costs an import duty imposed by a country importing the commodity—such a duty imposed by an exporting country would have no effects—or an export duty imposed by an exporting country, leads to a rise in the price of the good within the importing country and a fall in its price within the exporting country, coupled with an increased production of it and smaller sales of it in the importing country, and a decreased production and greater sales of it in the exporting country. We must now consider this matter in detail, and answer the questions: by how much will the price rise in the importing country? By how much will it fall in the exporting country? Must its price in the two countries differ to the full extent of the duty?[1] The answer to these questions depends upon the manner in which supply and demand in each of the two countries respond to a change in price. We must take account of (1) the elasticity of supply and of demand and (2) the absolute amount of supply and of demand, in each of the two countries.[1a]

We must, as we have already shown, begin with the fact that the first effect of an import duty is that foreign suppliers receive a price for their goods which is reduced by the amount of the duty. We have shown this graphically by lowering the whole curve system of the importing country, which we drew side by side with that of the exporting country. The further results of the import duty can readily be traced exactly on such a diagram. Nevertheless, in this case it may be useful to formulate our theorems in words.

(1) Up to the point at which it becomes prohibitive—that is,

---

[1] Pigou, *Protective and Preferential Import Duties*, pp. 94-95; H. Schultz, "Correct and Incorrect Methods of Determining the Effectiveness of the Tariff," in *Journal of Farm Economics* (1935), vol. 17, pp. 625 *et seq.*

[1a] We must distinguish between elasticity and absolute amount. In a diagram, the former is represented by the *shape* of the curve and in latter by its *position*. Elasticity is usually measured by the *percentage* change in amount divided by the *percentage* change in price. Thus, equal elasticities will have a different *absolute* significance according to whether they relate to a large or to a small country.

at which the home demand falls off so much or the home supply increases so much, that the good is no longer imported—an import duty upon a good previously imported must lead to a difference between the home and foreign price (or an increase in the difference previously existing on account of transport costs and so on) exactly equal to the amount of the duty. If this difference were greater than that, further import would be stimulated; and if it were less, importers would make losses and imports would be reduced. This price difference comes about through a rise in the home price and a fall in the foreign price; in certain extreme cases it comes about through either the one or the other.

We must remember that in practice a number of goods are imported and exported only intermittently, according for example to the seasons or to the size of crops. Thus the German duties on grain are so high that when the German harvests are good they become prohibitive and the German price of grain exceeds the world price by less than the amount of the duty. In such a case it is commonly, though not very accurately, said that the duty has ceased to be effective.

(2) Within the country imposing the duty the price, other things being equal, will rise less, and will therefore fall more abroad, the greater and more elastic is the home supply (and conversely)—that is, the greater the extent by which the home supply will increase in consequence of a small price-rise.[2] For this reason an import duty on a good which cannot be produced in the country imposing the duty will lead, under otherwise similar conditions, to a greater price-rise than a duty on a good whose production can be readily increased within the country. Duties on agricultural and mineral products, an increased production of which is usually accompanied by rapidly increasing costs, will lead to a greater price-rise than a duty on manufactured goods, the production of which can often rapidly be increased in response to a rise in their price. The more elastic the home supply, the more will the foreign price fall, since foreign producers, deprived of part of their export market by the duty, will turn to their own home market and thereby reduce the price there.

(3) For similar reasons the home price, in the importing country, will rise less, other things being equal, and the foreign price will therefore fall more, the smaller and less elastic is the foreign supply (and conversely).[3] If the foreign production does not decrease or

---

[2] Schüller speaks of the spread between the highest and lowest costs instead of speaking of elasticity.

[3] This can be set out diagrammatically in the following manner (fig. 22). Let the supply and demand curves SS and DD be given for each country. The price will be P and the quantity aa will be exported from country E to country I. Now let an import duty T be imposed in I and, in order to show this on the

decreases only slowly in consequence of a falling price (because, for example, it uses fixed capital which cannot be transferred to

diagram, let the whole curve-system of I be lowered by the amount T to S'S' and D'D'. The result of this is that the export is reduced to the quantity a'a' and

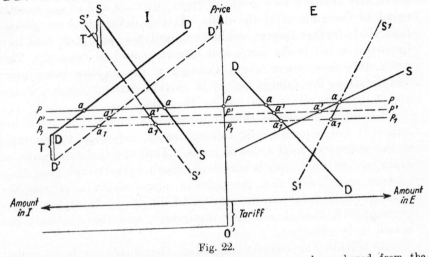

Fig. 22.

the price in E falls to P'. The price in I must now be reckoned from the lowered axis O'. The price in I has therefore risen by an amount equal to the difference between T and the strip PP' (the price-fall in E plus the price-rise in I must equal the duty).

Let us now assume a less elastic supply in E. This is shown by making its supply curve steeper ($S_1 S_1$ instead of SS). The result is that the price in E falls to a greater extent (to P_1) and rises less in I, while the amount exported becomes greater ($a_1 a_1$ instead of $a^1 a^1$).

A glance at the figure shows that the extent of the price-rise in I and of the price-fall in E depends partly upon whether the supply curve in E is relatively flat or relatively steep. The same is true *mutatis mutandis* for the three other curves. All this, of course, corresponds with the rules laid down in the text.

It is the *slope* of the curves and not their *position* which is decisive. If, for example, we move the whole curve-system of E to the right or to the left, this does not alter in any way the amount exported and the effects of the duty. For the distance between the curves, which is what matters, is not thereby altered. But we must not jump from this to the conclusion that it is only the *elasticity*

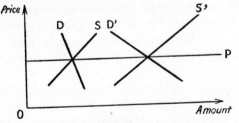

Fig. 23.

and not the *absolute amount* of the supply and demand which matters. For a horizontal movement of the whole curve-system to the right or to the left does *not* show an unchanged elasticity. Conversely, an absolute increase of supply and demand, due perhaps to an increase of population, results in an unchanged elasticity of the curves, *not* when the whole curve-system moves horizontally to the right, but when the curves move to the right and simultaneously become flatter, as is show in Fig. 23.

any other use), the foreign producers will be constrained to sell at a lower price than if they could readily change over to some other kind of production. The elasticity of supply is always less in the short run than in the long run.

(4) The price—other things being equal—will rise less in the importing country and, therefore, fall more in the exporting country, the larger and more elastic is the demand of the former, and conversely. If the demand in the importing country falls off considerably in response to a price rise, the home production there will not increase so much and, therefore, its costs will not rise so much, while, on the other hand, the foreign production will be reduced and its supply-price thereby lowered.

(5) The price—other things being equal—will rise more in the importing country and, therefore, fall less in the foreign country the larger and more elastic is the demand of the foreign country, and conversely. For in that case that part of the foreign supply now excluded by the import duty will be more easily absorbed in the foreign country itself and therefore the pressure upon the protected market will be lessened.

(6) Implied in the above conclusions is the rule laid down by Schüller, that the price-rise due to an import duty will be greater the smaller is the import in relation to the production of the exporting country and the greater is the import in relation to the production of the importing country. The reasons for this are obvious.

One case is worth special mention, since it can very easily be shown diagrammatically and something very like it often occurs in practice. This is the case in which the quantity of the good imported into a country forms an insignificant part of the total supply of the world market and, therefore, cannot influence the world price. For example, if Austria were to place an import duty or increase an existing duty upon an internationally-traded good such as cotton or copper or wheat or lead, the world price would not be affected thereby. The world supply is so large that any

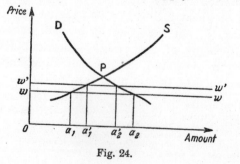

Fig. 24.

probable demand from a single country can be met at the existing price or at one very slightly higher. If we take as an example a commodity, such as grain, which is also produced within the country in question, this case can be presented diagrammatically in the following way (fig. 24).

If the commodity were not imported, the home price in the country in question would be P. The world price, Ow, would not change in consequence of increased sales in our country, since practically any quantity can be obtained at the world price. Under Free Trade the home price is determined by the world price. The home production is in fact Oa_1 and the import a_1a_2. If now a duty of the amount ww_1 is imposed, the consumption falls from Oa_2 to Oa'_2. The home production increases from Oa_1 to Oa'_1, the import decreases from a_1a_2 to $a'_1a'_2$. The home price is raised by the full amount of the duty and the world price remains unchanged. If a single country imposes a duty upon a mass-produced article with a world market, this simple diagram suffices to explain the direct effects of the duty.

It is possible to enlarge this diagram, without making it too complicated, in order to include those cases in which the world price is not independent of the amount sold in the country in question (fig. 25). Let us take as an illustration the import of

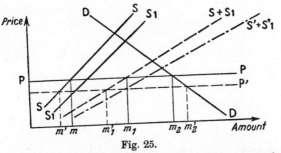

Fig. 25.

wheat into Austria. Austria can take any given quantity from the great Western market without influencing the world price. But the freight-situation is such that, in fact, Hungary provides most of her imports of wheat.[4] But the Hungarian export price, unlike the world price, is not independent of the amount exported to Austria. On account of the freight-situation, Hungary is constrained to sell to Austria. Hence the Hungarian supply curve must not be shown, like the supply curve to the world market, as a horizontal line, but must be shown as rising from left to right, like the home supply curve. We can now construct one single supply

---

[4] In reality differences of quality between Hungarian and Canadian and Russian wheat also play a part, but here we abstract from these differences.

curve for these three sources of supply to the Austrian market—the home production, the import from Hungary, and the import from the world market. The supply curve of the world market remains a horizontal line at the height (above the abscissa) of the world price *plus* transport costs and *plus* the import duty. The home supply curve SS rises as usual from left to right.

The curve S_1S_1 needs a word of explanation. It is the curve of the Hungarian supply *to the Austrian market*. It shows, for each price ruling in the Austrian market, what quantity will be exported (taking account of transport costs and of the import duty) at that price from Hungary to Austria. It must not be confused, therefore, with the curve of the *total* Hungarian supply. The curve S_1S_1 could be derived from the latter by deducting from the total quantity offered at any given price that part of it which would be sold in Hungary itself or in some third market. The curve S_1S_1 shows the quantity exported from Hungary to Austria as a function of the price in the Austrian market. We can now add together for each ordinate the abscissæ of the curves SS and S_1S_1 in order to obtain $S + S_1$, the Austrian-Hungarian supply curve.[5]

Our figure thus tells us that at a price P (=world price + freight + duty) in the Austrian market the Austrian production is Om, the Hungarian supply mm_1 and the import from the world market m_1m_2. If the price in Austria falls to P' (for example, because of a lowering of its duty or of a fall in the world price), the Austrian production contracts to Om', and the import from Hungary to $m'm_1'$, while the import from the world market rises to $m_1'm_2'$.

We may also mention that this diagram is especially suitable for explaining the effects of *preferential duties*. If Austria were to grant a reduction of duty upon the import from Hungary, the Hungarian supply curve would be pushed to the right. Hungary could now export more than before to Austria at a given price.[6] The curve $S + S_1$ would be pushed to the right; this is shown in our diagram by the dotted curve $S' + S_1'$. The import from Hungary would increase at the expense of the import from the world market. The home production and the home price would remain unaltered so long as the import from the world market was not completely excluded.[7]

---

[5] The horizontal distance of each point on the curve $S+S_1$ from the point at an equal height on the curve SS is therefore equal to the horizontal distance of the curve S_1S_1 from the vertical axis, which is equal to the import from Hungary at that price.

[6] If Hungary supplies also numerous other markets, its supply to the Austrian market will be only a part of its total supply, and this partial supply curve will thus be flatter or quite horizontal. The preference would then result in a price-fall, unless it was restricted to a small quota only.

[7] For an appraisal of preferential duties, *cf.* chap. xxi, § 5.

§ 2. The Indirect Effects of Duties.

The influence of a duty on the price and sales of the good in question, which we have analysed by the method of partial equilibrium, forms only a part of the total effects of the duty, albeit the part which is most obvious and which is paid most attention in trade policy. We must add to these direct effects the very important indirect effects; if these are not taken into account a politico-economic judgment on these questions cannot be formed.

The *first* of these indirect effects is *a displacement of the stream of demand*. If it so happens that the elasticity of demand for the good subject to the duty is exactly equal to unity, the purchasers will expend the same total sum upon it as before, but their relative demands for other commodities may be changed. If the elasticity of demand for it is less than unity, the duty will result in a greater sum than before being spent upon it and, therefore, less money will be available for other goods. If the elasticity of demand for it is greater than unity, money will be set free for the purchase of other goods.

A complete analysis of the effects of tariffs must take account, *secondly*, of the manner in which the State spends the money it receives from the duties. In setting out the pros and cons of import duties, these receipts must be counted on the credit side. But it is difficult to make any generalisation upon that subject.

Thirdly, import duties affect the structure of the economy in that they reduce exports. This point is often ignored by publicists and in the practice of trade policy. We must here distinguish between (*a*) *the long run effect*, that is to say the new equilibrium towards which the economy is directed by the coming of import duties, and (*b*) the *transition*, that is to say the path by which the new equilibrium is reached.

We can discuss (*a*) upon the basis of the conclusions reached in chapters X, XI, and XII. Every import duty finally results in a shifting of production away from the export industries and towards industries producing for the home market. Factors of production will be diverted away from the export industries. They will go either into those branches of industry protected by the import duties or, if such branches are not available (under pure revenue duties with an equivalent ' excise ' duty upon home production), into those industries towards which the diverted demand of consumers, or the increased expenditure of the State, is turned. We may further observe that the effects of import duties in diminishing total imports and therefore total exports may be lessened, and in extreme cases quite counteracted, if the purchasing power set free from other goods, or received by the State from the duties, is directed towards other *import goods;* for example, instead of tea more coffee may be imported or cloth instead of yarn or the means of production instead of the product or *vice versa.*[8] Thus every import duty—abstracting from the above borderline cases—leads to a shrinking in the volume of international trade and in the extent of international division of labour and to a loosening of the bonds which link the world economy together.

As to (*b*), the path by which the new import-export equilibrium is reached, this is associated with *inflationary phenomena.*[9] The imposition of import duties has a favourable influence upon the balance of payments. Imports from abroad decrease, so that the demand for foreign means of payment declines, while for the moment the supply of them remains the same. Hence the monetary and foreign-exchange mechanism is set in motion; the exchange value of the currency falls below gold import point; and gold flows in or the quantity of money in the country is expanded through increased bank credit. In a word, a mild inflation comes about, and this is frequently strengthened by an import of capital set in motion by the imposition of the duties. This inflation gives a certain stimulus to business, but, as in every inflation, this is only a temporary effect. This result comes about only if new duties are imposed or old ones raised; it is not produced by the mere maintenance of an existing duty, however high it may be. It forms part only of the transition from one equilibrium to another and the reaction comes all the quicker if the transition is to a position of reduced welfare due to the fall in the social product arising from the reduction in the international division of labour.

The removal of an import duty has the opposite effect. The balance of payments is rendered less favourable and the monetary mechanism brings about the new equilibrium by means of *deflation*.

In the other country—if we suppose there are only two countries —or in the rest of the world as a whole, the same process takes place in the opposite direction. If one country immediately counters increased import duties in the other country by raising its own, inflation and deflation cancel one another out and these transitional effects do not take place.

---

[8] See also the following section and chap. xvii, § 4.
[9] Well analysed by Hawtrey, *cf.* his *Good and Bad Trade* (1913), chap. 18, and *The Economic Problem* (1926), p. 289.

§ 3. Import Duties on Means of Production.

Import duties on means of production call for special mention. We include under means of production both original and produced means of both higher and lower orders; raw materials, intermediate products (such as steel, cement and yarn), and produced means such as machinery. One special characteristic of any means of production is its *complementarity*. (Consumption goods also are often complementary, but this characteristic is more universal and more striking in means of production.) One means of production is always used in conjunction with other means, the whole making a productive combination of factors. When the price of one means, or factor, is raised by an import duty, there is a danger that the demand for other means, with which it is complementary, may fall off also, the previous productive combinations being broken up. Another special characteristic of a means of production is that the demand for it is very often extremely elastic. This is always so when those industries in which it is most used have to face keen foreign competition.

Every tariff on a means of production which raises its price thereby raises the cost of every production process in which it is employed. Thus tariffs on iron and steel raise the costs of all industries which use iron and steel; tariffs on machinery raise the costs of all branches of production using machinery; tariffs on grain and fodder raise the costs of stock-raising and dairy-farming. When the industry which is damaged in this way exports its products, the tariff may result in a diminution of exports; and it may so happen that this equals the diminution in imports, so that the tariff does not disturb the balance of payments.

But it may happen that equilibrium in the balance of payments is preserved without the aid of the monetary and foreign-exchange mechanism not, as in such a case, by reduced exports, but by increased imports of other goods. For example, the imposition of a tariff on cotton yarn may raise its price so much that the cloth manufacturers can no longer meet foreign competition. In that case the import of yarn will indeed be reduced but the import of cloth will probably increase. In that event the original aim of the tariff, namely to increase the production of yarn within the protected country, would not be attained so fully, if at all.

In flagrant cases, in which the good subjected to the duty plays an important part in the costs of the industries using it, it is often the practice to take account of this. The interests harmed by the duty protest. The kind of compensation they may obtain will depend upon whether they are producing for export or for the home market. In the former event they may be given back the duty they have paid. This is known as a *drawback*. Alternatively, they may not be charged the duty at all if they announce at the time when they import the raw material or intermediate product that they propose to work it up and to export the finished goods.[1]

In the latter event, that is, when the industries concerned are producing for the home market, they may be compensated by an equalising duty upon the import of the goods which they produce. For example, if the duty on grain is raised, the duty on flour may be raised correspondingly, so that the flour-milling industry does not suffer. Through these and similar measures the effect of the duty upon the next stage in the production process is counteracted or weakened. But the indirect effects, mentioned in § 2, are not affected. In particular, the damage to the export industries, brought about through the play of the monetary mechanism, is not avoided.

---

[1] In such cases one sometimes speaks of an *active* ' improvement trade.' A *passive* ' improvement trade ' occurs when a country exports a good to be improved or worked up abroad and then imports the finished goods containing it duty-free while charging duty on similar finished goods made from materials produced elsewhere. A passive improvement trade for the home country is an active improvement trade for foreign countries.

CHAPTER XVI.

GENERAL ARGUMENTS FOR TARIFFS.

§ 1. INTRODUCTORY.

The arguments for Free Trade are clear cut and their application to trade policy is simple. This is not so with arguments for tariffs. On the one hand, there is a host of arguments which are in part inconsistent with one another and which set out from widely different axiological standpoints and theoretical considerations. On the other hand, if one accepts one of these arguments, its practical application is by no means clear. If we refuse to take seriously an extreme autarchism, which wishes a country to be completely isolated economically from other countries, there is no equally simple Protectionist maxim corresponding to the Free Trade maxim of no discrimination between internal and external trade. The dictum that tariffs are economically advantageous is not such a maxim, for it must also be stated under what conditions they are advantageous and exactly how high they must be. Even if one accepts unreservedly some particular argument for Protection, the answers to these questions are by no means easy to find. Therefore we must endeavour to divide the various arguments for Protection into groups for purposes of discussion. But it should be emphasised that the relative amount of space we shall give to any particular Protectionist argument by no means corresponds to its relative importance in affecting practical policy. On the contrary. Indeed, some arguments which are scientifically quite untenable and which can be refuted in a few sentences, have the greatest influence in practice, in Parliament, and in the discussion of the subject by interested parties and by the Press. But we shall concern ourselves here with a scientific treatment of the various arguments and not with a sociological analysis of political motives and forces.[1]

§ 2. REVENUE DUTIES AND PROTECTIVE DUTIES.

In order to make a survey of the various arguments for tariffs, we must first distinguish between revenue duties and protective duties. Revenue duties are usually taken to be those duties whose

---

[1] Pareto gives an interesting sketch of a Sociology of Protection in his *Manuel d'économie politique* (1927), 2nd edn., pp. 520 *et seq.*

primary purpose is to provide the State with revenue. They are a special form of taxation. Instead of a tax on the consumption of, say, tea or coffee, being imposed on the wholesaler or on the retailer, it is imposed when the goods cross the national frontier. The main motive for the imposition of protective duties, on the other hand, is not to create a new source of income for the State but to maintain and encourage those branches of home industry protected by the duties.

But this distinction is by no means clear cut. A distinction based upon the motives of legislators or other persons is always difficult to draw. The different persons concerned may have different motives, or one and the same person may have mixed motives. The majority of protective duties bring in something to the national Exchequer and on that account are welcomed by the Treasury, while many revenue duties indirectly provide some protection for certain home-produced products. For example, if a country which itself produces no wine raises its duty upon imported wine, part of the previous demand for wine will be diverted towards beer. Similarly, when a country in the temperate zone imposes revenue duties on tropical fruits its own fruit-growing industry is thereby benefited. Indeed, every tariff results in a shifting of demand, even in those cases in which the elasticity of demand for the good subjected to the duty happens to equal unity. The indirect consequences of tariffs described in the previous chapter apply just as much to revenue duties as to protective duties.

The best distinction between revenue duties and protective duties is an objective one, independent of the motives of the legislators or the interested parties, namely, whether there is any discrimination between the home and the foreign supply. If the home production bears the same taxation as similar imported goods, or if the good subject to duty is not produced at home, even after the duty has been imposed, and if no similar home-produced good exists towards which demand is diverted, then the duty is not a protective one. The following distinction can be drawn between protective duties and revenue duties with regard to their influence on the direction of production. A purely protective duty leads to a shifting of production away from the export industries and towards (a) the industries protected by the duty and (b) those industries towards which the diverted demand turns. A purely revenue duty without any discrimination or directly protective object finally leads to a shifting of factors of production away from the export industries towards (a) those branches of production, for example armaments or administrative services, upon which the

Government receipts are spent, and (*b*) those branches in which, owing to the general changes in demand, demand increases.

We must here point out that the two ends of getting the greatest possible revenue for the State and of affording the greatest possible protection to the home industry are to a large extent incompatible with one another. The duty which affords the maximum of protection is a prohibitive one which yields no revenue to the State. One the other hand, the revenue yielded by a duty will be the greater the less the import of the good falls off, that is to say the less the duty fulfils its protective function. This depends in turn upon two things: (*a*) how demand reacts—the less demand falls off, the higher will be the revenue from the duty; and (*b*) to what extent the home production is stimulated by the rise in price due to the duty. A duty thus fulfils its protective function when it leads to a great expansion of the home production; but if it does this it yields less as revenue. From the purely revenue standpoint, therefore, those duties are most useful which are imposed on articles of general consumption *not* produced at home. If the good in question is produced at home, then from the revenue standpoint it is advantageous—especially if the elasticity of the home supply is large—to impose a tax equivalent to the duty upon the home production, that is to say, to avoid any discrimination between the home-produced units and the imported units of the good. This is so even when we put on one side the fact that in addition to the income from the duty the State will receive an income from the taxation of the home-produced goods.

§ 3. ECONOMIC AND NON-ECONOMIC ARGUMENTS FOR TARIFFS.

A further distinction can be made between economic and non-economic arguments for tariffs. Tariffs may be regarded as desirable from either an ' economic ' or a ' non-economic ' standpoint. The significance of the distinction between these two standpoints has already been discussed (chapter XIII, § 2).

(*a*) The following *non-economic arguments for tariffs* or non-economic objections to international trade may be mentioned. It is said that from the standpoint of *national defence* each country should avoid too close a dependence upon other countries. If international division of labour is given full scope, it may lead to too great a specialisation, whether on industrial or on agricultural production. In times of danger such an over-specialised country would not be in a position to supply itself, even for a short time, with the goods previously imported. Hence too close a dependence upon the world economy should be avoided, even if such avoidance involves an economic loss. This argument may be used either for agricultural duties or for duties on those industrial products, such as iron and steel, which are needed for armaments in time of war.

Other non-economic arguments include that for *preserving the special ethos of the nation*, which, it is claimed, would tend to disappear under too close an intimacy with other peoples, and other more or less non-rational views.

Finally, tariffs may be advocated in order *to preserve certain classes of the population or certain occupations*, which it is thought would disappear under Free Trade, and the preservation of which is desired on political and ' social ' grounds. This argument is used almost exclusively for agricultural duties. These duties, it is claimed, should preserve a peasant class in large numbers and in prosperity. The agrarian population, it is said, forms a loyal and conservative element in the community, indispensable to the balance and moral unity of the population, and one should not, by giving free play to the price-system, allow it to fall into decay. Agriculture is the wellspring from which the human race is physically and mentally regenerated.

(*b*) We have already seen that it is difficult to say exactly what must be understood by *economic arguments* for tariffs. Certain it is that there is no pure economic ideal, which can be deduced by analysis from the science of economics without introducing meta-scientific value-judgments. It is not true that economic arguments for or against tariffs are to be judged by economics and non-economic arguments by other sciences or branches of knowledge. The effects of duties imposed for, say, military reasons—for example, in order to build up an armaments industry—fall within the scope of economic science just as much as those of duties imposed for ' economic ' reasons. The distinction lies simply and solely in the ends deemed desirable. The so-called ' economic ' ends are best conveyed, as we have seen, by some such phrase as the maximisation of the national income, or of the national wealth, or of the social product. Corresponding to them are those economic arguments which claim that the social product can be increased by Protectionist measures. Undoubtedly the great majority of the more plausible arguments for tariffs belong to this class, from the naïve error of acclaiming the increased production of the protected industries and ignoring the debit side, to the refined theories of Mr. Keynes and others, which advocate Protection as a means of avoiding certain disturbances in the economy.

Midway between the economic and non-economic arguments come those which are concerned not with the absolute amount of the social product but with its mode of *distribution* among the various sections of the population. In this connection there is, in addition to postulates of social justice, a purely ' economic ' standpoint, namely, that which takes account of the repercussions of the mode of distribution upon production. When Schüller, for example, declares that a rise of rents is an unfavourable consequence, and a rise of income from work a desirable consequence, of tariffs, he is introducing a value-judgment as to the right mode of distribution. On the other side, it is often admitted, even by Schüller himself, that a change in distribution in favour of the smaller incomes reduces the capacity to save and thereby diminishes the size of the national income in the future.

Indeed, the effect upon distribution can never be completely neglected; the greatest possible national income, irrespective of how it is distributed, is not an acceptable end. Nevertheless, it is possible to ignore effects on distribution which do not exceed a certain limit. Moreover, we can often be sure that a certain measure will increase the national income without being able to say how, especially in the long run, it will affect distribution. (*Cf.* chapter XII, § 3.)

§ 4. The Economic Arguments for Tariffs.

The economic arguments for tariffs, implying that in certain circumstances tariffs can increase the social product, contradict the view, which we have already set out, that Free Trade is economically advantageous. The following types of economic arguments may be distinguished :

(1) (*a*) *Long-run arguments* and (*b*) *short-run arguments*. The former claim to show that tariffs can increase the social product in the long run. The latter claim to show only that tariffs can lessen the difficulties of a transitional period. The argument for ' equalising tariffs,' both in its primitive form, as for example in American tariff legislation, and also in its developed form, as stated by Schüller, is a long-run argument. In general, the arguments worth discussing are for the most part short-run arguments. These short-run arguments mostly not only take account of the size of the social product, but also lay special stress upon its distribution. Even when the removal of a tariff or a change in the international competitive situation leaves the distribution of the national income unchanged, or influences it favourably, in the long run, the transitional period, nevertheless, always involves loss to some sections, and it is claimed that tariffs may prevent this loss.

I

(2) Closely related to the above division, but not identical with it, is the important division of arguments for tariffs into (a) those *which are based upon equilibrium theory* and (b) those *which imply that some disequilibrium is present.* Under (b) come those arguments which rightly or wrongly rely upon the assumption that in consequence of all kinds of disturbances and resistances the state of equilibrium portrayed by economic theory is in fact seldom or never attained. These arguments may be termed friction-arguments. Under this heading falls, for example, the view that a country which enters fully into the world economy may indeed be in internal equilibrium with full employment for part of the time, but that it will be very sensitive to external influences, and that these may involve it in a cyclical depression, the force of which could be lessened if it imposed tariffs. Under this heading falls also the view, put forward in England some time ago by Mr. Keynes and others, that to-day the frictionless working of the price-mechanism is *not* true of the labour market. This view points out that Free Trade doctrine assumes that all factors of production will be fully employed (unless their prices fall to zero); and that in reality this is not so, as the permanent existence of a large volume of unemployment bears witness. A further complication is the existence of unemployment benefit, which, it is claimed, is a circumstance which lessens the advantage of Free Trade.

(3) An important group of arguments is based upon the existence of *monopolies.* But the fear of monopolies takes two contradictory forms. On the one hand, injury is feared from a lower import price (dumping) and, on the other hand, injury is feared from exploitation by excessively high prices. The Free Trade country is said to put itself at the mercy of foreign monopolies, especially of raw materials.

(4) An important weapon against Free Trade doctrine is the notion of *economic development.* This takes account of a period of time longer than the theoretical ' long run.' Free Trade doctrine assumes that the quantity of original means of production is given or speaks in extreme cases of a short-run functional relation btween the price and the supply of existing original means of production.[2] It is indeed true that the classical economists, by including population doctrine within their system, i.e. by making certain assumptions as to the relations between increase of population and height of income, went beyond the boundaries of

---

[2] This is true of labour. Within certain limits the height of wages determines the amount of labour supplied.

static theory.[3]   Their population doctrine was inadequate and incorrect. We mention it only to illustrate the relation between the general theory laid down in this book and the problems of economic development.   Undoubtedly there are problems of development which go beyond the theory of Part I, which more or less accurately represents the present position of pure economic theory.   Nor is it the case that phenomena arising from economic development obey their own special laws and are quite independent of the phenomena discussed by the static theory; on the contrary, repercussions occur which affect the data assumed to be given.   In more concrete terms, the processes of production and exchange explained by the static theory upon the assumption of a given quantity of original means of production themselves affect the quantity of original means of production available in the future.

Such considerations provide some justifications for the infant industry argument. They also played a part in the discussion of the pros and cons of the development of Germany into an industrial country, in which Wagner, Pohle, Dietzel, Brentano and others took part in the years round 1900.

In this connection we must also consider whether tariffs, by inducing foreign producers to establish works within the protected country, may not draw into it additional factors of production. Finally, we shall have to speak of the famous controversy as to whether the export of machinery and of capital does not in the long run injure the exporting country, although at the time it appears advantageous on the basis of the principle of comparative costs.

(5) Finally, as a fifth group, we must name the arguments for *retaliatory* tariffs. These are based upon the belief that, while Free Trade may be correct in principle, nevertheless a liberal trade policy cannot be afforded by a country surrounded by neighbours who have all armed themselves with tariffs. Two different reasons are given in support of this view. (*a*) It is said that the Free Trade country is in a weak bargaining position, since, as it has no duties itself, it has no concessions to offer its neighbours to induce them to lower their tariffs upon its goods. (This is the

---

[3] The concepts ' static ' and ' dynamic ' in this connection are not unambiguous. We should really distinguish different stages in the extent to which an economy is dynamic. We should understand by a static theory one which, among other simplifications, assumes the *existence* of a given quantity of original means of production. The quantity in *existence* is taken as a datum which calls for no further explanation; this, however, by no means excludes the possibility that the quantity of means of production actually *supplied* is a function of their price and can thus be explained. On all this *cf.* Knight, " Statik und Dynamik " in *Zeitschrift für Nationalökonomie* (1931), vol. 2, pp. 1 *et seq.;* now reprinted in *Ethics of Competition* (1935).

tactical argument for tariffs in the proper sense of the term.) (*b*) But quite apart from these tactical considerations, it is claimed that one-sided Free Trade is harmful; why, is not clearly shown, but it sounds very convincing to declare that one sole Free Trade country delivers itself helplessly into the hands of foreign competitors unless it also provides itself with tariff weapons.

CHAPTER XVII.

PARTICULAR ARGUMENTS FOR TARIFFS.

§ 1. Arguments which do not Merit Serious Discussion.

It appears desirable to clear the ground by eliminating a number of arguments for tariffs which can be declared with absolute certainty to be based only upon errors and upon a complete lack of insight into the working of the economic system, and are therefore not tenable from any standpoint. But it must not be assumed, because we deal with them very briefly, that their practical importance is small. On the contrary. Indeed, it is these untenable arguments which carry the greatest weight in Parliament and with public opinion.

(1) The ' practical man ' and the layman are always greatly impressed by the ocular demonstration of the beneficial effects of tariffs in *expanding the production of the protected industries.* Is it not possible by means of adequate Protection to conjure up and develop great productive units and whole branches of industry? Has not extreme agrarian Protection in Germany and Austria resulted in a very short time in a considerable growth of agricultural production in those countries and in a sharp fall in their agricultural imports? Has not the agricultural country of Hungary within ten years brought whole industries into existence? Innumerable illustrations of this kind are available, and those who favour duties or who benefit by them do not fail to point to them with pride and satisfaction and to give them the widest publicity.

It is scarcely necessary to observe that such examples—even when the facts are as stated and the increased production is not really due to other causes—in no way prove that the tariffs have increased the social product. That the tariff increases the output of the protected industries is only *one* side of its consequences. Despite this increase of output in the protected industries, or rather, as our theory has shown, *because* of it, one branch of industry has expanded only at the cost of some other. If imports fall off, exports also must fall off, and if the producers of protected goods obtain higher prices, the consumers of these goods are paying higher prices for them. When one branch of industry expands and thereby attracts more factors of production, these factors of production are no longer available for other uses. Our theory has shown that the decrease in production elsewhere is greater than the increase of production in the protected industry. Whoever disputes this must prove the contrary, but in doing so he must draw up a complete balance-sheet of the effects of the tariff and not give only the credit side. If he does the latter, he merely proves that he does not understand the point at issue.

(2) The above remarks apply also to the catch-phrases about *creating and expanding a home market*. The home market is indeed expanded, but the export market is correspondingly contracted. The fall in imports is followed by a fall in exports. If it is contended, in opposition to this statement, that exports need not fall off immediately to the same extent as imports, maybe because the difference is lent abroad, we are drawn into a very complicated argument, which we discuss in § 3 of this chapter. The expansion of the home market in itself proves nothing. Nor is anything proved by the assertion, frequently made, that there is plenty of scope for work within the country, so that there is no need to seek export markets. Certainly it is true that there would be more than enough scope for work in supplying home demands (once the transition to self-sufficiency has been accomplished) but the work yields a smaller product than if some of it were devoted to producing for international exchange. Keynes has settled this argument once and for all: " If Protectionists merely mean that under their system men will have to sweat and labour more, I grant their case. By cutting off imports we might increase the aggregate of work; but we should be diminishing the aggregate of wages. The Protectionist has to prove not merely that he has made work, but that he has increased the national income. Imports are receipts and exports are payments. How, as a nation, can we expect to better ourselves by diminishing our receipts? Is there anything that a tariff could do, which an earthquake could not do better? "[1]

(3) We must next refer to the so-called *purchasing-power argument*, with which the parties who would gain by duties try to make their wishes palatable to others. Agriculture explains to Industry how advantageous agrarian protection would be for the industrial population, by increasing the purchasing power of consumers of industrial products. ' Hat der Bauer Geld, so hat's die ganze Welt '—when the peasant waxes fat, all the world grows rich on that. But this argument can be reversed : industrial tariffs increase the purchasing power available for agricultural products and therefore in the end benefit agriculture. Röpke makes some

---

[1] *The Nation and Athenæum* (1st Dec. 1923).

caustic comments on the ' Fata Morgana of the purchasing power mirage.'[2] Frederic Bastiat has delightfully exposed such arguments in his famous Petition of the Candle-makers, who request Parliament to protect them against the destructive competition of the sun. " If you would only block up as far as possible every means of entry for natural light and thus increase the need for artificial light, what industry in the whole country would not thereby benefit to some extent? . . . If the manufacturers gain by protection, this at the same time benefits agriculture. If agriculture gains, it has more money to spend on industrial products. If we were granted a monopoly of the provision of light, we should at once purchase large quantities of tallow, coal, oil, resin, wax, spirits of wine, silver, iron, bronze and crystal glass for the needs of our industry. We and our numerous suppliers, upon acquiring more purchasing power, would spend more and so increase the prosperity of every branch of national production. . . . It may perhaps be objected that light is a free gift of nature and that to throw away gifts is to lessen welfare. . . . You should consider, however, that up to the present you have always *on that account* cut down foreign imports, just *because* they approach to being gifts, and the more nearly they have been gifts the more have you shunned them. . . . When a commodity such as coal or iron or wheat or cloth comes from abroad and we thus obtain it with less labour than if we had produced it for ourselves, the difference is a gift which is being made to us. This gift is greater or less, the greater or less is this difference. It reaches a maximum when the giver, as the sun with its light, demands nothing from us in exchange. The question is, therefore, whether our country desires the alleged benefit of a costless consumption or the proved advantages of a work-creating production. We beg you to choose, but to choose logically. If you make your duties higher, as in fact you do, upon coal or iron or wheat or cloth from abroad, the lower is their price, how inconsistent would it not be to allow the sunlight, whose price is nil, to have free entry during the whole of each day! "[3]

(4) From the purchasing-power argument follows logically the postulate of *Protection all-round*, expressed by the catch-phrase ' Protection for national industry in both town and country.' If every duty assists not merely the industry whose products are thus protected but also, by means of increased purchasing power, benefits every other branch of production, it follows that the best course is

---

[2] *Weltwirtschaft und Aussenhandelspolitik* (1931), p. 54.
[3] *Sophismes économiques*, Nr. 7, Oeuvres complètes de Fr. Bastiat (1854), vol. 4.

to protect *every* branch by tariffs. Ever since Germany adopted high Protection with the new Bismarck tariff of 1879, this catchphrase—it can scarcely be termed an argument—has enjoyed great popularity in Germany. Bismarck at once realised its effectiveness from the standpoint of political tactics. In his well-known communication of 15th December, 1878, to the Bundesrat, concerning the revision of the tariff, he says: " Tariffs for particular branches of industry . . . have the effect, especially when they are unduly high, of a special privilege and therefore tend to arouse among the representatives of non-protected branches the kind of opposition which every special privilege encounters. A protective system which gives the total home production a preference over foreign producers in the home market encounters no such opposition. Such a system will not seem oppressive upon any section, since its benefits are shared equally by all producing sections of the nation." The tariff policy of nearly every country today rests upon this basis of solidarity. The various special interests adopt the attitude of *do ut des*: give me a tariff and I will raise no objection to a tariff on your product.

There is practically nothing to be said about all this from a scientific standpoint. The fact that all branches of production are protected by tariffs does not make the tariff-system one jot better. On the contrary. It should be clear that the more embracing and free from gaps is the tariff barrier, the more is the benefit of any particular tariff to the industry which it protects whittled away. For all members of that industry must now pay more dearly for all other imported goods and thus in their capacity as consumers they lose part of their gain as producers. Nevertheless, it is not true to say, as Free Traders often do, that an all-embracing tariff does not change the relative situation of different industries. It results rather in a strengthening of the position of those industries which have to face foreign competition and this takes place at the expense of the export industries. The more embracing is the tariff wall, the more is the country cut off from the world economy and from the benefits of international division of labour; the greater, therefore, is the loss to the social product. Those who declare that this loss should nevertheless be accepted must take the trouble to explain what are the advantages which in their view outweigh it. This would bring us to one or other of the more valid arguments for Protection. But the catch-word of *solidarity* in the matter of Protection has not the slightest contribution to make in this respect. It is not an argument at all but merely a phrase of great psychological and political effectiveness.

(5) Quite as untenable is the argument that tariffs *improve the balance of trade*. This argument is used especially in times of inflation and of acute monetary crisis. Since 1931 many countries in Eastern and Central Europe have imposed import prohibitions and increases of tariffs with the declared object of relieving the balance of trade or the balance of payments. In normal times a reference to the balance of trade is made more as a supplementary reason than as a main reason for Protection. The alleged favourable effects of Protection upon the balance of trade are regarded as a welcome secondary consideration which, in case of doubt, should turn the scale in favour of tariffs. This argument flows from the balance-of-payments theory discussed in chapter IV § 1 and is usually put forward with a complete lack of understanding of the monetary and foreign-exchange mechanism, which automatically brings about an equilibrium in the balance of payments. In this naïve form the argument is quite untenable. We shall discuss a more sophisticated form of it in § 3 of the present chapter.

We do not dispute that a passive balance of trade may be an unfavourable symptom. For example, it may lead to an undesired increase in indebtedness to foreigners or it may be a sign of the dissipation of property in such forms as the export of securities. But it is a gross error to believe that the diminution of imports will necessarily imply a diminution in the import *surplus*. A tendency to increase indebtedness to foreigners or to export property is not to be combated merely by diminishing imports. Nobody who wants to borrow abroad or to sell securities abroad will be deterred by the imposition of duties on imports. So long as the forces causing an excess of imports (for example, invisible exports or foreign indebtedness) remain in operation, a diminution of imports can only lead to a further corresponding fall in exports and will do nothing to reduce the surplus of imports; indeed, this surplus, if expressed as a percentage of the country's total external trade, will even increase. If a tariff leads to an import of capital—a possibility used as an important argument for tariffs, and discussed in § 4 of the present chapter—it will result in a greater worsening of the trade balance in the future.

(6) Equally untenable is the case for tariffs *to check the import of luxuries*. If this is advocated in order to induce different habits of consumption, and to lead people to spend less on luxuries, then, logically, there is no ground for discriminating between imported and home-produced luxuries; both should be taxed equally. If the price of imported luxuries only is raised, it is highly probable that the diverted demand will turn towards similar luxuries produced at home and not towards more ' useful ' goods.

(7) Despite the very widely held opinion to the contrary, *the simple argument for retaliatory tariffs* must be included among arguments which do not deserve discussion. The mere fact that other countries have tariffs is no reason whatever for imposing them. (We are not speaking here of the tactical possibility of thereby inducing the other countries to lower theirs.) If another country hinders our export trade, that is very regrettable; she thereby injures both herself and us, reducing both sides of the balance of trade and balance of payments account of both countries. If we then retaliate by also imposing tariffs, we inflict *further* injury both on ourselves and on the other country, our trade-partner, without in any way lessening the harm done by the tariffs of the latter. The Free Trade argument, as we have stated it, in no way depends for its validity upon the absence of foreign tariffs. For, it will be remembered, we introduced transport costs—which play the same role as tariffs—into our theory (chapter X, § 6). Our analysis of the effects of transport costs applies just as much if the transport costs are one-sided, being levied upon traffic in only one direction. But if the Free Trade case can be proved when there are one-sided transport costs, it can equally well be proved when there is one-sided Free Trade.

The popular belief that a country surrounded by a ring of hostile tariff walls cannot maintain her balance of payments in equilibrium is so primitive that we can pass it by.[4]

(8) Of quite special importance is the argument that tariffs *maintain wages*. We have already spoken (chapter X, § 4) of the view that tariffs can raise the general level of wages or, in other words, that a wage-level higher than that of other countries can be maintained only behind a tariff shield. When the *general* wage-level is meant, this view is proved false by the theory of comparative costs.[5] None the less, the *pauper-labour* argument is very popular in countries of high wages, especially the United States and England and her Dominions. The layman is impressed by the statement that the expansion of American industry could never have taken place, in face of the competition from Asiatic and European countries where wages are half or less than half American wages, without the protection of the American tariff. Nevertheless, the implication that trade between countries in *goods* leads to an

---

[4] This argument sometimes makes its appearance in a dynamic form. It then alleges not the *existence* but the *imposition* of foreign tariffs as a reason for imposing import duties. The sudden diminution of exports affects the monetary mechanism and makes inevitable a *painful* transition to a new equilibrium. The disturbances of this transition could be avoided at the expense of a permanent reduction of the social product. This form of the argument is discussed later (see § 3, pp. 269 *et seq.*).

[5] See specially Taussig in *Free Trade, The Tariff and Reciprocity* (1920).

equalisation of *factor-prices*, and in particular of wages, is fundamentally false. An equalisation of wages comes about only if labour is mobile and can move from districts where wages are lower to districts where they are higher. The appropriate weapon with which to create or maintain a wage-difference is therefore the prohibition of immigration, just as the appropropriate way to create a difference between the home and foreign price of a commodity is to prohibit or tax its importation.

But the question takes on quite another aspect when reference is made not to the general wage-level or to average wages but to the wages of particular groups of workers who are not in free competition with the others. This brings us back to the problem of the influence of a tariff on the distribution of the national income, discussed in chapter XII.

(9) The fear of lower foreign wages leads to the stupid idea that the object of a tariff should be to *counteract the lower costs* of foreign countries. Only then, it is claimed, will home industry be able to compete with foreign industry on a ' fair ' basis. It is clear that the complete and logical application of this postulate would destroy all international trade, since this arises only because of differences in costs.

Nevertheless, this view is very popular in the United States and has actually found expression in its legislation. The Tariff Act of 1922 declares: " In order to apply the policy laid down by the Congress in this Act . . . the President of the United States shall, . . . when it appears to him that a duty as laid down in this Act fails to equalise costs of production between the United States and competing countries . . . raise or lower the duty until the costs in both countries are equalised, provided that such an increase or reduction does not exceed 50 per cent. of the duty laid down in the Act." A special body, the Tariff Commission, was set up in order to calculate differences in costs. Similar statements appear in all subsequent American Tariff Acts. Much use has been made of these instructions. The Tariff Commission has made extensive researches into the cost of production of numerous goods in the United States and abroad; the duty has been raised in many cases but lowered in very few. Even if we put aside the difficult theoretical problems involved, arising from the many possible meanings of ' cost '[6] and from the fact that the production costs of a given

---

[6] As a rule the Tariff Commission has utilised for its calculations the average of the costs of particular concerns. Upon the results of such a method of calculation, and upon the theoretical significance of such ' statistical' cost-curves *cf.* Taussig, " Price-fixing as seen by a Price-fixer " in *Quarterly Journal of Economics* (1919), vol. 33. Upon the relation of such statistical cost-curves (the ' particular expenses curve ' of Marshall) to the cost-curves (especially the marginal cost-curves)

good are not everywhere the same even within one country, and even if we put aside also the technical administrative and statistical difficulties of such investigations, it is perfectly clear *a priori* that from the standpoint of a rational trade policy the whole business is meaningless. If a commodity is habitually imported, that fact alone in itself proves that its cost of production is lower abroad. No statistical investigation is needed.

The argument for tariffs to equalise costs of production is not any more valid if it concerns itself not with wages but with other circumstances giving rise to differences in costs. We have already shown (chapter X, § 4) that in Europe the desire to impose equalising tariffs against imports from America springs from the view that, although wages are relatively high in America, other conditions of production are more favourable than in Europe. In reality the one is a consequence of the other; wages are higher in America just *because* other conditions are more favourable; in other words, wages are higher because the labour, working under more favourable conditions of production, is more productive. The doctrine of comparative costs demonstrates that in such circumstances also international trade is advantageous.

Nor is the *general* burden of taxation[7] and the increase in production costs due to social measures such as the prohibition of night-work, the eight-hour day, and restrictions upon the employment of women and children, any reason for imposing tariffs, although it is often contended that these extra burdens should be offset by tariffs. In part such circumstances result in a reduction of money wages and to that extent have no influence on external trade; but, undoubtedly, they also cause a shifting in the scale of comparative costs. Those branches of production—for example, those especially suited to female or child labour—which are especially hit by such social measures, may now be unable to meet foreign competition. This naturally implies a reduction in the volume of production, since production is pushed out of some of the lines indicated by comparative costs and into others. But, in the opinion of the legislators, the reduction in the social product is

---

with which the theory works, see Viner, " Cost-curves and Supply-curves " in *Zeitschrift für Nationalökonomie* (1932), vol. 3. See also Simpson, " Average or Marginal Costs for the Flexible Tariff " in *Journal of Political Economy* (1926), vol. 34, pp. 514-24; and Sweezy, " Theoretische und Statistische Kostenkurven " in *Zeitschrift für Nationalökonomie* (1933), vol. 4, p. 515.

[7] The matter is different when a special tax is imposed on one product. In that case an equalising duty—a revenue duty—is justified. The fact that a particular product is especially suitable as an object of taxation in no way alters the advantages of specialising upon its production, and it would be irrational to prevent specialisation in the direction indicated by comparative costs by refusing an equalising duty to offset the tax. This was shown by Ricardo (*On Protection to Agriculture*, § 3, " On the Effects of Taxes imposed on a Particular Commodity ").

compensated by certain advantages, for example, by the stoppage of female or child labour. If, now, an equalising tariff is imposed, our theory shows that an additional injury is thereby inflicted, without in any way diminishing that due to the taxation or the social charges, and without throwing its incidence upon other countries. Thus the notion of ' equalisation ' as such is no argument at all. If the tariff is advocated in order, for example, to prevent unemployment in an industry previously using much female labour, on account of a prohibition of female labour, we are confronted with an argument which we shall consider later.

§ 2. The Protectionist Theory of Richard Schuller

Professor Schüller's exposition of the advantages of Protection ranks with justice as one of the most profound arguments for tariffs.[8] It is purely static in nature; it does *not* rest upon the assumption of disequilibrium or of losses due to friction nor upon considerations of economic development. This greatly simplifies the discussion of it. We have already considered (chapter XI, § 8, and chapter XV, § 1) the method, namely, that of partial equilibrium, which he uses in order to examine international trade and the effects of tariffs. He adopts two standpoints from which to judge tariffs: (1) their influence upon the *total income* of the population and (2) their influence upon the *distribution* of the total income; he considers a rise in income from labour at the expense of income from rent as desirable, and the opposite as undesirable. We shall here consider mainly the first, the ' purely economic,' criterion.

According to Schüller, every tariff has a twofold effect upon the national income. It hits consumers on the one hand and stimulates production on the other hand. In order to make a complete judgment upon the effects of any particular tariff, we must weigh the disadvantages under the former head against the advantages under the latter.

The advantages predominate when a tariff leads to a marked increase in production coupled with only a moderate rise in price; the disadvantages predominate when on the contrary the rise in price is great and the increase in production only feeble. Schüller then embarks upon a discussion of the circumstances which determine which of these two possibilities will occur in any particular case. These circumstances, according to Schüller, are, briefly, the structure of costs and the difference in costs between

---

[8] See his book *Schutzzoll und Freihandel* (1905).

home and foreign production, that is to say, in our terminology, the elasticity and the size of the home and the foreign supply, together with—although Schüller does not lay so much stress on this—the size and elasticity of the demand. It will suffice for our purposes to explain the principle upon which he strikes a balance between gain and loss by setting out two of his illustrations. He gives the following as an example of a duty which is without question advantageous:

"The home requirements of cotton yarn, at an average price of 200 kronen per unit, are 1,330,000 units a year, of which, in the absence of an import duty, only 100,000 units would be produced at home, the remaining 1,230,000 being imported. But the difference in costs is so slight that if the price were raised from 200 to 210 kronen per unit, almost the whole requirements, say 1,300,000 units could be supplied by home producers.

"The checking of imports by a tariff would therefore result in 1,200,000 units, for which previously 240 million kronen had been paid abroad, being produced at home. From this sum we must deduct 140 million kronen for the raw cotton, which now would have to be imported to make possible this home production of yarn. This would leave an importation to the value of 100 million kronen, for which home production would now be substituted. But the home consumers, who previously spent 266 million kronen on the purchase of 1,330,000 units at 200 kronen a unit, would now have to spend 273 million kronen, on the purchase of 1,300,000 units at 210 kronen a unit. They would thus have 7 million kronen more to pay and would receive 30,000 units less than before in exchange. On the other hand, production will increase to the extent of 100 million kronen. In this case, the advantages of a duty would unquestionably exceed its disadvantages."[9]

In the following case, on the contrary, a tariff would undoubtedly be harmful:

"Let us suppose that in a country every year 1 million units of flax, at a price of 80 kronen per unit, are used as raw materials, and that 400,000 of these units are produced at home, the other 600,000 being imported. Any considerable increase in the production of flax can take place only if its price rises very sharply. This is in fact the case in Germany, Austria, and other countries, and in consequence their output of flax increases only a little even at times when the price of flax has risen very considerably. It is therefore not an exaggerated assumption to suppose that the price of flax must rise from 80 to 150 kronen per unit in order that the home demand may be met, at that price, by home production. Naturally the consumption would fall off a good deal in consequence of such a rise in price. Let us suppose that it would fall from 1 million units to 600,000 units. Since 400,000 units were previously produced at home, this would mean an increase in production of 200,000 units, which were previously imported at a cost of 16 million kronen and are now produced at home at a cost of 30 million kronen, that is to say at 14 million kronen more. The price-increase of 28 million kronen for the 400,000 units of flax which were previously produced at home certainly benefits the home producers, but is disadvantageous from the standpoint of distribution, since it implies predominantly an increase of income from rent at the expense of income from work. The home consumption is supplied with only 600,000 units instead of 1 million, and must pay 10 million kronen more for these 600,000 than

---

[9] *Loc. cit.*, p. 130. Schüller points out that this example is not exaggerated, since the whole spinning industry of a country may depend upon just such a small difference in price.

it previously paid for 1 million; against that, an import of only 16 million kronen in value has been replaced by home production. In this case the disadvantages due to interference with Free Trade are beyond doubt much greater than the advantages."[1]

There are several comments to make upon this. This kind of balancing of the advantages and disadvantages of a tariff rests upon an inadequate and incorrect picture of the shifting of the structure of the economy brought about by the tariff. On the one hand, that circumstance from which, in Schüller's theory, the utility of the tariff arises, namely the increase in the *total* income (which, as we shall see later, can occur only by drawing into employment factors of production previously idle) is not explicitly present at all. On the other hand, the quantity used by Schüller as a measure of the credit side of the balance (namely, the increase in the home production of the protected commodity) perhaps includes the true credit—if a true credit is present at all—but in no circumstances can the *whole* of this increase be treated as a credit and used as a measure of the extent by which total income increases.

We can agree with Schüller in what he says about the debit side of the effects of tariffs. Consumers suffer by the consequent rise in price. Their loss in this respect can be measured, as by Schüller in the above examples, by the increased consumers' outlay on the good in question plus the value of the number of units of the good by which the amount consumed is diminished.[2]

The error in Schüller's reasoning concerns the credit side. He takes the increase in the home production of the good subject to the duty as equivalent to an increase to that extent in the total national income. This is a quite inadmissible proceeding. The question at once arises whether the increase in the production of the protected industry does not inevitably occur at the expense of reduced production in other industries. Will not the factors of production needed to increase the output of the protected industry be drawn away from other industries, so that the *net* effect on the national income is not an *increase* but merely a *shifting* of pro-

---

[1] *Loc. cit.*, pp. 129 and 130.
[2] Let us call the price of the good p_1 before the tariff and p_2 after the tariff and the quantity consumed q_1 before the tariff and q_2 after the tariff. Then the loss to consumers is measured by : $(p_2 q - p_1 q_1) + (q_1 - q_2) p_1$. I shall not discuss the question of whether the difference in quantity, in the second term of this expression, should be valued at the old price p_1 or at the higher post-duty price p_2. It should be observed that the first term of the expression may be negative. This will be the case if the elasticity of demand for the good is greater than unity, so that a rise in price reduces total consumers' outlay on it. In such a case the first term shows a ' negative loss,' that is to say a gain. But the value of the whole expression must be positive, whatever the elasticity of demand may be. This is easily seen by multiplying out : the result is $p_2 q_2 - p_1 q_2 = q_2 (p_2 - p_1)$, which must be positive since p_2 is higher than p_1. If we value the second term of our

duction towards the protected industry and away from the export industries or from those industries from which demand has been diverted in consequence of the duty?

Schüller naturally considers this objection, and tries to demonstrate, at some length, that it is not valid. This demonstration contains the heart of his theory. He goes into polemics against the ‘ error ’ of Free Traders in supposing “ that the size of a country’s production is fixed by the quantity of factors of production present in the country.” He contends that the factors of production within a country are never fully utilised, so that, in so far as a tariff causes previously unemployed labour or idle natural resources to be utilised or causes an import of capital or an immigration of labour into the protected country, it brings about an increase in its total production.

We have already observed (in chapter XII, § 2) that this argument, in so far as it is based upon the existence of unutilised factors of production, contains a fallacy. We shall return to this point in the following section; for the moment, let us ignore it. Even so, there is no reason whatever to assume that the increased production in the protected industry takes place entirely or mainly through the utilisation of factors previously idle. There exists no fourth dimension out of which factors of production can be conjured. When one branch of production expands, its expansion

expression at the higher post-duty price p_2, the result is $q_1(p_2 - p_1)$, which must also be positive.

In figure 26 DD is the demand curve. After the duty is imposed, the price rises from p_1 to p_2. The expression $q_1 (p_2 - p_1)$ is represented by the rectangle

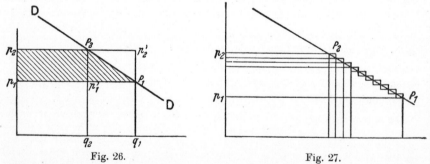

Fig. 26. Fig. 27.

$p_2p'_2p_1P_1$ and the expression $q_2(p_2 - p_1)$ by the rectangle $p_2P_2p_1p'_1$. The difference in consumers’ rent is represented by the shaded area $p_2P_2p_1P_1$ Thus one of the two expressions is greater and the other smaller than this difference. But if we allow the price to fall by steps from p_2 to p_1 as in figure 27, the two expressions approach one another and finally coincide with the increase in consumers’ rent.

In this figure $q_1 (p_2 - p_1)$ is represented by the area $p_2p_1P_1P_2$, bounded by the *outer* stepped line between P_2 and P_1; and $q_2 (p_2 - p_1)$ is bounded by the *inner* stepped line. We thus demonstrate that the measure used by Schüller for the injury to consumers caused by a tariff is the loss in consumers’ rent due to the rise in the price of the good.

must be to some extent at least at the cost of some other branches. Some part of its expansion *may* be due to the tapping of a reservoir of means of production previously unutilised. If so, the magnitude of this part is perhaps indicated by the amount of unemployment existing in that particular branch. But Schüller makes no reference whatever to this criterion. He merely declares in general terms that in every country and in every branch of industry—in all forms of agriculture and manufacturing alike—idle means of production will be present, without showing that more of such idle factors are present in *certain* branches than in others, and that, therefore, Protection to *those* branches would be beneficial. Nor is there any *a priori* reason to suppose that more idle factors exist in, say, the textile industry than in, say, agriculture. There is not sufficient connection between the circumstance which Schüller takes as decisive, namely the elasticity of supply, and the relative amount of unutilised factors in an industry. He lays down the following rule: " The smaller is, *firstly*, the spread between the highest and the lowest costs with which the home demand for the good can be satisfied by home production, and the smaller is, *secondly*, the comparative advantage of foreign producers in the case of goods which under Free Trade would not be produced at all in the home country . . . the greater is the increase in output due to a tariff relatively to the loss on the side of consumption caused thereby, and the more favourable, therefore, are the effects of the tariff upon the total income."[3] This is correct if instead of ' more favourable ' we write ' less harmful.' It is indeed obvious that, other things being equal, a tariff which hits consumers less—because the comparative advantages of foreign countries in the production of the good in question are only slight— does less harm than a tariff which does the contrary. But Schüller fails to prove that the former kind of tariff is not only less harmful than the latter, but is itself positively beneficial. Indeed, no such proof can be given.

It is very instructive to consider Barone's treatment of the problem of weighing the advantages and disadvantages of a tariff. Barone adopts the same methods and the same assumptions as Schüller. But he comes to the conclusion (*loc. cit.*, p. 104) that in international trade " the profits of those who gain in either market (country) are always greater than the losses of those who lose in that same market." He shows this with the aid of the following diagram (figure 28), which we have already had occasion to use.

If the two markets become one, the same price Om rules in each. If they are separated by a duty, the price rises in the importing country I to Oβ and falls in the exporting country E to Oa. The removal of the duty would result in a gain to the consumers of I equal to the area BCmβ. The loss to the producers in I

---

3 *Loc. cit.*, p. 136.

would be BDmβ. The gain is thus always greater than the loss, the net gain being equal to the shaded area BCD. Conversely, in the exporting country the

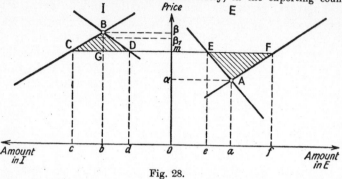

Fig. 28.

gain of the producers (AFmα) is always greater than the loss to the consumers (AEmα). Barone's method of reckoning the gain to consumers in I (and the loss to consumers in E, of which, however, Schüller says nothing) is the same as that of Schüller.[4]

The loss to producers due to the removal of a duty (or the gain due to its imposition) is reckoned by Barone in a quite different manner from that of Schüller. If production increases from Od to Ob, Barone reckons the gain of producers as equal only to the increase in rent (BDmβ). He does *not* count the increase in costs, BDdb, as a gain, since he takes it as obvious (without explicitly saying so) that the factors and goods upon which the extra costs are spent must be drawn away from other uses. Schüller, on the contrary, counts the whole area bdDmβB as representing an economic gain.

What, then, are we to conclude as to the view of Schüller that previously unutilised means of production can be brought into

---

[4] The area CBβm representing the gain of consumers measures *the increase in consumers' rent*. This concept is of very doubtful validity. I cannot here embark upon an analysis of it, but I believe that in the following form it may be accepted for our present purpose. Suppose a small fall in price from Oβ to Oβ_1. Then the gain of consumers, at any rate their money gain, equals a small strip Bβ of a height $\beta\beta_1$, since this is the sum which consumers save if they continue to buy the same quantity of the good as before. If we suppose the price to fall further by small stages, other strips are added to this one, until the sum of all such strips is the area CBβm. Leaving quite aside any vague references to the measurement of utility, we can define consumers' rent as *that sum of money which would exactly compensate the consumer for the given rise in price*.

But this method of measuring the gain to consumers, from the removal of a duty, is restricted within narrow limits. It can be used to measure the loss to consumers from *one* single duty, provided that everything else remains unchanged. The loss inflicted by a multitude of duties cannot be measured in this way, since as more duties are imposed the various demand curves must alter.

We may further observe that among the other things which must remain unchanged for our suggested method of measurement to be correct is the ' marginal utility of money.' And this will remain unchanged only if the price of only *one* good among *many* is affected, and even so only if not more than a small fraction of the total income is spent upon this good. We cannot here go into this matter in detail. But we may add that it is possible to explain the concept of the marginal utility of money—a concept which is usually enveloped in metaphysical vagueness and ambiguity—in terms of rational acts of choice.

We should perhaps add that there is a small difference, irrelevant for our purposes, between the technique of Barone and that of Schüller. The former moves, so to speak, by infinitely small steps, and therefore uses continuous curves, while the latter moves by discontinuous jumps, using arithmetical examples. This difference shows itself in the fact that neither $q_1 (p_2 - p_1)$ nor $q_2 (p_2 - p_1)$ exactly equals the increase in consumers' rent.

service by means of a tariff? In so far as these unutilised means consist of natural resources, such as fertile land, mineral deposits, and water-power, or of produced means of production, such as machines and factory buildings, his argument rests upon a fatal fallacy. This fallacy has already been pointed out, in chapter XII, § 2, and has been trenchantly exposed by Mackenroth in the article to which we there referred. With this exposure, the bulk of Schüller's objections to Free Trade fall to the ground. It remains only to enquire to what extent Labour is in a different category owing to the fact that the price-mechanism does not function without friction in the labour market,[5] and whether tariffs may lead to a *net increase* in the import of means of production from abroad and thereby to an increased use of means of production in the protected country. Both these enquiries relate to circumstances upon which many other authors have endeavoured to base a case for Protection. At this stage, therefore, Schüller's argument for tariffs merges into the arguments discussed in the following sections.

§ 3. TARIFFS AND UNEMPLOYMENT.[6]

1. INTRODUCTION.—The general public usually considers the existence of unemployment in an industry as a very good reason for the imposition of a tariff. Of course, it is beyond dispute that unemployment in one single industry—provided that its products do in fact compete with similar imported goods, and provided that the demand for such products is not completely elastic—can be diminished by a tariff on the competing imports. Such a diminution, the possibility of which is freely admitted by Free Traders, is one consequence of the expansion of production in that industry due to the tariff. But this proves nothing whatever as to

---

[5] Schüller does not make clear that the distinction here is between goods which are used so long as their price is above zero and goods, such as Labour, which may cease to be used long before their price falls to zero.

The Macmillan Report (see Addendum I, from the pen of J. M. Keynes) is by no means clear on this point. It says, on p. 201, sec. 40 : " The fundamental argument for unrestricted Free Trade does not apply without qualification to an economic system which is neither in equilibrium nor in sight of equilibrium. For if a country's productive resources are normally fully employed, a tariff cannot increase output, but can only divert production from one direction into another, whilst there is a general presumption that the natural direction for the employment of resources, which they can reach on their merits and without being given special advantages at the expense of others, will yield a superior national dividend. But if this *condition of full employment* is neither fulfilled nor likely to be fulfilled for some time, then the position is totally different, since a tariff may bring about a net increase of production and not a mere diversion." We shall consider in the following § how far this is correct.

[6] See Beveridge (editor), *Tariffs: The Case Examined*, chap. 6. Keynes and others in *The New Statesman and The Nation* (April and May 1931). Balogh, " Arbeitslosigkeit und Zölle " in *Weltwirtschaftl. Archiv* (1931), vol. 34, pp. 465 et seq.

the total effect of such a tariff. The real question in this context is whether *total unemployment* can be diminished or whether its diminution in some industries will be offset by its increase in others; in concrete terms, whether the number of workers dismissed in the export industries may not be as great as or greater than, the number of additional workers taken on in the protected industry.

Here again it is necessary to make clear the axiological standpoint from which this question is regarded. On the one hand, it may be believed that unemployment is in itself an evil, and that therefore a net diminution in unemployment is an adequate reason for a tariff. On the other hand, one may take as the sole or main criterion the change in the total social product. In the latter event, one must consider whether a diminution in unemployment may not be bought too dearly, since it is quite conceivable that the real income of other persons may fall more than the real income of the newly employed workers rises.[7]

The problem is further complicated by the existence of unemployment relief.

2. THE EFFECTS OF THE IMPOSITION OR THE RAISING OF TARIFFS UPON UNEMPLOYMENT IN THE SHORT RUN.—Let us suppose that unemployment prevails in some industry or other, say, the clothing industry. We need not for the moment concern ourselves with the causes and duration of this unemployment; we shall consider them in detail a little later. In considering the *short-run effects* of a tariff upon existing unemployment, it is immaterial whether this unemployment is fairly temporary, arising, for example, from a cyclical trade depression, or whether it is more permanent, arising from structural changes. It will suffice for our present purpose to set out the position as follows. A part of the workers in a given industry cannot at present find work, although they are prepared to work at the prevailing wage.[8] If the goods of the kind which that industry produces are normally imported in considerable quantities, then by means of an import duty home production can be increased and a part of the

---

[7] This latter standpoint is very clearly stated by L. Robbins : " The main object of economic policy is not to cure unemployment : it is to increase the social dividend. If by curing unemployment that end is accomplished, well and good. If the cure involves measures inimical to the increase of the dividend its desirability is more dubious." " Economic Notes on Some Arguments for Protection " in *Economica* (Feb. 1931), p. 50.

[8] We may suppose that through unemployment relief and trade-union resistance the wage has been prevented from falling and the unemployed from entering other branches of industry.

unemployed can thus be reabsorbed. (This is the *primary* effect of the duty.)[9]

But most Free Traders deny that this implies a diminution in *total unemployment*. They claim that a restriction of imports involves a falling-off of exports and therefore unemployment in the export industries.[1] As we shall see, it is broadly correct that a permanent reduction in total unemployment cannot be brought about by tariffs. Nevertheless, a mere reference to the falling-off in exports is not sufficient.

Two kinds of objections are made against such a reference. In the first place, the assumption that a restriction of imports is at once followed by an exactly equivalent diminution in exports is attacked as untrue. We deal later (pp. 272-3) with this point. But even when exports do fall off immediately, it does not follow that unemployment must thereby be caused in the export industries. We must not forget that the purchasing power which was previously spent by consumers on imported goods and used by the foreign recipients to purchase exports from the country in question is now spent by consumers on home-produced goods and may be used by the recipients to purchase goods from their own export industries, so that a new home demand for the products of the export industries may replace the previous foreign demand.[2] (This is the *secondary* effect of the duty.) The export industry E works now for the protected industry B instead of for foreign markets; the duty ' has increased the purchasing power of the home market '—this phrase, which we have previously criticised, is not without sense in this context. It must be admitted that in principle this contention is correct. Yet it by no means follows that the demands of the newly-employed workers will be for exactly those goods which were previously exported.[3] But if unemployment exists in any other branches of industry, and the new home demand flows towards any such branches, unemployment there will be diminished. This

---

[9] We should include also in the primary effect the influence upon those industries which supply means of production to the industry directly concerned—for example, upon the machine industry, in so far as the protected industry buys its machines at home and not abroad.

[1] Many authors who advocate tariffs take this dogma as their starting point and seek only to prove that it is not necessary for exports to diminish immediately and automatically by the same extent as that by which imports are restricted, e.g. Balogh, *loc. cit.*, p. 476, and Keynes, " Economic Notes on Free Trade " in *The New Statesman and Nation* (11th April 1931). " If a reduction of imports causes almost at once a more or less equal reduction of exports—obviously a tariff (and many other things) would be completely futile for the purpose of augmenting employment . . ." p. 242.

[2] A detailed analysis of this is given by R. Kahn, *Economic Journal* (1931), vol. 41, p. 173 : " The relation of Home Investment to Unemployment." It is true that Kahn is considering the repercussions of public works and not the effects of tariffs, but his analysis applies *mutatis mutandis* to the latter.

[3] Apparently this is asserted by Beveridge, p. 59.

diminution offsets the increase of unemployment in the export industries, and, in addition, there remains the diminution of unemployment in the protected industry. Thus runs the argument. But we cannot admit, without further discussion, that the labour set free in the export industries will flow into those branches of industry towards whose products the demand of the workers who have found employment in the protected industry has directed itself. Indeed, this assumption cannot be granted *in this context.* For we are speaking of the short run. There seems no reason at all for supposing that the workers in the export industries are perfectly mobile while other workers—namely, the unemployed from whose existence the whole argument arose—are not mobile. (If the latter were mobile, they would not be unemployed.)[4]

It can next be objected that the increased production in the protected industries is not entirely due to workers taken on from the reservoir of unemployed, but is partly due to materials and machinery and workers who were not previously unemployed,[5] and that these means of production must be diverted from some other branches of industry. It might be replied that possibly these means of production come from abroad. There might be, for example, less cloth but more yarn imported, so that the unemployed home weavers could work up the cloth. Of course, in such a case the imports would not diminish by the full value of the cloth now manufactured at home but only by the *value added* (to the yarn) by home labour. Even if the materials and so on are not at first imported, the increased demand for them will raise the price

---

[4] Let us call the consumers of the goods which will now be produced at home C, the home producers, who were unemployed and now by hypothesis become occupied, H, the exporters E, and the foreign countries F. Then the circulation of money *before* the imposition of the duty is represented by the arrows C⟶F⟶E, and *after* the imposition of the duty by the dotted arrows C ⁃ ⁃ ⁃> H ⁃ ⁃ ⁃> E (Fig. 29).

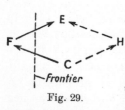

Fig. 29.

The foreigners F are now unemployed, and their place is taken by the home industries H who buy from E what used to be bought by F. We shall not here consider the further effects upon the foreign countries. The question remains whether all this implies—*e.g.*, as Robbins (*loc. cit.*, p. 53) declares—*an increased circulation of money* (due to an increase in either the quantity of money or its velocity of circulation), which prevents prices from falling. Robbins reaches his conclusion from the assumption that previously the circuit C⟶F⟶E, was shortened into one single payment C⟶E, whereas now the money changes hands more often by passing through H. But, of course, one may just as well assume that the new circuit in the home country is again shortened to one single payment C⟶E. We can speak of an increase in circulation only if we suppose that before the duty C⟶F⟶E was only *one* transaction, since foreign payments did not enter into the home circulation, whereas after the duty the payments C ⁃ ⁃ ⁃> H ⁃ ⁃ ⁃> E form two transactions. It is thus a question of definition whether we speak of an increase in circulation or not.

[5] Indeed, it is never possible to staff a works entirely with unemployed. Certain skilled jobs can be performed only by men in constant practice. Such men must be drawn from other works.

of the home-produced materials so that at least part of the demand
for materials and other production goods may be diverted abroad.

But it may also be true that part of the production goods now
utilised were previously idle—for example, an existing factory
building or an uncultivated field.

Nevertheless, in so far as labour or other means of production
must be diverted from other branches of home industry, there will
be a shifting of production and this, under the present assumptions
of relatively rigid wages and immobile labour, must result in
unemployment; this unemployment must be set against the
increased employment in the protected industries. The same result
comes about when the protected product is itself a means of production (for example, an intermediate good such as cloth). The
duty raises the price of the product and this hits the next step in
the production process (for example, the clothing industry) and
thereby causes unemployment there.

But in spite of these considerations it remains quite conceivable
that, if only a new or increased duty causes workers previously
unemployed to be absorbed in the newly-protected industries, the
result may be a net diminution in total unemployment. In such
a case, the magnitude of the diminution would vary with the extent
to which the protected industries employed labour and with the
smallness of the resulting rise in the price of the product (that is,
with the flatness of the cost-curve).

But does such a diminution in unemployment imply also an
increase in the social product? That is possible, but not necessary.
That it is possible, is shown by the following example. Suppose
that previously 10,000 q of a good were imported. Suppose that
now the import is restricted and the price raised by 10 per cent.
through a duty. Suppose that the elasticity of demand is equal
to unity, so that the total outlay of consumers remains the same,
and the amount purchased falls to some 9000 q. The consumers
thereby suffer a reduction in their real income to the value of some
1000 q[6]; the home production is by hypothesis increased by 9000 q.
Of course, we must not, like Schüller, count the whole value (or
even the whole value less that of imported materials) as a gain,
but only that part which represents the output of previously unemployed workers now found employment. If, for example, half
the value of the 9000 q goes to materials, and if of the pure labour-
costs less than 3500 go to workers who have been diverted from other

---

[6] For a more accurate reckoning, we should work with the difference in
consumers' rent in the sense defined above (p. 258). We could then of course
discard the assumption that the elasticity of demand is equal to unity. But it is
not necessary to go so closely into the matter, since we are concerned only to bring
out the theoretical possibility (not necessity) of an increase in the social product.

employments, then more than 1000 can be imputed to the workers previously unemployed and now found employment. This is greater than the loss (of 1000 q) to consumers, so that the net result—on the assumption that the repercussions do not cause unemployment elsewhere—is an increase of the national income. Clearly, such a result is more likely, the greater the amount of labour (relatively to other factors) employed in the protected industry.

But how does it come about that we reach a different conclusion, when speaking of the reabsorption of unemployed workers into the production process from that which we reached in chapter XII, § 2, when speaking of material, that is non-human means of production? We there concluded that the return from a previously-unutilised means of production, such as a closed-down coal mine, which was brought once more into employment by means of a duty, could not be regarded as a net increase in the national income. Why should the product and the income of workers be treated differently from those of material means of production, such as a field or a factory building, the earnings of which would provide an income for their owners? Is there not here a contradiction?

There is no contradiction. The distinction between the two cases lies in the circumstance, already mentioned, that as a rule material means of production rest unutilised only when their price has fallen to zero, whereas labour ceases to render services long before its wage has fallen to zero.[7]

We can most easily explain the consequences of this distinction if we consider, as we did on page 186, the moment in which the price falls so low, owing to increased foreign competition, that a diminution in production occurs in the home country—that is to say, the moment in which the marginal concern is obliged either to produce less or to close down completely. We have seen that this occurs when the value of the specific means of production has been written down to zero and when, nevertheless, the concern cannot pay the non-specific means of production their market-price (or, more accurately, the price which they could earn in another use). When in these circumstances the concern closes down, no loss is involved, for the specific means of production have already been written down to zero, so that their owners no longer have any income to lose, while the non-specific ones by hypothesis earn their incomes elsewhere.

If, however, the specific factors consist of workers, there is a significant loss at the moment when the concern is closed down. For their wages at that moment have not yet sunk to zero, so that their total wages are lost when the concern closes. The transfer to the foreign source of supply occurs, so to speak, at one blow. Hence there is a loss and, conversely, if the step can be avoided or retraced with the aid of a duty, there will be a gain. When the price of the product rises again beyond the critical point at which the concern can be reopened—and from that point upwards—the workers previously unemployed are paid *their old rate of wages at once*. In the other case, on the contrary, the price of the material factors has been written down to zero, so that if the concern reopens owing to a duty, their price begins to rise again only from the level of zero, which implies that the gain to the producers increases as a result of the increased price of the product only *pari passu* with the loss to consumers.

---

[7] This may happen in exceptional cases with material factors also : for instance, when their owner refuses to sell their products for a very small price, waiting in the hope that the price will rise. Nevertheless,, if his reason for refusing to sell is that the price does not repay him for his own efforts as an entrepreneur, or that in order to sell the products his factors must be combined with others (for example, when transport and marketing costs must be paid) and the receipts do not cover the cost of these other factors, then this is no exception to our general rule. In reality, in such cases his factors will be utilised unless their price sinks to zero.

3. GIVEN UNEMPLOYMENT, THE EXISTENCE OF UNEMPLOYMENT RELIEF IMPROVES THE PROSPECTS OF A NET FAVOURABLE RESULT FROM A TARIFF.—For then we must include on the credit side of the balance, together with the incomes of the re-employed workers, the *unemployment relief saved*. We have here an obvious case of so-called *external economies*. An individual entrepreneur can, by expanding his output, reduce the expenses to the community of unemployment relief. But he does not reckon the cost of unemployment relief in his own costs; it is a burden borne by the community as a whole. There is thus a discrepancy between what Professor Pigou calls private net product and social net product. In such a situation, and within narrow limits, an interference with the free play of economic forces may be of advantage if it has the result of somehow causing the gain to the community to enter into the private calculation of the entrepreneur. This can be done, for example, by a duty or by a bounty on production. But such a bounty should not exceed the saving in unemployment relief which is in fact made as a result of the increase in production.

The possibility of reducing this discrepancy underlies many schemes for diminishing unemployment. Although we have admitted that such schemes contain a certain amount of validity, we must, nevertheless, emphasise most strongly that no such scheme is really practicable. There are two reasons for this. *First*, such an interference can be of advantage only in those marginal cases in which the total subsidy does not exceed the *actual* saving which will be made on unemployment relief, and this latter is difficult to estimate. Moreover, if wages rise after the bounty has been granted, this condition may no longer be fulfilled and the bounty, therefore, no longer justified. *Secondly*, the practical difficulties of administering such a bounty or subsidy cannot be overcome. There is not even a tolerably reliable method of selecting those marginal cases—and only in marginal cases can there be a gain—which would make a bounty worth while. For it is necessary to estimate the net effects upon the whole complex of economic activity both at the moment *and in the future*. Moreover, it is administratively impossible to restrict the bounty to those expansions of production which would not take place without it.

4. THE VARIOUS TYPES OF UNEMPLOYMENT AND THE POSSIBILITY OF COMBATING THEM BY TARIFFS.—Although our analysis, up to this point, appears to show that it is not inconceivable to diminish unemployment and thereby increase the social product by means of tariffs, nevertheless a more far-reaching study of the problem, which considers the various causes and types of unemployment, will show that—leaving aside a few exceptional cases—a favourable result can be expected *only in the short run*, so that tariffs can be advocated on this ground only from a very short-run, and, indeed, short-sighted, standpoint.

For our purposes we can distinguish the following three types of unemployment:

(a) unemployment due to friction;
(b) unemployment due to the trade cycle;
(c) permanent unemployment.

(a) In every economy there is always a large number of persons who have been unemployed for a shorter or longer time, because they are treading the hard and weary path from one job to another.

Even in good times firms close down owing to the misfortunes or lack of capacity of their entrepreneurs; and works and, indeed, whole industries are closed down or change their location in consequence of a shift in the demand or in the relative cost of different locations. Technical progress continuously brings into being new processes, new concerns, and new industries, thereby undermining the capacity to compete of the older works and throwing workers out of their jobs. This is sometimes called ' technological unemployment.' The transition to another job, especially when it involves migration to another district, seldom takes place without friction and usually involves considerable loss and a fairly long spell of unemployment for the workers concerned. This is a *temporary* unemployment, but at every time and in every economy there are many such temporarily unemployed workers.

When an industry which has to face the competition of imports finds itself in difficulties because comparative costs have changed and more of the goods are now supplied from abroad, it is clear that unemployment in that industry could be diminished or avoided by means of a tariff. Obviously only the imposition of a new duty, and not the continued existence of an old one, can have this result. Such changes are constantly taking place in every economy, however high the protective barrier may be, and if one were to raise a tariff every time unemployment appeared anywhere one would incur lasting loss for the sake of a doubtful and temporary gain. One would forgo the immense gains of international division of labour and of technical progress for a mess of pottage. Certainly it is possible here and there to stop up a gap by means of a tariff. Indeed, this miserably short-sighted policy has long been followed with astonishing consistency by most of the nations of the world.[8] But such a policy involves abandoning all the fruits of technical progress, in so far as they can be enjoyed only through the medium of international division of labour.

Such a policy can indeed find theoretical support when it is believed that the superiority of foreign countries in the production of a certain good or goods is of *a temporary nature*, so that the imposition of a duty may enable the home country to avoid first adapting itself to this temporary situation and then going back to the previous position. But what is the basis of such a belief? It may be thought that in time the home country will attain the same standard of technical progress as the foreign ones. If so, and if it is also believed that a duty is the only available instrument, we come to the case for an *infant-industry duty*, discussed below in

---

[8] If this policy is followed by many countries simultaneously, naturally no country can reap even a temporary gain.

§ 5. Or it may be thought that a merely temporary shifting of demand due to a change in fashion has given foreign producers a momentary advantage. Such cases are conceivable. But who is in a position to make such a prognosis correctly? Hardly a Parliament or a Public Department!

(b) *Cyclical unemployment* accompanies those perplexing wave-movements of the trade cycle from which no capitalistic economy is free. Cyclical unemployment also can be lessened by tariffs, within the limits and under the conditions stated above. But the situation is complicated by the presence of such unemployment in numerous industries and countries. Here, once again, the alternative presents itself of a lasting loss due to the abandonment of the fruits of international division of labour, on the one hand, and a doubtful and temporary gain, on the other hand. The choice should not be difficult. But the fact is that *every* depression brings with it a great wave of tariff increases. With cyclical unemployment also, the imposition or raising of a duty, but not the mere continued existence of an old duty, may have some effect. It is indeed often contended that the separation of a country from the world economy insulates it from crisis. But this view will not hold water. Experience shows that the highly-protected countries—Germany, France, and the United States—are no less disturbed by crises and depressions than are countries pursuing a more liberal trade policy. Whether a country has high or low tariffs has nothing to do with the acuteness of its crises and depressions.

(c) Tariffs can possibly do something to correct *permanent unemployment* such as England, Austria, and to a less extent Germany have experienced since the War. But in this case also our previous analysis has shown that not much is to be expected. There is always the danger that a loophole will be made elsewhere. Such permanent unemployment is always the result of a marked increase in wages,[9] so that only *high* tariffs will have an appreciable effect. But this means that the unfavourable repercussions and the loss to consumers will be all the greater. We must also remember that even ' permanent unemployment ' does not last for ever. Again, even if the total number of the unemployed remains constant, the composition of that total is changing all the time. The effort to reduce this type of unemployment by tariffs will lead to the continuous imposition of duties, first here and then there, so that very soon the loss will outweigh the gain. Finally, every

---

[9] It makes little or no difference to our analysis whether the unemployment arises from too high a general wage-level or only from certain wages being too high and the dismissed workers being insufficiently mobile to transfer to other industries.

considerable increase in duties is followed by similar measures in other countries, and when that happens any hope of a net favourable effect must perish.

If the unemployment is concentrated in the export industries, the situation is hopeless. This was so in England[1] and, indeed, in most European countries during the post-War period. In such cases the unemployment—in so far as it is not due to purely national causes, notably to too high a wage-level—does not arise from foreign competition but from restrictions on international trade.[2]

Unemployment in the export industries can never be diminished by a restriction of imports, for this involves a further reduction of exports. One often hears the view that the home market must benefit by the curtailment of exports, and that no account should be taken of further damage to exports, since in any case the movement in all countries towards self-sufficiency must kill the export trade. This is like advising a consumptive person to eat less because in any event he will get thinner. If a rigid economy is constrained by the protectionist policies of other countries to become more self-sufficient, and if its flexibility and capacity for adaptation are insufficient to carry through this process in a short time without friction, one should do nothing to increase the amount of adaptation which must take place.

Up to the present we have supposed that there is unemployment in particular industries and that an import duty on the products of these industries has a *direct* effect in increasing employment in them. This corresponds more or less to the assumptions of Schüller. But during recent years many complicated theories have been put foward in England. These do not concern the direct effects of *particular* tariffs, but the *indirect* effects of a *general and equal* tariff upon *all* imports.

5. Tariffs as a Means of Reducing Real Wages.—Before England left the gold standard, in September, 1931, the opinion was often expressed by English, and especially Cambridge, writers that all imports should be subjected to a ' flat tariff ' of 10 to 15 per cent. in order to raise prices and *reduce real wages.* Unemployment was due to too high wages. The power of the trade unions prevented any lowering of money wages. Therefore, it was urged, some means should be found of reducing real wages—

---

[1] Compare, for example, the Report of the (Macmillan) Committee on Finance and Industry, 1931, sec. 108, p. 49 : " The mass of unemployment has been, and is, mainly concentrated in the heavy industries, and latterly in certain textile trades, all of which figure largely in our export business." *Cf.* Beveridge, pp. 70 *et seq.*

[2] Rail and sea transport, which have been especially hard hit in all countries by the depression, belong mainly to the export industries.

if possible without the workers realising it.[3] The devaluation of the pound was mentioned as a possible third course.

The following objection must be made against this whole scheme of reducing real wages by tariffs.[4] The entrepreneurs, and especially those producing for export, and these were the very ones worst hit in England, take account of *money wages* and not of real wages. If they must continue to pay the same money wages for the same services as before, it does not help them at all if their workers find that the purchasing power of their wages has been reduced by a rise in prices. The situation is somewhat different if it is proposed to use the receipts from the import duties to remove certain taxes which enter into costs of production. This is a proposal for a Public Finance measure, namely, the substitution of indirect for direct taxes. There are certain good arguments for it; but we are no longer in the realm of specific arguments for *tariffs*. The case here is for a general tax upon consumption.

6. TARIFFS AS A MEANS OF RESTORING EQUILIBRIUM IN EXTERNAL TRADE.—We owe to Keynes, however, a very refined version of the above theory. This version cannot be so easily dismissed. It demands a much fuller discussion.[5]

It is not easy to state Keynes' argument concisely. He has given several versions of it, and has not infrequently changed his mind upon points of detail. One never knows whether a given version correctly represents his present views. We must also observe that, unfortunately, he very often—especially in his popular articles in the *New Statesman and Nation*—puts forward quite superficial arguments for Protection in order to make his demand for a general tariff more acceptable to the general public. We shall not consider these lapses here. We shall restrict ourselves in the main to the exposition in his *Treatise on Money* and in the Macmillan Report.

Keynes arrived at his theory as a result of his analysis of the economic difficulties of England in the post-War period, and especially after her return to the gold standard in 1925. His proposal to reduce unemployment by means of a general tariff springs from a very definite diagnosis of the economic maladies of England. This does not imply that there was in post-War England a very singular combination of circumstances, which will never be repeated. On the contrary, one who accepts Keynes' views in this matter, must carefully study every case in which unemployment is present in an economy in order to see whether Keynes' assumptions about post-War England apply also to such a case. But of course his theory does not apply to *every* case of unemployment.

Keynes begins from his theoretical views, already known to us, as to the mechanism of international trade. In order to be in external equilibrium with the rest of the world, a country's credit or debit balance on capital account must

---

[3] This notion for obvious reasons did not receive much public discussion. See, however, the article by Sir Josiah Stamp in *The Observer* (15th March 1931), quoted by Beveridge, p. 71.

[4] *Cf*. Beveridge, p. 72, and Robbins, *loc. cit.*

[5] See the writings already mentioned of Beveridge (chap. 7), Robbins (pp. 57 *et seq.*) and Balogh. See also Keynes' *Treatise on Money*, vol. 1, chap. 21, and vol. 2, chap. 30, pp. 184-9, and the Macmillan Report, Addendum 1 (Keynes) and 3 (Gregory). In the *New Statesman and Nation* for April and May 1931, will be found a long discussion on these questions, in which nearly all the English economists participated.

equal its debit or credit balance on income account : its rate of foreign lending must equal its foreign balance.[6] A difference between these two balances cannot permanently exist. Such a difference can be removed only temporarily by gold movements. This equilibrium involves *two* series of conditions. The amount lent abroad depends on the relation between the rate of interest at home and abroad; whilst imports and exports depend on the relation between the price-levels at home and abroad (*loc cit.*, p. 326). Keynes then gives a condensed account of the working of the mechanism which keeps these amounts in equilibrium. His account more or less coincides with that given in the first part of the present work. His discussion of the equilibrium relations between interest rates, prices, incomes, and the balance of payments adds nothing to the ' prevailing ' theory which we have set out; his far too complicated but nevertheless effective exposition is not in disharmony with that theory.

What distinguishes Keynes from the orthodox writers, such as Taussig, is that he doubts the frictionless working of this mechanism. He believes that under certain conditions the transition from one equilibrium position to another is accompanied by painful and lasting difficulties. These ' disequilibria ' are none other than the transfer difficulties which we have considered in detail in chapter VII. They occur when large unilateral payments have to be made and when this cannot be done without worsening the terms of trade. Such a worsening of the terms of trade involves a reduction of wages (relatively to foreign wages), and if wages are rigid, this is accompanied by unemployment.

According to Keynes, England was in such a position from 1925 onwards. The pound, which had sunk in value owing to the war-time inflation, was then restored to its old parity. In order to return to the pre-War parity with gold and with the dollar, a deflation of prices and incomes to the extent of at least 10 per cent. was necessary. The opposition to this deflation was so strong that wages remained too high, the balance of trade worsened, and at the same time the export of capital did not diminish but actually increased, because the home opportunities for investment were rendered less attractive by the too high costs. The consequence was chronic unemployment.[7]

We must here distinguish between two different points, which are not always kept separate by Keynes and his followers. (1) It is, of course, not open to dispute that *a deflation* of the home currency which is not carried through in such a way as to cause *a reduction in incomes* does throw the rate of wages (rate of income), out of equilibrium and so cause unemployment. (2) But later on Keynes also stressed a second feature which arose from the fact that wages were above the equilibrium level, namely, an excessive *export of capital*.[8] In order to make possible this export, wages should have fallen still lower; and when they did not fall, the resulting unemployme t was greater than (1) alone would have brought about.

Upon this, we may make the following remarks. In chapter VII we have set out the circumstances which determine whether a unilateral payment will or will not worsen the terms of trade. We there saw that there is no *a priori* reason

---

[6] See " The Condition of External Equilibrium " in *A Treatise on Money*, vol. 1, p. 161.

[7] Keynes is in the pleasant position of being able to point out that he stressed the necessity of reducing incomes, if there was to be a return to the old parity, as early as 1925. See his pamphlet *The Economic Consequences of Mr. Churchill* (1925), reprinted in his *Essays in Persuasion* (1931).

[8] This feature has been especially stressed by certain other writers. For example, Balogh says : " The disturbance of economic equilibrium in England, in the accurate sense of the term, is a consequence of the tendency to lend too much abroad " (*op. cit.*, p. 476). This school of thought regards foreign lending as a bad habit of the English, in the prevailing economic circumstances, and one of which they should be cured by appropriate measures, such as differential taxation of income from foreign investments.

whatever why they *must* become worse. They may quite possibly improve. Indeed, Keynes now admits this. But he claims to have found good grounds for supposing that in the particular case of England the export of capital would lead to a worsening of the terms of trade; to a transfer-loss. Yet it is remarkable that Keynes, who as a rule applies quantitative analysis freely—indeed, that is one of the great merits of his work—does not in this case attempt a statistical verification. No great calculation would have been necessary. It is notorious that during the critical period the terms of trade became more favourable to England (as to all industrial countries)[9] : the prices of imports—raw materials and foodstuffs—fell relatively to the prices of exports, which consisted mainly of manufactured goods. The facts reveal no transfer-loss.[1]

But since we are concerned with the general theory rather than with the correctness of the diagnosis of the special case of England, we will assume for purposes of discussion that a part of the unemployment does arise from a transfer-burden coupled with rigid wages.

If unemployment exists owing to (1) and (2), then, according to Keynes, the following five solutions[2]—excluding the natural solution of a reduction in wages, which he takes to be impracticable[3]—are available.

(I) *An increase in the productivity of labour*, due to rationalisation, technical progress, and so on. Of course, this would be the ideal solution. But we cannot rely upon its happening.

(II) *Exchange Depreciation*, that is, letting the exchange value of the pound fall. It would have been possible to do this by *devaluation*, that is, by reducing the gold parity of the pound. This would retrace the step taken in 1925 and so bring English wages once more into equilibrium relatively to wages in other countries. This course was in fact taken in the Autumn of 1931, when England was constrained to leave the gold standard. The pound lost a third of its gold value; its exchange value in terms of the dollar fell from the old parity of 4.86 to 3.50 in the summer of 1932. With depreciation an accomplished fact, the other alternatives cease to exist. Keynes himself declared in a letter published in *The Times* of 29th September, 1931 (quoted by Beveridge, p. 77), that his proposal for tariffs (see V below) as an alternative to devaluation could now be abandoned.

(III) *A world-wide cheap money policy*, that is to say, an internationally-organised credit inflation. We cannot here discuss the problem of inflation.

(IV) *Discrimination between home and foreign investment*, in order somehow to promote home investment and thereby reduce the amount of capital exported. Technically, this can be done by means of an interest-premium on home investment, or a subsidy, or public works, or by making it more difficult to lend abroad. We shall not discuss the grave objections to such far-reaching intervention or the technical and administrative difficulties of carrying it out. But we must observe that these difficulties are out of all proportion to the result aimed at. Let us suppose that it were possible, for example by an embargo upon foreign lending such as the Bank of England has enforced on several occasions, to reduce the export of capital. What would be gained thereby? The very doubtful, not to say imaginary, transfer-burden would be removed and so would that part of unemployment due to it. But this would be attained only at the cost of a

---

[9] *Cf.* chap. xi, § 7.

[1] It might, nevertheless, be urged that the terms of trade would otherwise have been *still more* favourable. But that would mean that the transfer-loss had been more than offset by other circumstances. Another point of view is that the difficulties came about just *because* the terms of trade did not worsen. (That is the opinion of Robertson. See chap. xi, p. 158, note.)

[2] *Treatise on Money*, vol. 2, p. 186, and Macmillan Report, Addendum 1, p. 192.

[3] It should be observed that Keynes has altered his opinion on this point. At first he considered a reduction of wages as only unlikely to occur. In Addendum 1 of the Macmillan Report he declares that it is not at all to be desired.

painful process of adaptation. Previously the transfer was taking place, even if at the cost of friction and of a transfer-loss. The economy has adapted itself to the existence of a continuous transfer.[4] If now the export of capital becomes less or ceases altogether, the steps by which this adaptation was accomplished must be retraced. It is clear that, under the present assumptions of rigid wages and comparative immobility of labour, the need for such a new adaptation (or readaptation) would inevitably increase, rather than diminish, unemployment.[5]

(V) As a final possible means of restoring economic equilibrium without re-ducing money wages, Keynes suggests *a general duty on imports* combined with *a general bounty on exports*.[6] It is his view that this would have exactly the same results upon the imports and exports of a country as a devaluation of its currency, since it would directly increase the price of all imports and produce an all-round increase in the receipts, measured in the home currency, from exports. But it would have the advantage, as against devaluation, of not reducing the value of external sterling debts owed to England.[7]

How do the advocates of such a general duty on imports demonstrate that its effects would be favourable? It is not easy to find the answer to this question in Keynes' exposition of the scheme. (He always includes in his case for a tariff other arguments, which we have already considered, in addition to arguments relevant to the present issue.) He believes that the diminution of imports would not result in anything like a corresponding reduction of exports.[8] This, according to him, would be all right if England wanted to improve her balance of trade and to increase the gold reserve of the. Bank of England. But that is not the aim. The improved balance should be used rather to make possible an expansion of credit. This would have the result of increasing the import of raw materials and foodstuffs (which would have involved a *loss* of gold, had there not been a simultaneous restriction of imports) or of increasing the amount lent abroad.[9]

Thus the tariff is to be a means of permitting a mild inflation or of avoiding a deflation without any reduction in the foreign-exchange value of the pound and without any loss of gold. It can scarcely be denied that, within narrow limits, this is possible.[10] Indeed, the inflation is merely the *modus operandi* of the mechanism of international trade in response to a disturbance in the balance of payments. I do not question that in the short run this may produce a stimu-lating effect. But this stimulating effect is absolutely independent of the existence

---

[4] The export industries have provided the means of carrying out the transfer. The fact that in England the export industries were depressed is no objection to our *theoretical* conclusion. It contradicts only the *diagnosis* of Keynes, that England was suffering from transfer difficulties.

[5] We do not deny that, from a long-run standpoint, other aspects of the export of capital must be considered. It is by no means certain that a con-tinuous export of capital raises wages. It can be argued, for example, that if the capital had been invested at home at a lower rate of interest, instead of being exported, the roundaboutness of production would have been increased at home and the marginal productivity of labour and therefore its wage is thereby raised. On the other hand—and especially *sub specie æternitatis*—the economic development of the newer countries which is made possible by the export of capital is, of course, of great significance to the capital exporting countries themselves.

[6] He adds the suggestion of an export bounty in addendum 1 of the Mac-millan Report. The immediate consequence of such a policy would be that every country would impose additional compensatory duties upon imports from England. Thus, the effect would be a subsidy to the whole world from the pocket of the English taxpayer.

[7] Compare B. Whale, *International Trade* (Home University Library, 1932).

[8] See the Macmillan Report, p. 201, and Balogh, *op. cit.*, p. 476.

[9] Macmillan Report, p. 201.

[10] See chap. xv, § 2, and the references there given. *Cf.* also Balogh, *loc. cit.*, p. 476.

or non-existence of a previous transfer-burden. The complicated form in which Keynes presents his theorem is therefore quite superfluous.

The influence of the imposition of the tariff on the unemployment situation in England was probably not very great compared with the influence of the depreciation of the pound. If it were possible to calculate the adverse influence which both measures had through fostering throughout the world an unprecedented orgy of Protectionism, contributing markedly to the monetary chaos and thus depressing gold prices everywhere, one would probably arrive at a negative figure for the net effect.

7. SUMMARY.—We may draw the following conclusions. If the unemployment is *general* and *enduring*, then either the wage-level must be reduced or one must wait until technical progress enables the marginal productivity of labour to catch up with the unduly high wages—if one can not or will not make the suit small enough to fit, one can only hope that in time the body economic will grow large enough to fill it. If the unemployment is of a *cyclical* nature, it will disappear if a change in economic conditions brings about a recovery, but recovery may be delayed indefinitely if it is not aided by wage-reductions. The final case is that in which there is unemployment only in *one particular branch of industry*. Here the best course is to wait until the transition to full employment comes about without intervention, or possibly to assist the unemployed, for example by training them, to find jobs elsewhere. But to use the dynamite of tariff increases against the less pleasant aspects of economic progress is to destroy economic progress itself.

§ 4. THE IMPORT OF MEANS OF PRODUCTION AS A RESULT OF A TARIFF.

At the close of § 2 of the present chapter we saw that Schüller contests the central thesis of Free Trade doctrine, namely, that tariffs always produce only an irrational shifting of production and never an increase in the social product. His objection was that it is not true to assume that the available factors of production are given and fixed in quantity, and that they cannot be increased by tariffs. He contends that they can be so increased in two ways. In the first place, tariffs may cause home means of production previously idle to be utilised. This has been discussed in the previous pages. In the second place, tariffs may attract means of production from abroad. " The labour force of a country is not fixed in size . . . since the number of its workers can be increased by immigration and diminished by emigration."[11] Equally incorrect is the view that the size of the home production is limited by the amount

---

[11] Schüller, *loc. cit.*, p. 79.

K

of existing *capital*. If favourable openings for capital are available, capital flows in from abroad. " In spite of the difficulties which accompany a migration of capital, a considerable quantity does in fact migrate " (p. 81). The same argument is given by Ashley. " Adam Smith argued that protection could only divert capital from one industry to another; the Protectionist can reply that in many instances it has attracted capital into the country."[12] Ashley then gives a list of cases in which tariff increases in America have induced English firms to establish branches there.

The facts on which this argument is based are not open to question. Thousands of cases bear witness that the imposition or raising of tariffs may lead to an import of capital. It may be that foreign firms set up branches (so-called tariff factories) within the tariff wall, and to that end bring workers and machinery into the country. Or it may be that the establishment of new works, whether staffed by home or by foreign workers, is financed by foreign capital.[1] Very often negotiations are carried on, before the imposition of a new duty, with the foreign producers, and they agree to set up a factory when the duty is imposed.[2]

But it by no means follows from these facts either (*a*) that a *net* additional import of capital takes place, and that as much or more capital is not exported or lost as is imported, or (*b*) that even when a net import of capital does occur, the amount of the social product available for the inhabitants of the country is increased. Indeed, the following analysis will show that the latter is definitely *not* the case.

Let us suppose that a duty is placed upon a finished good, let us say cotton cloth, which was previously imported, and that the duty is high enough to bring into being home production and to diminish imports. The duty causes a shift in the location of industry from

---

[12] *The Tariff Problem* (1920), 4th edn., p. 78. Compare the trenchant criticism by Pigou in *Protective and Preferential Import Duties* (1906), pp. 9-12 (reprinted 1935). This argument of Schüller and Ashley is not new. It is found, for example, in the famous " Report on the Subject of Manufactures," written in 1790 by Alexander Hamilton, Washington's Secretary of the Treasury, who inaugurated the Protectionist policy of the United States. This model of Protectionist literature is reprinted in Taussig : *State Papers and Speeches on the Tariff* (1893), pp. 1 *et seq.* Now reprinted also in *Papers on Public Credit, Commerce and Finance* by Alexander Hamilton, New York, 1934.

[1] A good analysis of this train of events is given by Mackenroth, " Zollpolitik und Produktionsmittelversorgung " in *Weltwirtschaftliches Archiv* (Jan. 1929), vol. 29, pp. 93 *et seq.*

[2] In recent years in certain countries it has increasingly become the custom, in cases where there exists already an industry within the country, to prevent foreign firms from establishing factories subsequent to the restriction of import. In Austria, *e.g.*, the importation of textile machinery has been prohibited. The official reason is that " overproduction " should be avoided. The real motive is not to disturb the monopolistic exploitation of the domestic market by the existing firms.

foreign countries to the home country, and this shift is associated with an import of capital. Let us begin with an extreme case. Let us assume—to take a conceivable though improbable case—that *all the means of production are imported from abroad.* Then the result of the duty is that the industry has been diverted from its most favourable locations. Means of production are now imported in place of the finished product. The price of the latter rises, because the conditions of production are less favourable at home; plant and equipment must be installed which were already available abroad, transport costs will rise, and so on. The social product and the real income of consumers have diminished. There is no gain to set against this loss, although capital, perhaps in considerable quantity, has been imported. The form in which the import of capital takes place is immaterial. The means of production may be continuously imported or, through an issue of shares abroad, a large once-for-all investment may be made and the necessary machinery, materials, and workers imported with the proceeds.

Let us now pass from this extreme case to the typical case, in which only a part of the capital goods is imported, to be combined with home factors of production. In real terms, the following happens. Machinery, raw materials, intermediate products, and labour power are supplied from abroad either as a once-for-all investment or continuously, year by year. At the same time, home machinery, raw materials, intermediate products, and labour power are withdrawn from other uses, and so the new concerns are installed and kept going.[3]

How is the import of capital financed? The financing of the *stream* of current supplies presents no problem: raw cotton, or yarn, and so on are imported instead of cloth. The financing of *the installation of the works,* with their plant and equipment, may take place in various ways with either home or foreign capital. But there is a definite probability, especially if the industry is new to that country, that this will be financed by foreign producers, since they will be better acquainted with the kind of plant and equipment they need and with the firms which supply it and will be in a better position to get the necessary credit. Whether the foreign capital is provided by an issue of shares, or by the foreign producers themselves, or in some other way, there will be, *first,* an increase of imports and, *later,* spread over a series of years, an increase of exports. The increase of imports may come about

---

[3] If unemployment prevails, and this fact is most stressed in the argument, we come back to the reasoning of the previous section. As was shown earlier, the presence of unutilised means of production other than labour does not affect the argument at all.

because the new capital is used directly to import means of production or may come about through the usual working of the transfer-mechanism. The import of capital leaves a long-lasting impression upon the balance of payments, owing to the subsequent interest and amortisation payments which must be made upon it.

We are now in a position to draw conclusions as to the influence of this whole chain of events upon the social product. Without doubt, the supply of goods has suffered in that the price of the protected commodity has risen, so that less of it will be consumed than before. Is there any gain to set against this loss? The imported means of production must be paid for just as the previously imported finished products had to be paid for; if they are supplied on credit, interest on the foreign advances must also be paid. Such home means of production as are attracted into the new industry must be drawn away from other industries, and, finally, from the export industries. Since imports have fallen, exports also must fall.[4] Upon this transfer of resources from the export industries to the protected industries, nothing need be said here, since the discussion in chapter XII, § 2, and in § 3 of the present chapter, applies directly to it. That discussion showed that the consequence could be only an irrational shifting, and not an increase, in home production.

It is probable that the import of capital for certain purposes may be at least partly offset by the export of other capital. For if the export industries are depressed, the value of their specific factors, which cannot be put to other uses, will fall, and they will tend to migrate abroad. This tendency may be strengthened by a corresponding shift in foreign countries.

These considerations throw a further light upon the problems discussed in the previous section. They explain how the *imposition* of a tariff can have *at first* a favourable effect upon unemployment. For the favourable effects of a new tariff all display themselves at the outset. If there is an import of capital, and new investment, this makes possible increased activity. The import

---

[4] The original import of capital goods does not at once induce a corresponding export. For we have assumed that this import represents a *loan* from abroad. The corresponding exports will be spread over a number of years, during which interest and amortisation are paid upon the loan. The value of the total imports of means of production for the manufacture of the commodity is less than the value of the commodity previously imported, since the quantity of the product consumed is now less and a part of the means of production is provided at home. At the same time, an exception to this rule is conceivable. Given an inelastic demand and a sharp rise in price it may happen (if, for example, the home conditions of production or freight charges are very unfavourable) that the value of the imported means of production will exceed the value of the amount of the commodity which was previously imported. A duty which had such an effect would be quite clearly irrational in the highest degree, so that we need not further concern ourselves with such a case.

of capital improves the balance of payments,[5] gives more scope for a riskless expansion of credit, and strengthens the inflationary effect of the tariff.[6] But this stimulating influence must very soon disappear, and there will remain only the harmful effects of the tariff —the permanent penalising of consumption by higher prices and the injury to the national income.

Nearly every country has for years been under the spell of this economic morphinism. In one place after another the body economic has given itself an injection by imposing or increasing a tariff; the doses have become larger and larger; the volume of international trade has dwindled, the international division of labour has been curtailed, and the general welfare has diminished.

The effects of tariffs resemble those of many other phenomena in that the favourable aspects are concentrated in one place and can be seen plainly, whereas the other aspects are more diffused over the economy and extend over a longer time. They, too, can indeed be seen plainly, but their causes can be understood only by means of a theoretical analysis.

The following question remains. Granted that tariffs are unlikely to increase the income of the home population by attracting factors from abroad, may they not be a means of increasing that population and of making it greater than it would be under Free Trade? Beyond doubt it is possible, in certain circumstances, for protected industries to attract workers, especially business men, from abroad or to prevent them from emigrating. This may result in a *net* increase in the total population, but it will certainly not result in an increase in the social product per head of the population residing in the country before the protection was imposed. On the contrary. The average real income per head diminishes, and this diminution must cause a tendency to emigration rather than to immigration. In general, and in the long run, tariffs are not a suitable means for increasing the capacity of a country to maintain population.

Nevertheless, it may be possible by means of tariffs, or of subsidies in some other form, to overcome the frictional resistances against the immigration of particular categories of workers. These frictional resistances consist not so much of the money costs of moving as of the pull of associations and traditions, which may prevent a worker from emigrating although the wage-difference would more than cover his expenses of moving.

But this is a phenomenon which falls outside the field of

[5] But only when it takes the form of a foreign issue of shares and not of a direct import of resources *in natura*, without the aid of the transfer-mechanism.
[6] *Cf.* chap. xv, § 2.

equilibrium analysis. It is a phenomenon of development, to be considered in connection with the infant-industry argument for tariffs.

§ 5. INFANT-INDUSTRY TARIFFS.

1. HAMILTON AND LIST.—The infant-industry argument for tariffs was clearly formulated as early as 1790 by Alexander Hamilton in his *Report on Manufactures* (pp. 29 *et seq.*). His ideas enjoyed great popularity in America, where they were further developed by H. C. Carey and others. Later they were brought to Germany by Friedrich List. In his celebrated *National System of Political Economy* he expounds and popularises them with wearisome verbosity and a vast display of historical ' illustrations.' List was in principle a Free Trader. He realised the advantages of international division of labour. He rejects without hesitation tariffs to preserve certain sections of the economy from the growth of foreign competition, and especially tariffs upon raw materials and foodstuffs.

" With regard to the interchange of raw products, the [classical] school is perfectly correct in supposing that the most extensive liberty of commerce is, under all circumstances, most advantageous to the individual as well as to the entire State. One can, indeed, augment this production by restrictions; but the advantage obtained thereby is merely apparent. We only thereby divert . . . capital and labour into another and less useful channel.[7] To promote the home agriculture by protective tariffs is a bad beginning.[8]

" But the manufacturing productive power, on the contrary, is governed by other laws.[9] The school fails to perceive that under a system of perfectly free competition with more advanced manufacturing nations, a nation which is less advanced than these, although well fitted for manufacturing, can never attain to a perfectly developed manufacturing power of its own . . . without protective duties.[1]

" The reason for this is the same as that why a child or a boy in wrestling with a strong man can scarcely be victorious or even offer steady resistance. The manufactories which constitute the commercial and industrial supremacy (of England) have a thousand advantages over the newly-born or half-grown manufactories of other nations. The former, for instance, can obtain skilled and experienced workmen in the greatest number and at the cheapest wages, the best technical men and foremen, the most perfect and the cheapest machinery, the greatest benefit in buying and selling advantageously; further, the cheapest means of transport, as respects raw materials and also in respect of transporting goods when sold, more extended credit for the manufactories with banks and money institutions at the lowest rates of interest, greater commercial experience, better tools,

---

[7] *The National System of Political Economy*, translated by Sampson S. Lloyd, M.P. (1885), p. 217.
[8] This sentence is on p. 54 of the (1930) German text, in italics. It is not in the English translation, since this gives only extracts from the Preface (in which it occurs). There has been much dispute as to whether List favoured or opposed import duties on grain.
[9] *Ibid.*, p. 217.
[1] *Ibid.*, p. 316.

buildings, arrangements, connections, such as can only be acquired and established in the course of generations; an enormous home market . . . ; and consequently possess a guarantee for the continuance of their business and abundant means to sell on credit for years to come in the future, if it is required to acquire the control of a foreign market."[2] " It is (as a rule) incomparably easier to perfect and extend a business already established than to found a new one. We see everywhere old business establishments that have lasted for a series of generations worked with greater profits than new ones. We observe that it is the more difficult to set a new business going in proportion as fewer branches of industry of a similar character already exist in a nation; because, in that case, masters, fore-men, and workmen must first be either trained up at home or procured from abroad, and because the profitableness of the business has not been sufficiently tested to give capitalists confidence in its success."[3]

List stresses the advantages in culture and character which industrial occupations bring to a nation. " In a country devoted to mere raw agriculture, dullness of mind, awkwardness of body, obstinate adherence to old notions, customs, methods, and pro-cesses, want of culture, of prosperity, and of liberty, prevail.[4] This condition of things is entirely changed . . . by establishing a manufacturing power . . . the mental, moral, and physical stag-nation of the population is broken up.[5] Manufactories and manu-factures are the mothers and children of municipal liberty, of intelligence, of the arts and sciences, of internal and external commerce, of navigation and improvements in transport, of civilisa-tion and political power."[6]

Thus List arrives at the conviction that every ' suitable ' nation can reap an advantage, at a certain stage in its cultural and economic development, by fostering manufacturing, until it reaches large proportions, through protective tariffs. But the tariffs should be only temporary. They should be removed after they have per-formed their function of ' nursing,' and have built up a supply of skilled workers, technicians, and entrepreneurs, and have enabled a number of industries to become established and able to stand upon their own feet.

List is aware that such a policy involves abstinence and loss in the immediate future. " The nation must sacrifice . . . a measure of material prosperity in order to gain culture, skill, and powers of united production; it must sacrifice some present advantages in order to insure to itself future ones.[7] It is true that protective duties at first increase the price of manufactured goods; but it is just as true . . . that in the course of time, by the nation being enabled to build up a completely-developed manufacturing power

2 *Ibid.*, pp. 299-300.
3 *Ibid.*, p. 294.
4 *Ibid.*, p. 197.
5 *Ibid.*, p. 221.
6 *Ibid.*, p. 141.
7 *Ibid.*, p. 144.

of its own, these goods are produced more cheaply at home than the price at which they can be imported from foreign parts."[8] The present burden represents an investment of ' nursing capital ' which in a later generation will yield fruit to the nation at compound interest.

List warns us that this capital should not be invested in the wrong way.

" Measures of protection are justifiable only . . . in case of nations which through an extensive and compact territory, large population, possession of natural resources, far advanced agriculture, a high degree of civilisation and political development, are qualified to maintain an equal rank with the principal agricultural manufacturing commercial nations.[9] It may in general be assumed that where any technical industry cannot be established by means of an original protection of 40 to 60 per cent. and cannot continue to maintain itself under a continued protection of 20 to 30 per cent. the fundamental conditions of manufacturing power are lacking.[1]

List's exposition of these ideas, which are certainly very valuable and cannot be rejected out of hand, is unfortunately mingled with great exaggeration and gross Protectionist fallacies. It is also mingled with bitter and quite superfluous attacks upon the classical economists. He opposes his doctrine of ' productive powers ' to their ' theory of exchange value ' and the *national* system to their ' cosmopolitan doctrine.'

2. JOHN STUART MILL.—A more precise and correct formulation of the infant-industry notion, and one which at the same time shows that it is not inconsistent with classical and modern theory, is given by the Free Trader John Stuart Mill.[2] This illustrates the correctness of Viner's remark that all economically tenable arguments for tariffs come from Free Traders. Mill writes:

" The only case in which, on mere principles of political economy, protecting duties can be defensible, is when they are imposed temporarily (especially in a young and rising nation) in hopes of naturalizing a foreign industry, in itself perfectly suitable to the circumstances of the country. The superiority of one country over another in a branch of production often arises only from having begun it sooner. There may be no inherent advantage on one part, or disadvantage on the other, but only a present superiority of acquired skill and experience. A country which has this skill and experience yet to acquire, may in other respects be better adapted to the production than those which were earlier in the field : and besides, it is a just remark of Mr. Rae, that nothing has a greater tendency to promote improvements in any branch of production than its trial under a new set of conditions. But it cannot be expected that individuals should, at their own risk, or rather to their certain loss, introduce a new manufacture, and bear the burthen of carrying it on until the producers have been educated up to the level of those with whom the processes are traditional. A protecting

---

[8] *Ibid.*, p. 145.
[9] *Ibid.*, p. 309.
[1] *Ibid.*, p. 313.
[2] *Principles*, Bk. 5, chap. x, § 1. Mill wrote after List—the first edition of the *Principles* was in 1848—but was influenced by the Americans and not by List.

duty, continued for a reasonable time, might sometimes be the least inconvenient mode in which the nation can tax itself for the support of such an experiment. But it is essential that the protection should be confined to cases in which there is good ground of assurance that the industry which it fosters will after a time be able to dispense with it; nor should the domestic producers ever be allowed to expect that it will be continued to them beyond the time necessary for a fair trial of what they are capable of accomplishing."[3]

Since Mill gave it his approval, the infant-industry argument has been accepted in principle by many Free Trade economists.[4]

3. CRITICISM.—Taussig observes that the infant-industry argument, in contrast to other arguments for tariffs, bears fairly well the test of a critical analysis. The possibility, asserted by Hamilton and List, that a tariff may help an industry to survive the weaknesses of infancy, is not to be disputed. But it is very difficult to lay down general rules for ascertaining when such a possibility is in fact present. Only an examination of concrete cases can throw any light upon the matter. And, indeed, Taussig has written a large volume—*Some Aspects of the Tariff Question*—in which he examines the effects of a number of American tariffs (upon iron and steel, sugar, silk, rayon, and cotton) in order to see whether or not they have proved to be successful infant-industry tariffs.

The difficulty of such an examination is due, on the one hand, to the fact that the experiment of an infant-industry tariff is seldom or never brought to a conclusion. Nearly every industrial tariff was first imposed as an infant-industry tariff under the promise that in a few years, when the industry had grown sufficiently to face foreign competition, it would be removed. But, in fact, this moment never arrives. The interested parties are never willing to have the duty removed. Thus temporary infant-industry duties are transformed into permanent duties to preserve the industries they protect. Even if a part of the industry does become able to stand upon its own feet, there will always be *in addition* less efficient concerns which have come into existence behind the shelter of the duty and which would disappear were the duty removed. Moreover, even industrialists who could survive quite well under Free Trade strongly oppose the removal of the duty, either because they

[3] Ashley's ed., p. 922.
[4] Among these we must first name Marshall. The argument inevitably made a special appeal to him owing to his predilection for the phenomena of economic development. See numerous references in *Money, Credit and Commerce* and in *Industry and Trade*. See also his *Memorandum on Fiscal Policy* in the *Official Papers*. Pigou remarks : " of the formal validity of List's argument there is no longer any dispute among economists " (*Protective and Preferential Import Duties*, p. 13). See also Taussig, *Some Aspects of the Tariff Question*, 3rd edn., chap. ii, and *Free Trade, The Tariff and Reciprocity*, pp. 16 *et seq.;* Röpke, *loc. cit.*, p. 67; Clark, *Essentials of Economic Theory*, p. 522.

wish to continue making monopolistic profits under its protection or because they feel they may need it if foreign competition becomes keener. (Hence the fact that an infant-industry duty is not subsequently removed, as promised, does not prove that it has not in part fulfilled its purpose.)

The difficulty of such an examination is due, on the other hand, to the fact that even if a duty does create an industry which after some time can survive without it, and it is known for certain that this industry would not have come into existence without the duty, its capacity to survive is no proof that the duty has been advantageous. Suppose that a duty is imposed and that this causes much fixed capital to be installed, buildings to be erected, means of transport to be provided—in a word, causes what Wicksell calls ' Rent-Goods ' to be produced. Then it is possible that, even if the duty is removed, the industry will continue to produce, since much of the equipment and so on may be too specific to be put to other uses. Nevertheless, capital will have been lost, and must be written down in value. In such a case the duty will not have been advantageous.

But in this matter I cannot go all the way with Robbins,[5] who considers such an investment to be justified only when it yields compound interest at the prevailing rate. (The same applies to the ' nursing capital ' of List, which is invested by the present generation in the form of higher prices and bears fruit in the future, when the ' nursing ' has been successful, in the form of increased income due to the improved intelligence and skill of the population.) This involves somehow weighing against one another the burden and the gain of two generations. Such a valuation cannot be based upon the market rate of interest. The test of the rate of interest is relevant in this connection only upon the assumption that the invested capital would otherwise have been invested more profitably and would have yielded more benefit to future generations. But if it would have been consumed, and not invested at all, the test of the rate of interest has no application.

This discussion shows how very complicated the whole question is. Those who are perpetually advocating infant-industry duties usually have no notion of those difficulties. They believe that they, or others, are in a position to measure correctly and concretely all the various elements of the problem and so to strike a balance of gain or loss.

Some hold the view that infant-industry tariffs are unnecessary, since private enterprise will of itself perceive and utilise favourable

---

[5] " Notes on Some Arguments for Protection " in *Economica* (Feb. 1931), p. 47, footnote 3.

openings for production. In favour of this view is the fact that again and again without any Protection quite new industries have been set up in a country, when the conditions of production have been favourable and such other conditions as security and maintenance of law and order have been present. This is especially true of the great international migration of capital in modern times. The great Free Trade area of the United States affords very instructive instances. A powerful centre of industry was established in a relatively short time in the Middle West, without any protection from the established industries of the Atlantic States, although the latter enjoyed all the advantages enumerated by Hamilton and List. The same thing happened in the South, where, for example, a great cotton industry was set up, owing to the conditions of production and especially the supply of labour being favourable, despite the keen competition of the New England States. Thus favourable conditions of production were seized upon by private initiative although, as Taussig points out,[6] they could be fully utilised only after a preliminary period of experiment and uncertainty, during which the established industries enjoyed all the advantages against which Protection is alleged to be necessary.

The advocates of the infant-industry notion usually have in mind the creation of a supply of skilled workers. The view is often expressed that some branch or other of industry will not flourish in a country, because the supply of skilled workers is not great enough, although all other conditions are favourable. It is said that in such cases private initiative fails to take any action. It fails not only when the capital invested would not yield the prevailing rate of interest, but also—it is said—in some cases when the investment in itself would be profitable. The argument is that the investor is not certain of getting the fruits of his investment. Nobody guarantees him that his workers, after becoming skilled through practice, would not leave him for a competitor who paid them better or would not demand increased wages, so that the fruits of his ' nursing ' would be taken from him. This would be a case of the improvement of a factor of production, namely Labour, which *cannot be appropriated* by the entrepreneur. Such an improvement—apart from the difficulty of forecasting its value —would not enter into the monetary calculations of the entrepreneur : it would be an *external economy*. The same notion applies to other similar situations—for example, to the overcoming of a rooted but irrational preference of the public for a foreign brand of a certain commodity.

---

[6] *Free Trade, The Tariff and Reciprocity*, p. 21.

But we must remember that the infant-industry duty yields no advantage if it merely leads to workers being trained in an employment in which their productivity is only *equal* to what it was previously, elsewhere—as may quite easily happen in an industrial country with a large number of trained workers. An increase in the social product comes about only if the ' nursing ' attracts workers from employments where their marginal productivity was smaller. We have here the ' dynamic ' argument for tariffs upon which the theory of Manoïlesco is based.[7]

It is at least certain that in a modern industrial country, well supplied with skilled workers, trained technicians, and enterprising leaders of industry, a duty can be said to fulfil a ' nursing ' function only in exceptional cases. Or does one really believe that the German Steel Trust is to be regarded as a ' tariff baby '— it certainly requires enough nursing—and that the duty on benzine ' nursed ' into existence the German Dye Trust? The ' nursing ' function of duties on finished goods would, of course, be nullified by duties on foodstuffs and raw materials. Hence the all-embracing tariff walls of today cannot be justified by any infant-industry argument.

When Protectionists speak of the ' nursing ' function of a tariff, they often have in mind the *advantages of mass-production* which it would make possible, and the law of decreasing costs. This we have already discussed in § 4 of chapter XII. We there pointed out that the appropriate analytical tool with which to examine such consequences, alleged to be due to ' nursing,' is the concept of ' external economies.' We also showed how vague, muddled, and doubtful these alleged possibilities are, so that arguments for tariffs based upon them belong to the *curiosa* of theory rather than to a practical economic policy.

Anyone who bears all this in mind must surely agree with Röpke that it is doubtful whether a rational infant-industry duty has ever existed. In practice the infant-industry argument is nearly always a mere pretext. The Protectionists start from a false or grossly exaggerated account of the available possibilities, so that those rare cases in which a duty might possibly be advantageous, are never properly discussed.[8]

---

[7] *Cf.* chap. xii, § 3.

[8] Marshall tells how he was disillusioned when he studied the practice of tariff policy in America : " I for one was so much impressed by those arguments of Carey and his followers . . . that I went to the United States in 1875 to study the problems of national industry and international trade from the American point of view; and I was quite prepared to learn, not, indeed, that the American system was applicable to England, but that it might contain ideas capable of adaptation to English conditions.

" I came back convinced that a protective policy, in fact, was a very different

If, however, it is believed that these rare cases can always be detected, it is difficult to see why the industries in question should not be encouraged by a public subsidy instead of by a duty. As Mill emphasised, the former is much more rational, as the publicity enables everyone to realise what the cost is and lessens the danger that the protection will become permanent. Certainly in the case of ' forced saving,' mentioned above, a duty—owing to the difficulty of predicting its repercussions—is not the most rational method of taxing the present for the benefit of the future.[9]

§ 6. The Dangers of an Unbalanced Economy which Exports Manufactures.

1. Statement of the Argument.—In the second half of the nineteenth century Germany ceased to be a grain-exporting country and became a grain-importing country. This was the result of her very rapid industrial development, so much desired by List, and of the appearance of cheap corn from overseas, and especially from America, upon the European market. Germany was faced with the choice of following in the footsteps of England, sacrificing part of her agriculture to overseas competition, and becoming overwhelmingly industrial, or, on the other hand, of arresting this development by applying the brake of agricultural tariffs. The great influence of the big Prussian landowners was responsible for the decision she took. As Max Weber says (loc. cit., p. 110) Germany was Free Trade so long as the big Prussian landowners were Free Trade, so long as their motto—which one of them coined —was: '' I am a conservative and for that reason I am a Free Trader ''; she adopted tariffs at the moment when the march of events caused the big landowners to turn Protectionist.

Although she changed over to Protection in 1879, her development as a country exporting manufactures was not arrested. Her agricultural population fell from 47.3 per cent. of the total in 1871

---

thing from a protective policy as painted by sanguine economists, such as Carey '' (we can add : and List) '' . . . who assumed that all other people would be as upright as they know themselves to be, and as clear-sighted as they believe themselves to be. I found that, however simple the plan on which a protective policy started, it was drawn irresistibly to become intricate, and to lend its chief aid to those industries which were already strong enough to do without it. In becoming intricate it became corrupt, and tended to corrupt general politics. On the whole, I thought that this moral harm far outweighed any small net benefit which it might be capable of conferring on American industry in the stage in which it was then.

'' Subsequent observation of the course of politics in America and elsewhere has strengthened this conviction.''

[9] In pre-War Hungary industries were encouraged systematically and with success (but hardly with advantage) *without* tariffs. Hungary was prevented by her agreement with Austria from erecting a tariff barrier against the more efficient Austrian industries.

to 40 per cent. in 1882, 33.6 per cent. in 1895, 27.1 per cent. in 1907, and 23 per cent. in 1925. Her export of manufactures rose, as did her import of foodstuffs and raw materials. Many Germans viewed with concern the growing dependence upon other countries for raw materials and foodstuffs. The discussion[1] about this became most intense around the turn of the century, especially in the writings of Oldenburg, Pohle, Wagner, Dietzel, and Brentano. Thenceforward pessimistic prophecies as to the ultimate result of this dependence, which continued to grow in spite of the tariff, did not cease. The movement for Autarchy, which has become so prominent in recent years, has taken over the arguments of Oldenburg and Pohle and Wagner, although it presents them in a crude and unscientific form.

What are the dangers associated with a growing export of manufactures? (a) One is supposed to lie in *industrialisation as such*. Oldenburg, for instance, depicts a rural idyll disturbed by capitalistic and industrial development.[2] This question has only an indirect connection with the theory of international trade, and will not be examined here. We may point out, however, that those who are hostile to industry are diametrically opposed to List.

(b) This development is said to be especially dangerous in view of the possibility of war. *First*, the rural population supply the backbone of the army and are alleged to make far better soldiers than the flotsam of the cities. *Secondly*, a country which gets much of its food and raw materials from overseas can easily be reduced to submission by a blockade. Again, we shall not discuss this ' non-economic ' argument, beyond pointing out that a modern war demands complicated machines as well as men and that the former can be supplied in sufficient quantities only by highly-developed industries.

(c) But this development is said to be bad even from a purely economic standpoint. Here the danger, best stated by Pohle, is that sooner or later it must be reversed. The German economy comes more and more to resemble a structure which is built not upon its own ground but largely upon the uncertain foundations of imported raw materials and foodstuffs. The time must come

---

[1] From the Free Trade point of view, see the writings of H. Dietzel, "Agrar-und Industriestaat " in *Handwörterbuch der Staatswissenschaften* (2nd and 3rd edns.), *Weltwirtschaft und Volkswirtschaft* (1900), *Bedeutet der Export von Produktionsmitteln volkswirtschaftlichen Selbstmord?* (1907). The case for Protection was presented by Pohle, *Deutschland am Scheidewege* (1902); Oldenburg, *Über Deutschland als Industriestaat.* Speech before the 8. Evangelischsozialer Kongress (1897) (see, however, the effective answer of Max Weber, *loc. cit.*). Ad. Wagner, *Agrar- und Industriestaat*, 2nd edn. (1902).

[2] Similarly Méline, *Retour à la Terre* (1905), and against this thesis Brentano, *Die Schrecken des überwiegenden Industriestaates.*

when this flimsy structure will be overturned.   The countries which today specialise in the production of foodstuffs and raw materials want to have their own industries.   Their populations are rapidly increasing.   As time goes on, their export surplus of foodstuffs and raw materials must diminish, while simultaneously their increasing tariff walls will curtail the export of manufacturers by the older industrial countries.   Hitherto it has always been possible, when one foreign source of supply tended to dry up, to replace it by another.   Thus England obtained her grain in the first half of the nineteenth century from Germany; then Russia replaced Germany; then came the United States as a source of supply, and, finally, Canada and the Argentine.   But sooner or later all such countries will become industrialised, and then the older industrial countries will have to face a catastrophic reversal of their previous development.   It is relatively easy to absorb people from the country into the cities.   The opposite process is extremely difficult, if not impossible.   Experience shows that after two generations of city life industrial workers are neither physically nor mentally suited for agriculture.

A. Wagner underlines this prognosis by referring to the population question.   Following Malthus, he fears that the improved standard of living of the masses, arising from industrial development, must lead to a great increase in population.   The inevitable return to a more self-sufficient economy, with a smaller capacity to support population, will thus be all the more painful.   From this train of thought springs also the fear, expressed by Wagner and others, that the export of capital in the form of means of production spells economic suicide.   In particular, the English export of machinery and coal is regarded as a crime against all industrial countries in that it promotes the industrial development of the agricultural countries.

2. CRITICISM.—This prognosis contains nothing which can be refuted by an appeal to equilibrium theory.   Any criticism of it must rest upon a different valuation of the facts and of the direction which economic development is taking.

The main answer to those who fear the industrialisation of the agricultural countries is to point out, as Max Weber pointed out to Oldenburg, that in fact the best customers of the industrial countries are not the agricultural countries but—the other industrial countries.   Hitherto the industrialisation of agricultural countries has by no means led to a diminution in their imports from the older industrial countries.   On the contrary, their imports have continually increased.   The industrialisation of Germany was accompanied by a multiplication of her imports from England, and the same was true of the United States and of all other newly-industrialised countries. Of course, certain branches of industry, such as the cotton industry of England after the War, inevitably lost their markets, but other branches took their place. Indeed, it would be very remarkable if among countries with such different climates, geographical situations, and natural and acquired aptitudes of their workers, as England, Germany, France, Italy, the United States, Canada, Russia, India and so on, there were no differences in comparative costs. But so long as there are such differences a profitable exchange of goods is possible.

At the same time, the industrial development of agricultural countries is accompanied by a certain shifting in the composition of their trade with the older industrial countries. They become industrialised by stages. They begin by producing coarse qualities and semi-finished products, which demand no skilled labour. Their export of raw materials falls off somewhat. Instead of crude raw materials they come more and more to export semi-finished goods. Chilled meat replaces cattle, flour replaces grain, crude copper replaces ore, cellulose and paper replace wood. This development naturally involves a great saving in transport costs. But the finer qualities of many goods, together with means of production such as machinery, must still be imported. Nor does technical and industrial development stand still in the older countries. They turn to the production of more complicated machines, electro-motors, motorcars, aeroplanes, wireless apparatus, finer textiles, photographic and other optical apparatus, measuring instruments, and many other high-grade products. Their superiority in those fields requiring more skill and technical perfection is constantly manifesting itself.

It follows that up to the present the export of capital and means of production has not been economic suicide but rather has provided a basis for profitable exchange. Nor does there seem any reason why technical progress should not make possible a continuance of this development.

The ' pessimists,' such as Pohle, replied that the international exchange of finished products (of finer and finer quality) against raw materials must cease within a measurable time because the agricultural countries, owing to their increasing industrialisation and growing population, will no longer have a surplus available for export. They added that this natural development will be accelerated by the growth of extreme Protection in those countries, which will hinder the export of quality products from the older centres, even if it were still in the interests of all parties that they should be admitted.

Dietzel retorted that if this were indeed to come about it would not burst suddenly like a thunderstorm upon the older countries, but would be preceded and accompanied by a *general rise in the price* of foodstuffs and raw materials, which would give the various economies plenty of time to adapt themselves to the changing conditions.

But the decisive retort is a different one. It is that the pessimists overlook two important developments. The first is the application of technical progress and mechanisation to agriculture. The second is the fall in the birth rate in both old and young countries.

On the one hand, the technique of production has made such great strides in almost all branches of agriculture, in the widest sense of the term, and of mining, that there can now be no question of a shortage of raw materials. On the other hand, the rate of increase of population has fallen off so much, in the agricultural countries as well as in the others, that from this quarter also there is no danger to be feared.

It is true that nobody can tell what surprises the next hundred years may bring forth. But this much seems to be certain: the dangers which threaten the economy of industrial countries from within—such as social disturbances, socialistic experiments, increasing rigidity of their price structures owing to the growth of monopoly, currency experiments, and so on—are much more grave and acute than those which spring from the tendency of agricultural countries towards industrialisation and self-sufficiency.

§ 7. EMERGENCY TARIFFS AND TARIFFS TO ENSURE THE MARKET.

The emergency argument is of a dynamic nature, although different in kind from those considered above. Emergency tariffs are designed to remove or diminish the effect of a temporary crisis in some particular branch of industry. From a theoretical standpoint not much can be said about them. It is certainly conceivable that through some sudden change in conditions, such as an all-too-bountiful world harvest, especially if coupled with a poor harvest at home, a crisis may come about which can be banished or softened by a rise in price through a tariff. A change in technique, or in fashion, or a tariff war between two foreign countries, which robs a foreign industry of its usual market, can lead to increased imports and thus to an emergency situation. The emergency may be one which will soon pass away or, if it is coupled with a permanent shifting in comparative costs, its suddenness may make a sufficiently quick adaptation unlikely. In such cases tariffs may soften the crisis or make easier the transition to a new equilibrium.

But experience shows that even when tariffs have been imposed to meet a quite temporary emergency they are not subsequently removed without the greatest difficulty. In the past each economic crisis has produced a rich crop of tariff increases and has left behind it higher tariff walls. Hence great caution in imposing them is desirable.

Other considerations reinforce this conclusion. When emergency tariffs are simultaneously imposed upon a number of different goods, they must to some extent work against one another. Political tactics demand that a duty desired by one group should be purchased by other duties desired by other groups. Duties on raw materials and intermediate products involve also duties on the corresponding finished product. An emergency tariff in one country is extremely likely to cause other countries to retaliate with similar measures. In view of all this, the only possible conclusion seems to be that emergency tariffs bring more harm than benefit and therefore should be strictly avoided, especially if less dangerous means of alleviating the crisis are available.

A favourite excuse made by interested parties when demanding a duty is that the object of the duty is not to raise prices or to increase home production at the expense of imports, but merely to ensure the market and provide protection against occasional imports. Clearly this plea can be taken seriously only when there is *not* a regular import of the good in question. This happens less often than might be supposed. Owing to the freight-situation, some districts in a country often import a good which, for the country as a whole, is an export commodity. Again, certain special qualities or grades of a good may be imported although on balance the good is an export commodity. For such districts, and for such special qualities or grades, a tariff ' to ensure the market ' would be protective and price-raising.

§ 8. Tariffs as a means of Improving the Terms of Trade (' The foreigner pays the duty ').

In earlier tariff controversies the argument was frequently put forward that the foreigner pays the duty. If, after the imposition of the duty, the home price does not rise or does not rise by the full amount of the duty, then the duty is borne wholly or in part by the foreign producers. Bismarck remarked in his well-known message to the Bundesrat of 15th December, 1878, which introduced the definite change of Germany from a liberal to a protective trade policy: " In the case of goods . . . which home producers are in a position to produce in large quantities for home consumption, the duty must be paid entirely by the foreign producers in order to enable them to compete upon the German market. If in such cases a part of the home consumption is still supplied from abroad, the foreign competitors must pay at least a part and often the whole of the duty, thus reducing their previous profit. . . . If the increased duty is indeed borne by the home consumer, then its raising will have been a matter of indifference to the foreign competitors."[3]

This passage certainly shows no deep economic insight. It in no way depends upon the circumstances mentioned whether or not it is possible to shift the duty onto the foreigner. But it is not to be denied that under certain conditions it is possible so to shift part or even the whole of the duty and that the gain to the country whose Government receives the income from the duty *may* exceed the loss to its consumers, so that the duty on balance may be of advantage to the home economy. This, therefore, is one of the few arguments for tariffs of a purely *static nature* which are worth discussing.[4]

The problem is the same as that presented by the imposition of any other indirect tax. We must examine the shifting and incidence of the tax, or of the duty, in order to discover whether it is finally borne by consumers or by producers or shared between the two. In the case of an import duty the producers are foreigners. An analogous problem is of course presented by export duties.

Suppose that Germany imposes an import duty upon wheat of 20 marks per quintal. If thereupon the German price rises by 20 marks, the German consumer pays the whole duty and the foreigner pays none of it.[5] But if the diminished demand of Germany causes the foreign price to fall, say by 2 marks, and the home price to rise, therefore, by only 18 marks, one can say that the foreigner makes a contribution of 2 marks per quintal of wheat imported into Germany. It is even conceivable that the foreign supply is so inelastic that a small diminution of the German demand causes the

3 Poschinger, *Bismarck als Volkswirt*, 1, pp. 170 seq.

4 The problem is discussed in the whole literature on the shifting and incidence of taxation. Compare especially Seligman's big book *Shifting and Incidence of Taxation* which gives a survey of the literature. Marshall has discussed the problem with special reference to tariff duties in his *Money, Credit and Commerce*, pp. 177-209 and Appendix J. See also his memorandum on *The Fiscal Policy of International Trade* (1903), now reprinted in *Official Papers* by Alfred Marshall. Edgeworth, *Papers relating to Political Economy*, vol. 2, pp. 39 *et seq.*, and Pigou, *Public Finance*, 2nd edn., pp. 198 *et seq.*

5 This, however, does not mean that the foreigner is not injured. He is injured in so far as the increase in German production reduces his market. In such a case, strictly speaking, the home price cannot rise by the full amount of the duty. But if we consider the world market in relation to that of one single country, we can abstract from this small difference.

price to fall by 20 marks. In such a case the German price would not rise at all and the foreigner would bear the whole of the duty.[6] So long as we restrict ourselves to the direct influence of the duty upon the price of the good concerned, and ignore the further effects, we may speak of the incidence of the duty in the narrower sense of the term.

The fact that there is a difference equal to the amount of the duty between the home price and the foreign price clearly tells us nothing at all as to how much, if any, of the duty is borne by the foreigner.[7] So long as some imports continue to come in, such a difference must exist. The proportion in which the incidence of the duty is shared between the home country and foreign country depends upon the extent to which this price difference is due respectively to a rise in the home price and a fall in the foreign price.

This in turn clearly depends upon the circumstances analysed in § 1 of chapter XV. We may summarise the results as follows:—

Let us first take the response of the home demand as given. Then the fall in the foreign price will be the greater, and the foreigner will therefore bear a larger proportion of the duty, the greater is the relative importance of the protected market to the foreign producers, that is to say, the smaller are their other foreign markets, the less favourable is the freight situation for exporting to them, and the higher are their import duties. Another relevant factor is the cost-situation of the foreign producers. How much will marginal cost fall when their production is curtailed? To what extent can factors of production move out of this industry and into other lines, which have become relatively more profitable owing to the duty?

Let us next take the response of the foreign supply as given. Then the determining circumstances are the conditions of the home demand and of the home supply. The more the home demand falls off in response to a rise in price, the less will the home price rise and the greater, therefore, will be the proportion of the duty borne by the foreigner, but at the same time the less will be the total receipts of the taxing Government from the duty. The more elastic is the home supply—the greater, that is to say, is the extent to which the home production expands in response to a small rise in price—the less will the home price rise, the more will imports be curtailed, and the greater will be the proportion of the duty borne

---

[6] This is least unlikely when the foreigner has a monopoly of the good in question as, e.g., Greece has of currants.

[7] This point is nearly always ignored. Schüller gives examples of writers who ignore it. H. Schultz, " Correct and Incorrect Methods of Determining the Effectiveness of the Tariff," in *Journal of Farm Economics* (1935), vol. 17, pp. 625 et seq.

by the foreigner but at the same time the less will be the total receipts of the taxing Government from the duty.

It follows that the protective aim of the duty and its function of providing revenue at the cost of the foreigner are inconsistent with one another.[8] For when the protective aim is fully attained, the duty yields no revenue, and, conversely, when the foreigner bears the whole of the duty, the home production receives no protection, since the home price remains unchanged.

In general, one country is seldom able to make the foreigner bear part of its import duties (in the sense defined above), and even when this is possible the share borne by the foreigner is likely to be small. For, as a rule, the imports of a good by any one country form such a small proportion of the total exports of that good that a restriction of its imports is unlikely to have a perceptible effect upon the price at which it imports them. This generalisation is obviously likely to apply in a greater measure to a small country than to a large one.

Nevertheless, it may be possible *in the short run*, as Marshall says, to snatch a small gain from a suddenly imposed import duty at the cost of foreign producers and merchants who have specialised in exporting and who are not in a position immediately to liquidate their businesses or to cut down their exports sufficiently to avoid bearing part of the duty. But ' practical men ' and politicians, who always consider only the immediate effects of tariffs, greatly exaggerate the frequency and importance of such cases. In the long run such a shifting of the duty very seldom occurs to any significant extent. Moreover, there is always the danger that other countries will impose retaliatory duties, thereby nullifying any such chance of gain.

But, so far, we have considered only the direct effect of a particular duty upon the price of the good on which it is imposed, that is to say, we have spoken only of the incidence of the duty in the narrower sense. If there are a number of tariff changes, this ' partial-equilibrium ' method gives a very incomplete picture. We should consider also the *indirect effects*. The *first* of these is the diversion of demand due to the change in the prices of the goods subjected to duty. The *second* is the shift in production both at home and abroad which occurs owing to the influence of the duty upon those branches of industry which it affects. The *third* arises from the response of the monetary mechanism, in restoring equilibrium in the balance of payments, The *fourth* arises from the manner in which the State distributes the expenditure of its receipts from the duties over different goods and services.

It is conceivable that these indirect effects may make the net result of a duty just the opposite of what one would deduce by considering only the direct effects. For example, let us suppose that the latter are the most favourable we

---

[8] But this is valid only if we restrict ourselves to the particular prices directly affected by the duty and ignore the further effects (see below).

can conceive. The foreign price falls by the full amount of the duty, so that the whole of the duty is borne by the foreigner. This means that the income of foreign producers will fall by the full amount of the duty. Let us now suppose that they, therefore, restrict their purchases of certain goods which the first country specialises in exporting, and that this causes a substantial fall in their price. Let us further suppose that the Government of the first country buys mainly foreign goods with its receipts from the duties. In such circumstances it is quite possible that on balance the first country will lose more by the reduced prices of its exports and by the increased prices of some of its imports than it gains by the fact that the incidence of its import duties, in the narrow sense, is entirely upon the foreigner.[9] But it is also conceivable, to take a different case, that the monetary mechanism operates in such a way as to turn the terms of trade still further against the foreigner, so that the latter both bears the whole of the original duties and also sells some of his other exports more cheaply and pays more for some of the other goods which he buys from the first country, than before. This will occur, broadly speaking, in the not improbable event of (a) the receipts from the duties being spent upon home goods and (b) the reduction in the incomes of foreign producers leading to a reduction in their demand for goods produced in their own countries and in part exported to the first country.

It will be seen that the possibilities are incalculable. Absolutely anything is conceivable. Those who declare that the foreigner will bear the duty certainly have no idea of the complexity of the problem. How is it possible, in view of this complexity, to form a final judgment? How can it be said, in any significant sense, that the foreigner pays the duty?

The classical economists and Marshall, closely following Mill, find the criterion not in the price of the good subjected to duty but in *the terms of trade* in the sense of all the import prices relatively to all the export prices. If the imposition of a duty or of duties—for in this connection there is no need to limit the discussion to one duty—leads to an improvement in the terms of trade (that is, if a unit of exports purchases more imports than before or, in other words, if import prices fall relatively to export prices), then part of the burden of the duty or duties has been shifted onto the foreigner. The ' reciprocal supply-and-demand curves,' with which we became acquainted in chapter XI, are used in analysing this. The analysis is made in great detail by Marshall, and it would be superfluous to repeat his results here.

We should, however, say a word about the very narrow limitations of this method. To take the reciprocal supply-and-demand curves as given is to make a very large assumption. It is to assume that the final result brought about by the various changes in demand and supply, by the monetary mechanism and all the other factors mentioned above is already known. Hence everything which has to be explained is included as a datum in these complex curves. Thus the curves express no empirical law, but merely provide (in the range of their possible shapes and positions) a catalogue of all the conceivable possibilities. The result is what was to be expected *a priori*, namely that almost everything is conceivable.

Any practical application of these curves is scarcely conceivable, since it is not possible to discover their shape in any concrete case. These curves do not provide a short-cut enabling us to dispense with a careful analysis advancing step by step

---

[9] Again, the case of a positively-inclined demand-curve in the protected country is not beyond the bounds of possibility. Suppose the duty is imposed on grain. The standard of living in the protected country falls. Large sections of its population may thereby be constrained to buy more bread and less meat, milk, and so on. If these latter products are produced mainly at home, while grain for bread-making is mainly imported, the result may be an increase in the demand for the imported grain, despite the duty, and a fall in the demand for home-produced meat, milk, and so on.

and varying the necessary assumptions as required in consideration of all the factors mentioned above and their complicated interactions. Only in such a way can one determine these curves or rather their shape in the neighbourhood of the point we are interested in. Having done this, the task is accomplished and we can " read off " the result. Moreover, as we explained in § 6 of chapter xi, any statistical attempt to discover, after the event, how the terms of trade have changed must encounter very great difficulties. Marshall was well aware of all this, as his sceptical footnote on page 177 of *Money, Credit and Commerce* indicates.

In the present state of our knowledge it is out of the question to deduce an argument for tariffs from these considerations. Whoever does so proves only that he has not realised the full complexity of the problem.

CHAPTER XVIII.
DUMPING, CARTELS, MONOPOLIES, AND EXPORT BOUNTIES.

§ 1. INTRODUCTION.

Hitherto we have usually supposed free competition to prevail both at home and abroad. We must now enquire to what extent our conclusions as to the effects of tariffs and as to trade policy are changed if free competition is either absent or curtailed. There is no need to stress the great significance of this question in an epoch of trustification, giant concerns, and cartels. We have, then, to ask what are the effects of imposing or increasing duties if at home and/or abroad monopolistic organisations are already in being. Are tariffs a suitable weapon against monopolistic exploitation? What is the effect of a duty, and how are we to appraise it, if under its protection a cartel is formed or some particular concern obtains a monopolistic position? The most important phenomenon to consider in this connection—a phenomenon which spreads its tentacles into the domain of free competition but which is the child of Monopoly and Protection is that known as ' dumping.'

§ 2. THE NATURE AND FORMS OF DUMPING.[1]

1. DUMPING AS SELLING ABROAD BELOW THE HOME PRICE.—It is fortunate that during recent years theorists have attained a greater uniformity in their use of terms. The term ' dumping ' is now almost universally taken to mean the sale of a good abroad at a price which is lower than the selling price of the same good at the same time and in the same circumstances (that is, under the same conditions of payment and so on) at home, taking account of differences in transport costs. From the standpoint of economic theory the general definition proposed by Viner: " Dumping is

---

[1] Literature on Dumping : Taussig, *Free Trade, the Tariff and Reciprocity* (1920), pp. 10 *et seq.;* Viner, *Dumping: A Problem in International Trade* (1923); same author, " Dumping " in *Encyclopædia of the Social Sciences;* Döblin, *Theorie des Dumpings* (1931); Plant, " The Anti-Dumping Regulations of the South African Tariff " in *Economica* (Feb. 1931); Yntema, " The Influence of Dumping on Monopoly Price " in *Journal of Political Economy,* vol. 36; Federal Trade Commission, *Antidumping Legislation in U.S.A. and Foreign Countries* (1934) and Robinson, *Economics of Imperfect Competition* (1933). A. Cabiati, " Betrachtungen über das Dumping " and Paul Szigeti, " Monopolpreis und Dumping " both in *Zeitschrift für Nationalökonomie,* vol. vi (1935).

price-discrimination between two markets," is to be preferred; for three reasons. *First*, the price-laws which underlie the phenomenon of dumping are the same whether it occurs between two independent countries or between two regions of the same country. *Secondly*, this definition includes the case of ' reverse dumping,' in which the foreign price is *higher* than the home price.[2] *Thirdly*, price-discrimination may occur not between home and abroad but between two foreign markets. But we shall confine ourselves, unless otherwise stated, to what is by far the most important case, namely, that in which the foreign selling price is below the home price, leaving the reader to apply our results *mutatis mutandis* to other cases.

We must insist upon all the qualifications and limitations in the above definition—not from pedantry but because a neglect of them gives rise to serious errors in transferring the concept of dumping into anti-dumping legislation.[3] In comparing the export-price with the home-price, we must be careful about (*a*) the point of time to which the comparison refers. It should refer to the moment when the sales contract is concluded. If it refers to the moment when the goods actually *cross the frontier* of the exporting country, anti-dumping measures may be incorrectly applied, for the home-price may have risen in the interval. (*b*) Account must also be taken of transport costs. Dumping may exist if the c.i.f. price quoted for exports exceeds the home price by less than the full cost of transport. The true comparison is between the home-price and the export-price, both taken at the factory or other place of production before the addition of transport costs. (*c*) We must also consider a number of circumstances, such as the cost of special packing for export, the conditions of payment, rebates for quantity,[4] and so on, in order to arrive at a true comparison of price.

2. OTHER DEFINITIONS OF THE CONCEPT OF DUMPING.—In the Press, in political speeches, and in the statements of interested parties, the term ' dumping ' has become a vague catchword with which to abuse every kind of foreign competition. In 1919 the United States Tariff Commission, in response to its enquiries, received 146 complaints about foreign dumping. Of these, only 23 related to foreign sales below the home-price. In 97 cases the complaints were simply of acute competition from foreign pro-

---

[2] This will happen only with a given constellation of cost- and demand-curves. (See § 3 below). Viner gives an example : *Dumping*, p. 5.
[3] Examples are given by Plant in *Economica* (Feb. 1931), pp. 70 *et seq.*
[4] Foreign sales are often in larger lots than home sales, and for that reason, without any dumping, the export-price may be the lower.

ducers. The others related to such practices as using deceptive trade-marks, describing the goods falsely, and declaring a false value to the customs officials.[5] Plant describes exactly the same experience in South Africa, where the dumping argument has played a great part in the agitation for Protection.

Even in scientific discussions the term ' dumping ' is often used to mean simply sales at a price below that prevailing in the foreign country or below that at which the foreign producers can compete. Clearly, this applies to all exports in the usual sense of the term.

Dumping is often defined as *foreign sales below cost of production*. This definition is usually combined with the further statement that the loss on exports is covered by the profit on home sales, or that the lower export-price is made possible by an unduly high home-price. This gives us a double criterion of dumping: (1) foreign sales below the home-price and (2) foreign sales below the cost of production.

From the practical standpoint this definition is open to the objection that the cost of production can be determined only with much greater difficulty than the home-price. But in addition to this the concept of ' the cost of production ' is in itself ambiguous. If it means the *average cost* per unit, and the cost of management and interest and amortisation on the fixed capital are included in the total costs, then export often does take place below the cost of production.

But sales below average cost in this sense in no way involve selling at a loss. There is a loss only if the total product is sold at a price below its average cost. But when dumping takes place, as a rule the fixed costs (the general overhead costs), or a greater proportion of them than the proportion of home to total sales, are covered by the home sales and the export-price need cover only the variable costs of the quantity exported in order to be profitable. The lower limit of the export-price is thus determined by the *marginal cost*, that is, by the additional cost due to expanding the output for export. The marginal cost lies below the average cost in all those very frequent cases in which production can be expanded within the existing productive unit, that is, without increasing the buildings or plant or equipment or administration or book-keeping, or at least without increasing them in the same proportion as production is increased.

Moreover, the expression ' selling at a loss ' is ambiguous. Suppose that the price covers the current costs of the concern (both

---

[5] See *Information concerning Dumping and Unfair Foreign Competition in United States and Canada's Anti-Dumping Law* (Washington, 1919).

those which vary more or less proportionately with the output, such as materials and wages, and those which are more or less fixed, such as the general expenses of management) but does not permit interest or amortisation on the fixed capital. If to sell at this price is ' to sell at a loss,' then selling at a loss is the general rule in times of depression. If, however, the expression is applied only when the current expenses of a concern definitely exceed its current receipts, then selling at a loss is a short-run phenomenon which occurs only because the entrepreneurs concerned hope that conditions will soon improve.

The two rival definitions of dumping: (1) ' foreign sales below the home-price ' and (2) ' foreign sales below the home-price *and* below the cost of production (in the sense of full average cost) ' will lead to the same results in numerous cases; if the export price is below the home price, it is usually, as we shall see shortly, below the full average cost also. There is a discrepancy between the two definitions in those cases in which the export-price is indeed below the home-price but *above* the average cost. In such cases the home-price, unduly high owing to monopoly, exceeds the average cost by *more* than the export-price exceeds it. In such cases dumping is present upon the first definition but not upon the second.

Leaving aside the practical difficulty that average costs can seldom be determined exactly, the following considerations are relevant in deciding which definition to choose. Those cases which the second definition excludes result, as we shall show, from exactly the same economic laws and circumstances as other cases of dumping. The second definition thus splits into two groups phenomena which all belong, economically, to the same group. Moreover, the second definition is not a suitable one to use when making judgments upon trade policy. For it is a matter of complete indifference, both to the exporting and to the importing country, whether the dumping price does or does not exceed the average cost.

Frequently the concept of dumping is made to include a certain *motive* on the part of the dumper. For example, some speak of dumping only when the dumper intends to drive out of business his foreign competitors or to force them to join him in a cartel. The term may even imply moral disapproval and may be restricted to those cases in which the methods of supplying the market are deemed to be ' unfair.'

But all these definitions have the disadvantage that they either split up a single economic group of facts or class heterogeneous cases together. They may nevertheless seem useful in framing anti-dumping legislation, since one may not want blindly to prevent every single case of price-discrimination. But all that is needed for this legislative purpose is a classification of different kinds of dumping.

It may be observed that the so-called 'exchange-dumping,' which occurs when, in time of inflation, home costs and prices have risen less than the exchange-value of the currency has fallen, is not genuine dumping, since no price-discrimination is present. Nor is the so-called 'social-dumping,' which is said to occur when the producers in one country pay lower wages or give their workers poorer conditions than do their foreign competitors.

A phenomenon which is *sui generis* is the 'Russian dumping': the foreign sales of the Soviet economy. The question whether these sales are made below the home-price or below the cost of production has no meaning, since the price-mechanism does not operate anything like freely in the Soviet Union. Of course, it is not to be denied that this phenomenon presents an important problem and that, theoretically, it is possible for the Soviet Union to harm certain branches of the capitalist economy by selling at very reduced prices.

8. CLASSIFICATION OF THE FORMS OF DUMPING.—It has become customary in Anglo-Saxon writings to distinguish between (*a*) *sporadic* or *occasional*, (*b*) *short-period* or *intermittent*, and (*c*) *long-period* or *continuous* dumping.

(*a*) *Sporadic* dumping occurs, especially at the end of a selling season, to get rid of 'remainders' which are practically unsaleable on the home market. It is a phenomenon of no special interest, although it may be very annoying to foreign competitors.

(*b*) *Intermittent* dumping is the sale abroad, from time to time, at a price below the home-price, and may involve selling at a loss in the strict sense of that phrase. It may be resorted to (*a*) in order *to get a footing in a foreign market* or to prevent the loss of it through temporary underselling by foreign competitors; (*β*) in order *to destroy a competitor* or to render him amenable to the wishes of the dumper; (*γ*) in order *to prevent the establishment of rival concerns*. This aggressive form of dumping is the spectre often used to frighten public opinion into imposing tariffs. Nevertheless, this form of dumping very seldom occurs. For the cost of such a campaign is very high and the danger is always present that the foreign country will resort to defensive measures, such as the imposition of an anti-dumping duty; (*δ*) in order to serve as a *measure of retaliation* against dumping in the opposite direction ('defensive dumping').

(*c*) *Long-period* dumping is not possible at a loss, that is, at a price below the marginal cost. It can and will be undertaken with profit (α) when the export will permit the existing fixed capital to be fully used or the output to be expanded by adapting or transforming the fixed capital—especially if this leads to a reduction in costs—without lowering the home price. The home-price, which cannot be a purely competitive price, remains *above* the marginal cost. The export-price must at least cover the marginal cost, or the goods would be exported at a loss. This kind of dumping occurs especially—but not only—when the output can be expanded at a decreasing cost. Into this category fall the most striking cases of dumping by great trusts and cartels, such as the dumping of German and American iron and steel products. (β) Such long-period dumping may also occur, and the goods may even be sold abroad at a loss, if the State or some other body grants *an export bounty*.

We must distinguish between cartels which monopolise the home market and are thereby enabled to dump and the so-called *export cartels*. The latter are associations which do not attempt to monopolise their home markets but devote themselves exclusively to raising the export-price. Their practice is thus almost the opposite of dumping. For the most part, they do not monopolise the export markets but only promote exports and reduce the cost of making foreign sales by reducing advertising expenses, establishing common sales-offices, and similar measures.

On the basis of a report of the Federal Trade Commission (*Report on Co-operation in American Export Trade*, 1916) the American legislature passed the Webb-Pomerene Act, which permitted the formation of cartels, otherwise illegal, for export purposes.[6] The Copper Trust came into existence under the ægis of this law.

4. NECESSARY CONDITIONS FOR DUMPING: PROTECTION AND MONOPOLY.—The *first* necessary condition for successful dumping is that the goods are prevented from coming back again, for if they were not, then home consumers would buy them on the cheaper foreign market. The means by which they are prevented is usually a duty, but transport costs, or an agreement on the part of foreign buyers not to resell to the home market, may also serve. In the case of sporadic dumping, the uncertainty of finding buyers in the home market is a sufficient deterrent. But in the case of long-period dumping on a large scale—and this is the case which will claim most of our attention—the necessary condition is a duty protecting the home market.

The *second* necessary condition is monopoly upon the home market. If free competition in the strict theoretical sense is present —that is to say, if no one producer can perceptibly influence the

---

[6] See W. F. Notz and R. S. Harvey, *American Foreign Trade, as promoted by the Webb-Pomerene and Edge Acts* (1921).

price of his product, so that each producer is confronted with a practically horizontal demand curve—the home price must be forced down. The monopoly may take several forms. *One* concern may have a monopoly, either because it is so large relatively to the market that no other concern can profitably enter or because it alone has some secret process of production or possesses a patent or some similar legal privilege. *Several* producers may have a tacit agreement, or may be explicitly united in a cartel, for the purpose of limiting the amount produced.

§ 3. The Theory of the Dumping-Price.

1. Statement of the Problem.—Dumping will clearly lower the *foreign price*. But by how much? And how will the *home sales* and the *home price* be affected? Hitherto economists have not all given the same answers to these questions. Schumpeter has expressed the view that dumping *raises* the price in the exporting country. " If the goods now exported could not be dumped, they would not cease to be produced but a large part of them—not the whole—would be sold on the home market, thereby reducing the price there." [7] This is certainly true of *sporadic* dumping; indeed, little more than this can be said as to its influence upon the home price. But if the dumping is continuous and systematic—and this is the only kind of dumping which we shall consider in the following paragraphs—we cannot take the quantity produced as a datum. We must ask *whether it would, in fact, be produced* and placed upon the home market if dumping were not possible. Clearly this would be determined by the conditions of cost and of demand.

The most usual view is that dumping enables cartels to increase their output and thereby to lower their costs and reduce the home price.

Viner, on the contrary, believed that dumping has *no* influence upon the home price. Upon the assumption that the concern which begins to dump has already fixed that price for the home market which maximises its profit and will continue to make its total profit as great as it can, " resort to dumping will not make any change in the domestic price profitable. . . . *There is no conceivable combination of demand schedule and cost curve having any relation to actual conditions which can render profitable an increase in the*

---

[7] " Zur Soziologie der Imperialismen " in *Archiv für Sozialwissenschaft* (1919), vol. 46, p. 301.

domestic price which was not equally profitable before resort to dumping of this type."[8] Mayer seems to hold the same opinion.[9] Now this thesis is untenable. Dumping will alter the home price most favourable to the monopolist, because the increased production for export changes the cost of production for the home output also. So far as I know, the correct, although not complete, solution of the problem was given for the first time by Yntema.[1] He reaches the following very important results: (1) If the (dumping) monopoly is working under falling marginal costs, dumping will reduce the home price which maximises its profit. (2) If the marginal cost is rising, dumping raises the most favourable price.[2] The proof of these results is not easy to set out. It requires some knowledge of the theory of monopoly and of the theory of costs—indeed, such knowledge is in any case indispensable to a serious student of the problem of dumping.

The problem of how dumping influences the home price of course involves a comparison between the home price when there is dumping and the home price when there is no dumping. For the latter we must not take the home price as it would be under competition but as it would be under monopoly in the absence of dumping. (Obviously the price under monopoly, with or without dumping, will be higher than under competition.) But even this is not unambiguous. We may compare the home price, given dumping, with either (A) the home (monopoly) price, assuming no export to take place or (B) the home (monopoly) price, assuming that export does take place, but that the exports are not sold at a price below the home price, that is, that there is no dumping. We shall call these two problems, which we shall examine presently, Problem A and Problem B. In the second problem we are comparing the home price when discrimination is present with the home price in the absence of discrimination.[3] Both problems may be of significance, and can be solved, but formally B corresponds more closely to the definition of dumping—discrimination between home and abroad—than A. There are, however, cases where

---

[8] *Dumping*, pp. 102-3. Viner's italics. But since then he has changed his opinion. See his article *Dumping*, in the *Encyclopædia of the Social Sciences*.

[9] Art. on *Preis (Monopolpreis)* in *Handwörterbuch der Staatswissenschaften*, 4th edn., p. 1034; "The injury to the home economy from dumping is not due, as is often asserted, to the cheap sales abroad, for the monopolist has already fixed the price and the quantity of sales most favourable to him upon the home market *without taking any account of such foreign sales*" (my italics).

[1] Yntema, "The Influence of Dumping on Monopoly Price" in *Journal of Political Economy* (Dec. 1928), vol. 36, pp. 686 *et seq.*

[2] *Loc. cit.*, p. 693.

[3] Yntema has considered only Problem A. On B *cf.* Viner, Art. *Dumping* in the *Encyclopædia*. Other writers quite overlook this important distinction.

nothing will be exported, if, for one reason or another, price-discrimination is not possible.

In the following pages we shall explain the method of analysing these problems and shall state, with all necessary reservations, the most important results without, however, attempting to give an exhaustive analysis of all conceivable cases.

2. ELEMENTS OF A THEORY OF MONOPOLY PRICE.—We begin with the assumption that a monopolist—either a single producer or a cartel—exists, that he wishes to maximise his profit, and that he has the power to fix whatever selling price seems to him the most favourable. (If for some reason, such as fear of State intervention or of potential competition, he is satisfied with a lower price than that, this lower price replaces his most favourable price for purposes of analysis.) The monopolist can fix *either* the price *or* the quantity produced (and sold) as he wishes. But once he has fixed the price he must content himself with the volume of sales which the market will take at that price; or, conversely, once he has fixed the quantity he will sell he must accept the price at which the market will just absorb that quantity. The monopolist will therefore try to find that price at which the product of the price and the quantity sold is a maximum,[4] or, rather, taking account of his costs of production, that price at which *the price times the quantity less the cost is a maximum*.

The monopoly price and the amount produced thus depend upon the conditions of (a) demand and (b) cost. We can take the demand conditions as given once and for all, since dumping will not change the home demand.[5]

As to the costs, the following may be said. Fixed costs, which are independent of the quantity produced and represent a fixed

---

[4] Geometrically (fig. 30) he will try to find that point P ('the Cournot point') on the demand curve at which the inscribed (shaded) rectangle reaches a maximum.

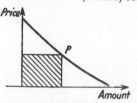

Fig. 30.

[5] This is not always quite correct. Dumping may *indirectly* influence the home demand. For example, if the German steel dumping were to promote Dutch shipbuilding, the German shipbuilding industry would be injured and its demand for steel would fall. As a rule such repercussions are small enough to be ignored. On the general problem whether the supply curve and the demand curve can be assumed independent of one another, *cf.* Mayer, "Die Wert- und Preisbildung der Produktionsmittel" in *Economia Politica Contemporanea* (1930), vol. 2, pp. 4-51.

deduction from the total receipts, have no influence upon the most favourable price, since they must be paid whether much or little is produced. (Naturally we assume that the receipts exceed this fixed sum).[6]

The price is influenced, from the cost side, only by the *marginal cost* : that is, the addition to total costs caused by the production of one unit more. When the marginal cost is rising, that is to say when output can be expanded only at an increasing cost, production will expand up to that point at which the continually diminishing increase in the total receipts[7] equals the increase in the total costs. Exactly the same generalisation applies to the case of falling costs : production in every case will expand up to the point at which the increase in total costs equals the increase in total receipts, or, more briefly, at which marginal cost equals marginal revenue. Clearly, other things being equal, the price will be lower if marginal cost is falling than if it is rising, for the output at which marginal cost equals marginal revenue will be greater in the former case.

These relations are best shown with the aid of a diagram. This involves a fuller explanation of the *marginal revenue curve,* derived from the usual demand curve and showing the successive increases in total receipts (or revenue) as sales increase.

In figure 31 SP is the demand curve and ST is the marginal revenue curve derived from it. The total receipts are shown on the demand curve by the rectangular area formed by drawing perpendiculars from the relevant point upon it to the axes. For example, at a price Op the total receipts are shown by the rectangle OMPp. On the marginal revenue curve, the total receipts are shown by the area between the curve and the two axes. For example, at a price Op (and therefore a sale of OM) they are shown by the area SRMO (which equals OMPp, so that SpL equals LPR). The increase in total receipts as the price falls and the sales increase is shown by the increase in this area. The marginal revenue curve cuts the abscissa when total receipts reach their maximum. After that, the increase is negative, since total

---

6 If, with increased sales, total receipts remain the same or fall off—that is, if the demand curve has an elasticity equal to unity or less than unity, throughout the relevant portion—then a quite small quantity will give the greatest receipts. Such a case. is, therefore, not of any further interest to us.

7 The curve showing the change in total receipts due to a change, in output is now usually called the ' marginal revenue ' curve. Yntema calls it the ' marginal gross revenue ' curve, Harrod the ' increment of total demand ' curve, and Pigou the ' marginal demand ' curve.

L

receipts are falling.[8] Figure 31 shows also the total receipts (or total revenue) curve. The ordinate of this shows the magnitude of total receipts (quantity times price) for that quantity of sales shown

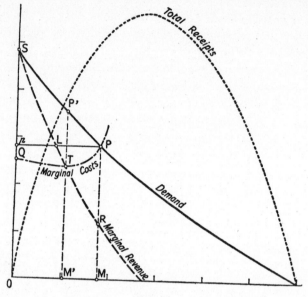

Fig. 31.

on the abscissa. It begins in O and reaches its maximum with that quantity at which the marginal revenue curve cuts the abscissa.

Let us now consider the marginal cost curve. Let it cut the marginal revenue curve at T. Then the most favourable quantity to produce (and sell) is OM′. Up to the quantity OM′ the increase in total costs is always less than the corresponding increase in total receipts, and the total profit rises. After the point T the increase in total costs is greater than the increase in total receipts. Therefore the quantity OM′ will be produced and will be sold at the price M′P′. At this point the monopoly profit reaches its maximum: QST. It will be observed that under monopoly the marginal cost, in equilibrium, is lower than the price. Under free competition the price is forced down till it equals the marginal cost, production being expanded until this is the case and the monopoly profit has vanished.

All this applies equally to the case of falling marginal cost, shown in figure 32. It will be seen that in this case, with other

---

[8] Up to this point the elasticity of demand is greater than unity, at this point it is equal to unity, and beyond this point it is less than unity.

data unchanged, the most favourable output is greater and the monopoly price is lower than when marginal cost is rising.

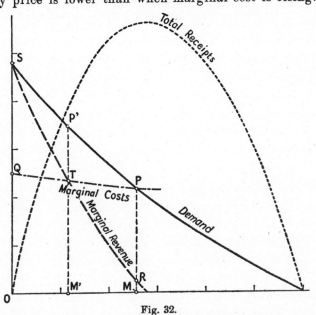

Fig. 32.

3. DETERMINATION OF THE EXPORT (DUMPING) PRICE. PROBLEM A: COMPARISON BETWEEN THE HOME (MONOPOLY) PRICE WHEN THERE IS NO EXPORT AND THE HOME (MONOPOLY) PRICE WHEN THERE IS DUMPING EXPORT.—We have just described the situation on a closed monopoly market. We must now ask what happens when export is possible. How high must the foreign price be in order that export may take place? What quantity will be exported, and at what price, and how will this export affect the most profitable home price?

To answer these questions, we start from the marginal cost prevailing at home (MT in fig. 33) and trace the course of the marginal cost curve beyond T. Let us suppose that the marginal cost falls. Clearly, export is then profitable, provided only that the foreign price covers the marginal cost.[9] We then draw, side by side with our diagram showing the situation in the home market (origin at O), the demand curve confronting our monopolist in the foreign market (origin at o). Let us assume that there are several competitors on the foreign market. This implies that the

---

[9] But this statement needs a qualification. It may be that the marginal cost curve, although falling throughout the relevant range, *at first* lies above the marginal revenue curve, subsequently falling below it, and finally cutting it. Thus, so to speak, the loss on the first units is transformed into a gain when output is further expanded. This special case involves no difficulty, and I leave the reader to work it out in detail for himself.

demand curve confronting our monopolist approaches the horizontal,
since the demand for his products is very elastic.[1] We next insert
the marginal revenue curve which is derived from this demand

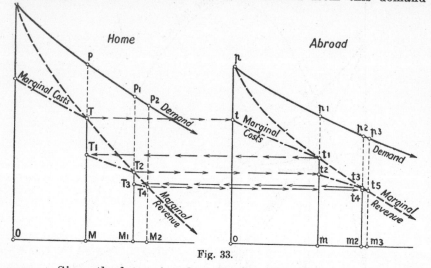

Fig. 33.

curve. Since the latter is relatively flat, the distance between the
two is small. In the extreme case, when there is free competition in
the strict sense of the term, the demand curve will be quite horizontal and will coincide with the marginal revenue curve. That
would be the case if the foreign market were the world market and
we could assume that our monopolist could sell any quantity which
he is likely to be in a position to offer, upon the world market, without perceptibly affecting the world price. This assumption would
simplify our exposition; I refrain from making it, but discuss
instead the more general case of a demand curve sloping downward
from left to right.[2]

The marginal cost MT applies also to exports. We transfer the
point T, as the arrow shows, to t and continue the marginal cost
curve from there. Then production for export can expand up to
the point t_1 at which the marginal cost equals the marginal
revenue. But at this stage the marginal cost has fallen to mt_1;

---

[1] We must suppose the demand curve for the product of our monopolist (not
to be confused with the *total* demand curve for the product) to be constructed
as follows. At any given price, his foreign competitors are prepared to supply a
certain quantity. The difference between that quantity and the total amount
demanded at that price represents the sales which our monopolist can make.

[2] I am aware that this exposition is inaccurate, since not all the various intermediate cases between complete monopoly and free competition can be adequately
distinguished by changing the inclination of the demand curve. But, unfortunately, economic theory has not yet provided us with definite and certain conclusions about Duopoly. The difficulty is that a duopolist cannot assume with
certainty a given demand curve (either horizontal, as under free competition, or
sloping, as under complete monopoly).

it is thus once more smaller than the marginal revenue at home (MT). Hence home sales can again be expanded. We transfer the point t_1, as the arrow shows, to T_1 on the home-market diagram, continue the marginal cost curve from there, and expand the home sales by MM_1. The home price sinks to P_1.

We can now transfer the point T_2, and can keep repeating this process. Equilibrium will be finally reached when the marginal cost, the marginal revenue at home, and the marginal revenue abroad are all equal to one another.

The same situation is shown in fig. 33a in another way. We there show the marginal cost curve as a continuous curve, inserting the relevant portions of the home and foreign demand curves. We begin with the home demand curve and

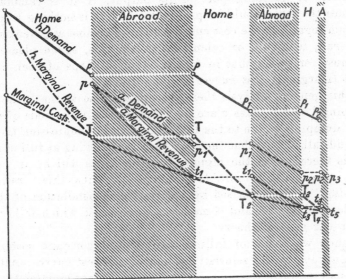

Fig. 33a.

the marginal revenue curve derived from it and follow the latter until the marginal cost curve cuts it at the point T. Thereafter, in the next (shaded) section of the diagram, we confront the continuation of the marginal cost curve with the foreign demand curve and marginal revenue curve until the latter cuts it at t_1. (We could equally well have begun from the other end, with the foreign market.) In the third section of the diagram we then continue the home marginal revenue curve, prolonging it from T to T_2, and so on. The final solution is the same as that reached by the other method, in fig. 33.

Thus, when there are falling marginal costs, dumping leads to a reduction in the home price. In a similar manner it can be shown that when marginal costs are constant there is *no* change in the home price and that when marginal costs are rising dumping raises the home price. For, it must be noted, dumping may be possible and profitable even when marginal costs are rising. But in such a case the amount dumped will scarcely be large, since, clearly, the marginal cost will more quickly equal the marginal revenue.

We may perhaps add the following remarks. We began with the home market and supposed the monopolist to regard foreign sales as, so to speak, secondary. This is likely to correspond with reality. But this should not lead us to assume (as some writers do) that dumping can take place only when a concern, with all its fixed capital, is already in existence and producing for the home market, having been established solely for this purpose, and regarding dumping (when that possibility presents itself) as a fortunate but unforeseen occurrence. This is not so. Dumping—discrimination between two markets—may also be advantageous from the long-run standpoint; and a concern may be set up with the deliberate intention of dumping part of its output, if it is calculated in advance that this would be profitable. There is nothing to prevent us from regarding the cost curve which we assume as given as either short-run, long-run, or calculated in advance, as we please. But we must remember that in fact the typical shape of each of these three (marginal) cost curves will be different.[3]

This general analysis therefore applies also to the ' trade-cycle dumping ' which takes place on a large scale in periods of slump. Such dumping is due to the fact that with the depression the home demand falls off, so that the concern is not working at full capacity, and is therefore in the region of falling costs which, as we have seen, is especially favourable to dumping. Thus, this ' trade-cycle dumping ' is characterised by a particular constellation of the cost and demand curves, and is merely a special case which falls readily within our general theory.

When we speak of falling, rising, and constant costs, these relate always to the relevant portion of the cost curve. Although costs may be falling over a certain range, sooner or later they will rise again. This must occur in the short-run because sooner or

---

[3] In the short run we can assume both the marginal and average cost curves to be of the typical U-shaped form shown in fig. 34. In the long run this form is not so likely.

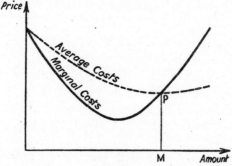

Fig. 34.

later the optimal capacity of the existing concern will be passed; and in the long-run because the enlargement of the concern also has its limits and because sooner or later the increased demand by the concern for means of production will tend to raise their price.

When we discard the assumption that competition prevails on the foreign market, we can no longer lay down the general rule that the foreign price must be lower than the home price. Under certain conditions it is then possible that the converse discrimination, namely a higher price abroad than at home, yields a greater profit. The following generalisation can be made. The greater is the foreign market, the stronger is competition there, and the smaller is the influence of the exporting monopolist upon the foreign price, the more probable is it that the foreign price will be below the home price and the greater will the price-difference in favour of the foreigner tend to be. For the stronger the competition, the flatter will be the demand curve and the smaller will be the vertical difference between the marginal revenue curve and the demand curve at the price-point. Therefore P and P_1 will be lower than p and p_1. In other words, when competition prevails there is no scope for a monopolistic raising of the price.

The following rule, stated in exact terms, is valid. The price is lower in that market in which the elasticity of demand at the equilibrium point is greater. If it so happens that the elasticity is equal in both markets, the price in both markets will also be equal; that is to say, in this case no advantage is to be gained by discrimination. Here, again, we refer not to the elasticity of the total demand in the foreign market but to the elasticity of the demand upon which our monopolist can count.

It will be remembered that we referred some pages back to another definition of dumping, namely, foreign sales below both the home price and the cost of production. We may now briefly consider what circumstances determine whether the dumping price, arrived at in the way we have shown, lies below the average cost.

This depends, in the first place, upon the relation between the marginal costs and the average costs. The average costs lie *below* the marginal costs when the latter rise from the start. The average costs lie *above* the marginal costs when the latter fall from the start. When the marginal costs first fall and then rise—the case usually taken as typical—the average costs continue falling after the marginal costs have already begun to rise. They lie above the marginal costs up to the point at which the latter have moved up to them. From this point onwards (which is the lowest point of the average cost curve—point P in figure 34) the average costs begin to rise and thenceforward lie *below* the marginal costs. For after this point each addition to total costs (due to the production of one more unit) is greater than the previous average cost.

When both marginal *and* average costs are rising, the foreign (dumping) price, which cannot be less than the marginal cost, is *above* the average cost. But this is of little importance, since dumping occurs mainly when costs are falling, and in that event the average costs *exceed* the marginal costs. Everything then depends upon the extent to which the price exceeds the marginal costs. If free competition prevails abroad, the demand curve approaches the horizontal, and the difference between the marginal revenue curve and the demand curve is small. Therefore the price is close to the marginal costs, for export is expanded until the marginal costs have almost reached the price. Hence the price lies *below* the average costs. This situation can also be expressed in more popular language by saying that the entrepreneur covers his general overhead costs, or a more than proportionate part of them, by home sales and that the high home price makes possible the cheap foreign sales.

But if our monopolist has something approaching a monopolistic position in the foreign market also, it is quite possible that the dumping price may *exceed* the average costs, without our having to alter anything in our theory.

These considerations demonstrate again that the second definition of dumping is not an appropriate one from the standpoint of economic analysis. It is undesirable to distinguish between foreign sales below the home price which are also below average costs and those which are not, since the actual course of average costs is not in itself of any importance.

4. PROBLEM B: COMPARISON BETWEEN THE HOME (MONOPOLY) PRICE WHEN THERE IS EXPORT AT THAT PRICE AND THE HOME (MONOPOLY) PRICE WHEN THERE IS DUMPING EXPORT.—We have now answered the first of our two problems. This covers the case in which no export would occur if price-discrimination between the two markets were not possible because exports at the home price would not be profitable; solution A applies to this case. The second case is that in which export would occur at the home price if dumping were not possible. We have to ask how, in such a case, the possibility of dumping affects the home price.

Economists have not yet fully analysed this problem. But the following conclusion seems certain. If the elasticity of demand is greater in the foreign market than in the home market, then discrimination between the two must raise the home price, whether marginal costs are rising or constant or falling.[4]

We must once more point out that the foregoing analysis assumes that the monopolist is in such a strong position that he can fix the price which maximises his profits. If he must take account of other considerations such as the fear of State intervention, his (home) price will be lower than this. Again, our conclusions must be modified if ' the monopolist ' is a cartel which restricts production not by closing down those works operating under the least favourable conditions but by causing all its production-units to work below their optimal capacity. They must also be modified if the tariff protecting the home market is not high enough to enable the monopolist to charge his optimal price in that market.

§ 4. ECONOMIC APPRAISAL OF DUMPING.

In order to make a value-judgment of the phenomenon of dumping, we must first distinguish two different problems.

The narrower problem is this. We can assume the necessary conditions for dumping, namely Monopoly and Protection, to be given and unalterable. We can then pass an opinion upon the effects of dumping, first, from the standpoint of the importing country and then from the standpoint of the exporting country.

The broader problem is this. We can assume that these conditions—Monopoly and Protection—may be altered. We can consider whether the situation under them is more or less desirable than under free competition, and if we prefer the latter we can enquire how the conditions which make dumping possible can be removed.

We begin with the narrower problem. Nearly all the outcry against dumping comes from those countries into which goods are alleged to be dumped. Complaints are very frequent in countries, such as England, which follow a liberal trade policy. The reason is that in such countries interested parties have less chance of

---

[4] Unfortunately, we have not space for the somewhat complicated proof of this conclusion. The author, together with Dr. Gerhard Tintner of Vienna, has worked out a graphic solution which it is not possible to reproduce here. If the demand curves are assumed to be straight lines, we get the important result that the possibility of discrimination leads neither to an increase nor to a decrease of output but only to a different distribution of the same output between the two markets. In the graphic solution of the problem it must be remembered that the collective marginal revenue curve derived from the collective demand curve (=the sum of the demand curves of each market) is not always identical with the horizontal summation of the two marginal revenue curves. Since this was written, a brilliant graphic solution of this problem has been provided by Mrs. J. Robinson in her well-known book *Economics of Imperfect Competition* (1933), pp. 190 *et seq.*

obtaining protection for their own products and realise that in the absence of a duty they themselves cannot dump abroad on a large scale.

In general, the outcry against dumped imports is far greater than the facts warrant. But even when imports do come in at a lower price than that charged in the exporting country or below cost of production, the importing country is in no way injured if the cheap imports are going to continue. It makes not the slightest difference from the standpoint of the importing country whether the goods come in cheaply because the exporting country enjoys a natural comparative advantage or because they are dumped, nor does it matter in the least whether the dumping is due to monopoly abroad or to export bounties given by the foreign Government or by some other body. Not one of these circumstances disturbs the fundamental Free Trade argument. They are significant only in so far as they indicate whether or not the cheap imports are likely to continue. They are more likely to continue for an indefinite period when they take place owing to climatic or other natural advantages possessed by the foreign country than when their low price is due to the dumping policy of a foreign monopolist, which may be changed at any moment.

Dumping is harmful only when it occurs in spasms and each spasm lasts long enough to bring about a shifting of production in the importing country which must be reversed when the cheap imports cease. Such intermittent dumping may be harmful even when there is no competing home industry. For it may lead to the establishment of an industry which uses the cheap imported goods —if they are producers' goods—and which cannot continue when they cease to come in. When the dumped goods are consumers' goods, the dumping may lead to a shifting of demand which must later be reversed and may thus cause injury.

'Cut-throat dumping,' pursued in order to drive out competitors and then impose a high monopoly price, is of course also harmful. For example, the Match Trust tried to break its competitors by selling at very low prices in order later on to include the country in question within its monopoly. But in practice this kind of thing very seldom happens, for such a price-war is very expensive and there is always a great danger that the monopolist may himself be robbed of the fruits of his costly victory by legislative intervention.

Let us now consider dumping from the standpoint of the country which exports the dumped goods. Of course, we need not concern ourselves with the mercantilist argument, so willingly embraced by the dumping concerns as a justification of their trade policy, that dumping is beneficial to the country because it increases exports and brings in money.

If we exclude dumping by export bounties, to be considered in our next section, and if we accept the monopolisation of the home market as an ineluctable fact,[5] we can say that dumping is advantageous if it reduces the price of the goods in question to the home consumers. As we have seen, this happens only when marginal costs are falling.

When the home price rises owing to dumping it is more difficult to form an opinion. The fact that the price rises is not in itself a condemnation, for every export tends to raise the home price of the exported good. In order to make an objective judgment we must balance the increased price to consumers (measured by the loss in consumers' rent, discussed in chapter XVII, § 2) against the increased profits of producers. Viner believes[6] he can prove that the former must exceed the latter. If this is so, then dumping must be regarded as injurious when it raises the home price.

The *dumping of producers' goods* has always attracted much attention. An especially glaring example was and is the German dumping of iron and steel, sold abroad (for example, to Holland and formerly to England) at a price often 50 per cent. below the German price. Clearly this greatly benefits the iron- and steel-using industries in such countries. It is well known that the Dutch shipbuilding industry lives directly upon the German dumped exports. Often quoted is the remark of Palmer, President of the English shipbuilding company of that name: " Let them sell at cut prices, so long as they can. We shipbuilders are only too pleased." Another example often quoted is the encouragement of the English jam and other sugar-using industries by the Continental sugar-dumping before the Brussels Sugar Convention of 1902. Free Traders always point to such cases to show what an advantage dumping is to the importing countries.

And this is undoubtedly correct. But we must ask how this dumping of producers' goods is to be judged from the standpoint of the exporting country.

The home industries using such goods, for example, in Germany, all the iron- and steel-using industries, are of course severely hit by the cheap sales (of pig-iron and ' semis,' in this case) to their foreign competitors.[7]

---

[5] At the same time it is conceivable that it is only the possibility of dumping which keeps the home monopoly in existence. For example, effective anti-dumping measures by foreign countries might cause the home cartel to break up.

[6] In private correspondence.

[7] A similar problem is presented by the export, without dumping, of producers' goods, such as raw materials, intermediate products, and machinery. Such

It is often sought to counteract this in a twofold manner. The home monopoly-price is reduced upon materials to be worked up and exported in a more finished form[8] and the home market is assured to the finishing industries by an equalising duty.

The reduction of the monopoly-price to assist exports is certainly to be welcomed, even when it takes the form of an export bounty. But equalising duties stand on a different footing. Before passing judgment upon them, we must again ask whether the unduly high monopoly-price at home is regarded as an unalterable fact. If so, we must say, in opposition to the prevailing view, that the finishing industries have no economic right to exist if they cannot compete with the foreign industries which are enabled to undercut them by the dumped materials. In other words, *upon the assumption that the high monopoly-price at home is an unalterable fact*, it is more rational to purchase the finished products more cheaply from abroad than to expand the home finishing industries by imposing equalising duties. But we must also remember that it cannot be profitable for the monopolist to charge a price so high as to strangle his customers, the finishing industries. Often the result of imposing an equalising duty to protect the finishing industries is simply to make possible a higher monopoly-price for the producers' goods.[9]

We now turn to the wider problem of forming an opinion upon the whole complex of circumstances which lead to dumping. Here there can be no doubt of the injurious effects. The monopolistic raising of the price both of consumers' goods and of producers' goods implies an irrational shifting of production away from the economic optimum. In addition to that, the current Protectionist outlook means that dumping leads, on the one hand, to equalising duties for the finishing industries and, on the other hand, to retaliatory measures by the other countries, not to mention the frequency with which dumping is (wrongly) used as a reason for Protectionist interventions. But we must again stress the fact that

---

export always harms the finishing industries of the home country and assists those of the foreign countries. But this is no reason for forbidding or taxing exports of this kind. If country A enjoys a comparative advantage in the production of a raw material and country B in working it up, a ' vertical ' division of labour between them is in principle just as advantageous as a ' horizontal ' one.

[8] The so-called ' Avi ' agreement between the German iron and steel industry and the German industries using iron and steel fixes the rebates to be given to the latter upon their purchases of iron and steel to be exported as finished products. Indeed, this enables these industries themselves to practise dumping.

[9] A tariff on iron and steel products shifts the demand curve for iron and steel of the industries using it in such a way that the Cournot point lies higher than before. In other words, when the finishing industries are not protected from foreign competition, their demand for the monopolised product is more elastic. We have already examined the relation between the elasticity of the demand and the dumping price. Here we have not space to explain the present conclusion in detail and with the necessary qualifications.

any considerable and permanent dumping is possible only under
Protection. It is thus itself a consequence of a Protectionist outlook
and again illustrates the truth that such an outlook breeds a host
of ills.

In conclusion, we can say with Mayer that dumping, that is
cheap foreign sales, is nothing like so harmful as the monopolisation
of the home market and the consequently higher home price which
is bound up with it. Given the existence of a monopoly in the home
market, the advent of dumping is of relatively minor significance
and may equally well be either beneficial or harmful.

§ 5. Export Bounties.

1. Historical Examples.—Export bounties were always one
of the main instruments of a mercantilist trade policy. In the
relatively liberal period of West European trade policy, in the
second half of the nineteenth century and the first decade of the
present one, they more or less disappeared; the most important
exception was the sugar bounties. The neo-mercantilism of the
post-War period showed no desire to make any extensive use of
them. This was partly due to the difficult state of the public
finances in most countries, but it was also due to the ease with which
the effects of an export bounty can be destroyed by a counteracting
duty imposed by the importing country, so that the bounty flows
directly into the Exchequer of a foreign Government.

Up to 1814 England gave export bounties on grain, which varied with the
home price and were accompanied by import duties. But in effect this system
ended about 1766,[1] at which time England became a grain-importing country.
In the same period she granted production bounties, which of course served also
as export bounties, to herring-fishing and whaling.[2] Well-known also are the
bounties given to the linen industry from 1740 to 1830 in Ireland, and later in
England and Scotland, with considerable apparent success. France had a widespread system of export bounties under the *ancien régime;* it was abandoned
during the Revolution, but revived in the beginning of the nineteenth century,
and remained in force until 1860.[3]

In modern times the most important example of export bounties is that
afforded by the international history of the sugar trade in the second half of
the nineteenth century up to the Brussels Sugar Convention of 1902.[4]

The export bounties on sugar were at first in a concealed form : sugar exported was relieved from payment of the sugar tax or excise duty. But soon—

---

[1] See Fay, *The Corn Laws and Social England* (1932), and Barnes, *A History
of the English Corn Laws* (1930).

[2] Smith, *The Wealth of Nations*, bk. 4, chap. 5. Article *Bounties* in *Dictionary of Tariff Information* (1924).

[3] Lexis, *Die französischen Ausfuhrprämien* (1872).

[4] A great deal has been written about the sugar bounties. See especially
Kaufmann, *Weltzuckerindustrie und Internationales und Koloniales Recht* (1904)
(which contains a history and bibliography) ; Viner, *Dumping*, pp. 178-186.

usually as a reply to concealed bounties elsewhere—there was a switch to open bounties : by Austria-Hungary in 1888, Germany in 1891, France in 1897. The result was increased Protection given by other countries to their sugar industries, and especially by England to her refineries. As early as 1864, England, France, Belgium, and Holland had concluded an agreement in which they bound themselves to grant no concealed export bounty by means of rebates from the tax. This convention remained in force till 1875. In the last two decades of the century the bounties were so general that they largely cancelled one another out and were quite a burden upon the public finances. Then England, in the interests of her sugar-producing colonies, prepared to fulfil her threat (which the Free Traders had hitherto prevented her from doing) and impose equalising duties to the amount of the bounties. This led to a Convention in 1902 between England and all the important beet-sugar producers, except Russia. All the countries present agreed not to grant any bounties, direct or indirect, upon the production or export of sugar. They also agreed to take action against any other country which granted bounties by prohibiting imports from it or imposing duties equal to its bounties. They agreed further, in order to prevent the dumping of sugar by private cartels, that the protection afforded to sugar-refiners by the excess of the import duty over the excise duty should not exceed 6 francs per 100 kilogrammes of refined sugar. A permanent Commission was set up in Brussels to supervise the working of these agreements. Later Russia joined the Convention, which was renewed in 1908 and enjoyed complete success, being brought to an end only by the War.

Another well-known example of export bounties are the so-called *import certificates*, first used by Germany, in 1894.[5]

These filled a gap in the system of agrarian protection, from which Eastern Germany was receiving little benefit owing to the freight-situation.

In the course of the nineteenth century Germany as a whole had changed by degrees from a grain-exporting to a grain-importing country. But this was, so to speak, the resultant of different movements in different districts. The west has long been on balance grain-importing, so that there import duties have been effective, but the east—and especially the estates of the large landowners in East Prussia—has until very recently exported grain.

The world price of grain fell heavily in the seventies, owing to the large supplies from overseas countries with lower costs. Before then, the west of Germany had imported grain and the east had been able to export it profitably, northwards and eastwards, at the world price. After the fall in the world price, this export was no longer profitable. The agrarian duties imposed in 1879 were intended to provide a market in Germany itself, at a price higher than the world price, for the excess production of the east. But this aim was not at first attained, owing to the relatively high cost of transporting grain by rail from the east to the west of Germany. It cost much less to send it by sea to Northern and Eastern Europe.

Thus the duties on grain did not help the east at first. From 1880 to 1894 the price of wheat in Cologne was considerably above the world (London) price; but the price in Königsberg was little higher than the world price and, indeed, in several years was below it. This meant a reduction of profits, and later a positive loss, to the east. The following figures from the German Statistical Yearbook show how sharply the export of grain from Germany fell off :—

---

[5] Beckmann, *Einfuhrscheinsysteme* (1911) and " Erneuerung der Einfuhrscheine? " in *Archiv f. Sozialwissenschaft* (1925), vol. 54.

	Export of			Export of	
	Wheat. Tons.	Rye. Tons.		Wheat. Tons.	Rye. Tons.
1880	178,169	26,586	1887	2,840	3,137
1881	53,387	11,563	1888	1,112	2,262
1882	62,502	15,755	1889	758	608
1883	80,758	12,133	1890	205	119
1884	36,193	6,286	1891	337	134
1885	14.080	4,020	1892	244	890
1886	8,293	3,188	1893	293	270

Attempts, through differential railway rates and similar measures, to enable the wheat of the east to be sold in the west, met with no success.

Then came the law of 4th April, 1894. Each exporter of grain received, for every complete 500 kg. exported, an import certificate. This was a right to import, within a certain time, free of duty, an equal quantity of grain (since 1906 not necessarily grain of the same kind as that exported) or certain quantities of other imports, such as petrol, spices, and cocoa. This certificate could be sold by the exporter. In general an importer would pay for it a sum about equal to the amount of the duty it saved him.

In this way the eastern exporter was given a bounty on his exports about equal to the import duty. The export of grain from the east to other countries again revived.

	Export of			Export of	
	Wheat. Tons.	Rye. Tons.		Wheat. Tons.	Rye. Tons.
1892	244·0	890·8	1895	69,910·9	35,992·3
1893	293·1	270·5	1896	75,214·4	38,321·5
1894	79,170·7	49,711·8			

In this way the import certificates made possible an export bounty upon the grain of the east which enabled that region to benefit from the German import duties upon grain imposed in 1879.

At the outbreak of the War the grain duties and the import certificate system were abolished. The latter was re-established in 1926 and extended to other commodities (cattle, pigs, sheep, and the products of millers and maltsters).

In general, export bounties have been quite frequent since the War, but mostly in a concealed form, such as special railway rates, rebates on taxes and import duties, tax privileges, special credit facilities, and export credits guaranteed by the Government. Under this head falls also the whole system of State subsidies to shipping, which are, in effect, bounties upon the export of transport services. There have also been overt export bounties, for example, those which Hungary has long given upon the export of grain.[6]

---

[6] During recent years reciprocal reductions of duties, in which third countries, although enjoying most-favoured-nation status, do not share, have been made in the form of agreements between two countries to grant export bounties. Instead of lowering its import duty, each country permits the other party to get an equivalent benefit for its exports by granting an export bounty. The payment of such a bounty costs the Government as much as an equivalent reduction in its import duty upon a good imported from the other country would cost it. Thus such reciprocal export bounties are equivalent to reciprocal reductions in duties

2. EFFECTS OF EXPORT BOUNTIES.—The working of export bounties can be analysed in just the same way as that of import duties. The direct effect upon the home price and the foreign price of the good in question is most readily shown by our usual import-export diagram. It should be borne in mind that an export bounty must be accompanied by a corresponding duty. Otherwise, in so far as the bounty exceeds the cost of transport both ways, exported goods will flow back to be sold on the home market, and the export bounty will act as a bounty on production rather than only on export. Let us assume that such re-import is prevented. Then figure 35 shows the effect of the export bounty in shifting the foreign supply curve from SS to S'S' and the foreign demand curve from DD to D'D', the shift in each case being equal to the amount of the bounty.

The consequences are as follows. Exports and home production both increase. The foreign output is diminished. The price falls abroad and rises at home, causing a price-difference equal to the bounty. The amount sold increases abroad and diminishes at home.

If the re-import were not prevented, the export bounty would be equivalent to a general bounty on production, to be represented by a lowering of the home supply curve. The effects on the foreign price and on the foreign sales would be qualitatively the same as those of a pure export bounty; but the home price also would fall and home sales would expand.

As to the indirect effects, it is practically certain that export bounties worsen the terms of trade of those countries which grant them (although it is possible by the exercise of sufficient ingenuity to conceive cases in which the opposite would be true).

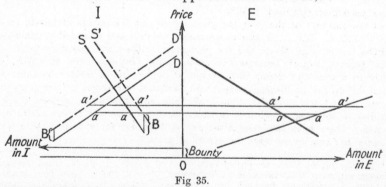

Fig 35.

(preferential duties) by the two countries concerned. Such agreements, covering fixed quotas of a long list of goods, exist between Austria and Hungary and between Austria and Italy, the export bounties taking the form of cheap export credits. The necessary comments upon such excrescences of trade policy are made in chap. xxi, § 5.

3. APPRAISAL.—One must concede that export bounties fit very well into the mercantilist system. The money paid out in bounties benefits the home producers, thus ' remaining in the country,' exports are promoted, the balance of trade improved, and gold brought into the country.

Adam Smith attacked this superficial view of the matter, and argued against bounties, although his arguments were not always completely sound—they were ably criticised by Ricardo in chapter XXII of his *Principles*.

In order to make an appraisal of export bounties we must distinguish between (a) *pure export bounties* and (b) *compensatory export bounties*. The former are granted in order to encourage some branch of production although that branch is in no way handicapped, relatively to its foreign competitors, by special taxation or a monopolistic enhancement of the prices of its means of production or any similar burden. The latter are granted solely to counteract some such burden.

The decisive argument against pure export bounties, stated by Adam Smith and in a still better form by Ricardo, is the same as that against tariffs. Export bounties divert trade away from the lines indicated by comparative costs. Such bounties are a gift to the foreigner. Either they induce the economy to produce goods which could be obtained at less expense from abroad in exchange for others, or they induce the subsidised industries to expand their production beyond the point at which (owing to diminishing returns) it ceases, from the rational standpoint of comparative costs, to be profitable.

Thus bounties of this kind are in principle similar to tariffs. All the arguments for and against tariffs which we have already considered apply *mutatis mutandis* to them also.

Compensatory export bounties are to be judged differently. We may divide them into several groups. (1) If a consumption tax is imposed on a certain commodity, for example spirits, it is of course quite proper to refund the tax when it is exported. Whether this refund should be called an export bounty is a question of terminology. (2) The same holds good of those cases in which the bounty is merely a compensation for the duties imposed on the imported raw materials and means of production used in making it. (3) The same holds good again of export bounties given to finishing industries by cartels and trusts making producers' goods in order to compensate them for the unduly high price of such goods and to enable them to meet the competition of foreign industries which have bought such goods (from the cartels or trusts) at a dumping price. The best-known example of this is the system of bounties by which the German iron- and steel-using industries are in some measure compensated for the high home price of iron and steel fixed by the German cartels.[7] (4) Under certain conditions it is also proper for a country A to grant an export bounty which only just compensates for a duty imposed by country B. In this case, as in the first three, the bounty restores the situation which would exist under unrestricted Free Trade. Country A, in effect, gives some tribute to country B as the price of a restoration of the situation existing before the duty was imposed, and it is possible—but not certain—that the price may be worth while.

But these considerations do not justify export bounties as compensation for *a higher general level* of taxes than prevails abroad.

It must further be remembered that in all these cases the favourable effect can be destroyed through the imposition of an equalising duty by the foreign country.

§ 6. ANTI-DUMPING DUTIES.

The arguments for and against ordinary protective duties apply also to anti-dumping duties.

This is true of long-run as well as of sporadic and intermittent dumping. The effects upon the importing country of imports which are cheap because they are dumped are in no way different from those of imports which are cheap for some other reason. Temporary dumping may harm the importing country, but so may the temporary import of cheap goods due to some other cause. There is a valid distinction between dumped imports and other cheap imports only when the former are due to ' cut-throat ' dumping, undertaken in order to destroy competitors and later raise the price. We may perhaps add that the probability that the cheap imports will continue is less when they are dumped than when they are cheap for other reasons.

There is no doubt that tariffs may be a suitable weapon with which to fight dumping. However great the financial resources of the dumper, an anti-dumping duty of appropriate height will soon bring the dumping to an end.

A question which demands more discussion is whether duties are a suitable means of preventing, as well as of curing, dumping. Protectionists always claim that a Free Trade country, or one with

---

[7] This is simply an extended form of price discrimination. The foreign demand for the unmonopolised (finished) goods of that country is very elastic. It therefore pays the monopoly to fix a lower price for those of its products which are destined for export, embodied in the unmonopolised goods. But other motives also affect the behaviour of the monopoly : for example, fear that the protective tariff may be removed.

low duties, is far more exposed to dumping than a Protectionist country. They have long pointed to England as the dumping ground of the world. This argument for tariffs is closely bound up with the argument, already discussed,[8] for tariffs to ensure the market. Here we need only add a little to what we said in that connection.

I believe that Dietzel[9] was the first to protest against the view, then universally accepted, that tariffs are a good prophylactic against dumping. But his reasoning is not altogether free from faults. We shall not examine it in detail, but shall try to state it briefly in a more correct form.

Dietzel is absolutely right in declaring that the existence of tariffs, no matter how high, *provided they are not prohibitive*, affords *no* protection against future dumping. Since, in spite of the tariffs, some imports do come in, there must be a price-difference between home and abroad equal to the amount of the duty plus freight. In other words, the price of an imported good stands at the import-point in the protected country and at the export-point in the foreign country, so that any fall in price or export bounty, however small, in the latter must at once lead to increased imports. A duty of 100 per cent. in no way hinders the foreign producers from increasing their exports, if the price of the good is 100 per cent. higher in the protected country.

These considerations, of course, apply equally to non-dumped imports, due, for example, to exceptional harvests abroad. Thus the mere *existence* of agrarian tariffs affords no guarantee against a crisis in home agriculture due to increased imports, if there is normally some import in spite of the tariffs. The tariffs extend the margin of profitable home cultivation, but there are always marginal concerns which may be in difficulty if imports increase, and prices fall, owing to large foreign harvests.

Always provided that imports do come in, a temporary crisis can be relieved only by *raising duties* or *imposing new ones:* the existing duties can do nothing to soften it.

Of course, even prohibitive tariffs cannot protect a country from an agricultural crisis due to over-production at home. They can do so to a limited extent only if before the crisis they were not fully utilised, the margin of cultivation not being extended as far as it could have been, so that even the marginal concerns can stand a certain fall in the price.

Ricardo pointed out[10] that prohibitive tariffs not merely failed to afford protection against agricultural crises, but were also themselves a source of price-disturbances which the country would not suffer, or would not suffer to the same extent, in the absence of such tariffs. If a Free Trade country has good harvests

---

[8] Chap. xvii, § 7.

[9] " Free Trade and the Labour Market " in *Economic Journal* (1905), vol. 15 (published in German in 1902); Pigou, " Professor Dietzel on Dumping and Retaliation " in same vol. of *Economic Journal;* Viner, *Dumping*, chap. ix.

[10] Ricardo, *On Protection to Agriculture*, § 7 : " Under a system of Protecting Duties, established with the view to give the Monopoly of the Home Market to the Home Grower of Corn, Prices cannot be otherwise than fluctuating."

then—unless the rest of the world also has good harvests—there is no need for the home price to fall at all sharply, since the surplus can be exported. If the tariffs, although they may be high, are not prohibitive, and imports do come in, a good harvest at home leads not to a sharp fall in price but only to a diminution in the amount imported. But if the tariffs are prohibitive, so that there is no import, a plentiful harvest at home must cause the home price to fall to the level of the world price before relief can be obtained by exporting.

Thus tariffs prevent dumping only when they are prohibitive. Every duty which is so high that import has ceased must be greater than the difference between the home price and the foreign price. The home price stands below the import-point and the foreign price above the export-point. Therefore the export bounty must reach a given height before it permits the foreign exporter to surmount the tariff wall. It is not enough for the dumping-price to be a shade lower than the price prevailing abroad; it must be lower by the excess of the duty over the price-difference between the foreign and home market. The foreign export-price must be reduced to the export-point; and this is a financial burden. The higher is the prohibitive duty, the more effective is it in preventing dumping.

It follows that ordinary tariffs are in part ineffective against dumping and in part prevent it only at the cost of a permanent contraction in international division of labour. The only cases in which a favourable result is conceivable are those in which normally there is no import, so that a duty does no harm.

There is something to be said only for *ad hoc* anti-dumping duties, to meet each case as it arises. But the administrative difficulties of such a system and the danger of its being misused for purely Protectionist ends are very great. Nor does the history of anti-dumping duties offer any encouragement.

§ 7. International Monopolies of Raw Materials and International Cartels.

1. General Remarks.—Protection is a necessary condition for any considerable amount of dumping. But in addition the monopolistic organisations which practise dumping owe their very existence, for the most part, to protective duties. As Havenmeyer, the American sugar producer, remarked before the Industrial Commission of 1900, " The tariff is the Mother of Trusts." Perhaps it would be an exaggeration to say that *every* cartel and *every* trust is the child of a tariff, but beyond doubt the *majority* of cartels hold together only because of a protective tariff. It is far more easy for the few producers of a small country, sheltered by duties, to act together than it is for the numerous producers of a large economic region. If all tariffs were removed tomorrow, very many entre-

preneurs would lose the monopolistic position which each today possesses in his own line and country, while most of the existing cartels would vanish or would cease to exercise any power. For without a tariff each producer has only the natural protection of transport costs; as soon as his price exceeds the level at which foreign producers can profitably sell in his country they will commence to do so.

These views are confirmed a thousandfold by experience. Cartels have developed much less in England than on the Continent. This is partly due to such factors as the proverbial individualism of the English entrepreneur, but it is largely due to the absence of protective tariffs. Nor is it a mere coincidence that the rapid growth of cartels in Germany began just after she adopted Protection in 1879.

There are two kinds of exceptions to the general rule that monopolies are due to tariffs. In the first place, there are *local monopolies*, protected by transport costs. In the second place, there are *international* monopolies. These range from the complete control of the supply of a commodity throughout the world to the control of a large part of the supply—or at least sufficient to affect the market price—within two or more customs areas, protected from outside competition by tariffs or transport costs or both.

We must distinguish two classes of such international monopolies. Each class presents problems of its own. (*a*) *One country or a small group of countries* has a monopolistic position on the world market, which it endeavours to exploit by charging high prices to the rest of the world (for example, the monopoly of quicksilver by Spain and Italy or the Franco-German potash syndicate). (*b*) The producers of *all* countries, or at least of a large number of countries form (through their national cartels, if these exist) an international alliance or cartel in order jointly to restrict production and control price.

International monopolies of the first class are based almost always upon control of raw materials. One country may contain most or all of the sources of supply of an important raw material. But the further processes of working up these raw materials can be carried out in many different places, even if the cost of doing so is higher in some places than in others.

International monopolies of the second class raise the question of whether, as many people suppose, international cartels provide a means of escape from the errors of Protection.

2. INTERNATIONAL MONOPOLIES OF RAW MATERIALS.[1]—The mere fact that the sources of supply of a given raw material lie wholly or mainly within the territory of one State does not make possible a monopolistic exploitation of the rest of the world or, more exactly, of the consumers in other countries (and perhaps also of the consumers in the country in question). There is a further condition necessary to enable such a monopolistic exploitation to take place: the producers must somehow be organised for the purpose of restricting production and supply. Nearly all the raw materials which fulfil the first condition are agricultural or mineral products produced not by a few large undertakings but by numerous small ones. Thus the intervention of the State is nearly always necessary in order to create an organised monopoly and to restrict supply. Wallace and Edminster, in their *International Control of Raw Materials* enumerate twenty raw materials which in recent years it has been sought, with at least temporary success, to bring under monopolistic control. Only in two of these twenty cases— quinine and quebracho bark—did the State play no part. The following cases are the most important from the standpoint of world trade: currants (Greece), camphor (Japan), coffee (Brazil), quicksilver (Spain and Italy), nitrate (Chile), potash (Germany and France), rubber (British Malaya), silk (Japan), tin (British Malaya), sulphur (Italy and the United States). Two of the most important of these attempts to restrict supply have since broken down: the Rubber Restriction Scheme and the Coffee Valorisation Scheme.

The State may intervene for any of the following purposes: (1) *to obtain revenue* for itself, at the cost either of its own producers or, where possible, of foreign consumers. This was the main object of the Chilean export tax on nitrate. As the Chilean nitrate met with no competition, it was possible to shift the burden of the export duty, to a certain extent, upon the foreign consumers. Since then, the development of synthetic nitrate has fundamentally changed the situation. (2) *To stabilise the price* and, if possible, to ensure a higher price to producers. The schemes for rubber and coffee provide illustrations of this. (3) *To afford Protection* in order to establish or maintain industries working up the raw material within the country. An example is the tax on tin ore exported from British Malaya to countries outside the British Empire. (4) *To favour home consumers* as against foreign ones.

---

[1] See Viner, " National Monopolies of Raw Materials " in *Causes of War* (1932), Wallace and Edminster, *International Control of Raw Materials* (1930); Rowe, " Artificial Control of Raw Material Supplies " in *Economic Journal* (1930), vol. 40; and *Memoranda* by the same author published by the London and Cambridge Economic Service.

Thus the Prussian State enabled German agriculture to obtain potash relatively cheaply. The Webb-Pomerene Act of the United States, which permits cartels only for export purposes, is another example. (5) *To conserve the resources* of the raw materials in question by preventing too rapid a rate of production.

The State may adopt any of the following methods to raise the export price of the monopolised commodity : (1) *the imposition of a State monopoly,* or of a monopoly of production or trade controlled by the State. Examples are the German potash monopoly and the Japanese camphor monopoly. (2) *The formation of a private monopolistic organisation* which the State compels producers to join. Examples are the sulphur syndicate in Sicily, the nitrate syndicate in Chile, and the Spanish-Italian quicksilver cartel. (3) *Duties or quotas upon exports.* (4) *Restriction of Production.* Examples are the Rubber Restriction Scheme and the taxes on new coffee plantations in Brazil. (5) *The fixing of a minimum price.* This usually implies some restriction of production. (6) *State purchases* of the commodity in order to raise its market price. This method has been much used by the Brazilian Government to support the price of coffee.

In general, attempts to monopolise raw materials have not met with much success. They have sometimes been of benefit to the producers, but more often, especially in the long run, they have been of considerable injury to them. For the world economy as a whole all these attempts have been of relatively minor significance; and most of them have not lasted long.[2] Either it proves impossible to restrict permanently the total supply, owing to the growth of production in countries outside the scheme or technical progress evolves substitutes, as in the case of synthetic nitrate, which compete with the monopolised commodity. The former alternative is, of course, more likely if the price is maintained (as it was in the case of rubber) at a level which yields abnormally high profits to outside producers. The fear that certain countries will be able, through their control of certain raw materials, to extort tribute from the rest of the world—a fear which is the opposite of the fear of dumping—has at present no real basis.

3. INTERNATIONAL CARTELS.[3]—The question of international cartels, that is of uniting the producers, in a given branch of

---

[2] The unprecedented fall since 1928 in the prices of raw materials cannot be said to be attributed to previous monopolistic excesses; it is nevertheless a good illustration of our thesis.

[3] The whole literature on cartels deals also with international cartels. The League of Nations and the International Chamber of Commerce have published various memoranda reports on the question by M'Gregor, K. Wiedenfeld, C.

industry, of as many countries as possible into an organisation to exercise a single planned control over production and price and possibly to divide markets between the different producing countries, has aroused much interest since the War. It has been discussed at many international conferences and has afforded an outlet for the phantasies of numerous writers. The motive has been less the fear of monopolistic exploitation of consumers than the hope that agreements among the producers of different countries, united in international cartels, might prepare the way for the removal or lowering of tariff barriers. We shall confine our remarks upon international cartels to the question of whether this is desirable or possible, since to examine international cartels in all their aspects would involve an analysis of the whole cartel-problem and would take far too much space.

The hope in question seems very dear to the French. They have declared again and again at conferences of the League of Nations and of the International Chamber of Commerce that a far-reaching cartellisation of as many branches of industry as possible in order to exercise an international control over production—that is, to eliminate free competition—is an indispensable preliminary to a general lowering of tariffs. It is interesting to note that it is France, the country which has moved less than any of the great European States in the direction of collectivism, who is the strongest advocate of this sort of planning in the international sphere.[4] Germany—the classical home of cartels and intervention, taking an important share in all the international cartels—remained, on the whole, sceptical and unsympathetic to the French thesis of forming international cartels in order to lower tariffs.

The French industrialist and politician Loucheur, one of the most influencial advocates of the cartel idea, explained, in a speech before the World Economic Conference at Geneva in 1927, that the only way to solve the European economic problem seemed to be " to organise the European industries upon the horizontal method, that is, by branches of industry. Only in this way can we begin to make the important adaptations which are necessary, and . . . the international cartels will . . . also in part solve the question of reducing tariffs."

At the international conferences the French thesis was opposed by the representatives of countries with a liberal trade policy— England, Holland, and the Scandinavian countries—together, as

Lammers, R. Conte, Domeratzky, *The International Cartel Movement* (*Trade Information Bulletin*, Washington, annual report); Costa, *Le rôle économique des unions internationales de producteurs* (1932); A. Plumer, *International Combines in Modern Industry* (1934).

[4] The French liking for import quotas also illustrates this curious attitude.

we have observed, with Germany. And it was opposed with good reason. The thesis proves on closer examination to be a false one, introduced as a red herring by Protectionists.

(I) The first thing to do is to get at least an approximate notion of the scope and significance of the existing international cartels and to estimate the proportion of total world trade formed by commodities under their control. This is no easy problem, since not much work has been done in this field. Liefmann estimates the number of international cartels at the beginning of the century at 40, Harms estimates it for 1912 at 100, and Wagenführ estimates it for the post-War period at 320, of which 230 were industrial cartels.[5] But this is of little help, since their economic significance cannot be counted in figures but must be estimated qualitatively. But ordinary observation and general considerations suggest that one should not rate too highly the part played by international cartels in world trade.

The general remarks which writers have made as to the suitability for cartellisation of various branches of industry of course apply also to international cartels, but with the qualification that all the difficulties and obstacles in the way of cartellising a branch of production increase in geometrical proportion to the number of participating countries. It is much more difficult to bring together the producers of several countries than those of one country. But, in addition to that, national cartels—the indispensable forerunners of international ones—are not equally developed in different countries, nor are all countries equally willing to take part in an international agreement. Thus the possibility of forming an international cartel at all, and the length of time for which it will hold together if formed, depend upon whichever country is the weakest link in the chain. For example, the cartellisation of industry is less developed in England than elsewhere; hence England is not a member of most international cartels, and this fact greatly limits their power. Moreover, the fact that England would remain outside prevents a number of international cartels from coming into existence.

Cartels can achieve their aim of raising the price[6] for any considerable period of time only if they can in some measure control the production, and this in turn is possible only when the output is not too widely distributed among different producers. Hence the cartellisation of agriculture is out of the question. Thus the

---

[5] The world crisis has greatly lessened the importance, and to a less extent the number, of international cartels.

[6] Price in the widest sense, including conditions of payment. Cartels which divide the market regionally among their members thereby also affect the price.

proposal for international cartels can contribute nothing towards the solution of the problem of agrarian protection, which plays such a dominant part in the Protectionist system of most countries.[7]

Again, every industry in which the bulk of the output is contributed by small or medium sized firms is unsuitable for cartellisation. This rules out all industries in which individual craftsmanship or design or taste, or frequent changes of fashion, play a large part. All the textile and wood-working industries are very little suited to cartellisation.

The following groups of industries are the most suitable for cartellisation on an international basis:

(*a*) Industries closely based on raw materials and able to prevent the entry of outsiders by a strict control of the raw-material supplies. Apart from the raw-material monopolies already mentioned, the international lead, magnesium, copper, aluminium, and zinc cartels belong to this group, as do in part the cartels of the chemical industry. But all except the last named are concerned with raw materials upon which most countries levy *no* import duties. Hence they hold no interest for tariff policy and are important only in that they exploit the consumers.

(*b*) Very important are cartels to exploit patents. These play a large part in the electrical and chemical industries. Examples are the incandescent lamp cartel and the ball-bearings cartel.

(*c*) Most important of all are cartels in those industries in which the advantages of large concerns are especially great and in which, therefore, there is most concentration. Newcomers are deterred by the large amount of capital (which must largely be transformed into very specific forms) required to set up a concern approaching optimal size. The iron and steel industry falls into this group, together with part of the chemical and artificial-silk industries. Probably the best-known example of an international cartel is the Continental Crude Steel Cartel. But, in addition to this, the iron and steel industry has established a whole series of cartels for rails, tubes, and so on. Those who hope to reduce tariffs through international cartels produce the international cartels of this industry as their show-piece.

Nevertheless there is not much ground for this hope, for international cartels cover too small a sector of world trade and

---

[7] But this has not prevented various proposals, especially by the French, to set up agricultural cartels, *e.g.*, a wheat cartel. These, however, do not relate to cartels in the usual sense but to State intervention, Government purchases, and so on. The Canadian 'wheat pool' is well-known, but its attempt to keep up the price of wheat was soon frustrated. The American New Deal has evolved various methods to reduce and control agricultural output and was very successful in solving the problem of poverty amidst plenty by removing the plenty.

have nothing like sufficient cohesion to do much in this direction. If one does not wish to resort to the strongest kind of intervention, in order to compel firms to join international cartels—a course already urged by influential French exponents of the cartel idea[8]— it is clear that for purely quantitative reasons the existing international cartels are not a suitable instrument for demolishing tariff walls within any measurable time. And our next point, which follows, strengthens this view.

(II) Many of the present international cartels *owe their own existence to tariffs*. They are therefore scarcely adapted for destroying tariffs. Unless the industry in question happens to be about equally strong in every participating country, the weaker national groups would not and cannot give up their tariff protection. The members of the so-called international cartels are usually united by rather loose agreements, and the allocation of quotas and sales areas is made only for a short period at a time. Negotiations, often very difficult, as to the allocation of quotas and markets among the members when the existing agreements expire, are going on nearly all the time. It cannot be too strongly emphasised that in these struggles, in which each member-country tries to get better terms from the others as the price of its adherence, the strongest means of exerting pressure is the existing tariffs and, in particular, the possibility of raising them. Indeed, in recent years many tariff increases have taken place or have been definitely threatened with the expressed intention of strengthening the position of the national industry in its negotiations with its international cartel. Hence the weaker members of international cartels will not willingly forgo their actual or potential tariff protection.

Of course this is not to deny that if tariff walls were removed, let us say in Europe or in Central Europe, then European or Central European cartels would replace national ones. But this would happen only *after* tariff walls were removed over a certain area. Without such a removal, this development would take place only in those exceptional cases in which, in spite of the tariffs,

---

[8] The experts of the League of Nations have strongly denounced this course. " The experts expressly point out that the establishment of international industrial cartels should not be brought about artificially by measures of compulsion. It is much better to let them arise from the free initiative of the participating groups as a result of the prevailing economic circumstances. Both the foundation and the actions of the cartels should be quite free from the influence of Governments, which may use them to promote their own aims in the sphere of trade policy." Report of the Economic Experts of the Europa-Commission of the League of Nations.

approximately the same situation prevailed as would prevail under Free Trade.[9]

We now turn to the decisive argument against this whole idea.

(III) *International industrial cartels can facilitate the reduction of tariffs only when they themselves serve as substitutes for tariffs*, so that the Protectionism of cartels replaces the Protectionism of tariffs. For in what way could international cartels facilitate tariff reductions? Clearly by guaranteeing to the weaker members the same relative position which they enjoy under the existing tariffs. This is most plainly seen in the case of international cartels to allocate markets. (The majority are of this type.) Such cartels divide the total market among their members and delimit the sales areas of their various member-groups or individual firms. If they agree upon the same division, despite the tariffs, as that which would prevail under Free Trade, both the tariffs and the agreements are superfluous and the removal of the tariffs makes no difference in this respect. But if the division is *different* from this, then its effect is similar to that of tariffs; it maintains an irrational situation and makes more difficult, or prevents, an international division of labour.

International cartels may be of advantage in other directions. They may make possible a pooling of knowledge and may eliminate some waste, such as that due to competitive advertising. They may perhaps be welcomed as the forerunners and pioneers of an economy united on an international basis. They may be expected to lessen the severity of economic crises (although this hope is not altogether supported by experience). But as a means for reducing tariffs and for painlessly enabling the advantages of international division of labour to be enjoyed, they are not suitable. If we shrink from the difficulties of adaptation, we must renounce the advantages of the international division of labour. But the conflict of interests is too strong to offer any hope that the various parties will voluntarily unite in an international cartel in order to renounce tariff protection and to carry out under their own banner all the adjustments required to give full effect to the international division of labour.

Another question, which would demand very careful consideration, is whether the adjustments which would follow a reduction of tariffs might not be facilitated by planned intervention by the

---

[9] The fact that industrial groups are of equal strength (that is, working under the same cost-conditions) in the participating countries is no proof that they would remain so if tariffs were removed. Under Free Trade it might easily be profitable to expand one group and liquidate another.

State in the form of subsidies and bounties to hasten the consequent adaptations. But at present, when there is not general agreement upon the desirable goal, it is too early to bother about the detailed technique. The simplest way to facilitate the transition is to agree upon a general reduction of all tariffs.

PART II.

C.—THE TECHNIQUE OF TRADE POLICY.

CHAPTER XIX.

THE CONTENT AND FORM OF TARIFF LAWS AND THEIR APPLICATION. OTHER KINDS OF PROTECTION.

§ INTRODUCTORY.

We have hitherto supposed the height of the import duties, together with the customs area and the goods to which they apply, to be definitely given. We must now enquire how it is decided in any particular case whether a good is subject to duty, and, if so, how much duty must be paid and at which place and at what time. If such matters are not to be left to the arbitrary decision of the customs authorities, and if as much uniformity as possible is to be secured in carrying out the various regulations, those responsible for framing the relevant laws and decrees have a very difficult task to perform. The general terms and expressions which must be used often prove in their application to be ambiguous and not sufficiently precise. Take, for example, the phrase, ' the value of the good.' Does this mean its value at the place from which it is sold, or its value at the frontier, or its value when finally received by the buyer? Again, it is often not easy to determine exactly the various facts upon which the amount of the duty depends. To secure uniformity of practice, detailed instructions as to procedure must be given to the customs officials. Examples of such instructions are those describing how to ascertain the value or the *net* weight of the good subject to duty.[1]

§ 2. THE TARIFF SCHEDULE AND THE CUSTOMS AREA.

A tariff schedule is a list of all the existing import duties. An import duty may be laid down in a law or in a decree or in an inter-State agreement. Hence one can distinguish between *autonomous* and *agreed* (or ' *conventional* ') duties. Moreover, the tariff law or agreement may provide either for one or for two or more different rates of duty upon the same good. Hence we can distinguish between a *single tariff*, a *double tariff*, and a *tariff with*

---

[1] The best general treatise on the technical problems of commercial policy is Gregory, *Tariffs: A Study in Method* (1921). See also Gruntzel, *System der Handelspolitik*, 3rd edn., *Dictionary of Tariff Information* and *The Tariff and Its History*, both published by the U.S. Tariff Commission, Washington, 1924 and 1934; Culbertson, *International Economic Policies* (1925); Greiff, *Die neuen Methoden der Handelspolitik* (1934).

more than two columns. Under a single tariff, no distinction is made between the import of the good from one country and from another, except that it may be allowed free entry from certain countries. The tariff with several columns (or ' decks ') discriminates according to the country of origin of the good, or the country from which it is consigned. The double tariff distinguishes either between autonomous and conventional duties or between maximum and minimum duties. Conventional duties apply to goods coming from countries with which there is a relevant trade treaty or agreement, and autonomous duties to goods coming from other countries. *Minimum duties* are usually laid down by Parliament in the tariff law and fix a lower limit to any concessions which the Administration may make. The minimum duties may apply automatically to all countries with which there are relevant trade agreements, the maximum duties applying to the other countries. Sometimes a distinction is drawn between ' deferred ' duties, which are held in reserve to be applied, for example, if a tariff war arises, and the *normal* tariff ordinarily in force.[2] These various distinctions are easy to understand from an economic point of view. But the terminology used to describe them is not quite uniform. Different terms may be used owing to some peculiar feature of the political or legal situation or to overcome some tactical difficulty in negotiating a trade agreement.

Most countries distinguish between the Customs law and the tariff law. The former lays down general rules as to the method of executing the law, the competence and rights of the various official bodies and persons, and other matters which do not further interest us, together with instructions as to methods of valuation. Hence its provisions are not very often changed. The tariff law, on the other hand, fixes rates of duty, which may frequently be altered. A kind of official commentary, which very often has the force of law, enumerates and describes the various goods subject to duty, stating under which tariff number each falls. The various goods often used to be listed in the tariff schedule in alphabetical order[3] or according to the height of the duty, but under the highly protective tariffs of today they are always classified according to their country of origin, characteristic features, uses, and materials. A modern tariff schedule is a formidable affair: for example, the

---

[2] Of course, the duties could be raised in case of need by law. But since the legislative machine does not always work promptly, general powers to impose or increase duties in special circumstances may be given to the Administration.
[3] For example, until 1924 Belgium had an alphabetically-arranged schedule with few and low duties.

present German one contains 19 divisions, again divided into sub-divisions, and many hundreds of individual items.

Since the brief period of Free Trade in the third quarter of the nineteenth century came to an end, the general tendency has been, and still is, for tariff schedules to become more extensive, their classifications more complicated, and their individual items more numerous.[4] This is due both to the wider scope of Protection and to the growing specialisation of modern production. Increasing care is shown in grading the various duties and in relating them one to another, especially in connection with the successive stages in a production process. A duty on undyed yarn to benefit spinners implies a correspondingly higher duty on dyed yarn to protect the dyers and this in turn necessitates a duty on cloth and finally on clothes, and so on. Account must be taken also of the numerous possibilities of substitution as, for example, between natural silk, artificial silk of various kinds, and other textile fabrics.

Another reason for the increasing complication of tariff schedules is the effort to evade the Most Favoured National Clause. To this end, the specialisation of tariff items is sometimes carried so far that a slight difference of quality, if it is found only in goods coming from a certain country or countries, is listed as a separate item. In this way it is possible, if desired, to reduce the duty on goods coming from one country without also reducing it—under the provisions of the Most Favoured Nation Clause—upon similar goods from other countries. The example of this always quoted is a provision in the German tariff, dating from 1902 and still valid, which is clearly meant to apply to Switzerland and Austria, relating to " brown or dappled cows reared at a level of at least 300 metres above the sea and passing at least one month in every summer at a height of at least 800 metres."

Thus a modern tariff schedule is a complicated instrument which could not have been created at one stroke. It has acquired its present form as the result of decades of continuous alterations. Every separate sub-division and item has its history and is the result of struggle and intrigue. Only a few specialists are at home in its thicket of clauses and are in a position to judge the significance of their finely-drawn distinctions.

There can be no doubt that the increasing complication of tariff schedules is in itself an increasing hindrance to the inter-

---

4 For example, the first schedule of the German Customs Union (1834) contained 190 items, the first of the German Reich in 1871, 230. This grew to 490 in 1888, 1800 in 1902, and 2600 in 1928. At that date the French schedule comprised 6000 items. *Cf.* Memoranda by T. W. Page and Trendelenburg submitted to the World Economic Conference, 1927 (League Documents).

national division of labour. The administrative difficulties and annoyances to be faced are thereby increased; and the general level of tariffs is thereby made higher than it would otherwise be, since it is much easier to increase the duties upon special subdivisions or items than to obtain an increase covering a large number of goods simultaneously. Moreover, the protective effect of a duty can be enhanced without raising the average height of the duty if one tariff item is divided into a number of separate items each with its own rate of duty.

The World Economic Conference of 1927, appreciating these facts, demanded (at the instance of Germany) a simplification of tariff nomenclature. The League of Nations set up an international committee of experts to work out a uniform scheme for this purpose. They produced a scheme very similar to that of the German tariff. The aim should now be to induce as many countries as possible to adopt this proposed standard classification and, if possible, to promise not to create any further divisions or subdivisions. But the prevailing Protectionist spirit offers little hope that this aim will be attained. We cannot assume that Protectionism will be outwitted by such a manœuvre.[5]

Today the *customs area* usually coincides with the area of the country. It is well known that this was not always so. Before and during the Mercantilist era, and even later, there were numerous internal tariff districts, although then the tariffs were mainly for revenue.[6] Even today there are exceptions to the rule that tariff boundaries coincide with State boundaries. It may happen that a part of one country belongs to the customs area of another. Thus the German customs area includes two small Austrian villages which are excluded from the Austrian customs area on account of their geographical position. Again, it is well known that the French hinterland of Geneva formed part of the Swiss customs area until 1918. The Hague International Court declared that the provision of the Treaty of Versailles which transferred this district to the French customs area was not valid. Other exceptions to this general rule are provided by customs unions (discussed later) and by colonies.

---

[5] The complications of the modern tariff schedule afford interested parties rich opportunities to work in the dark and to obtain special advantages at the cost of the community without the general public realising it. Some glaring examples are given by Taussig, *How Tariffs should not be Made* in *Free Trade, the Tariff and Reciprocity*, p. 163. But such things do not happen only in America.

[6] Some internal tariffs still exist in the form of taxes upon foodstuffs entering certain cities ('octrois').

§ 3. Specific and *Ad Valorem* Duties.

The amount of any particular import duty can be fixed in either of two ways. It may be laid down either that a fixed sum of money must be paid upon each unit of quantity (for example, hundred-weight) imported, or that a fixed percentage of the value of the amount imported must be paid. Duties of the former kind are termed *specific* and of the latter, *ad valorem*. If the true value of the good is known, then, of course, a specific duty can be expressed as an *ad valorem* duty, and conversely. But since it is usually difficult to determine accurately the value of an import, and since each specific duty, however specialised the tariff schedule, usually covers a range of different qualities and therefore of different values, the two kinds of duty are very different in their application. Each kind has both advantages and disadvantages. In general, *ad valorem* duties are the more difficult to collect, especially when they are high and therefore offer a greater incentive to evasion. Hence most countries have adopted the system of specific duties. But *ad valorem* duties still prevail in Free Trade countries with low tariffs, such as Holland, and in some overseas countries, including the United States.

Specific duties have the following disadvantages:

(1) They are regressive in their operation, since the cruder and cheaper qualities of a commodity are taxed more heavily (per unit of value). In consequence the home production of the finer qualities is less protected. *Ad valorem* duties, on the other hand—always assuming that the value can be properly determined—allow for differences in quality and ensure equal treatment. This disadvantage of specific duties can be overcome to a certain extent by increased specialisation of the tariff schedule. To this end the amount of the duty must be made to vary with each special feature of the good which affects its value. Thus yarn can be divided into categories, for tariff purposes, according to its fineness, cloth according to the number of threads per square inch, petrol according to its specific gravity, and so on, in order that the burden of the duty may be approximately equal as between more valuable and less valuable grades. Another method of avoiding the regressive effect is to impose a basic specific duty plus a supplementary *ad valorem* duty.

(2) The real burden of specific duties varies with the price-level. When prices are rising the real burden of specific duties, and therefore their protective effect, becomes less; and conversely when prices are falling. Thus in recent years there has been a general

automatic increase in the real burden of duties owing to the sharp fall in prices. Governments have learned to allow for this circumstance in times of inflation by stating the sum to be paid in terms of gold and receiving whatever amount of their own currency is equivalent to that at the time. But this expedient fails when, as in recent years, the value of gold itself changes. No country has so far made its duties vary with the purchasing power of gold, as shown by some general index of prices.

(3) Specific duties cannot be applied to certain goods, such as works of art. A picture cannot be taxed according to its weight or surface area.

The great advantage of specific over *ad valorem* duties is that the physical and chemical properties of a good can be determined much more easily than its value, although one should not underrate the difficulties of specific duties under a very specialised tariff —indeed, they often involve complicated chemical and physical researches.

Ad valorem duties have the advantage that the burden of the duty can be clearly expressed and the duties levied by different countries can more easily be compared. It means much more to say that a duty takes thirty per cent. of the value than to say that it takes so many shillings per hundredweight.

The difficult problem under *ad valorem* duties is to determine the value of the good. Upon which price is the duty to be based? The f.o.b. price or the c.i.f. price, the price including or excluding the cost of packing? The market price at the time when the sales contract is made, or at the time when the goods are dispatched, or at the time when they cross the frontier? Is the invoice price or a specially declared value to be taken as the basis for the duty? The market price often fluctuates considerably during a single day, and varies with the grade or quality of the good, with the credit of the buyer, with the length of time allowed for payment, and with the amount bought. In order to obtain anything approaching a reliable valuation, a complicated system of controls and penalties, with rights of complaint and appeal, is necessary. For example, the State may have the right to purchase the goods at their declared value or to examine the books of the firm (thus exposing it to the dangers of economic espionage)[7] or may demand invoices certified as correct by its consuls abroad (involving extra expense to the traders). Even so, sometimes, as in the case of gifts, there are no invoices and the market value cannot be deter-

---

[7] The methods of the American Customs Authorities, in particular, have led to increasing complaints in Europe.

mined. In such cases the American tariff takes the cost of production as representing the value, but clearly—for example, in the case of a picture—this is not always satisfactory.

In order to overcome once and for all the difficulties of determining the value of a good with a constantly fluctuating market value, resort is often had to official fixation of values. When such an official value can be revised if proof is given that it is wrong, the duty is still an *ad valorem* one. But when this is not possible, and the official valuation cannot be challenged, the duty becomes in effect a specific one.[8]

§ 4. SLIDING-SCALE DUTIES.[9]

A very interesting problem, which has not so far been fully analysed by modern economists, is that of the so-called sliding-scale duties, which vary with the price of the commodity. These could be either specific or *ad valorem*, but in practice they are always specific. Historically, they have been confined almost entirely to duties on grain. They have been applied to grain because its price frequently changes owing to harvest variations, and it is such an important staple commodity that, on the one hand, its price can be readily ascertained and, on the other hand, Governments have sometimes endeavoured more or less to stabilise its value.

Sliding-scale duties on grain were in force in England for hundreds of years. The details varied but the principle was maintained from 1463 to the repeal of the Corn Laws in 1846. This principle is simple and obvious. In order to keep the price of corn as stable as possible, the duty was to be lowered when the price rose and raised when it fell. Thus, for example, the law of 1827 declared that when the price was from 62 to 63 shillings the duty should be 20s. 8d., and that for each fall in price of 1s. the duty should be raised by 2s. and for each rise in price of 1s. the duty should be reduced by 2s. The duty should be determined afresh each week upon the basis of the average price of the six previous weeks.

The experience of England with sliding-scale duties was very

---

[8] A League of Nations memorandum prepared for the World Economic Conference, 1927, gives an international survey over the methods used in various countries. *Cf.* also Gregory, *loc. cit.*, p. 299.

[9] Literature : Henningsen, *Die gleitende Skala für Getreidezölle* (1912); Diehl, " Über die Frage der Einführung beweglicher Zölle " in *Jahrbücher für National-ökonomie und Statistik* (1900), series 3, vol. 19; Gregory, *Tariffs*, pp. 133 *et seq.*; article, " Sliding Scales " in *Dictionary of Tariff Information;* Barnes, *A History of the English Corn Laws from* 1660 *to* 1846; Fay, *The Corn Laws and Social England* (1932).

unfavourable and brought the system into disrepute.[1] It suffered from the inconvenience that it was possible to bring about a decrease in the duty by withholding supplies and an increase in it by speculatively forcing down the market price. Scarcely was the duty lowered than large quantities were imported in the expectation that it would shortly be raised again; this caused the price to fall and the duty again to be raised. In short, the effect was not to stabilise the price. Traders and speculators could not freely fulfil their function of smoothing out fluctuations in the price, and the fluctuations were in fact much greater than they would have been under fixed duties.[2]

Most economists who have studied the question are of opinion that the failure of the system was due not only to the unfortunate way it was managed (especially before 1822) but also to its inherent defects.

We cannot here discuss this matter fully. Instead, we shall set out some fundamental considerations, upon which a judgment of the whole arrangement must depend.

Clearly an effective price-regulation through movable *import* duties is possible only in a country which imports grain, and which imports it, moreover, in amounts not too small relatively to its consumption, since otherwise a good home harvest would make the duty ineffective.[3] Further, success is more likely when the import is small in relation to the world market, so that the world price is independent of the height of the sliding-scale duty. For if the amount imported has a marked influence upon the world price, then an increase, for example, in the sliding-scale duty will push down the world price and thus weaken the effect of the increase upon the home price. If, then, the duty is further increased, this implies continuous fluctuations, especially if the market is much influenced by speculation. Theoretically, in order to stabilise the home price, such a duty must be levied as will have that result after allowing for its repercussions upon the world price. But it is almost impossible to discover what size such a duty should be, since this can be done only by trial and error, and during the process the market situation will probably alter.

The necessary conditions for a satisfactory working of sliding-

---

[1] The same applies to the experience of other countries, *e.g.* Bavaria in 1826, Sweden in 1830, France in 1831, and Belgium and Holland in 1834-35.

[2] Henningsen takes a different view, but this does not seem to me to be borne out by the statistical data he gives. Against him we can set the well-founded judgment of Marshall : " Her (England's) perverse mixture of prohibitions and sliding scales rendered it an act of gambling rather than of sober business to grow wheat " [*Official Papers* (1926), p. 380.].

[3] We have already shown that *fixed* duties also may lead to undesired fluctuations in price. See chap. xviii, § 6.

scale duties were only very incompletely present in England in 1846. When these conditions, implied above, are present, it is theoretically correct to make the height of the duty vary with the world price and not with the home price, as usually happens. It is necessary to make a firm decision as to the level at which the home price is to be stabilised and to make the duty equal to the difference between this desired price and the prevailing world price.

Even so, the danger that such a stabilisation policy may be defeated by speculative manœuvres is not thereby abolished.[4] In order to overcome all these difficulties, the regulations must become ever more complicated until, finally, the only resource is an *import monopoly*. Switzerland has had a monopoly of the import of grain during and since the War and her experience, as regards the stabilisation of the home price, has been by no means unfavourable.[5]

It must also be remembered that, in view of the inelastic demand which usually prevails for grain, stability of the home price often is less favourable to agriculture than a variable price. Suppose that a bad harvest at home coincides with poor world-harvests and the world price is therefore high. Under either Free Trade or fixed duties the farmers would find at least some compensation for the small harvest in an increased price. But if at such a time the duty is lowered and the price therefore does not rise, the returns to the home producers of grain must fall. To stabilise the price is by no means the same thing as to stabilise the corresponding branch of industry.

---

[4] Henningsen has proposed that the duty, to be fixed in a complicated fashion by means of a basic duty and two supplementary duties, shall be both decided upon and levied at the close of the period of time during which the imports subject to it have come in. Clearly, this would turn the trade in grain into a mere gamble.

[5] The advocates of this scheme contend that the main advantage of restricting imports by means of an import-monopoly is that the same protection can be given to producers by imposing a smaller burden upon consumers than they would have to bear under a duty. Suppose that under free import the price of wheat would be 20s. a quarter and that producers have been guaranteed a price of 40s. Then under a tariff, a duty of 20s. must be imposed and the price to consumers is raised to 40s. An import monopoly would give producers the same benefit more cheaply. If we suppose that the import is about equal to the home production, then the monopoly can sell the wheat at a ' mixed price ' of 30s. to consumers, without producers getting any less. It can use its profits on the imported wheat to keep down its home price. (In an accurate calculation, of course, account would have to be taken of the expansion of demand.) It is clear that this advantage of a monopoly is possible only if the State renounces its receipts from a wheat duty. Moreover, the import must not be too small relatively to the home production. For example, an import monopoly of grain into Germany would have, for this reason, only a quite small effect in cheapening the price to consumers. See Gross, "Zoll- oder Monopolischutz für den österr. Getreidebau?" and Fischmeister, "Zoll oder Monopol?" both in *Zeitschrift für Nationalökonomie* (1930), vol. 1. On the Swiss experiences, see Landmann, *Die Agrarpolitik des schweizerischen Industriestaates* (1928); Hainisch, *Das Getreidemonopol* (1929).

§ 5. IMPORT PROHIBITIONS, EXPORT PROHIBITIONS, AND QUOTAS.

Import prohibitions closely resemble prohibitive duties, so that what we have already said about the latter applies to them also, and need not be repeated here.

We shall not consider import prohibitions imposed for reasons other than those of trade policy, such as Security (for example, arms), Health (for example, prohibitions under veterinary regulations), Morality (for example, pornographic writings), and so on. Import prohibitions imposed for reasons of trade policy, that is to say in order to discriminate between the home and the foreign supply, were frequent in Western Europe in the first half of the nineteenth century and earlier, especially on finished products. During the War and the period of inflation which followed, they again became a permanent feature of trade policy, being imposed for purely Protectionist reasons and upon the pretext of safeguarding the currency by preventing too great an adverse balance of trade.   After the period of inflation their importance again dwindled. In 1927 the League of Nations tried to get an international agreement not to impose import and export prohibitions. But the application of this agreement was made conditional upon the adherence of certain States, and, with the refusal of Poland to ratify the project, it came to nothing. During the recent years of depression numerous countries have again resorted to prohibitions, either open or concealed, upon imports. The pretext is usually the protection of the currency. But the case presented for such prohibitions always contains Mercantilist misconceptions of the most primitive kind.

Export prohibitions were numerous, upon raw materials and other producers' goods, during the Mercantilist period, but in modern trade policy they play only a subordinate part. During the War many countries prohibited the export of essential raw materials and foodstuffs in order to ensure sufficient supplies for their own civil and military needs. But after the War they were soon removed. Such export prohibitions as there are today, apart from those imposed upon non-economic grounds (for example, of national works of art), apply to raw materials, with the object of ensuring that they are worked up within the country.   Thus Rumania prohibits the export of crude oil, in order to protect its refineries. Many countries prohibit (or tax) the export of hides and bones. In 1928 seventeen European countries made an international agreement not to hinder the export of these commodities, and this came into force in 1929.[6]

---

[6] Other examples are the prohibition of the export of ostriches and ostrich-

Protectionism leads to really grotesque situations when the country producing a raw material prohibits its export in that form and importing countries restrict its import in a more finished form. We have already remarked that Rumania prohibits the export of crude oil. But Austria, which is a natural market for Rumanian oil (coming up the Danube), restricts the import of refined oil in order to protect her refineries. This dilemma has been resolved in the following way. The crude oil is refined and separated into its constituent parts in Rumania; then these parts (benzine, petrol, and so on) are again brought together and imported as so-called ' mixed oil ' into Austria, where they are again separated in the Austrian refineries. Hungary's demand for Rumanian oil is met in a similar way.

We turn to *the system of quotas*.[7] Sometimes a given quantity of a good is permitted to enter duty-free or upon payment of a relatively low duty, imports in excess of that quantity being charged a relatively high rate of duty. But our remarks will relate mainly to *import quotas*, under which the fixed amount which may be imported cannot be exceeded. One can distinguish between *autonomous* quotas, fixed by law or by decree, and *agreed* quotas, fixed by some trade agreement with one or more other countries.

Each quota has a similar effect upon the amount imported to a duty of a given height, in the sense that under given conditions it is always possible to find a rate of duty which will curtail imports by just as much as any given quota. But a duty, so long as it is not prohibitive, does not sever all connection with the world market; it does not prevent the amount imported from varying in response to changed conditions and needs. A quota, on the other hand, cuts all links between the home price and the price on the world market.

The quota system, in any form, raises problems which tariffs alone do not raise. Under tariffs, the market-forces of supply and demand determine who shall import, and how much. Anybody may import as much as he pleases, but, of course, he must pay the duty, just as he pays the costs of transport. But if the amount imported is restricted to a certain quantity, then—always provided that the restriction is effective, in the sense that less is imported under the quota than would be imported under the free play of the

eggs by South Africa, and of date-palm shoots by Egypt and Tunis, and of pineapple seedlings by Cuba, in order to prevent their cultivation in other countries. Several important countries prohibit or limit the export of scrap-iron.

[7] The literature is mainly in German. An extension of the argument in the text is to be found in my book *Liberale und planwirtschaftliche Handelspolitik* (1934). *Cf.* also Häfner, 'Zur Theorie der mengenmässigen Einfuhrregulierung,'' *Weltwirtschaftliches Archiv* (1934 and 1935), vols. 40 and 41. F. A. Haight, *French Import Quotas. A new Instrument of Commercial Policy* (1935).

market—a new principle of selection is introduced which is divorced from the play of the market. The fixing of import quotas, like the fixing of maximum prices, is an interference with the price-mechanism which is *alien to the price-system*.

When the import of a good is subjected to quota, a difference comes about between the home price and the foreign price which is not covered by the cost of transport plus the duty. Thus it becomes unusually profitable to import such a good, and it must somehow be decided who shall have the privilege of importing it. The most primitive method, adopted for example by France for certain commodities in 1931, is to permit all the units of the good to enter the country until the moment when the quota for the period is filled. The result of this is that at the beginning of each quota-period as large a quantity as possible is rushed into the country. There is no need to labour the point that this is not a rational method of selection.

Another method is to sell licences to import to those who will pay the most for the privilege. This is perhaps the most rational principle of selection, from the standpoint of the importing country; but it has not been used by any Government. In some countries it has been used unofficially to a certain extent, in that would-be importers must bribe the body entrusted with the distribution of import licences in order to obtain the right to import.

It is customary to distribute concessions to import (usually in the form of licences) among the importing houses or—if the goods are consumed industrially—directly among the consumers. Usually the total quota is distributed among the traders or consumers concerned upon the basis of the relative amounts they imported in the year before the quota was imposed. But this is only a provisional, and not a permanent, solution, for as time goes on this basis must become obsolete. A permanent solution, in the case of a producers' good, involves ascertaining the relative needs of each industrialist who uses it; this in turn implies a control of production; and the economy comes more and more under the sway of the State and of those bodies or associations to which it may delegate its powers.

The import licences may be distributed, especially if the good is a consumers' good, among traders. These then make large profits without corresponding effort. Skill in trading ceases to be a principle of selection. Instead, those who happened to be importing the good when the quota system came into force, or those with the most influence or the greatest skill in bribing, are the ones selected. But it is unlikely that a number of fortunate traders will be allowed indefinitely to obtain abnormal profits in this way.

The system will probably end in a State import-monopoly, or in something approaching it. This will have the advantage, from a Protectionist standpoint, of permitting the amount imported to be rapidly varied according to the situation in the home market.[8]

It is a fact recognised by both friends and foes of the present economic system, that import quotas lead directly away from Capitalism towards a planned economy. We may leave planners themselves to decide whether it augurs well for the planned economy of the future that it should be ushered in by the system of import quotas, so lacking in rationality and flexibility, and involving, through its inroads upon the international division of labour, such a great diminution in productivity. But it seems unlikely that the system will continue to find much support, for already, in a relatively short time, its errors have been too glaring and its evils too obvious.

§ 6. OTHER PROTECTIONIST DEVICES.

1. GENERAL REMARKS.—In addition to tariffs and import prohibitions, there is a whole arsenal of expedients for discriminating between the home and the foreign supply, in order to restrict importation and to make it more expensive, and to hinder the international division of labour and divert factors of production from the rational lines into which the mechanism of comparative costs would direct them. A complicated system of affording underground and indirect Protection has been created, of which it is often difficult to discover the full details; and it is often as potent in destroying wealth as the open system of tariffs. This system of administrative Protection has grown to full stature under the increasing influence of interventionist ideas and socialistic experiments. It is an aspect of the trend towards greater State interference in economic affairs: a trend which is making for the destruction of the liberal economy and for compromises between different special interests at the cost of the community as a whole. It springs, on the one hand, from a change in intellectual outlook. The fear of State intervention and the belief in the beneficial results of the free play of economic forces (both, it may be conceded, often

---

[8] If country A agrees with country B upon an import quota, the extra profits thereby created may go either to the importers or industrial users in A or to the exporters or producers in B, or may be divided in some proportion or other between the two groups. The division will depend partly upon whether import licences are granted by A or export licences by B. Recently it has become customary to include a provision as to this in the trade agreement. But it is of course necessary for the exporters or producers or importers or users to be united in an organised association. This development has gone especially far in Austria.

held on irrational grounds) are disappearing. It springs, on the other hand, from the perfection of technical administrative instruments and devices, which enables the modern State to undertake tasks that were quite out of the question twenty years ago.[9]

This kind of Protection causes great trouble to traders. No trade agreement can adequately cope with it, since it is always appearing in new forms not covered by the agreements. This indirect preference given to home production is more dangerous than an import duty of corresponding height, for it rapidly changes its nature in an unpredictable manner, thus introducing an injurious uncertainty into the economy.

2. We shall now attempt to make a grouping of interventions of this kind and to offer some illustrations. Of course, our enumeration can make no claim to be exhaustive, since in this realm it is not possible for science to keep pace with the developments of practice.

(A) We may first mention customs regulations which make it more expensive to import by imposing unfavourable conditions for the payment of the duty and by similar devices. Thus the duty may be made payable at the frontier, which is a nuisance, for example, when goods are sent by post. Again, especially when for some reason the goods can claim a ' preferential ' rate of duty, it may be laid down that the duty must be paid at one or other of certain customs offices; and those offices are selected which are most unfavourably situated, so that transport costs are increased. The regulations may demand expensive evidence of the country of origin of the goods, or special packing, or the use of the language of the importing country in the attached documents, or a mark of origin upon each separate unit in a consignment. Many countries deliberately make their customs regulations complicated and make it difficult for traders to discover exactly what they are. The investigation of claims is made expensive and caused to drag on for a long time and high ' supplementary ' fees are charged for examining the goods; duties are charged on the gross weight; and so on.

(B) A favourite device is the unfair use of veterinary regulations. Thus a long period of quarantine may be imposed upon living cattle or the import of slaughtered cattle may be permitted only in whole carcasses with the entrails still adhering. Helfferich

---

[9] It is true that in many countries too great a strain has been placed upon the capacity of this apparatus, and it has therefore worked badly. But this in no way alters the fact that there has been a marked increase in its capacity.

declares that the German Inspection Laws do not so much protect the health of the German consumers as compel them (by keeping out foreign competition) to pay the highest possible price for meat.[1]

(c) Discriminating freight-rates for transport by rail and by ship have a quite analogous effect to that of tariffs. This device is used to promote exports as well as to check imports.

(D) Measures of the kind under discussion are not confined to making importation more expensive. Some measures have the object of making it more difficult for importers to do business with foreign suppliers and, where possible, of nipping potential new import business in the bud. Thus difficulties are placed in the way of foreign commercial travellers: they are subjected to special taxes and are not allowed to bring samples across the frontier without paying duty upon them. Similarly, goods sent by post as samples or advertisements may be subjected to heavy duties.

(E) In addition to making importation dearer and foreign competition more difficult, the State may directly or indirectly exert pressure upon home buyers to forgo foreign goods, even if they are cheaper and better than the competing home products. The State sets a ' good ' example by purchasing supplies for the Army and Navy, the State railways, and other publicly-controlled services, from home producers. This preference for home suppliers, which partly openly and partly secretly is nearly everywhere the rule, is of great importance owing to the large volume of expenditure made by public bodies. The difference in price between home and foreign supplies may be very great, especially in countries which are industrially backward, so that this practice of placing public orders with home producers often involves a considerable loss to the community.

(F) The State also offers inducements to its citizens to buy home products. The means used are the granting of tax- and other concessions, together with administrative dodges of all kinds. Thus in Italy there are black lists of businesses which are guilty of the crime of purchasing from what happen to be their cheapest sources of supply, namely foreign countries. When the State purchases supplies for itself, it imposes upon its home suppliers the condition that they shall use as far as possible materials, and other means of production, which also are produced at home.

(G) Mention should also be made of the psychological influence exerted upon the buying public by propaganda and business

---

[1] *Handelspolitik*, p. 85.

pressure. The 'Buy British' campaign has a parallel in most countries. Regular boycotts are often instituted against goods coming from certain foreign countries, appeals being made to national feeling and patriotism or, as in China and India, to hatred of the foreigner. In Finland, Holland, and Denmark an attempt has been made to organise a boycott of German goods as a measure of reprisal against increased German duties.

(H) The positive complement of propaganda against imported goods is to make the use of home produce compulsory. Thus German regulations compel (home) butter to be added in the manufacture of margarine and (home) alcohol to be mixed with benzine, while in Austria home coal must be mixed with imported coal, and so on.

(I) Protection by making it more difficult to effect payment is by no means a new phenomenon, but it has again come to the forefront in recent years. In nearly every country it is endeavoured to use the regulations as to foreign exchange for purposes of trade policy. A distinction is drawn between ' good ' and ' bad ' imports and it is made difficult or impossible to pay for the latter.[2]

(J) A leading example of indirect Protection is afforded by tax concessions and subsidies to certain branches of production and individual firms, in order to strengthen them in their fight against foreign competition.

3. APPRAISAL.—The uninstructed public doubtless considers a number of these devices to be completely justified and not open to objection. Is it not a matter for congratulation when consumers, in consequence of an appeal to their patriotism, turn to home goods although the foreign goods may be cheaper? Is it not good that the State should spend the money which it takes from the economy in taxation only upon the products of home firms, so that it remains within the country? We must reply that in all these cases the effects upon the supply of goods and the satisfaction of wants[3] and the diversion of production from the rational lines of the international division of labour are exactly the same as those due to the diversion of demand towards home products through a tariff. These measures hence have in the main the same merits and defects, and are to be judged, and deplored or welcomed, in exactly the same way as tariffs. Thus we need add nothing about them to the remarks we have already made upon the effects of tariffs.

---

[2] On the problems of monetary policy raised by exchange control, cf. chap. vii, § 7.

[3] Possibly the desire to buy only home products might be regarded as a want in itself.

§ 7. ADMINISTRATIVE MITIGATIONS OF TARIFF PROTECTION.

We shall mention, only briefly, various arrangements which are designed to remove or to mitigate certain harsh features of a tariff system. These arrangements can be distinguished from tariff reductions in that they are not meant to affect the protective function of tariffs. Nevertheless, the border-line between devices of this kind which do not affect the amount of protection afforded and those which are virtually equivalent to a reduction in duties can seldom be clearly drawn in practice; and measures taken ostensibly to remove unnecessary severities (for example, the institution of a duty-free improvement trade) often represent important reductions in tariffs.

We can distinguish two groups of measures: (a) measures to relieve trade, and especially transit trade, and (b) measures to free certain uses of goods from the burden of import duties, notably to free the export industries from the burden of duties upon their means of production. The reason for measures of the second group is that if the prices of means of production are raised to the export industries, and export thereupon ceases or is greatly diminished, the home producers of such means of production obtain no benefit therefrom. The same applies to an industry producing for the home market and using imported means of production, if a duty on the latter greatly diminishes the sales of the industry.

The first group of measures includes free ports, duty-free zones, and the permission for goods to enter and move across the country, under customs supervision, without paying duty. In favourably-situated places (such as a place where the journey is broken, a harbour, or a centre of trade or consumption) small Free Trade zones are created within the customs area. Here the goods can be brought, and transhipped or stored or repacked, and possibly worked up, without payment of duty, and subsequently exported to another country or to another Free Trade zone. A duty is levied only when the goods leave the free port or Free Trade zone (which may be under either public or private administration, but is always under the supervision of the customs authorities) to be sold upon the home market. All this in no way diminishes the protection afforded to home production, while it greatly relieves and promotes trade, and especially transit trade.

Measures of the second group relate mainly to the active and passive improvement trades. Under a duty-free active improvement trade, goods are permitted to be imported duty-free under the condition that they are not to be consumed at home but only to be worked up and re-exported in their more finished form. Thus,

1 A

for example, cloth is imported, is dyed or printed, and is then re-exported either to the country from which it came or to a third country. Provided that the home dyers or printers could not obtain this business if the imported cloth were subjected to duty or if they had to use the dearer home-produced cloth, there can be no objection against such a duty-free active improvement trade even from home cloth manufacturers who desire protection. But it often happens that the home producers (for example, of cloth) do lose orders, which they would otherwise get, from finishing industries working up similar goods imported free of duty to be sold abroad; and hence such exemptions from duties always give rise to disputes among the various parties concerned.

Under a duty-free passive improvement trade, home-produced goods which have been worked up abroad are permitted to be imported again in their finished form free of duty. The active improvement trade given above as an example is a passive improvement trade from the standpoint of the other countries from which the cloth was exported in order later to be imported again in its dyed or printed form.

Freedom from duties can be claimed for a passive improvement trade upon exactly analogous grounds to those relating to an active improvement trade, yet present-day Protectionist practice is far more favourable to the latter than to the former. In this respect, it is somewhat short-sighted, if not inconsistent. For if country A imposes hindrances upon a passive improvement trade, which is an active improvement trade from the standpoint of country B, then B is very likely to retaliate by placing difficulties in the way of an improvement trade which is passive for B but active for A. The natural solution is for the countries concerned to make reciprocal concessions, and, in fact, this often occurs.

There are also quite a number of other administrative and legal devices which may enable means of production to be imported duty-free for certain purposes, but these are of interest only from the administrative standpoint and present no new economic problems.

Another method of relieving export industries from the burden of duties upon their raw materials is *to refund the duties* when the (finished) goods are exported. But it is often very difficult to determine how much duty has been paid upon the raw materials embodied in exported goods, and this device, therefore, provides opportunities for concealed export bounties and subsidies.[4]

---

[4] We should also remark here that an export bounty under the name of a tax-refund is justified only in the case of a *special* tax. In this case the export

A special case of the refunding of duties is presented by the German import certificates for grain, which we have already discussed. The same kind of thing must come about if proofs are not demanded of the identity of the goods used in an improvement trade. Thus there may be an active improvement trade in which the goods said to be ' re '-exported, and for which the exporters receive an alleged ' refund ' of duties, are not identical with those which have been imported, in a cruder form, to be worked up. In such a case it may happen that the goods enter one part of the country and *other* units of these goods (in a more finished form) are exported from another part of the country. The improvement trade then brings about, in effect, a lowering of duties upon goods imported into one part of the country and an export bounty upon similar (finished) goods exported from another part. It is easy to justify the reduction of duties upon the goods imported. But it is not at all clear why this should be linked with virtual export bounties, which tend to divert production from its natural locations to locations nearer the export markets.

§ 8. The Concept of ' the Height of a Tariff ' and the Methods of Measuring It.[5]

Those concerned with economic policy are frequently called upon to make a judgment as to the height of a tariff (in the sense of a tariff-wall). This nearly always involves a comparison between the height of the tariff in one country and in another, or between the height of the tariff in a given country at two different points of time.

But the attempt to prove such a judgment as to the comparative height of a given tariff, and to express it in an exact numerical form, must face the greatest difficulties. These are not only of a technical statistical kind. They also arise from the fact that the concept ' the height of a tariff ' proves on examination to be by no means clear and unambiguous.

Attempts have been made to measure the height of a tariff wall by the percentage of the total imports which consists of imports subject to duty. But the decisive objection to this method is obvious. The more closely a duty approaches the level at which it

---

bounty compensates for an interference with international competitive relations. The refund of a *general* turnover tax (such as many countries impose) simply resembles a general export bounty.

[5] Literature : Loveday, " The Measurement of Tariff Levels " in *Journal of the Royal Statistical Society* (1929), vol. 92, reprinted in *Britain and World Trade* (1931); *Memorandum on Tariff Level Indices* prepared by the League of Nations (1927); *Survey of Overseas Markets* (Balfour Committee) (1925), p. 543; Crawford, " Tariff Level Indices " in *Economic Record* (1934), vol. 10.

becomes prohibitive, the smaller will be the percentage of the total imports formed by imports subject to this duty. A country which has only prohibitive duties, allowing free entry to goods not subject to these duties, will have an extremely low tariff wall as measured by this method. Thus the figures given in the Statistical Abstracts of the United States show that under the Fordney MacCumber tariff of 1922 the share of total retained imports formed by duty-free imports from 1923 to 1931 was on the average 64 per cent., whereas from 1898 to 1909, under a much lower tariff, this share was only 45 per cent.

The same objection applies to the methods, frequently used, of measuring the height of the general level of a tariff by the average burden of import duties upon the total imports. These methods take the percentage of the total value of all imports, or of the total value of all imports subject to duty, which is formed by the sums paid in import duties, as the measure or index of relative height. They also have the absurd result that prohibitive duties do not affect the index obtained. As judged by these methods, England in 1925 (on account of her high revenue duties) had a higher tariff than Italy or Germany! Again, to take another example, the average duty-burden upon American imports averaged, according to this method, 13.70 per cent. from 1926 to 1930 as against 23 per cent. from 1906 to 1910. A similar result is obtained if the receipts from duties are expressed as a share not of the total value of imports but of the total value of imports subject to duty (40 per cent. 1926 to 1930 as against 42.86 per cent. 1906 to 1910).

In order to avoid these ridiculous results, other methods have been adopted. These all rest upon the following principle. Data are collected for as many goods as possible—ideally for every good which is subject to a duty—showing the amount of the duty as a percentage of the value of the good subjected to the duty. This involves converting specific duties into *ad valorem* duties for purposes of reckoning. An average is then taken which shows the average percentage of the value which is taken in duty. In the case of tariffs which apply a uniform *ad valorem* rate of duty—for example, in the case of the present Dutch tariff which imposes, apart from a few exceptions, a uniform and general *ad valorem* duty of 10 per cent.—there is no need to compute such an average. It will be seen that the methods under discussion endeavour to represent an assortment of different duties, some *ad valorem* and some specific, by an index showing the uniform general *ad valorem* rate to which the assortment is about equivalent.

In carrying out such computations, a number of different possibilities and problems present themselves. These can be solved only if one is completely clear as to the aim which the computations are intended to achieve.

I leave on one side the technical statistical difficulties. For example, it is often very difficult to convert a specific duty into an *ad valorem* duty, since the value of the good is not known or since there is not a uniform market price, the specific duty covering a range of different qualities and, therefore, of different values. For this reason, and also on account of the very large number of different goods which enter into international trade and the great specialisation of modern tariff schedules, it is necessary to select a limited number of goods from which to derive an index. The computation of the Austrian National Committee of the International Chamber of Commerce[6] covers 402 goods; that of the League of Nations is restricted to 78 goods.

In computing the burden of a duty upon a particular good, one must choose as a basis its price in either the exporting or the importing country. But there is always the difficulty that the duty influences the price. Thus the importance of a given duty will vary with the elasticity of supply and of demand in both the exporting and the importing country. Again, every duty must not be allowed to have the same influence upon the resulting average. Clearly, for example, a duty on steel is more important than a duty on mustard. A weighted average must be constructed. This raises the question of the basis upon which different weights are to be assigned to different duties. One possible basis is the share of the good in the total imports of the country or countries in question. Another is its share in the total exports. Another is its share in the volume of world trade. Another is its share in the volume of production of one or more countries. But, whichever of these bases is chosen, the difficulty remains that the size of this share will be decisively influenced by the height of the duty.

How is one to select the goods which are to enter into the computation of the index? Here, again, there is quite a number of possibilities. Should the goods be chosen only from those imported by the country in question? If so, then as soon as any duty becomes prohibitive it ceases to influence the index. Another possibility is to select instead of goods imported into one country goods exported from another; or, again, one could choose the goods which have most importance in world trade.

A grave objection against the whole method is that once a duty

6 *Zollhöhe und Warenwerte* (1927).

has exceeded the level at which it becomes prohibitive any further increase in it is irrelevant. And one duty may reach this level when it is, say, 20 per cent. *ad valorem* and another when it is, say, 200 per cent. *ad valorem*. A further point is that the effectiveness of duties ' of equal height ' varies between different countries owing to their different economic structures.

In order to answer all the questions which we have raised in the preceding paragraphs and to decide which of the various possibilities shall be adopted, one must be clear as to exactly what one wishes to measure. This means defining in other words what one understands by ' the comparative height of a tariff wall.' It is obviously not enough to reduce the various duties to one uniform *ad valorem* duty. Moreover, even if, for example, country A imposes a uniform *ad valorem* duty of 40 per cent. upon all its imports and country B imposes a uniform *ad valorem* duty of 50 per cent. upon all its imports, it would be rash to assume that the tariff wall of country B is unconditionally to be regarded as the more protective of the two. For it may be that the imports of A react far more strongly to a tariff of 40 per cent. than those of B react to a tariff of 50 per cent.

Thus one must decide exactly what is to be established or indicated by such a proposed index. Is the index to be merely a kind of shorthand note of the trade policies of different countries? If one wishes to form a judgment as to the extent of the divergence caused by a tariff wall from the situation which would prevail under the policy of Free Trade, this is not enough. In that case, one must not rely only upon the height of the tariff wall as measured by a value-percentage; one must also take account of the effectiveness of the tariff wall, and this varies with the different circumstances of different countries. Mr. Loveday holds the view that it is completely false to assume that a tariff-index can and should provide a measure of the amount of protection thereby ensured by a State to its agriculture and industry.[7] He proposes to approach the problem from the standpoint of the exporting, and not of the protected, country. The tariff-index should measure not the relative degree of protection but the relative degree of obstruction.[8] It must be conceded that the amount by which imports are curtailed is not necessarily a measure of the effectiveness of the tariff in protecting home production, since in certain circumstances the tariff may lead merely to a reduction in consumption. Nevertheless, the degree of obstruction imposed upon imports depends not only upon

---

[7] *Journal of the Royal Statistical Society* (1929), vol. 92, pt. 4, p. 513.
[8] *Ibid.*, pp. 493-4.

the height of the tariff but also upon the elasticity of supply and demand—and these are circumstances which the methods of computing a tariff-index, considered above, do not take into account. Indeed, from this standpoint it is, strictly speaking, insufficient to compute only *one* tariff-index for a given country. It often happens that the tariff of a given country strikes severely imports coming from certain countries whilst leaving imports from other countries undisturbed. For example, before England adopted Protection in 1932, she might well have been regarded as a country with high Protection from the standpoint of Switzerland, since her few but fairly high protective duties (the MacKenna and Safeguarding duties) happened to apply to precisely those goods which Switzerland exported. Thus one should really compute for each country a whole series of tariff-indexes, one for each country from which it imports. Recognising this fact, the British computations (in the Blue Book of 1904 and in the Survey of Overseas Markets of 1925) rightly confine themselves to giving an average of the tariffs of the most important countries upon *British* exports. The computation of the League of Nations endeavours to determine an *international* index for every country. Whether such an international index has any practical value depends upon the extent of the dispersion of the individual indexes. A judgment as to the extent to which the various indexes (compiled for different purposes) are capable of being united and therefore expressed by one figure can be formed only upon the basis of statistical experiments. Hitherto such a basis has been completely lacking.

CHAPTER XX.

COMMERCIAL TREATIES: THE FACTS.

§ 1. CONTENT AND FORM.

Commercial treaties may cover a very wide range of subjects. They may relate to: the rights and competence of consular representatives; the establishment of foreign firms and the status of foreign commercial travellers; legal and police protection for foreigners and their property; the execution of legal judgments; the protection of patents, trade-marks, copyright, and so on; import duties and other taxes and charges upon imports; customs formalities; veterinary regulations concerning the import of cattle; the rights and treatment of foreign ships in home harbours; freight rates and regulations applied by railways and other means of transport. We may group all such subjects under the four heads of (a) consular matters, (b) rights of foreigners, (c) transport questions, and (d) tariff and trade questions.

In the course of development, the economic relations between States have become more and more complex, and it has therefore become usual to regulate certain matters (such as questions of copyright, of double taxation, and of legal aid) by special agreements. A tendency has also come about to reserve the expression 'commercial treaties' for agreements on *tariff questions*. We, too, shall use it in this sense, unless otherwise stated.

Concerning the form of commercial treaties, we need mention only the distinction between *bilateral* treaties (between two countries) and *multilateral* treaties (sometimes known as collective agreements or International Conventions), between more than two countries. But it may happen that a whole series of treaties, each of which is formally bilateral, are the result of collective discussions and decisions, and all have the same content. In the realm of international trade, the following International Conventions, which have been concluded under the auspices of the League of Nations and ratified by numerous States, should be mentioned: Convention concerning the Freedom of Transit Trade (Barcelona, 1921); Convention for the Simplification of Customs Formalities (Geneva, 1923); Convention concerning the Transmission in Transit of Electric Power (Geneva, 1923). Many others have been planned, but have come to nothing—for example, the so-called

' Tariff Truce,' an International Convention to stabilise tariffs for two years (Geneva, 1931). The sole example of an important and successful collective agreement about tariff matters was the Brussels Sugar Convention of 1902.

As to the methods by which States pledge themselves in commercial treaties to maintain a certain relation with one another, an important distinction is to be drawn between *direct* and *indirect* methods. Examples of *direct* methods of fixing the treatment to be given to foreign citizens and goods are, in general terms, as follows. One State may agree that the consul of a foreign State shall have such and such rights and obligations; or that a foreign firm must fulfil such and such conditions in order to have the right to establish itself; or that an import duty of such and such an amount will be imposed upon such and such a good coming from the country with which the treaty is made. *Indirect* methods consist in laying down a measure or yardstick by which the treatment accorded to the other party is to be regulated. Three such measures are customary and each of these has its corresponding Treaty Clause: *the Parity Clause, the Reciprocity Clause*, and *the Most Favoured Nation Clause*. Under the *Parity Clause*,[10] the treatment given by a State to the citizens and goods of the State with which the treaty is made must not be worse than that given to its own citizens. Under the *Reciprocity Clause*,[1] this treatment must correspond to, or at least must not be worse than, that given to the citizens and goods of the State in question by the other State. Under the *Most Favoured Nation Clause*, this treatment must not be worse than that given to any third country. The three clauses may be combined, in which case the other State can choose whichever of the three measures is most favourable to it. Thus, for example, if both Parity and Most Favoured Nation treatments are agreed upon, the one State must not treat the citizens of the other worse than its own and it must also give them any privileges which it accords to citizens of any third State.

In the treatment of foreign nationals, for example in the rights of actual and legal persons before the law, civilised countries as a rule content themselves with being placed on an equal footing with the home country. But exceptions are not infrequent. Either (a) foreigners are treated *worse* than home nationals, the latter, for example, receiving preference in certain occupations, or (b) the foreigners receive *better* treatment in certain respects than home nationals: this is especially frequent in treaties between civilised and backward countries.

---

10 Also sometimes called *formal* reciprocity.
1 Also sometimes called *material* reciprocity.

We now turn to trade policy in the narrower sense of tariff policy. In this sphere, naturally, little use is made of the Parity Clause, since it is the object of tariffs to discriminate between home and foreign supply, and it is the Most Favoured Nation Clause which has by far the greatest importance. There is very seldom a reciprocity *clause* in commercial treaties, although in the concluding and interpretation of treaties the reciprocity *principle* plays an important part.

We can divide commercial treaties in the narrower sense—that is, those which concern the imposition of import duties and their height—into *pure Most Favoured Nation Treaties* and *Tariff Treaties*. Under the former, a State binds itself not to impose any higher duties upon goods coming from the other State than it imposes upon similar goods coming from any third country. Under the latter, the concrete provisions of particular tariffs are stated: for example, the import duty on butter must not be more than so many shillings a hundredweight. But most tariff treaties also include a Most Favoured Nation Clause. Under a pure Most Favoured Nation treaty, the amounts of the import duties are left to the autonomous decision of the State which imposes them, but every reduction in duties which it grants to a third country it must grant also to any country with which it has such a treaty.

§ 2. The Content and Forms of the Most Favoured Nation Clause.

1. Introductory.—The European States began as early as the seventeenth century to include the Most Favoured Nation Clause in their commercial treaties. As time went on, it became more and more customary to do this; several different variants of the Clause were introduced, but by the second half of the eighteenth century scarcely a commercial treaty was concluded without the Clause being either expressly stated in one or other of its forms or implied in the text.

No other feature of commercial treaties is so much discussed and so hotly disputed both in legal and economic writings and by politicians and publicists as the Most Favoured Nation Clause. Some see in it a guarantee of peace and a symbol of a liberal trade policy; others regard it as an obstacle to reductions of duties; and yet others attack it on the ground that it prevents an increase of duties.[2]

---

[2] A large part of the literature on the subject is to be found in treatises on international law and law-journals. The most important monographs are: Glier, *Die Meistbegünstigungsklausel. Eine entwicklungsgeschichtliche Studie*, Berlin

2. UNCONDITIONAL AND CONDITIONAL MOST FAVOURED NATION TREATMENT.

—When a State binds itself not to give worse treatment to imports from another State than it gives to imports from any third State, this obligation can be interpreted in two ways. It can mean either (a) that the other State receives any concession, such as reduction in duties, which the first State grants to any third, immediately and automatically and without any special reciprocal concession or (b) that it receives such a concession only if it grants to the first State the same concession, or an equally valuable one, as that granted as a *quid pro quo* by the third State to the first. Most Favoured Nation treatment is unconditional if interpreted in the former sense and conditional if interpreted in the latter sense. The unconditional sense is also referred to as the European interpretation, because European countries adopted it *de facto* as early as the first half of the nineteenth century and after 1860 adopted it explicitly and without any exceptions. The Government of the United States made the conditional interpretation its own and until 1922, with only insignificant exceptions, held to it. President Wilson included a demand for unconditional Most Favoured Nation treatment in his famous fourteen points, but it was not until 1922 that the United States suddenly changed over to the unconditional form. Thereafter it defended this form with as much conviction and zeal as it had previously shown in defending the conditional form.[3] As an example of the unconditional Most Favoured Nation Clause, we may quote the following extract from article 7 of the Commercial Treaty between the United States and Germany, signed 8th December, 1923, and ratified in 1925, but now no longer in force.

" Each of the High Contracting Parties binds itself unconditionally to impose no higher or other duties or conditions and no prohibition on the importation of any article, the growth, produce or manufacture of the territories of the other than are or shall be imposed on the importation of any like article, the growth, produce or manufacture of any other foreign country.

" Each of the High Contracting Parties also binds itself unconditionally to impose no higher or other charges or other restrictions or prohibitions on goods

(1905); Hornbeck, *The Most Favoured Nation Clause in Commercial Treaties*, Madison, U.S.A. (1910); Mazzei, *Politica doganale differenziale e clausola della nazione più favorita* (1930), vol. 1; Riedl, *Exceptions to the Most Favoured Nation Treatment* (1931); U.S. Tariff Commission, *Reciprocity and Commercial Treaties* (1919); Arndt, *Die Zweckmässigkeit des Systems der Meistbegünstigung* (1901); Lusensky, *Unbeschränkte gegen beschränkte Meistbegünstigung* (1908); Viner, " The most favoured nation clause in American commercial treaties," *Journal of Political Economy* (Feb. 1924); Viner, " The most favoured nation clause " in ' *Index* ' (Stockholm, Jan. 1931), vol. 6; G. Haberler and Verosta, *Liberale und Planwirtschaftliche Handelspolitik* (1934). *Louise Sommer, Neugestaltung der Handelspolitik. Wege zu einem intereuropäischen Präferenzsystem* (1935) (contains an extensive bibliography).

[3] The conditional form was also frequently inserted in European treaties in the first half of the eighteenth century. But it was never applied with logical completeness and therefore, for reasons to be given presently, it was ineffective.

exported to the territories of the other High Contracting Party than are imposed on goods exported to any other foreign country.

" Any advantage of whatsoever kind which either High Contracting Party may extend to any article, the growth, produce, or manufacture of any other foreign country shall simultaneously and unconditionally, without request and without compensation, be extended to the like article, the growth, produce or manufacture of the other High Contracting country . . .

" With respect to the amount and collection of duties on imports and exports of every kind, each of the two High Contracting Parties binds itself to give to the nationals, vessels and goods of the other the advantage of every favour, privilege or immunity which it shall have accorded to the nationals, vessels and goods of a third State, and regardless of whether such favoured State shall have been accorded such treatment gratuitously or in return for reciprocal compensatory treatment. Every such favour, privilege or immunity which shall hereafter be granted the nationals, vessels or goods of a third State shall simultaneously and unconditionally, without request and without compensation, be extended to the other High Contracting Party, for the benefit of itself, its nationals and vessels."[4]

Under the Most Favoured Nation Clause, therefore, every reduction in duties which one State grants to another is immediately extended to all those States which stand in a Most Favoured Nation position towards the first one. The Most Favoured Nation Clause thereby establishes a nexus between all the commercial treaties of a country; and, if the country applies it universally (which hitherto has nearly always happened), gives it one tariff level which applies to imports from every other country. (The exceptions to this rule will be considered under point 4 and its economic advantages in the following chapter.)

Until 1922 the United States held firmly to the conditional interpretation. It took the standpoint that it could not permit every country to which it had granted Most Favoured Nation status to benefit, without doing anything in return, from every favour which the United States granted to a third country in return for a reciprocal concession. Such another country could receive a similar favour from the United States only if it paid the same price as the third country. Moreover, the United States insisted upon stating this interpretation clearly in black and white. Their very first commercial treaty, that with France in 1778, contained the conditional formulation of the Most Favoured Nation Clause; and article IX of the Treaty of 1828 between the United States and Prussia, which remained in force until the World War, declares that if in the future one of the contracting parties shall grant any favour to any other nation without receiving a reciprocal compensatory concession, the same favour shall be granted to the

---

[4] The older formulations were much simpler. Countries were constrained to adopt more and more complicated formulations owing to their unpleasant experiences with States with whom they had made treaties : these States had tried to avoid their obligations by adopting a restricted interpretation of the Clause.

other contracting party, but that if the other nation makes such a concession as the price of this favour, then the other contracting party shall enjoy the favour upon payment of the same price.

The American interpretation led to continued diplomatic disputes,[5] for three reasons. *First*, the United States insisted upon applying the conditional interpretation even when the relevant treaties were not unambiguously expressed in this form. *Secondly*, the concept of a reciprocal compensatory concession which was ' the same or of equal value ' was open to many interpretations. Suppose that country A lowered its steel duties to country B upon condition that country B lowered its wheat duties to country A. Suppose, further, that country C has a Most Favoured Nation treaty with country A. Is C justified in demanding the same reduction in steel duties from A upon condition that C grants A the same reduction in its wheat duties as B has granted A? What if there is no export of wheat from A to C? Or what if C has already reduced its wheat duties, before the arrangement between A and B was made? What other reduction in duties by C would be equal in value to A to the reduction in the wheat duties of B? Obviously it is for A to decide whether it considers a concession to be of equal value, and whether or not it can enforce its view will depend upon its political and economic power. Hence the conditional Most Favoured Nation Clause is to be regarded, from a juristic standpoint, only as a ' *pactum de contrahendo*,' as an obligation to enter into negotiations with the other contracting party. In practice the conditional Most Favoured Nation Clause means little more than a refusal to grant Most Favoured Nation treatment at all.

Thirdly, inconveniences arose because a country which had both conditional and unconditional Most Favoured Nation treaties was bound to feel itself at a disadvantage relatively to those countries with which it had treaties of the former kind. For the conditional clause has the peculiarity that it leads to just the same results as the unconditional clause unless it is included in *all* the commercial treaties which a country makes. For example, Germany had numerous unconditional Most Favoured Nation treaties with other European States, in addition to the conditional one (of 1828) with the United States. Thus, for example, she granted unconditional Most Favoured Nation status to France in the often-quoted article XI of the Peace of Frankfort. Suppose that Germany granted a reduction of duties to Austria in return for a reciprocal concession. France, by virtue of her unconditional

---

5 *Cf. Reciprocity and Commercial Treaties.*

Most Favoured Nation status, had the right to the same reduction without giving Germany anything in return. But if Germany gave France such a concession for nothing, then the United States by virtue of her conditional Most Favoured Nation relation to Germany, would also have the right to it for nothing. Thus the United States enjoyed *de facto* unconditional Most Favoured Nation status towards the European countries, whilst she herself granted only conditional Most Favoured Nation status.[6] The Free Trade countries especially must have found it unfair to be treated worse, because they had nothing to offer as a reciprocal concession, by the United States than Protectionist countries which continued to -place great obstacles in the way of American exports even after they had made some relatively small reductions in their duties upon American goods.

3. The So-called Reciprocity Treaties.—A number of so-called reciprocity treaties were concluded by the United States, before it abandoned the conditional interpretation of the Most Favoured Nation Clause. Before the unconditional interpretation became supreme in Europe, reciprocity treaties were concluded there also. The Treaties of Sardinia, concluded under the gifted leadership of Cavour from 1838 to 1851, and based upon the conditional interpretation, are a famous example.

Reciprocity treaties, in the sense spoken of here, are tariff treaties in which two States grant one another tariff reductions without the intention of allowing other States to share automatically in these reductions. In this respect they differ from tariff treaties based upon the unconditional Most Favoured Nation Clause, which became generally accepted in Europe after 1860.

The United States concluded such Reciprocity Treaties with Canada in 1854, with Hawaii in 1875, with various European and South American States in 1890 and 1897 and with Cuba in 1902. (This last is still in force.) In 1910-11 she endeavoured to enter into a reciprocity relation with Canada; the Canadian Government and the American Congress reached a complete agreement, in the form of parallel legislation to come into force simultaneously in the two countries, but the Canadian Parliament refused to sanction it.

These agreements, which are grouped together under the name of Reciprocity Treaties, differ considerably from one another. Some of them—for example, those with Canada, Hawaii, and Cuba—

---

[6] Viner has pointed out that it would be possible to rule out such a result by using an appropriate formulation of the Most Favoured Nation Clause. But, so far as I am aware, this has never happened.

definitely forbade either of the contracting parties to extend the concessions it made therein to any third State, even if the third State was prepared to give in return the same reciprocal concessions as those given by the other contracting party. The very threadbare legal grounds for such a prohibition are usually that every country is unique in its geographical situation and other relevant characteristics, so that it is impossible for a third country to offer concession of equal value.

The treaty with Cuba is a normal preference treaty. In the more recent American commercial treaties, the tariff reductions granted by the United States to Cuba are always expressly excluded from the operation of the Most Favoured Nation Clause. One should therefore speak not of reciprocity, but of exemptions from the Most Favoured Nation Clause.

RECIPROCITY CLAUSES IN AMERICAN TARIFF LEGISLATION.—We should say a few words about the so-called contingent duties, often incorrectly termed ' countervailing duties,' of America. The American tariff laws of 1922 and 1930 contain a pure Reciprocity Clause. § 369 of the ' Fordney-Macumber ' Tariff of 1922 declares that there shall be a general import duty upon automobiles of 25 per cent. *ad valorem*, but that if any country imposes a higher import duty than 25 per cent. upon American automobiles, the same higher duty shall be imposed by America upon automobiles imported from that country. Similar provisions apply to a number of other goods. These Reciprocity Clauses are without doubt contrary to the Most Favoured Nation principle, in either its unconditional or its conditional form. Moreover, they are a very unsuitable means of applying the Reciprocity notion, since as a rule two countries are not both equally interested in taxing the import of the same good : a country which imports American automobiles will probably have no interest in the American tariff upon automobiles.

4. RESTRICTIONS UPON AND EXCEPTIONS TO THE MOST FAVOURED NATION CLAUSE.—In addition to the distinction between the conditional and the unconditional form of the Clause, there is a distinction between *unilateral* and *bilateral* Most Favoured Nation agreements, depending upon whether the obligation to give Most Favoured Nation treatment is binding upon one or both of the parties to the contract. As is well known, the Treaty of Versailles contained a unilateral undertaking by Germany to give Most Favoured Nation treatment to the Allies for five years.

There is a further distinction between *restricted* and *unrestricted* Most Favoured Nation agreements, depending upon whether they apply to all matters (rights of foreigners, heights of duties, veterinary regulations, and so on) and to all countries, or are limited to certain matters, goods, and countries. Professor Schüller distinguishes between the restriction of the content of a Most Favoured Nation agreement, when it does not cover all matters or *topics* and restrictions in its *ambit*, when it does not cover all States. Thus, for example, the Most Favoured Nation agreement concluded between Germany and France in article XI of the Peace of Frankfort was formally restricted to those concessions which France or Germany granted to one of the following States: England, Belgium, Holland, Switzerland, Austria, and Russia.

Of course, it is open to the contracting States to insert whatever limitations they wish into a Most Favoured Nation agreement and to state exceptions to it. As a rule two kinds of exceptions, which could almost be held to be implied in any such agreement, are explicitly stated. The first relates to the small trade of the frontier districts. The inhabitants of these districts may bring small quantities of goods across the frontier either duty-free or upon payment of reduced duties, without a third State having the right to claim the same concessions by virtue of its Most Favoured Nation status. The second relates to the possible future formation of a *complete Customs Union*. If such a Union is formed, no third State can claim that duties should be abolished upon its goods also.[7]

In recent years there has been lively discussion as to the treatment of an *incomplete* Customs Union. When two countries with high tariffs form a Customs Union, one cannot expect them to abolish at one stroke their duties on one another's goods. They are far more likely to reduce them by stages, for example by 10 per cent. yearly, as Belgium and Holland have agreed to do in the Treaty of Ouchy of 1932.[8] The 1931 proposal for a Customs Union between Germany and Austria also provided for the gradual reduction of duties during a period of transition. During such a period, which may be quite a long one, there are two possible interpretations of the legal position. The reduced duties between the two countries may be regarded either as constituting *an incomplete Customs Union* and paving the way for a complete one, or as *preferential duties*. Under the former interpretation, a third State has no right to claim similar treatment by virtue of its Most Favoured Nation status, but under the latter interpretation it has this right.

From a purely legal standpoint the latter interpretation must be adopted as the one which corresponds to the text of the treaty: otherwise every preferential reduction of duties could be declared to constitute the first step towards a complete Customs Union and in that way Most Favoured Nation obligations could be avoided. But in reality the problem is not one of positive law

---

[7] Whether an *express* provision must be made for each of these two cases is disputable. In fact, it is very frequently made and, even when not explicitly stated, is universally acknowledged.

[8] Which never came in force mainly because Great Britain objected on the basis of its most-favoured-nation rights.

but one of *lege ferenda*. Is it more helpful to hinder the formation of Customs Unions by a strict interpretation of the Most Favoured Nation Clause or to help their formation by permitting exceptions to the Clause? If it were made possible for one country to grant preferential duties to another and, by declaring that they formed the first steps towards a Customs Union, to avoid extending them to third States, would this possibility be abused? Once these questions have been decided, the corresponding interpretation of the Most Favoured Nation Clause can be applied, and, if necessary, the text of the treaty can be altered or disregarded, provided that the relative political strength of the parties concerned permits such a course. We shall deal with the economic considerations in the following chapter.

A number of regional exceptions to the Most Favoured Nation Clause have long been customary and accepted. A number of States make provision in their commercial treaties for granting special advantages to countries with which they are closely linked by special geographical, political, historical, and economic ties, without being obliged by their Most Favoured Nation agreements to extend such advantages to other countries. The Scandinavian countries form a closely-linked group of this kind, the Russian border States insert the so-called ' Baltic Clause ' in their treaties, the United States reserves the right to grant preferential duties to Cuba, and so on.

But the most important reservations of this kind are those made by the countries of the British Empire—Great Britain and her Dominions—for the benefit of their mutual economic relations, and those which have always been made to cover colonial possessions. The British treaties declare that imports from the other contracting party shall not receive less favourable treatment than similar imports from any other foreign country. The reservation lies in the word ' foreign.' British Dominions, Colonies, Protectorates, and Mandated Territories come under British rule and are not foreign countries.

THE PREFERENTIAL TARIFFS OF THE BRITISH EMPIRE.—Until the middle of last century, when England ceased to be Protectionist, her tariff schedules provided for preferential duties upon imports from her colonies, and the tariff schedules of her colonies made similar provision for imports from England. When she abolished her duties on corn in 1846, her preferential treatment of Canadian wheat automatically lapsed. In 1860 the last tariff preference granted by a colony to Great Britain was removed, and during the next forty years Great Britain enjoyed no preferential tariff treatment from her colonies.

Canada was the first country to establish once more preferential duties for Great Britain. She began in 1897 by granting a general reciprocal tariff, with duties an eighth lower than those of her general tariff, which applied to Great Britain, New South Wales, and British India. In the following year Canada

N

changed her tariff law. In addition to a general tariff and to a reciprocal tariff which she applied to *all* countries which gave her tariff favours, she instituted a preferential tariff exclusively for goods imported from the Empire; the reductions granted to Great Britain represented at first 25 per cent. and later 33⅓ per cent. of her general tariff. Preferential duties were also granted to British goods by New Zealand and South Africa in 1903 and by Australia in 1905.

Until the post-War period the Dominions granted a one-sided preference to Great Britain, since she admitted nearly all goods duty-free. But during the War Great Britain made many departures from her Free Trade system, and at the Imperial War Conference of 1917 the Dominions expressed the wish that she should give preferential treatment to their goods. In 1919 she did so, reducing her duties upon tea, coffee, cocoa, sugar, tobacco, and other similar imports by one-sixth and upon goods subject to the recently-imposed 'MacKenna Duties' by one-third, if they came from her Dominions or Colonies. After the stabilisation of the pound her preferential duties on sugar and a number of other goods were revised. In general, the preferential duties were a third lower than the general ones. Preferential treatment was given to finished goods only when at least 25 per cent. of their value was due to labour expended upon them within the Empire.

Conversely, in the post-War period all the Dominions and other members of the British Empire granted preferential duties to the mother country. In order. to get the benefit of this preference, a good had to derive either the whole or at least a minimum percentage (varying from 25 to 75) of its value from Empire labour and raw materials. The preferential reduction represented up to 50 per cent. of the general duties.

England's departure from Free Trade in 1932 led to a further expansion of this system of preferences. At the noteworthy Imperial Economic Conference held at Ottawa in August, 1932, both Great Britain and the Dominions pledged themselves to grant far-reaching preferential treatment. A new feature, and one of the greatest significance, was that Great Britain bound herself not only to refrain from raising a number of her duties upon Dominion products but also *to refrain from lowering* a number of her duties upon foreign products and to impose certain duties upon foreign products—foreign products being, of course, those coming from countries outside the British Empire.

THE MOST FAVOURED NATION CLAUSE AND IMPORT QUOTAS.—An interesting controversy has been aroused as to the legal claims of countries enjoying Most Favoured Nation status relatively to a country which subjects a good to an import quota. No definite practical solution has yet been reached, since the imposition of import quotas by the civilised countries whose practice constitutes international law based on custom was not sufficiently frequent before the present period of depression. But the International Chamber of Commerce has considered the question and has proposed various solutions : for example, that import quotas of equal size should be granted to all countries enjoying Most Favoured Nation status, or that the quotas granted to the various States should bear the same relation to one another as did their respective shares in the total imports of the country in question before it imposed quotas. But it is most unlikely that a method can be found which all will accept as correct, and it is to be hoped that the pernicious system of import quotas will quickly disappear, and that therefore there will be no need to find a definite solution of this question.

Another disputed point is whether the Most Favoured Nation Clause permits anti-dumping duties. Viner,[9] after a long discussion, in the course of which he refers to legal writings on the subject, comes to the conclusion that, unless the contrary is stated, one contracting party has *not* the right to impose anti-dumping duties upon the goods of the other contracting party to a Most Favoured

---

[9] *Dumping*, pp. 298 *et seq.*

Nation agreement unless it imposes them also upon imports from other countries. This view is supported by the practical consideration that experience shows countries to be very ready to seize upon the pretext of dumping and that proofs and counter-proofs are often very difficult to produce. An exception can perhaps be made for 'equalising' or 'countervailing' duties to offset export bounties given by foreign countries. Such duties would induce countries to cease granting export bounties.

CHAPTER XXI.

COMMERCIAL TREATIES: APPRAISAL OF THE VARIOUS SYSTEMS.

§ 1. THE COMMERCIAL TREATIES OF FREE TRADE COUNTRIES.

This chapter attempts to judge the value, from an economic and political standpoint, of the various systems of commercial-treaty policy.

Nobody disputes that the most suitable trade policy for Free Trade countries is the Most Favoured Nation system. Free Trade countries can conclude no tariff treaties, as they have no compensatory concessions to offer—they can only threaten to abandon Free Trade. They must try to conclude at any rate Most Favoured Nation treaties, to prevent other countries from discriminating against them. England was in this position during her Free Trade period, and she is still, together with the United States, the leading advocate of the unconditional and unrestricted Most Favoured Nation Clause.[1] She has managed to obtain Most Favoured Nation treatment for all her exports, with only unimportant exceptions. For this success she has to thank mainly her political strength; but it is partly due also to the fact that other countries cannot ignore the argument that it would be unjust to give worse treatment to a country which places no obstacles in the way of their exports than they give to a country whose only merit is that it has made a small reduction in its high protective tariffs.

§ 2. THE SYSTEM OF RIGID TARIFFS.

A number of countries refuse upon principle to make the height of their tariffs dependent upon agreements with other States. The appropriate treaty policy for such countries, just as much as for Free Trade countries, is that of pure Most Favoured Nation agreements. For example, since 1922 the United States has taken the stand that her tariff schedule is to be determined solely by the needs, as she conceives them, of *her own* economy; and she has avoided hampering herself by tariff treaties from erecting

---

[1] But this in no way prevents her from excluding the preferential tariffs of the British Empire from her Most Favoured Nation agreements.

an ever higher tariff wall. She has thus become a convinced adherent of the unconditional and unrestricted Most Favoured Nation Clause.[2] She ensures all countries 'equal rights'; she does not discriminate but treats all equally, which means equally *badly;* but she in turn demands full equality of treatment[3] from all other countries. The Tariff Law of 1922 (section 117) commands and fully empowers the President of the United States to retaliate, by means of tariff increases and import prohibitions, against any country which discriminates in any way against the trade of the United States.

It must be conceded that there is a great deal to be said for this principle of neither seeking nor granting any special advantage. If tariffs are regarded as unavoidable, then without doubt equality of treatment is beneficial in maintaining peace and good relations between States, for without such equality innumerable potential causes of conflict would arise. It is of especial and vital importance for small countries that the world should keep, at least in principle, to this policy. If a short-sighted policy of discriminating treatment came into fashion, the small and weak countries, who cannot offer such important economic concessions as the large ones and who have not sufficient political influence to prevent others from discriminating against them, would suffer heavy loss. Nevertheless, as we shall show very soon, the principle of unconditional Most Favoured Nation treatment is in no way incompatible, despite the widespread opinion to the contrary in America, with the conclusion of tariff treaties.

A further advantage of the unconditional Most Favoured Nation system, provided that its application is universal, is that a country has one and the same duty upon any given import, whatever its source. Thus it becomes superfluous to furnish the customs authorities with proofs of origin, and the collection of duties is thereby greatly simplified and cheapened. Nobody who knows the bureau-

---

2 The policy inaugurated in 1922 is very understandable if one remembers her very unfortunate experience with the system of conditional Most Favoured Nation treatment. A further reason for the policy is that, owing to the permanent antagonism between President and Congress, together with other difficulties arising from her Constitution and from her internal political circumstances, it is unusually difficult for her to conclude tariff treaties with other States. In 1934, President Roosevelt was given special powers to conclude trade agreements and to lower duties by not more than 5 per cent. He has made use of this in concluding a number of treaties—with Brazil, Belgium, Sweden—which brought substantial tariff reductions and contain the Most Favoured Nation Clause in its unconditional form.

3 When in 1922 the Secretary of State Charles Evans Hughes inaugurated this policy, the United States returned to the principle laid down by her first President, who said in his farewell address : " Our commercial policy should hold an equal and impartial hand; neither seeking nor granting exclusive favours or preferences . . . "

cratic system of certificates of origin, with all its accompaniments of chicanery and expense and evasion and recrimination, as it has broken out again in Europe during recent years of crisis, will hold this advantage cheap.

§ 3. TARIFF TREATIES AND THE PRINCIPLE OF EXCHANGING PARTICULAR TARIFF CONCESSIONS.

1. GENERAL REMARKS.—In most countries it has become usual not only to grant reciprocal Most Favoured Nation treatment but also to exchange concessions as to the height of particular duties. It may be that the contracting parties bind themselves not to raise their existing tariffs, or it may be that they agree to reduce particular duties enumerated in the Tariff Schedule attached to the Treaty.[4] The resulting reduction of duties may be *general*, all duties being reduced one or more times by a given percentage,[5] or *particular*, a number of duties, agreed upon in the course of the negotiations, being reduced by various percentages.

One aspect of the Protectionist development of the last fifty years is that countries have quite given up[6] the large-scale method of making general reductions. They now restrict themselves to exchanging a greater or smaller number of particular reductions in duties. Even so, they have become more and more niggardly. Duties are imposed for purposes of negotiation: that is to say, the existing level of duties is raised before negotiations are begun in order that it may not be reduced by the concessions which may be made; and the general level constantly rises. It has become increasingly more difficult to carry through negotiations, and substantial reductions in tariff-levels have become more and more rare. Indeed, very often the purpose of the negotiations is not in the least to obtain a reduction in tariff-levels but is, on the contrary, to obtain the consent of the other contracting

---

[4] We must here omit certain technical details arising out of the special circumstances of the contracting countries—their constitutional law, their political practice and so on. For example, many countries prefer to embody the concessions which they are prepared to make if absolutely necessary in a minimum tariff passed as a law by their Parliament, whilst others leave the Administration a free hand to negotiate whatever reductions in their duties it pleases, subject to ratification by their Parliament, and so on.

[5] Under the famous Cobden Treaty of 1860 between England and France, the latter bound herself to lower her duties to 30 per cent., and from 1864 to 25 per cent. *ad valorem*.

[6] The Treaty of Ouchy between Holland and Belgium (1932) is a happy exception. It contemplates a yearly reduction of 10 per cent. in the existing duties during five years, at the end of which time the duties will be half their original level. But the reduced duties are to be preferential duties : third States are *not* to benefit from them. The consent of all the Most Favoured Nation countries has not been obtained, and therefore the treaty has not come into force.

party to the raising of certain duties. Country A does not say to country B: " If you will give my export industries a chance by reducing these or those duties, then I am prepared in return to lower such and such duties." Instead, it says: " If you will permit me to increase such and such duties, although this is contrary to my obligations under our existing agreement, then I am prepared in return to make no protest if you increase a number of your duties, which you have pledged yourself not to increase."

Moreover, the length of time for which countries bind themselves has constantly shortened. The so-called Caprivi Treaty, concluded by Germany at the beginning of the nineties, and the Bülow Treaties, which she concluded in 1904 and 1905 with Belgium, Russia, Switzerland, Serbia, Italy, Austria-Hungary, and Bulgaria, all involved tariff obligations for ten to twelve years. After the War, the period was reduced to one to two years (only pure Most Favoured Nation agreements being concluded for a longer period than this) and the length of notice to be given before denouncing a treaty was at most three months, and often only two months or even one month. The consequent uncertainty and instability greatly accentuated the effects of tariffs in affording protection and causing economic loss. For naturally the risks of a large investment are multiplied if the products are destined partly for export and if the entrepreneur must reckon with the possibility that at any moment notice may be given that within a short time foreign duties upon them will be increased, and their export thereby rendered unprofitable.

2. THE PREVAILING TONE OF TARIFF NEGOTIATIONS.—It is now fifty to sixty years since Protection, after a brief interlude of Free Trade, again became dominant. Ever since then, countries have entered into tariff negotiations with the intention of securing as far-reaching reductions as possible in the duties of the other contracting party and sacrificing as little as possible of their own tariff. Each reduction of the latter is regarded as an evil and an economic burden which is worth while only if other countries reduce theirs to at least the same extent.

This outlook dominates not only in practice, but also in scientific discussions upon the appropriateness of the various methods and systems of tariff negotiation. With rare exceptions, such discussions try to answer the question of which system will permit a country to purchase the greatest possible reductions in foreign tariffs at the cost of the smallest possible ' sacrifice ' of her own. But this method of stating the question is completely false. It springs from the belief that one-sided Free Trade is economically impossible and that a tariff-level substantially below that of other countries is injurious; and this belief, as we have already shown,[7] is untenable. It is usually accompanied by the primitive mercantilist notion that concessions to foreign countries should be given only if the resulting increase of debits in the balance of payments is at least equalled by the resulting increase of credits.

Yet, if all these false notions are abandoned and if one accepts the fact that one-sided Free Trade is beneficial and that there is no need to worry about the balance of payments, it by no means follows that the whole problem ceases to exist, since there is no longer any purpose to be served by tariff negotiations. This is not so, for even countries which are in principle Free Trade must face the *tactical* problem of inducing their Protectionist neighbours to lower their duties. And one may well hold the view that a country wishing to achieve this aim will find duties of its own an appropriate instrument, always supposing that it is ready to remove them effectively when the right moment comes and—herein lies the difficulty of the situation—to keep them on in case of need.[8] (If a country is not prepared to keep them on if necessary, they lose their effectiveness as an instrument of bargaining.[8])

Thus a rational trade policy does not aim, in tariff negotiations, at obtaining as 'favourable a balance' as possible between reductions in its own duties and reductions in foreign duties. Its aim is to sell its own duties at as high a price as possible, in the sense of obtaining as far-reaching a reduction of foreign duties as possible in return for the removal or lowering of its own. The peculiarity of such an 'exchange' is that the surrender of its own exchange-object—the reduction of its own duties—is in reality *no* sacrifice.[9] The sacrifice or burden is borne only by a small section of interested

---

[7] Chap. xvii, § 1.

[8] If a country is not prepared to keep them on if necessary, they lose their effectiveness as an instrument of bargaining. The risk of being left ' sitting on the duties '—that is to say, the danger that the country overestimates the concessions which its neighbour is prepared to make if absolutely necessary and therefore demands a higher price than he is prepared to pay—of course will be appraised differently by the Free Trader and by the Protectionist. The latter may be secretly pleased if the negotiations break down and the blame can be placed upon the intractability of the other countries. The risk is especially great since even when duties are imposed solely for bargaining purposes it is very difficult to remove them, as interested parties will have become accustomed to the higher prices and will have invested capital in the protected industries, and so on. This makes it very easy to understand why many Free Traders wish to have nothing to do with retaliatory or bargaining duties. No conclusions of general validity can be laid down upon this point. Everything depends upon the concrete political and economic circumstances and upon the attitude of the persons responsible and the skill of the negotiators. History shows that now and then such duties have attained their object, but that on the whole they are to be regarded with mistrust and to be used only with caution.

[9] Abstracting from the hardships of the transition, which can be avoided or greatly softened by making it a gradual one.

parties for the benefit of their fellow-countrymen. It is the increase and not the reduction of duties which is the real economic burden!

If people realised all this, they would conduct negotiations for trade agreements in quite a different spirit. They would not be afraid of ' purchasing ' a reduction in foreign duties with a much greater reduction in their own; they would not cling as tightly as possible to every single duty; and they would spare themselves the pains of trying to solve the quite insoluble problem of how much reduction in their own duties is exactly equivalent to a given reduction in foreign duties.

Clearly negotiations undertaken in this spirit would achieve their end far more easily than negotiations which set out from false assumptions to haggle about particular duties, as is customary today. And this applies also, although to a smaller extent, when the other contracting party is a close-fisted Protectionist. In such a case one would merely obtain smaller reductions in duties than from a liberal country and would give *relatively* greater concessions in return.[1]

We must also emphasise that the considerations set out above by no means hold good only from the standpoint of a 100 per cent. Free Trade doctrine. One does not reach any different result even if one takes account of the exceptions to the general rule of Free Trade which we have discussed earlier. Exceptions which might possibly be justified, consisting of cases in which a duty may bring an advantage, are of the second order of smalls relatively to the existing tariffs of today and should present no serious obstacle to agreement in negotiations for commercial treaties.

§ 4. THE DISPUTE OVER THE MOST FAVOURED NATION SYSTEM.

1. GENERAL REMARKS.—The dissatisfaction with the system of unconditional and unrestricted Most Favoured Nation treatment, which had long been felt, became more intense and widespread after the War. Nevertheless, this system was re-established after the War, despite the resolve of the Allies at their Economic Conference of 1916 to continue the War in the realm of trade policy by a systematic discrimination between Allied and Enemy Powers. This return to the unconditional Most Favoured Nation system was due to the new trade policy of the United States, to the efforts of

---

[1] The tactical situation is especially difficult, for one should not give the other party the impression that one is prepared in any case and at any price to remove the bargaining duties or that one will not, in fact, fulfil a threat of imposing retaliatory duties.

Great Britain, and to the strong support of the system by Germany. In 1927 the German Government succeeded, under great difficulties, in arranging with France a commercial treaty containing an unconditional and unrestricted Most Favoured Nation Clause.   This treaty formed the backbone of the European Treaty System in the post-War period.   At the end of 1932 the Most Favoured Nation undertakings (between Germany and France) were renewed, with some limitations, for a further five years.

The attacks on the system have become more numerous and insistent; people demand to be freed from its chains.   During the period of depression since 1931 there have been, especially in Central and Eastern Europe, countless breaches in the system, many of them contrary to existing treaty obligations.   But its future will not be prejudiced by the excesses of irrational small States impelled, by a crisis partly of their own making, to carry on a guerilla economic warfare against one another and to vie with one another in evading their mutual obligations under the system. Whether the Most Favoured Nation system will remain the basic principle of international trade policy in the future will depend far more upon the decisions of the great Economic Powers.   At present it does not seem that any changes will be made.   One International Conference after another, without exception, has adhered to the unconditional and unrestricted Most Favoured Nation principle, and hitherto the concessions which have been made to its opponents scarcely exceed unimportant exceptions to be applied in times of emergency.[2]

What, then, are the alleged disadvantages of the Most Favoured Nation system?   What should replace it and what are the supposed advantages of the systems which are proposed as substitutes for it?

We need not concern ourselves with those writers who attack the system because they see in it merely a device for promoting Free Trade.   We shall not consider autarchists or isolationists who storm at the system because they want to abolish completely the individualistic basis of the modern world economy and to replace it by a planned system of international exchange or by something similar, in which the principle of unconditional Most Favoured Nation treatment plays no part.   We shall deal here only with those arguments against the Most Favoured Nation principle which rest

---

[2] Cf. the Report of the Preparatory Committee for the World Economic Conference (Geneva, 1933).   Some writers on trade policy, such as Schüller and Riedl, advocate the recognition of general regional exceptions to the Most Favoured Nation Clause, for the sole purpose of preventing these unregulated violations of the Clause, which threaten to undermine from within the principle, essential to world trade, of equality of treatment.

upon an acceptance of the individualistic world economy and the international division of labour.

2.—THE ARGUMENT THAT THE UNCONDITIONAL MOST FAVOURED NATION SYSTEM IS UNJUST.—We begin with the most attractive and powerful argument against the unconditional Most Favoured Nation system. It is an argument which was formerly always used by Americans in support of the conditional interpretation and which has recently found much favour in Europe, especially in France. It is that it is unjust to permit countries which make no reciprocal compensatory concessions to enjoy favours which other countries must purchase dearly. This argument derives mainly from the untenable Protectionist belief that every unilateral reduction in one's own tariffs is a sacrifice.

But, apart from this fact, in most cases it is not watertight. In order to judge its validity, we must distinguish between cases in which the other contracting party itself grants unconditional Most Favoured Nation treatment and cases in which it does not.

When it does, its reciprocal concessions fall under two heads:

(a) *It binds itself, for its part, to grant unconditional Most Favoured Nation treatment*, so that any discrimination in favour of a third State is ruled out. It is unfortunately far too little realised that this in itself, quite apart from any concrete tariff obligations or reductions in tariffs, is a valuable concession. Helfferich has seen this clearly and has stated it plainly. " But those who judge these [namely, the Most Favoured Nation Treaties of Germany with the United States and with the Argentine] unfavourably usually overlook an important circumstance. The absolute height of import duties is, of course, important for German trade with the Argentine and other countries and above all with the United States . . .; but it is far more important that her goods should not be subjected to heavier duties than those of other competing countries. An increase of duties in the United States and in the Argentine may cut down German exports to those countries; but a so-called differential treatment of German goods must destroy her export trade with them and transfer these markets to France, England, and other competitors. We have, indeed, a great interest in low duties upon our exports, but our interest in receiving the same tariff treatment as other countries is immeasurably greater."[3]

The possibility of such adverse tariff discrimination implies that in addition to the danger, present even under complete Most

---

[3] *Handelspolitik* (Leipzig, 1901), p. 97; similarly, Viner, *loc. cit.*, and Arndt *loc. cit.*, p. 32.

Favoured Nation treatment, that the uniform tariff may be raised at any moment, there is the further danger that one day a competing country may obtain for itself reductions of duties. Thus a departure from the strict Most Favoured Nation policy quite significantly increases the risks of foreign trade, and therefore the assurance of full Most Favoured Nation treatment is in itself a valuable concession.

(b) *Any concessions which it makes to third countries must be extended, without compensation, to the other contracting party, just as it must receive concessions made by the latter to third countries.*

This concession, however, has no value if the State in question completely abstains from concluding any tariff treaties. For example, the United States participates, by virtue of its Most Favoured Nation treaties, in all the reductions in duties made to one another by the European countries, without itself making any reduction in its skyscraper tariffs.[4] This policy of the United States has done more than almost any other circumstance to bring the unconditional Most Favoured Nation Clause into disfavour in Europe.

If one believes that a country which imposes high duties and will not enter into tariff negotiations can be brought to reason if other countries discriminate against it and refuse it Most Favoured Nation treatment, then the best course is to denounce existing Most Favoured Nation treaties with it or to follow the example which has been set for a long time by Germany in making the grant of full Most Favoured Nation treatment dependent upon the readiness of the other party to make tariff concessions. The grant of Most Favoured Nation treatment would then become the crown and coping-stone of the treaty edifice, and not something which the other party could count upon receiving ever afterwards in all circumstances.

But this course is worth while only if there are good grounds for the belief that it will induce the refractory high-Protectionist country to come into line. In the case of the United States, such grounds are lacking, owing, on the one hand, to her political and economic strength and, on the other hand, to her constitution and political arrangements, which make it very difficult for her to carry through tariff negotiations. This being so, there is nothing for it but to concede her unconditional Most Favoured Nation

---

[4] This has changed to some extent since 1935 when America began to negotiate tariff reductions with other countries.

status. This course involves no sacrifice. It merely rules out a gain which, in the circumstances, could not be reaped.

When the other contracting party receives unconditional Most Favoured Nation treatment, but grants no Most Favoured Nation treatment in return or grants it only in the conditional form (a policy which, as we have seen, was adopted by the United States towards Europe until 1922, and which amounts in practice to a refusal to give Most Favoured Nation treatment), then the situation is similar to that in the case just discussed. One must consider whether there is a prospect of bringing the country in question to reason by refusing it Most Favoured Nation treatment and by imposing retaliatory duties upon its goods.

In judging this prospect, one should ask what are the exports of the country upon which it is proposed to bring the pressure. The position of the United States was formerly so strong partly because her exports were mainly staple commodities: raw materials and foodstuffs, such as wheat. If Germany had imposed a differential duty upon American wheat, it would have had to import more wheat from other countries and the American wheat would have filled the resulting gaps in the imports of England, Holland, and other countries. A country which, on the contrary, exports manufactured goods which are not staple articles and whose origin cannot be concealed, is far more vulnerable to discrimination.[5] Those responsible for German trade policy have realised this and Germany has therefore adopted the unconditional Most Favoured Nation system.

3. THE ARGUMENT THAT THE UNCONDITIONAL MOST FAVOURED NATION SYSTEM IS AN OBSTACLE TO TARIFF REDUCTIONS.—It is sometimes urged that, although in periods when a Free Trade tendency prevails and duties are moving downwards, the unconditional Most Favoured Nation system does bring about, by a general extension of every reduction in duties, a general lowering of tariff-levels, yet in periods when Protection is in fashion it has the opposite effect, since then a country is averse from making a tariff reduction which must be extended to the whole world.

When country A is negotiating with countries B, C, D, and E, and has already concluded tariff treaties with B, C, and D, it may be that E, by virtue of its Most Favoured Nation status, has already obtained all the reductions in A's duties for which it can hope, and therefore has no incentive to reduce its own. If E had not the right, given to it by its Most Favoured Nation status,

---

[5] Of course its vulnerability will depend also upon the transport-cost situation and upon whether or not it has a monopoly in some particular branch of production.

to benefit from every reduction in duties granted by A to B, C, and D, it would then be prepared to reduce its own duties in order to obtain these concessions. Thus, in the absence of a Most Favoured Nation system, a country could make use of one and the same concession several times over, in negotiating with different countries.

Moreover, it often happens that A withholds certain concessions in its negotiations with B, C, and D because it must reserve them for its negotiations with E; hence tariffs in B, C, and D will be reduced less than otherwise they might be. Then possibly no agreement is reached with E, and therefore A does not make the further reductions in its duties which it was prepared to concede.

We may reply to this that as a rule A will still have duties for whose reductions E will be prepared to pay an acceptable price. If, however, A believes it can go no further along the path of tariff reductions or that it could get more from E by means of the concessions which it has already made to B, C, and D than by means of such further concessions as it can make, then it is always open to A to make the grant of Most Favoured Nation status to E conditional upon tariff concessions being granted to it by E. Viner has pointed out that it is possible to guard against negotiations being prejudiced in the way described above by doing what countries, following the lead of Germany, endeavoured to do before the War—namely, by prolonging all tariff treaties until the same point of time and then, in the so-called comet year of trade policy, simultaneously concluding them all anew, so that the grant of Most Favoured Nation status would depend upon the successful conclusion of the tariff negotiations.

This method of proceeding is based upon a view of the Most Favoured Nation system which finds adherence especially upon the continent of Europe. This view regards Most Favoured Nation status not as the *premise* upon which the relations between two countries as to trade policy are based, but rather as the *final seal* upon those relations. It is in opposition to the view, held mainly by Anglo-Saxon peoples, that a country has a kind of natural right to claim Most Favoured Nation status.

But the policy of simultaneously negotiating trade treaties with numerous States is often, for one reason or another, impracticable. Even so, it is by no means obvious that greater reductions in tariffs could be obtained *without* the burden of Most Favoured Nation obligations. Further, against this alleged advantage must be set the risk that no treaty may be concluded at all. Nobody who bears in mind the advantages of equal tariff treatment, discussed above, will deem this danger a small one. Most Favoured Nation status is a prize of such value that one should not wantonly forgo it for the attainment of problematic advantages by haggling over particular duties.

For small countries especially, it is quite vital that the principle of equal rights in international economic relations should continue to be recognised as fundamental. If the world embarked upon a short-sighted policy of weighing mechanically concessions against counter-concessions, those countries which have nothing to offer in markets and purchasing-power at all comparable to what the Great Powers can offer would be the first to suffer.

Another reproach levelled against the unrestricted Most Favoured Nation system is that it hinders the conclusion of preferential-tariff treaties or so-called ' economic unions,' which might bring about at least a partial reduction in tariffs. It very often happens that one country is prepared to grant another a reduction in duties, but only on the condition that the whole world does not participate in it. It is urged that neighbouring countries especially, which are bound to one another by geographical and economic ties, by close trade relations and a long common frontier, and possibly by the ties of blood and of a common culture, should have the right to grant one another *preferential duties* without States outside this closely-linked group being able to participate by virtue of their Most Favoured Nation status. In order to judge the economic justification for this claim, we must get a clear notion of the advantages of such desired ' economic unions.'

§ 5. PREFERENTIAL DUTIES.

1. GENERAL REMARKS.—During the post-War period a very queer notion came into vogue as to the desirable aim of international trade policy and the routes by which it should be attained. A general ' schematic ' and ' inorganic ' reduction of tariffs was not desired; people either did not understand the case for Free Trade or did not believe in it; international division of labour was out of favour as being too reminiscent of the classical theories; but economic unions and the creation of larger economic areas (but not on any account Free Trade areas) was the solution of the day. Attempts to prove the economic advantages of these ' areas ' and ' unions ' left much to be desired. Political, geographical, and pseudo-economic arguments were flung together promiscuously in support of fantastic proposals concerning the countries to be included in such areas: Central Europe, the Danube Basin,

Paneuropa with or without England, and so on. In particular, much mischief was caused by the excessive use of inappropriate military concepts and analogies under the rubric of ' Geopolitik.' Military language, containing expressions such as ' economic front ' and ' defensive positions,' is especially inappropriate to the analysis of problems of international trade and of division of labour between countries because it constantly brings into prominence the fundamentally false mercantilist notion that the gain of one country must mean the loss of another. It suggests that a ' front ' of economic conflict lies always between two countries, whereas in reality the conflict is between groups having different interests *within* each country.

The content of these planned ' economic unions ' varies from a complete Customs Union at one extreme to more or less substantial tariff or other preferences to imports at the other extreme. We shall postpone the problem of Customs Unions to the following section.

2. ECONOMIC APPRAISAL OF PREFERENTIAL DUTIES.—What are the advantages that are claimed for preferential duties? Wherein lies their superiority over a general reduction in duties? (We are here interested only in the *economic* advantages. We shall not take any account of the aims of Nationalism, real or imaginary, which are held either clearly or vaguely, avowedly or tacity, by many exponents of this notion.)

It is clear that the economic advantages of the preferential system can lie only in its leading to a reduction of tariff-levels which could not be attained by other means. The Preference is an instrument for making a breach in the tariff walls. And this partial reduction of tariffs is to be judged, in principle, in the same way as a general reduction, namely, as a means of extending the international division of labour and increasing the social product. Preferential duties can be justified only upon the general Free Trade principle. The argument runs somewhat as follows : There is no difference of kind, but only one of degree, between the grant of lower preferential duties upon imports from certain countries and a general reduction in tariffs. A partial reduction is better than none at all (although, of course, a general reduction would be still better, from an economic standpoint). Conversely, an increase of tariffs with preferential exceptions is to be preferred to a general increase. But preferential duties are not justified when they merely provide a pretext or an inducement to raise duties against outsiders without any diminution in the obstacles to trade between the countries enjoying the reciprocal preferences.

It is necessary to emphasise that preferential duties can be justified from an economic standpoint only by means of the Free Trade argument. For many advocates of preferential duties are opponents of the Free Trade principle without being aware of the contradiction.[6]

Some objections which merit consideration have been made against the above reasoning. Viner, for example, attacks the view that a preferential reduction in tariffs is in all circumstances better than none at all. The possibility that new discriminations between countries may be imposed or existing ones removed increases, as we have shown already, the insecurity and risks of international trade. Apart from this evil (which can be obviated by creating stable relations through long-term tariff agreements), the main objection against preferential duties is that tariff discrimination leads to a greater diversion of trade away from the rational lines which it would follow under free exchange than would be brought about by uniform duties, even if they were higher ones. " Suppose that under free trade country A would find it to its advantage to import a particular commodity from B, and that even with a high duty it is still not possible to produce the commodity at home at a profit to its producers, so that it continues to be imported from B. While the tariff reduces the volume of trade, it does so only as a revenue measure, and still permits the commodity to be produced there where it can be produced most cheaply. Suppose, now, that the duty is reduced by half on imports from a third country, C, and that by virtue of this preferential treatment C can undersell B and capture A's trade. The result of the discrimination is . . . that the commodity . . . is now produced in C, where the conditions for its production are comparatively unfavourable."[7]

This argument is correct from the standpoint of the world economy as a whole. From a nationalistic standpoint, however, which takes into account only the interest of A and C and disregards

---

[6] There has never been any attempt, so far as I am aware, to show, from the standpoint of any of the arguments for Protection, that a preferential reduction of tariffs should be judged differently in principle from a corresponding *general* reduction. This last phrase does not imply a general reduction of tariffs *by the same proportion* but one which has the same significance in increasing the international exchange of goods—broadly speaking, one which brings about the same increase in imports and exports as does the preferential reduction. Thus a preferential reduction of certain duties by 10 per cent. may correspond, for example, to a general reduction of these duties by 7 per cent. Neither the infant-industry argument nor the cost-equalisation argument nor any other of the Protectionist arguments provide any basis for asserting that preferential reductions are superior in principle to general reductions. Such a superiority could be only a *tactical* one, due to the fact that the responsible persons were prepared to concede preferential duties but would not agree to a corresponding general reduction.

[7] *Index, loc. cit.*, p. 5.

N*

the loss of B, the situation may be different. As a result of the preferential reduction in the duty, A obtains the good more cheaply and C is enabled to export it. By all the rules of the Theory of International Trade this must be advantageous to A and to C. (It may be that the loss of customs revenue or a change in the terms of trade outweighs the gain to the economy, but this may happen just as well under a general reduction.) B is injured, but that is another question; and whether the injury to B may not be greater than the gain to A and C is yet a third question.[8]

Very important, however, is the following objection against preferential duties, which Taussig brought forward as early as 1892.[1] When country A grants country B a preferential reduction in duties and B is not in a position to supply all the import-requirements of A, the reduction in duties represents simply a subsidy from the State Exchequer of A to the producers in B. For if A must supplement her imports from B by resorting to the world market, the home price in A will *not* alter[2]; even after the grant of preferential duties to B it remains as before at the level of the world price plus the original duty, and the consumers in A are not relieved of any of their burden, but the producers in B gain by the reduction in duties. In such a case, the reduction in duties is indeed a sacrifice for A, although not for its producers but for its State Exchequer.[3]

Preferential duties of this kind, which leave the home price unchanged, increase neither the volume of trade of the country which grants them nor the international division of labour. The total imports do not increase at all; more is taken from B but less from other supplying countries. Preferential duties of this kind

---

[8] Viner's reasoning has a very limited application owing to his assumption that A itself would not produce the commodity even under a high import duty. If we turn to the far more important case in which A, under a high import duty, does itself produce the commodity but still imports a part (becoming ever smaller as the duty increases) of its supply from B, and in which the grant of a preferential duty to C causes its own production to cease or to diminish, we see at once that by all the rules of international division of labour the preferential régime must be of advantage for both A and C and that the benefit to them may be far greater than the injury to B.

Thus Viner's analysis does *not* lead to the *general* conclusion that preferential duties and Customs Unions are of economic advantage only if they divert trade into those channels which it would follow in the absence of all tariffs. The argument would be only quantitatively and not qualitatively different were one to urge that Free Trade upon the Earth is harmful because trade would follow quite different channels if exchanges of goods took place with the planet Mars.

[1] "Reciprocity," *Quarterly Journal of Economics* (Oct. 1892), reprinted in *Free Trade, the Tariff and Reciprocity* (1920), pp. 120 *et seq.*

[2] When the world-market price cannot be assumed to remain constant, the principle remains the same—there is only a difference in degree.

[3] Taussig and Viner give as an example the preferential reduction in the sugar duty which the United States granted (and still grants) to Hawaii and Cuba. See *Reciprocity and Commercial Treaties*, pp. 103-36, and Taussig, *Some Aspects of the Tariff Question* (1931), 3rd edn.

are worthless as measures of trade policy and should not be placed in the same class as a general reduction in tariffs. This is especially true when the preferential reduction is restricted to a relatively small quota, a practice which has become more and more frequent during recent years in trade between the States of Central and Eastern Europe. Indeed, today—let nobody deceive himself on this score—the Protectionists are making use of the catchword of Preference. Its popularity is due simply to the fact that preferential duties have become a means of making *sham concessions* to liberal ideas of trade policy. People are prepared to let a greater quantity of grain come in, under favourable conditions, from the East, provided that imports from the West are simultaneously reduced by the same amount.

But the possibility of exporting more, is, of course, an advantage to the country which is granted a preferential duty. For that country the volume of trade increases and the international division of labour is intensified. It follows that if two countries reciprocally grant one another such tariff preferences, a moderate extension of international division of labour comes about. Even if these reciprocal preferences are restricted to quotas so small that they do not affect the price in the importing country, the exports of both the countries will increase and hence their imports also must somehow increase—perhaps *via* their trade with third countries.[4]

The same effects upon the volume of trade and the international division of labour could clearly be achieved through a general reduction in duties by a smaller amount, and such a general reduction would be far preferable to a preferential one. Moreover, the bias in favour of preferential duties, and of their restriction to fixed quotas, springs mostly from the naïve belief that such preferential quotas provide a means of promoting exports without either increasing imports or reducing any home prices. Nevertheless, it must be conceded that the reciprocal granting of such preferential quotas is preferable to no reductions whatever in duties.

Such ' preferential agreements ' have been concluded between Austria and Hungary and between Austria and Italy. In order to veil the evasion of their existing Most Favoured Nation obligations, they granted the ' preferences ' or export subsidies not in the form of reductions in duties but in the form of ' credit privileges.'[5]

---

[4] Import under a preferential duty implies only a redistribution of the total amount imported among the different supplying countries, and not a net increase in this total, so long as the home price is not affected.

[5] Both parties to the ' credit privileges ' (or export bounties) assist their *exporters* and not their *importers*, this plan being adopted in order to prevent third countries from claiming equal treatment by virtue of their Most Favoured

The East European countries for some years have been carrying on a campaign to get open preferences granted to their exports of grain by the grain-importing countries of Western and Central Europe. This course, which they have urged at all international economic conferences (and especially at the Conference of Stresa in August, 1932) and at the League of Nations, turns simply upon the granting of subsidies to the bankrupt Balkan countries. Since these countries are at the same time debtors of the Western countries, the problem is simply one of creditor-policy: should one try to give a helping hand to these debtor countries, who at present are unable to pay, by granting them assistance? In this case, a point in favour of granting such preferences is that the subsidy may come partly out of the pocket of foreigners—as would happen, for example, were France to succeed in persuading Germany to grant preferences to the Balkan countries. Another, and far preferable, possibility is that the Eastern countries might be induced, by the grant of subsidies in the form of preferences, to make a general reduction in their tariffs. Germany has followed this path in her treaties with Rumania and Hungary. But so far the protests of Most Favoured Nation countries have prevented these treaties from being put into force.

When the one-sided grant of a preferential duty leads to no reduction in price, it is completely or almost completely worthless; and in the other extreme case, when under Free Trade the commodity would be imported only from the country receiving the grant, it is superfluous to clothe the removal of the duty in the garb of a preference.

Between these two extremes lie those cases in which the grant of a preferential reduction in duties is of advantage—assuming that a general reduction of duties by the same (or by a somewhat smaller) amount cannot be attained. These favourable cases are characterised by the fact that the grant of lower preferential duties leads to a reduction in prices, an increase in the volume of international trade, and an extension of the international division of labour—although to a smaller extent than would be brought about by a *general* reduction in duties of the same amount.[6]

Nation status. But it does not follow that these subsidies should not be regarded as preferential duties. They lose, however, their character of preferential duties if the subsidies are given for the export of goods which can be imported duty free into the other contracting State. In such a case it is a question of an export bounty and not of a preferential duty. This is frequently the case in the 'credit privilege' agreements mentioned above between Austria and Italy and between Austria and Hungary.

[6] To this category belong the numerous preferential reductions in duties which Riedl, Schüller, and others demand for certain groups of countries, upon the assumption that all the countries in such a group would succeed in making a common agreement. It is proposed that other States should be given an induce-

We have still to examine an argument which plays a very great part in the writings of publicists and in discussions at international conferences. It is urged over and over again that geographical proximity, kinship of culture and race and speech, and economic ties and political friendship between two countries render a preferential system between them especially advantageous to both of them and that the rest of the world ought to permit it. On this point, Viner[7] has rightly observed that the same and also additional economic advantages could be attained through a general reduction in duties.[8] Moreover, when two countries are really so closely linked economically, an extension of their reciprocal tariff reductions to the rest of the world will have no great significance, since third countries will not be able to face the competition of one of them in the markets of the other. The fact that two countries are, so to speak, economically complementary, means only that the nature of their respective resources and therefore of their production possibilities, the conditions governing the location of industry, and so on, make an intensive exchange of goods between them especially favourable since differences in comparative costs between them are especially great and, possibly, transport costs between them relatively low. The criterion for this is the intensity of their mutual trade relations, provided that these are not artificially disturbed by interventions, such as differential duties.

The significance of a reduction in a duty depends fundamentally upon the extent to which the import increases, the price falls, and the exchange of goods is intensified. From an economic point of view it is a matter of complete indifference whether the country upon whose imports the duty is reduced is or is not in close political or other relations with the country which makes the reduction.

Hence such a closeness of relations is no argument for a preferential reduction in duties. But from a *tactical* standpoint it may be more easy to influence public opinion and get a reduction in

---

ment to join such preferential agreements, in order that as many countries as possible might benefit from the original preferential reductions in duties, by the inclusion of *Accession* or *Adherence* or *Equity Clauses* in the suggested agreements. That is to say, in the *first* place, that it shall be quite open for third States, who are prepared to grant the same reductions in duties and other aids to the exchange of goods as the original contracting parties, to join the preferential agreements, and that, in the *second* place, the benefit of every preferential reduction in duties shall be extended automatically to every third State which pursues a liberal trade policy (such as Free Trade countries) and whose import duties are lower than the reduced duties of the signatory States to the preferential agreements.

7 " The Most Favoured Nation Clause in American Commercial Treaties," *Journal of Political Economy* (Feb. 1924), p. 108.

8 It cannot be denied that most advocates of preferential duties are greatly influenced by the false Protectionist belief that it is an advantage to restrict tariff concessions to as few countries as possible.

duties carried through if an appeal is made by suitable propaganda to the feeling that there are bonds of unity with the other country or countries. We discuss the alleged tactical advantages of preferential systems in § 7.

§ 6. Customs Unions.

It follows from the foregoing observations upon the economic appraisal of preferential duties that, from an economic standpoint based upon Free Trade reasoning, complete Customs Unions are to be wholeheartedly welcomed; and the same applies, in a lesser degree, to Customs Unions with moderate duties between their constituent parts. This is not only for the reason given by Viner,[9] namely, that such Unions are usually recommended only for neighbouring States, and that a great part of the trade between two neighbouring States which comes about when duties between them are removed would remain if the tariff walls between them and the rest of the world were also removed. No, Customs Unions are always to be welcomed, even when they are not between neighbouring or complementary States. A Customs Union must be especially advantageous for small States, since these are particularly injured if they exclude one another's goods. We must emphasise that the economic advantages of a Customs Union can be proved only by exact Free Trade reasoning as to the international division of labour and the Theory of Comparative Cost, and not by any reference to racial, cultural, and other relations. It follows also that, from an economic standpoint—and with the reservations we have made earlier—a general removal of duties by the States concluding the Customs Union would be better than a removal of duties only between themselves, their duties against other countries being retained.

It is an erroneous Protectionist belief that a Customs Union brings with it any advantage which could not be attained in a still fuller measure by a general removal of duties. A Customs Union is, of course, equivalent to the case in which duties are removed only between the countries forming the Union and not between them and other countries.

When freedom of trade is linked with freedom of movement of workers and of other factors of production capable of movement, this gives rise to special problems, which I cannot here examine.

The removal of tariff walls between two States gives rise, like any reduction of duties, to general Protectionist resistances. But,

---

[9] *Index* (Jan. 1931), p. 11.

in addition to these, a Customs Union raises a host of very difficult political and administrative problems. Two Governments, two Parliaments (or one Tariff Parliament with delegates from both the States), two groups of interested persons and organisations, must agree upon a common Tariff Schedule. When one reflects how difficult it often is, even in a unified State, to fix upon a tariff, owing to the conflict of wishes and opposition of interests of the various parties concerned, and when one remembers what a painful process it was to get an agreement between the two halves of the old Austria-Hungary, despite the bonds of a common monarch and a common army, one is forced to the conclusion that, apart from exceptional cases, these problems are practically insoluble. Moreover, an agreement must be reached as to the division of the customs revenue, as to questions of taxation, and as to measures of customs administration. Indeed, modern history presents us with one sole example of a successful Customs Union: the German Customs Union, leading to the German Reich. And it should be noted that the German Customs Union came about in a liberal era, when a duty of 20 per cent. *ad valorem* was considered high. It is very unlikely that such an agreement could be reached peacefully in the present era of extreme Protection.

§ 7. TACTICAL CONSIDERATIONS UPON THE PATH TO FREE TRADE.

All far-reaching schemes for a Customs Union to embrace all or most of the European States are quite Utopian and fantastic. They are completely ruled out by the spirit of Nationalism and Protection which prevails today. But these schemes are not merely quite without any present prospect of realisation: this is true also of schemes of universal Free Trade and of many other ideals and ends, for which, nevertheless, the more high-minded and intelligent of mankind have always fought and for which, it is to be hoped, they will always continue to fight, despite the discouraging prospects. The schemes in question suffer, in my view, from the further disability that they contain an inner contradiction. They are to be condemned, not because present conditions rule out a European Customs Union but because the end which they envisage as an ideal is both too limited and at the same time more difficult to attain than the final end to which it is subordinate. They propose a detour towards an intermediate goal which is harder to follow than the direct road towards the final goal.

To be more precise, there seems no reason why the reduction of duties should stop at the frontiers of Europe. From the standpoint of Sociology and Politics and History as well as of economics, it is very crude to think in terms of geographical continents. For example, Western Europe stands much closer, spiritually and economically, to many overseas countries than to the East of Europe. One should not forget that the seas which divide continents form a barrier to commerce in goods and in ideas which is far more easy to overcome than the barrier of great stretches of land.

All the political and administrative difficulties,[1] mentioned above, which must be faced by ordinary Free Trade propaganda, the object of which is simply to reduce duties, stand also in the way of a Customs Union; and to conquer false Protectionist doctrine —especially that which declares high tariffs an essential feature of a national economic policy—is just as much a necessary preliminary to the establishment of a complete, or nearly complete, Customs Union as to the establishment of Free Trade or of a general reduction in duties.

These remarks apply just as strongly to the less ambitious schemes for economic unions and preferential duties. To believe that a better trade policy can be obtained by some change or other in its technique, by giving up the principle of unconditional Most Favoured Nation treatment, by permitting regional exceptions to it, and so on, is to follow an illusion. The trade policy of today has been shaped not by the Most Favoured Nation Clause in commercial treaties but by the Protectionist spirit of the time, springing from a false conception of Nationalism and from Mercantilist errors.

It is an error to think that any radical demolition of duties can be brought about by small reforms in the technique of trade policy without a frontal attack upon the Protectionist outlook. Protectionism cannot be outwitted; it must be conquered. The weapons are not made more effective by speaking of Customs Unions and preferential duties instead of Free Trade and reductions in tariffs.

It is true that European politicians, who will have nothing to do with Free Trade and reductions in tariffs, are today speaking everywhere of preferential duties as if they were the philosopher's stone of trade policy; they seem to be willing to grant in this form reductions of duties which they would not consider for a moment if they were demanded by Free Traders for straightforward economic reasons. But we should not deceive ourselves. If the whole thing is not merely a deliberate manœuvre to create a

---

[1] One should further remember that these difficulties do not only present obstacles to the actual formation of a Customs Union : they remain as permanent sources of friction and conflict, even after it is formed.

diversion and postpone any action, it springs only from a naïve belief that the preferential system provides a means of reaping part of the advantages of Free Trade without hurting anybody, a way of increasing the volume of trade without any reshuffling and without any of the pains of transition, a method of increasing exports without importing any more than before. So long as such notions prevail, so long as people fail to realise that increased exports involve an extension of the international division of labour, an increase in imports, and a reshuffling of home production, a conversion of opinion is out of the question and no substantial reduction of tariffs can be hoped for by way of preferential duties. Either the concessions which are made will be only sham ones, which neither hurt the interested parties nor benefit the community, or the opposition to preferential duties and economic unions will become just as strong as the opposition to Free Trade and general reductions in duties. There is only one way out. It is to take the bull by the horns, to fight the spirit of Protection, to spread far and wide correct ideas about international trade, and to confront the organised forces of sectional interests which support Protection with a powerful organisation drawn from those who suffer from it, that is, from the vast majority of the people of the world.

1 D

INDEX OF NAMES

NAMES OF SUBJECTS